DATE DUE

MAR 2 6 2010

The Madisonian Constitution

The Johns Hopkins Series in Constitutional Thought

Sanford Levinson and Jeffrey K. Tulis, *Series Editors*

The Madisonian Constitution

GEORGE THOMAS

The Johns Hopkins University Press
Baltimore

© 2008 The Johns Hopkins University Press
All rights reserved. Published 2008
Printed in the United States of America on acid-free paper
2   4   6   8   9   7   5   3   1

The Johns Hopkins University Press
2715 North Charles Street
Baltimore, Maryland 21218-4363
www.press.jhu.edu

Library of Congress Cataloging-in-Publication Data
Thomas, George
The Madisonian constitution / George Thomas.
p.   cm.
Includes bibliographical references and index.
ISBN-13: 978-0-8018-8852-6 (hardcover : alk. paper)
ISBN-10: 0-8018-8852-2 (hardcover : alk. paper)
1. Madison, James, 1751–1836. 2. United States. Constitution.
3. Constitutional law—United States. 4. Constitutional history—
United States. I. Title.
KF4520.T46 2008
342.7302′9—dc22   2007052654

A catalog record for this book is available from the British Library.

*Special discounts are available for bulk purchases of this book.
For more information, please contact Special Sales at 410-516-6936 or
specialsales@press.jhu.edu.*

The Johns Hopkins University Press uses environmentally friendly book
materials, including recycled text paper that is composed of at least
30 percent post-consumer waste, whenever possible. All of our
book papers are acid-free, and our jackets and covers are printed on paper
with recycled content.

For Courtney

1 Madison's Complex Constitutionalism   14

2 Congress, the Supreme Court, and the Meaning
   of the Civil War Amendments   39

3 The Progressive Reconstruction of
   American Constitutionalism   65

4 Discontinuities in the "Constitutional Revolution of 1937"   94

5 Unsettling the New Deal and the Return
   of Originalism   126

CONTENTS

In drafting the Massachusetts Constitution of 1780, the oldest constitution currently functioning, John Adams spoke to "The Frame of Government," famously putting forward the axiom that in the commonwealth "the legislature, executive, and judicial power shall be placed in separate departments, to the end that it might be a government of laws and not of men." Such an understanding, as James Madison would later argue, positions the separation of powers as foundational to the nature of constitutionalism and essential to maintaining its form. Yet, in our own day, this understanding has been taken to illustrate the unique position of the judiciary in upholding a constitution. Notice, however, that this axiom speaks not merely to the judiciary but to the whole of the separation of powers.

The Madisonian Constitution attempts to recover this understanding of constitutionalism, which underlies the U.S. Constitution. It is an understanding rooted in political science, offering what might be dubbed a *constitutional* perspective, which is not the same as a legal perspective. Indeed, I offer a Madisonian understanding in contrast to a legalist perspective, which collapses the Constitution into law explicated by the Supreme Court. In sketching a Madisonian vision, I illustrate the importance of diffuse and separate powers to American constitutionalism, which also illuminates the hazards and limits of a legalist mind-set. I should note at the outset, however, that this book does not offer an exhaustive account of the Madisonian Constitution. Rather, it is preoccupied by the separation of powers and clashes over constitutional interpretation—that is, only a portion of the whole Constitution, though the portion scholars tend to focus on the most. Even in this arena of constitutional interpretation, which is taken to be the essence of the judicial duty, the legalist Constitution does not capture the nature of our Constitution.

This understanding is not James Madison's alone. The book could plausibly have taken its name from others of the founding generation or even later generations. Insofar as I focus on constitutional interpretation within the national separation of powers, Abraham Lincoln might have a unique claim here. Yet, because Madison played such a profound role in theorizing about the underpinnings of modern constitutional government, it is best to situate Lincoln (and numerous others) within the contours of Madison's vision, rather than the other way around. It was Madison, after all, who had such a heavy hand in making the Constitution of 1787 a real constitution.

For comments on various portions of the book, I would like to thank Dean Alfange, Beau Breslin, Bryan Garsten, Shelly Goldman, Gary Jacobsohn, Ken Kersch, Charles Kesler, Sandy Levinson, Wayne Moore, and Keith Whittington. I would like to thank James Stoner in particular. He brought his subtle and penetrating mind—much in the common-law manner he so admires—to bear on the entire manuscript. He offered numerous helpful suggestions, often capturing precisely what I wanted to say better than I had. In time, I am sure to regret not following more of his wise counsel. I owe a special debt to Jeffrey Tulis, whose careful reading of the manuscript was invaluable. His suggestions, comments, prodding, and insight helped me write the book I wanted to write. I would also like to thank Henry Tom of the Johns Hopkins University Press for his encouragement, as well as his patience. Peter Berkowitz and Frank Buckley of the George Mason Law School provided funds to help work on the manuscript and, perhaps more importantly, provided an environment where I made lasting friends.

Two individuals bound up with Williams College have been invaluable teachers. James McAllister listened often to my ideas over coffee, lunch, or a stroll around campus. He is a truly extraordinary teacher, who tutored me in the art of teaching Williams's remarkable students (and much else). He is a good friend to whom I owe far more than I can say. Gary Jacobsohn (my predecessor at Williams) taught by his scholarly example. It was an honor to assume his old position—all the more so as it came with his approval. If I might borrow his language, he provided a model of scholarship to aspire toward. No doubt, as he reminds us about constitutional aspirations generally, there is sure to be a gap between aspirations and practice.

Much as the Constitution grounds and shapes us, and in ways that we take for granted, so it is with my family. It was my parents who put the scholarly world on my horizon. They have fostered and sustained me to that end, while imparting a sense of what is most important, which included giving me a brother who is also a best friend. Angelo and Isabella make me even more appreciative of the charms of college life. All the more so as Angelo's curiosity has taken us along Boston's Freedom Trail, through Lexington and Concord, and back home to Chapin Library at Williams, which houses original printings of the Declaration of Independence and Constitution (as well as George Washington's copy of *The Federalist,* which, it turns out, is not quite so captivating as his "soldier guy book"). Happily, his mom is there, in this as in all else, to help answer his many questions and remind us "one at a time." Courtney has heard the arguments in this book for far too long, usually with me beginning apropos of nothing, leaving her to sort it out as she so often does. Busy producing her own history books, she remains my best editor—in life, as well as in prose.

The Madisonian Constitution

Introduction

> To make a government requires no great prudence. Settle the seat of
> power, teach obedience: and the work is done. To give freedom is
> still more easy. It is not necessary to guide; it requires only to let go
> the rein. But to form a free government; that is, to temper together
> these opposite elements of liberty and restraint in one consistent
> work, requires much thought, deep reflection, a sagacious, powerful,
> and combining mind.
>
> *Edmund Burke*

The great innovation of written constitutionalism, it is often asserted, is that it brought fundamental law down to earth by making it legally binding in courts of law.[1] Casting his eye at this great innovation, Edward Corwin noted that, paradoxically, prior to this development "the *supremacy* of constitutions was a real barrier to their *legality*."[2] We have taken this lesson to heart. So strong is this disposition in our polity that our understanding of constitutionalism begins from the axiom that the judiciary is "the one institution above all others essential to the preservation of the law."[3] This sentiment, perhaps not surprisingly, finds expression in the Supreme Court's insistence that our attachment to constitutionalism is inextricably bound up with our faith in the Court: "If the Court's legitimacy should be undermined, then, so would the country be in its very ability to see itself through its constitutional ideals."[4]

In this way, Chief Justice John Marshall's famous insistence in *Marbury v. Madison* that "it is emphatically the province and duty of the Court to say what the law is"[5] has come to be seen as articulating the unique position of courts in maintaining constitutional government.[6] Judicial review is seen as *the check* that maintains the Constitution. Far more than deciding the case before it in accord with the Constitution (judicial review), the Court acts as the sole expositor and enforcer of constitutional meaning, its opinions authoritatively binding on the Congress and the president (judicial supremacy). If it were otherwise, constitutional government would be rendered meaningless. Thus, while the conventional understanding of judicial review—which implies judicial supremacy—is frequently mentioned in the same breath as James Madison's separation of powers, they point to divergent, if not contradictory, conceptions of constitutionalism.

This book offers a Madisonian vision of American constitutionalism. Drawing on the thinking and practices of James Madison—often dubbed the "father of the Constitution" and who, we should recall, was not a lawyer—I argue that American constitutionalism is primarily about countervailing power and not about the legal limits enforced by courts.[7] Put another way, the essence of the Constitution as fundamental law is its foundational division of power and authority and not its legality. This political division provides the constitutional order within which the constitutional text can take shape as law. Thus, while the Constitution is legally binding, precisely because it founds the political order, it cannot easily be enforced as ordinary law. The central question for Madison was how to make constitutional text binding. This book examines the Madisonian solution to this problem and its subsequent import for American constitutional development. It offers an argument about the nature of the Constitution that takes its bearings from Madison's political science, which is put forth as a corrective to our tendency to view the Constitution from the lens of the Court.[8] It then turns to how the diffusion of power between the branches has brought the word of the Constitution to life.[9] The result of this Madisonian solution is that, in practice, the Constitution does not find coherent expression as a whole. This is so even when the different branches of government offer and act from an understanding of the whole Constitution. These branches often offer competing conceptions of constitutional authority and meaning, which, at times, turn on different conceptions of "what" the Constitution is.[10] And these constructions have inevitably shaped how we see the Constitution. Let me bring this down to earth, which is precisely what I argue the Madisonian Constitution does for fundamental law.

The Madisonian vision begins from the nature of the written Constitution, founded on the natural rights and popular sovereignty of the people. But the Constitution is not an act of writing alone.[11] The written constitution calls forth institutional forms that are central to maintaining it as fundamental law.[12] Because the written Constitution does not speak for itself, if not properly contrived, as Madison argued in *Federalist* 48, constitutional forms might become a "mere demarcation on parchment."[13] Yet to vest authority to "speak" for the fundamental law in any one body is effectively to make that body sovereign. Rather than vesting authority in any one branch of government, the Madisonian Constitution is driven by principle and prudence: the fundamental law is best maintained when each branch adheres to, and defends, its understanding of the Constitution. This is not simply a departmental understanding, where each branch may interpret the Constitution (though it entails that).[14] Nor is it captured by "constitutional dialogue" (though this, too, does occur).[15] More foundationally, the purposeful division of power is based on a refusal to vest sovereign authority in any single body—including in "the people themselves," even if the Constitution implicitly recognizes the people's *revolutionary* right to "alter or abolish" this particular constitution.[16]

The diffusion of sovereign authority—what Aristotle called the distribution of offices—speaks to the fundamental nature of the polity: it is neither "democratic" nor "undemocratic," as recent scholarship would have it.[17] Rather, the Constitution is a "complex and skillfully contrived" blend of liberalism and democracy that is characterized by tension.[18] This tension is evident insofar as natural rights and popular sovereignty both provide the foundation of our Constitution. These two elements do not sit easily together, yet preserving the tension within this compound may be central to preserving our constitutionalism.[19] The deliberate fostering of tension within the separation of powers, drawing on different features of liberalism and democracy, is more than a mere means. "Where the constant aim is to divide and arrange the several offices in such a manner as that each may be a check on the other," the separation is also intrinsically valuable, as Sotirios Barber argues, in fostering "the institutional embodiment of a national aspiration to rise above accident and force by governing ourselves by the claims of reason."[20]

This book seeks to describe the practice of American constitutionalism in a number of historical studies that manifest these foundational tensions as they are encoded into the nature of the American regime. But, as a partisan of the Madisonian Constitution, I also hope that describing and analyzing these aspects of our constitutionalism will help sustain the Madisonian vision. Thus, political science itself can play a role in fostering the amalgam that makes up the American Constitution. Recognizing that tendencies toward judicial supremacy stem, for example, from liberal and legal elements within the constitutional order might more readily help us keep this tendency in check.[21] There is also, however, the possibility of overcorrection, drawing on democratic elements within the regime. These tendencies have been featured when democracy is viewed as the primary value, giving us not only the putative "countermajoritarian dilemma" but the now fashionable understanding of "popular constitutionalism" where "we the people" can simply begin telling a "different" story about ourselves and, in so doing, alter the identity of the Constitution in a revolutionary way.[22] In this way, *The Madisonian Constitution* rejects both judicial supremacy and popular sovereignty as mechanisms for making the Constitution authoritatively binding.

The refusal to repose trust in any one branch of government to give a coherent accounting of the whole Constitution is, for Madison, the necessary result of human nature. After all, Madison's great fear was the concentration of all powers in a single authority, which "may justly be pronounced the very definition of tyranny."[23] The ineluctable result of this move, so much at the heart of American constitutionalism, is to make the Constitution "resistant as a whole to any sustained settlement of the kind that either a demagogue or a sovereign authoritative point of view might try to impose."[24] The central point here is the *imposition* of a sustained settlement. Many constitutional issues are foundationally settled because they are never contested.[25] Where there is ready agreement, an external sovereign authority is unnecessary. Where there is active disagreement, an external sovereign authority is likely to be harmful, as it is either impractical or tyrannical. Because conflict cannot be avoided, or settled with acceptable costs, it is channeled. In order to channel conflict, Madison's constitutionalism is structured around a set of agonistic institutions and principles. Yet, within this framework, "the differences between Jeffersonians and Hamiltonians, Federalists and Anti-Federalists, are ultimately reconcilable within a broad consensus of agreement on political fundamentals."[26] Beneath the surface of these clashes is a remarkable stability, as the public seems to have bestowed upon the Constitution that "veneration which time bestows on everything, and without which perhaps the wisest and freest governments would not possess the requisite stability," as Madison put it in *Federalist* 49.[27] We may have, in this manner, a sort of constitutional faith, but the faith is in the constitutional framework and the foundational principles it rests upon, which provide for a deep clash over the particulars of constitutional meaning in different circumstances, continually revisiting how our constitutional commitments should be ordered.

Describing how these tensions have been a central feature of American constitutionalism and seeking to nourish them, rather than dissolve them, are, I hope, central contributions of this work. For even while the Constitution is founded on fixed principles and presuppositions, and has "a meaning of its own,"[28] protecting these principles by way of countervailing power and applying them to changing circumstances make it likely that different, even competing strands of constitutional thought will be developed by the independent branches of government. Although written fundamental law traces its origins to Thomas Hobbes, often regarded as the father of modern constitutionalism, the Madisonian vision rejects Hobbes's unitary sovereign. With Hobbes, fundamental law is written so that it can be deciphered by "every man"; in contrast, unwritten law is based on the "artificial reason" of judges.[29] Those who insist on judicial supremacy, effectively vesting sovereignty in the Supreme Court, even if it is justified by way of an original act of popular sovereignty, pull against the very nature of the written Constitution by making it the peculiar province of courts and lawyers rather than fundamental law accessible to those who made the political compact.

Popular constitutionalists are right, then, to claim, along with Judge John Bannister Gibson, that written constitutionalism does not necessarily call for or depend on courts and lawyers: "The principles of a written constitution are more fixed and certain, and more apparent to the apprehension of the people, than principles which depend on tradition and the vague comprehension of the individuals who compose the nation, and who cannot all be expected to receive the same impressions or entertain the same notions on any given subject."[30] Like Gibson, popular constitutionalists insist that the "people themselves" are the primary enforcers of constitutional meaning through the legislature and elections: "for, after all, there is no effectual guard against legislative usurpation but public opinion, the force of which, in this country, is inconceivably great." Therefore, "it rests with the people, in whom full and absolute sovereign power resides, to correct abuses in legislation, by instructing their representatives to repeal the obnoxious act."[31] For Gibson, the public would measure a legislative act against the fixed written Constitution. Popular constitutionalists, unlike Gibson, dissolve the notion of a fixed constitutional foundation, positing democracy as the defining feature of the American regime, which means that "We the People" can remake the Constitution in a Rousseauian act of popular sovereignty outside of Article V.[32]

This concept is alien to the Madisonian Constitution. Madison insisted, constitutionally speaking, not only that it was a great virtue of the Constitution that it deliberately excludes the people *in their collective capacity* from any share of the government but that government itself was based on the fact that men were not angels: "In framing a government which is to be administered by men over men, the great difficulty lies in this: you must first enable the government to control the governed; and in the next place oblige it to control itself."[33] From the Madisonian perspective, which takes constitutional forms seriously, popular constitutionalism conflates the people's constitutional right of amendment with their revolutionary right to "dismember or overthrow" the Constitution.[34] We must be attuned to the difference between the sovereign people as the legitimate authority establishing the Constitution and the people as the authoritative interpreter of the Constitution once established: "whilst the Constitutional compact remains undissolved, it must be executed according to the forms and provisions specified in the compact."[35]

The binding authority of the Constitution, perhaps given a sort of constitutional faith, has rarely been challenged. But as a polity, we have disagreed profoundly about its meaning. Such disputes often involve deeper questions of "what" the Constitution itself is and might be aptly characterized as an extended debate about our constitutional identity.[36] In canvassing a number of constitutional disputes, I treat these efforts to construct, and reconstruct, constitutional authority as an open-ended empirical inquiry, describing how the constitutional actors themselves justified their understanding of constitutional meaning and authority. I then seek to trace these different trajectories. I do so, in part, because I take seriously the notion "that thought might constitute politics."[37]

The Constitution has shaped these conflicts, but efforts to construct constitutional authority have inevitably shaped how we see the Constitution. The practical result might be a more Aristotelian view of the Constitution insofar as it speaks to how the political life of the nation is constituted by the diffusion of offices. We might characterize this process as an interaction between America's small "c" constitution, which has aptly been described as America's constitutional soul, and our large "C" formal constitution.[38] To be sure, debates about constitutional ideas are historically rooted in struggles to justify particular policies and political projects. But they also illuminate what it has meant to bring the Constitution to life. These ideas, moreover, shape how we think and speak about the Constitution, even while the Constitution shapes the horizon in which such political struggles take place. This is an inevitable result of making fundamental law binding in practice, not simply in theory. And we could not overcome this dilemma by vesting sovereign authority in a single body. Even then, we could surely point to disjunctions between the sovereign authority's decision and the Constitution itself. Is this not just what we do as a polity, even when giving lip service to judicial supremacy?

At least this contention is maintained throughout the book, insofar as I argue that the Court has not acted as the authoritative articulator of constitutional meaning. Rather, given the centrality of maintaining the Constitution by formally separating power, conflicted understandings of the Constitution exist side by side. In describing and analyzing how this has worked in practice, I hope to extract two deeper lessons for our polity that are inextricably bound up together. First, I suggest that we cannot avoid constitutional politics, even by turning to the legal constitution, and therefore we cannot avoid our responsibility for rendering constitutional judgment. Second, I hope we can become more explicitly comfortable with constitutional conflict and thus, perhaps paradoxically, more appreciative of constitutional forms, allowing us to distinguish far more vividly than we do *constitutional propriety* from *constitutional meaning*.

First, constitutionalism does not remove our responsibility for constitutional judgments; it is not a way of avoiding politics so much as framing politics in a particular manner. As a polity we cannot trust that the Court alone will maintain our constitutional commitments, or absolve us from the responsibility of doing so. Such a view encourages irresponsibility in the legislature, allowing it to evade its constitutional responsibilities by deferring, often surreptitiously, to the Court. One scholar has recently captured this most evident failing of the Madisonian Constitution, in a review of constitutional deliberation in Congress, with the simple title: "James Madison Has Left the Building."[39] Yet Congress, even while rhetorically indulging judicial supremacy, has resisted what it views as "unconstitutional" judicial decisions. In this way, the Congress acts in a Madisonian fashion while adhering to the rhetoric of judicial supremacy. It is torn between the Madisonian Constitution and the legal Constitution. The rhetoric affects practice, though, as Congress often disputes what it views as unconstitutional Court decisions tepidly, as if it is unsure of its constitutional grounding to do so. Thinking of the Constitution in Madisonian terms, and recognizing the robust lineage of the Constitution in Congress, might foster bolder and clearer constitutional arguments from Congress. Here, paradoxically, rhetoric and thought might actually serve to correct what is, at times, a Madisonian failing rooted in the narrow self-interest of congressional representatives. This breakdown might be most evident in the Senate hearings of judicial nominees, where many members of Congress all too willingly give lip service to judicial supremacy, irresponsibly evading the necessity of rendering constitutional judgment in a highly visible public forum where the issues are squarely constitutional.

Second, this approach should make us more comfortable as a polity with constitutional quarrels, which, paradoxically, might help make us more appreciative of constitutional forms. Because the Constitution does not remove the responsibility of constitutional judgment from each branch, constitutional quarrels about meaning, and who has the authority to do what, will be an ordinary feature of our politics. Such disputes will often require "judging" other constitutional actor's constructions of constitutional meaning. We should recognize as a matter of constitutional propriety each branch's right—indeed, obligation—to form independent judgments about constitutional meaning. This acknowledgment should encourage each constitutional actor to take the Constitution more seriously as he or she must focus on and articulate arguments about constitutional meaning and authority. Knowing that no institution will simply settle such disputes, as a polity we might attend more carefully to constitutional meaning, even, perhaps, to how such meaning fits within the whole of the Constitution. In doing so, we might usefully distinguish constitutional meaning from constitutional propriety. Even while disagreeing profoundly about *meaning*, we should recognize the constitutional *propriety* of the Congress, the president, and the Court adhering to their understanding of constitutional meaning.

Here is precisely where we might learn to appreciate constitutional forms more than we do. Viewing the Constitution from the outside, we may see it as a coherent whole. But, for reasons I have explained, when we bring it down to earth, it is partial and conflicted. There is the temptation to dispense with constitutional forms in favor of grander and nobler constitutional ends. We might read the preamble for inspiration, as it calls us to "establish justice" and "secure the Blessings of Liberty to ourselves and our Posterity." We would be hard pressed to find such inspiration in the mundane technicality of Article I. Or, for those of us swept away by the Court as great defender of individual liberty, Article III, Section 2: "The judicial Power shall extend to all Cases, in Law and Equity, arising under this Constitution, the Laws of the United States, and Treaties made, or which shall be made, under their Authority." Demands for justice, finality, and efficiency, all articulated to some degree in the Constitution's preamble, are often behind the insistence on judicial supremacy or popular sovereignty in rejecting the Madisonian vision. But Madison views complex constitutional forms as a means of achieving justice. In his most famous discussion of the separation of powers in *Federalist* 51, Madison concludes his exposition on the virtues of the separation of powers by attaching it to the sentiment that "Justice is the end of government." This thought is brought more vividly to light in a subsequent sentence, "It [justice] ever has been and ever will be pursued until it be obtained, or until liberty be lost in the pursuit."[40] The point is that justice might be best achieved by preventing quick or authoritative action under the Constitution, particularly authoritative or quick action that is done in the name of justice. The separation of powers can be both means and ends: a means in preventing "usurpations" and an end in "promoting sober deliberation"[41] about the ends toward which the Constitution aspires.

This makes a virtue out of necessity.[42] In attempting to bring to life an actual government, not merely to theorize about government, Madison was creating a regime in *deed,* not in *speech.* Forging the Constitution itself was a mix of principles and possibilities based on history and experience. As he argued in *Federalist* 41, "the choice must always be made, if not of the lesser evil, at least of the GREATER, not the PERFECT good."[43] Consider that the preamble of the Constitution aspires "to form a more perfect Union," suggesting the inevitably imperfect nature of such a Union: or that the president swears an oath to protect, preserve, and defend the Constitution "to the best of my ability." In defending the Constitution, *The Federalist* speaks of "aptitude and tendency" or, in the language of modern political science, probability, not certainty.[44] This recognition of imperfection led Madison to be much less sanguine than later critics of countervailing power, like Woodrow Wilson, about maintaining constitutional government (as well as achieving justice). Crafting our institutions to this end may indeed foster disharmony, but it may also foster deliberation and reflection—and foster deliberation and reflection precisely because it fosters disharmony. In this manner, the constitutional order that Madison created *sought* to turn potential vices in a positive direction; and it did so by drawing on the lessons of experience as distilled by the "new science of politics."

In chapter 1, I explain more fully the Madisonian understanding of the Constitution that I have sketched here, turning to Madison's own efforts in constitutional construction to do so. I argue that it draws, more than is usually thought, on ancient constitutionalism insofar as it seeks to replicate the tension and balance within the "mixed regime." This understanding is perhaps most evident in attempts to situate John Marshall's argument for judicial review in *Marbury* as a corollary of the Madisonian Constitution. While I argue that judicial review, but not supremacy, can be situated within the Madisonian separation of powers, I also note that it does so somewhat uneasily. It is not simply the potentially aristocratic nature of the Court and its power of judicial review in the midst of republican institutions. The executive, too, at least as originally conceived, manifested many of these qualities. And our attempt to constitutionalize executive power also speaks to how it sits ambivalently within republican institutions.[45] More problematical than the judiciary's potentially antirepublican cast is the tension between institutions called forth by fundamental law, and the Court's peculiar concern with legal forms, which has given birth to arguments for judicial supremacy and attempts to reduce the whole of the Constitution to a sort of "super" positive law explicated from a legal mind-set.[46]

In chapters 2–5, I then examine four crucial episodes of constitutional conflict that have profoundly shaped how we view our Constitution. In these instances, the branches of government struggled with one another to construct constitutional authority and meaning as part of maintaining the Constitution. While many of the issues and debates I canvass are familiar, I want to situate them more thoroughly and wholly within the Madisonian framework. My hope is to illuminate how these struggles have played out in Madisonian terms, casting light on both the struggles themselves and the Madisonian Constitution.

My primary concern in chapter 2 is to examine Abraham Lincoln and the Republican Congress's attempt to construct constitutional authority in a manner that would make the Union they saved "forever worthy of the saving." For the antislavery and free labor Republicans, this attempt rested on the Declaration of Independence's promise of liberty and equality, which ultimately entailed the passage of the Fourteenth Amendment. By amending the Constitution, the Republicans sought to settle a bundle of constitutional questions that had vexed the American polity, giving their understanding permanent constitutional authority by entrenching it in constitutional text. This promise, however, was only partially realized, as struggles turned from the authority of the Fourteenth Amendment to its meaning. Democrats situated the Civil War amendments within the contours of antebellum constitutional thought in an effort to limit the Republican reconstruction of constitutional meaning. The Republican constitutional understandings—despite formal constitutional amendments—only found partial expression, rather than a grand synthesis of Founding and Republican constitutionalism forging of a "new" constitutional regime.

If Republicans of the Civil War era sought to understand the antebellum Constitution as rooted in Jefferson's Declaration, in chapter 3 we see the progressives reaching back to Alexander Hamilton. Progressives sought to draw upon and rework the constitutional thought of Hamilton (and others) to reorder our constitutional understandings of the national government's power to regulate economic life. For progressives, as a living organism the Constitution had to be adapted to the needs of the day, bringing all of the branches together to insist on the will of the people. This required jettisoning earlier strands of constitutional thought—including, for instance, Lincoln's free labor vision and, at root, the notion that the Constitution had a fixed meaning—in a "deconstructive" process. But much like the Republicans of Reconstruction in seeking to reorder our constitutional understandings, the progressive reconstruction was partial and incomplete. Progressives were able to lay the foundations of the administrative state, even while differing views of the commerce power and due process sat uneasily together for decades.

Turning to the New Deal, chapter 4 argues that while FDR drew deeply on progressive constitutional thought, in reconstructing our constitutional understandings he linked the progressive notion of an evolutionary constitution to the Founders. If he was expanding government beyond traditional understandings, it was necessary to preserve the constitutional order itself and thus was consistent with it. Roosevelt rejected traditional views of liberty and limitations on government. These views would have to be reconstructed to make way for governmental regulation and control in order to protect liberty itself. But FDR was only partly successful. While his reconstruction of national authority was entrenched for decades, and he further solidified the administrative state, particularly giving birth to new "constitutional" commitments, FDR did not fully succeed in bringing about a new constitutional understanding of liberty. Here, New Deal foundations were essentially negative, leaving us deeply conflicted about "civil liberties" to the present day.

Chapter 5 turns to Ronald Reagan's attempt to dismantle FDR's constitutional reconstruction. Yet, in interesting ways, elements of his constitutional thought were rooted within the constitutional change wrought by the Progressive and New Deal eras. In advocating original intent, Reagan sought to return to pre–New Deal understandings, particularly on the issues of federalism and the enumerated powers of the national government. His view of original intent also rejected the notion of evolving constitutional meaning, and the judicial balancing that had grown up around it, at the heart of the New Deal constitutional changes. While Reagan did not fully reconstruct our constitutional understandings, federalism and the notion of limited national power have become vibrant strands of thought in our constitutional discourse, taking solid root in some areas. Yet aspects of Reagan's originalism, at least as expressed by some within his administration and his court appointees, were deeply rooted in the New Deal's deconstructive constitutional vision. These originalists digested the New Deal reconstruction insofar as they rejected earlier originalist lines of constitutional thought. Here again, we witness partial reconstructions of constitutional meaning and authority, as these various strands of constitutional thought sit uneasily alongside one another.

Taken together, *The Madisonian Constitution* argues that these episodes do not reveal grand moments of constitutional transformation, where the political branches play an unusual role in constitutional development, but after which we return to the norm of constitutional settlement. Nor do they show the Supreme Court settling contested constitutional issues, or falling into line with the essentials of the political branches. Rather, these cases illustrate that constitutional conflict is a perennial feature of our constitutionalism. And while these are four separate though wide-ranging cases, they build on one another historically. They capture wide swaths of our constitutional history where constitutional meaning and authority remain conflicted and unsettled, revealing that alternative views of constitutional meaning and authority persist within the independent branches of government. These historical studies are not an *exhaustive* account of the Madisonian Constitution; rather, they seek to frame the house within which American constitutionalism takes shape. The central focus in these studies is the interaction between the president, the Congress, and the Court over constitutional interpretation. These studies seek to reveal the limits of judicial supremacy and the legal Constitution insofar as constitutional interpretation has been seen as essentially judicial, when in fact the political branches have frequently shaped constitutional meaning. Here I hope that this work not only opens new vistas that future scholarship might help flesh out more fully but also situates current scholarship within the general contours of the Madisonian understanding.

This understanding of our constitutionalism has surely been submerged or been overlain with the veneer of judicial supremacy and the legal constitution.[47] Yet, beneath this veneer of a legal Constitution articulated and enforced by the Court lies the reality of the Madisonian Constitution, which, I argue, continues to capture much of the actual functioning of our polity. That is, the Madisonian vision best captures the translation of word into deed that is central to bringing fundamental law down to earth.

This is not, however, a story of happy endings.[48] A Madisonian understanding of the Constitution recognizes imperfection and the possibility of failure.[49] The Constitution is established to foster and protect America's creedal commitments, but no framework can guarantee success. Statesmanship has often been necessary to maintain the Constitution. But statesmanship cannot be guaranteed.[50] As a polity, we have not always adhered to the Constitution. And though new circumstances have often led us to develop constitutional meaning, not every such reconstruction is constitutionally grounded. Constitutional meaning is not infinitely malleable; the Constitution is not a mere framework the substance of which we may alter with ever-new constructions. Yet, the attempts to construct or reconstruct constitutional meaning and authority that are canvassed in the chapters that follow are frequently arguments over precisely what constitutional ends and foundational principles require.[51] And such debates have shaped how we see the Constitution, giving us a layered "text-polity" where recent constructions overlay, and conflict with, the Madisonian Constitution without displacing it.[52]

Before turning to the chapters ahead, let me pause to say a word about the scholarly turn to constitutional politics. I have a tremendous debt to this work,[53] which I acknowledge in citations throughout the book. This book, however, departs from the most prevalent approaches—a political regimes understanding and a constitutional regimes understanding—which offer sophisticated and subtle variations on Robert Dahl's notion that the Court follows the election returns.

Much of this scholarship has turned from constitutional theory to constitutional politics as a way of examining how changes in judicial understandings of the Constitution are, at root, due to changes in American electoral politics. This is especially true of a "political regimes" approach that takes its bearings from Dahl in examining how the Court reflects the various political desires of the "governing-coalition." With some irony, these approaches, while institutionalist, end up replicating, although in far more subtle and sophisticated ways, Dahl's behavioral approach.[54] To say that the Court acted in line with the "governing-coalition" leads us to ask how we know that any particular outcome is what the "governing-coalition" wanted. The answer often is, Because that is the way the Court *behaved*. But why did the Court act thus? Because that is what the governing coalition allowed.[55] This perspective runs the risk of tautology as it does not pay enough heed to how the Constitution itself, that great independent variable as idea and structure, might provide for, even cause, such behavior.[56] While this empirical bent of mind is refreshing, it is at times disconnected from thought, which runs the risk of reducing the Constitution to electoral outcomes, neglecting how constitutional thought might operate autonomously in structuring politics. Moreover, in examining how the political branches might attempt to use the courts, such approaches have little to say about this from a *constitutional* perspective.[57] Long ago, Alexander Hamilton in *Federalist* 16 voiced concern that judges "might be embarked in a conspiracy with the legislature."[58] And Lincoln, after all, saw *Dred Scott* as part of just such a conspiracy. The decision might well have been grounded in the interests of a "governing-coalition," but that did not make it constitutionally sound. It was all the worse, according to Lincoln, because the Court allowed itself to be used by the likes of President Buchanan and Judge Douglas in an attempt to silence a foundational constitutional dispute.[59]

Attending more fully to constitutional thought, but also following a variation of Dahl's analysis, scholars have detailed the construction of different *constitutional* regimes over the course of American history. In extraordinary moments of constitutional politics, we, by way of critical elections and reconstructive presidents, forge new constitutional understandings and create "new" constitutional regimes. In this telling of our constitutional history, the political branches and the people are primarily responsible for transforming constitutional meaning in these extraordinary constitutional moments. The reconstituted Court, then, becomes the primary defender of the "new" Constitutional order.[60] The common theme of a constitutional regimes narrative here is the focus on extraordinary constitutional moments or reconstructions that ground judicial power in the political commitments of each particular constitutional order.[61] Such a packaging of our constitutional history also masks persistent constitutional conflicts and disputes that are a recurrent feature of our constitutionalism—a feature, I argue, that is called forth by our Constitution.[62] In this way, *The Madisonian Constitution* illuminates how countervailing power plays an ongoing role in maintaining, creating, and recovering constitutional meaning and authority.

CHAPTER ONE

Madison's Complex Constitutionalism

Constitutionalism in the American tradition is defined by the insistence upon a written constitution as fundamental law that "prescribes the limits of all delegated power."[1] This move, so much a part of early American constitutional thought, attempts to empower and limit government. But how do we make the written constitution effective? The act of writing itself is no guarantee that fundamental law would be translated from word to deed. The question is how to bring this fundamental law down to earth.[2] How do we bond the polity to the word of the Constitution?[3] Scholars of constitutionalism have often suggested that a constitution's being fundamental law was a hindrance to making if enforceable. Thus, it has been suggested that the great innovation in American constitutionalism was not just in providing a written constitution but in making that written constitution enforceable as law.[4] As Gordon Wood has argued, "What in the final analysis gave meaning to the Americans' conception of a constitution was not its fundamentality or its creation by the people, but rather its implementation in the ordinary courts of law."[5]

This legal view of the Constitution, as well as its solution to the problem of making fundamental law binding, remains the conventional understanding of constitutional enforcement.[6] Exercising the power of judicial review, the Court binds the polity to the law of the Constitution. The Supreme Court itself has pushed this argument, insisting that it "speaks" for the Constitution and that, once it has spoken, we—the president, the Congress, and the people—are bound by its interpretation of the Constitution.[7] The nature of the Constitution as law inexorably means that the Court—whether exclusively or finally—is its authoritative "voice."[8] If judicial review is frequently spoken of in terms of checks and balances, it has really come to be seen as the one "check" that maintains the Constitution. This led Charles McIlwain to insist that "the doctrine of the separation of powers has no true application to judicial matters." And, indeed, this is because "the one institution above all others essential to the preservation of the law has always been and still is an honest, able, learned, independent judiciary."[9] Notice the easy confla-tion of "law" with Constitution. Such an understanding of constitutionalism is profoundly at odds with James Madison's separation of powers.[10]

To draw out the Madisonian vision of the Constitution, I begin this chapter with a conceptual and theoretical discussion.[11] Although the Madisonian vision begins from the written nature of the Constitution, the written constitution calls forth institutions that, at the risk of sounding opaque, "constitute" the Constitu-tion. It is a merger of words and forms; it is symbol and instrument.[12] The written text brings institutional forms to life that look back to the text as part of bringing the Constitution to life—making fundamental law an *actual* constitution.[13] To this end, rather than being entrusted to a single body, power is deliberately divided among institutional forms as a central feature of maintaining the Constitution. This division necessarily invites "a concurrent right to expound the constitution,"[14] yielding multiple and conflicting views of the Constitution as an inherent—even healthy—part of the constitutional order.[15]

Next, I examine Madison's participation in early constitutional debates to fur-ther elaborate his vision. Madison suggests an intimate connection between thought and practice. Indeed, commenting on Madison's constitutionalism, Thomas Jeffer-son said it belonged to the category of political science rather than political theory.[16] Concerned with creating and sustaining a durable form of republican government with the materials at hand, Madison's thought was informed by history and experi-ence grounded in nature, not abstract Newtonian physics.[17] As Madison himself put it, experience should be our guide, rather than the musings of "an ingenious theorist" planning a constitution from the closet of his imagination.[18] Unlike much of contemporary constitutional theory, Madison's constitutional thought does not try to dissolve the tensions within the constitutional order. Examining the interac-tion between thought and practice invites us to see how this dynamic has actually worked (and changed) in regard to constitutional interpretation. This topic is taken up far more extensively, though more narrowly, in chapters 2, 3, 4, and 5.

Finally, I seek to situate judicial review within the Madisonian separation of powers as one facet of the constitutional order. From the Madisonian perspective, we can see judicial review as one part of the whole of American constitutionalism, rather than viewing American constitutionalism through the lens of judicial re-view. Even here, however, there is some tension as is evidenced by efforts, dating to the early years of the republic, to draw on the legal nature of the Constitution as inexorably calling forth judicial supremacy. Yet this move threatens to subvert the constitutional framework, even while drawing on Madison's separation of powers to do so. By making constitutional questions legal questions, and therefore the peculiar province of courts, the Court is placed above the Constitution rather than within it.[19]

Madison's Complex Constitutionalism

Much like Thomas Jefferson and John Marshall, Madison agreed that a written constitution was our "peculiar security," the great improvement of our "political institutions."[20] A written constitution "prescribes the limits of all delegated power"[21] by writing those limits down for all to see; they are thus subject to neither the whim of the legislature nor the will of the judge.[22] A written constitution has come to be seen as the defining feature of constitutionalism as it legally defines the powers of government and the rights of citizens.[23] But can the polity be bound by words? Madison insisted that the mere act of writing the Constitution, "a mere demarcation on parchment,"[24] did not make it self-enforcing. One could surely imagine, as Marshall did in *Marbury,* a government overstepping its prescribed constitutional limitations—and doing so despite the fact that those limitations are clearly demarcated. If constitutional limits were not somehow enforced, Marshall said, then "a written constitution was an absurd attempt on the part of the people to limit a power that is illimitable."[25] On this score, Madison agreed with Marshall. To be effective, the Constitution's written limits had to be maintained.

Structure: Countervailing Power and the "Self-Governing" Constitution

Madison's great innovation was to make the constitutional framework "self-governing."[26] Key to constitutional maintenance is the structure the written constitution calls forth. The division of power between the national and state governments, the large republic, and the separation of powers and checks and balances are all institutional innovations that structure, or form, our politics. These institutional innovations, the invention of modern political science, would make certain actions more probable, but—just as we could not trust that "enlightened statesmen will . . . be at the helm"—they would not alleviate us from attending to self-government.[27] Rather than being a "machine that would go of itself," the Madisonian vision calls on us to continually engage in the process of constitutional self-government.

This vision is particularly evident in Madison's initial skepticism about a bill of rights, where he insisted to Jefferson that a people who reject constitutional limits are unlikely to be restrained by textually enumerated rights. Surveying the various bills of rights in the state constitutions, Madison noted "that repeated violations of these parchment barriers have been committed by overbearing majorities in every state."[28] Madison's idea was to contrive the institutional framework so that it would have an "aptitude and tendency" to thwart "the physical and political force of the nation" when such a force was heedless of constitutional limits. Thus, the Madisonian Constitution depends not on the "people themselves" but first and foremost on institutional forms that seek to refine and shape popular opinion, tempering its vices, in order to maintain constitutional government.[29] For Madison, "public liberty" rejected the notion of "government in one center."

Thus, the Madisonian vision created a diffusion of offices, all of which would share in maintaining the Constitution, but none of which would be superior in that regard. The result is a complex constitutionalism that Madison viewed as sui generis.[30] Surveying the history of republican government, Madison sought a cure for the diseases most incident to republican government, but focused his search on a cure found in nature and experience, not in abstract theorizing.[31] This approach was founded in a realistic (not necessarily pessimistic) view of human nature, which, according to Madison, is why government needed to be *powerful and limited* in the first place. As one legal scholar has put it, written constitutionalism depends "on 'the trust men repose' in the ability of human beings to change their behavior in response to law."[32] But this is precisely what Madison refused to do. Instead, Madison sought to simultaneously create and contain the polity by an institutional framework, which, so contrived, would also contain itself. This concept entailed not a legalistic separation of powers, or the simple fact of a written constitution, but a separation of powers rooted in countervailing power.[33]

Its implementation begins with a functional separation of the different institutions—executive, legislative, and judicial—so that no single individual, or institution, holds all power. But these institutions are not hermetically sealed from one another; on the contrary, each has a portion of the others' power, providing for checks and balances between the institutions. This countervailing power occurs not just in giving the executive a portion of the legislative power (i.e., through the veto), for example, but in the foundational construction of each institution. That is, each institution is constituted in such a manner that it draws its power from a different constituency, making each institution independent of the others, as well as cultivating an agonistic balance of power between them.[34] Thus, the Congress—because the legislature was the most feared power—is itself divided. Representatives in the lower house draw their power, and depend for their reelection, directly from the people of their particular districts. Senators, on the other hand, depended initially on their state legislatures and today on the people of the whole state. The executive depends on the people of the whole nation acting through their state institutions and the Electoral College. The Court depends on the appointment of the president and confirmation by the Senate, but is then independent of each, catering to no immediate constituency. In drawing their power from different groups, these institutions have different interests, which deliberately foster disharmony, if not conflict, between them (making constitutional deliberation a necessity). This independence is evident even in the overlapping terms of office: representatives serve two years, senators serve six, and presidents four, while members of the Court serve for life.[35] Constituting a government in such a manner makes each branch truly independent. As Madison said at the Constitutional Convention, referring to Montesquieu's separation of powers without naming him, "If it be a fundamental principle of free Government that the Legislative, Executive, and Judiciary powers should be *separately* exercised, it is equally so that they be *independently* exercised."[36]

This design takes it as given that human beings may well act to increase their power. Countervailing power in this manner fosters the virtues and independence of the different institutions in a positive direction, while maintaining constitutional boundaries, and independence, by having them police one another. The creation of this complex institutional order brings to mind ancient understandings of constitutionalism and "mixed government."[37] The blending of monarchy, aristocracy, and democracy, with action and reaction between the different features of these political orders, moderated and contained government. This complex constitutionalism is most evident in the thought of Montesquieu whose "gothic constitutionalism" is perhaps best understood as a blend of ancient and modern political thought.[38] Not coincidentally, "the celebrated Montesquieu" is the most cited authority in *The Federalist*.[39] Prior to the dissemination of these essays, Montesquieu offered the most thoroughgoing discussion of the separation of powers and was the first thinker to insist that there will be no "liberty if the power of judging is not separate from legislative power and from executive power."[40] His teaching about the separation of powers was, at root, a moderating one aimed at self-government:

> Political liberty is to be found only in moderate governments; and even in these it is not always found. It is there only when there is not abuse of power. But constant experience shows us that every man invested with power is apt to abuse it, and to carry his authority as far as it will go. Is it not strange, though true, to say that virtue itself has need of limits? To prevent this abuse, it is necessary from the very nature of things that power should be a check to power. A government may be so constituted,

as no man shall be compelled to do things to which the law does not oblige him, nor forced to abstain from things which the law permits.[41]

In Montesquieu, the separation of powers combines elements of the institutional function of each branch (executive, legislative, judicial) along with elements from Aristotelian regimes (monarchy, aristocracy, democracy).[42] In Madison's hands, the separation of powers is wholly republican. Each branch traces it power, albeit in complex ways, to the people. Yet Madison draws heavily on Montesquieu in crafting an institutional structure in which each branch represents a different aspect of republicanism—that is, drawing on both its liberal and democratic features—imitating the tension and balance within a truly "mixed" constitutional regime to protect the people's liberty.[43] As the very Montesquieuian Alexis de Tocqueville would later note in speaking of this new science of politics, the constitutional system attempted to foster pride as a spur to action by fusing it with self-interest, using a modern virtue to imitate an ancient virtue.[44] Thus, Madison sought to "transform simple quantitative majority rule into a more complex qualitative majority rule."[45] And he did so by combining features of democracy and liberalism. The Constitution created and channeled different versions of the people as the foundation for different institutional forms in a manner that would contain and inspire both the government and the governed—as both are potential threats to constitutional liberty as well as necessary defenders of it.

Although the emphasis is on structure, the Madisonian Constitution is not simply a process, devoid of any substance, as some jurists and legal scholars have attempted to render it.[46] The Madisonian framework is structured to protect and further the substantive ends, or aspirations, of the Constitution.[47] Contrary to some views of "interpretive plurality," Madison does not reject the notion of "fixed" meaning or first principles in favor of constitutional indeterminacy. As I noted in the introduction, the discussion of checks and balances in *Federalist* 51 culminates with the insistence that the end of government is justice. As Madison puts it in *Federalist* 43 in defending the legitimacy of the proposed Constitution, "the transcendent law of nature and of nature's God . . . declares that the safety and happiness of society are the objects at which all political institutions aim and to which all such institutions must be sacrificed."[48] For Madison, the substantive principles on which the Constitution rests are best furthered by this complex constitutionalism.

Consider, in this light, Abraham Lincoln's notion that the Constitution ought to become the political religion of the nation, or Franklin Delano Roosevelt's suggestion that it ought to be read again and again by citizens like the Bible.[49] The religious imagery is unmistakable and might be seen to promote what Sanford Levinson has called "constitutional faith."[50] Madison himself, without naming the Bible, once noted that interpreting the Constitution's words might, at times, involve the same sort of disputes about meaning that occur even "when the Almighty himself condescends to address mankind in their own language."[51] But Lincoln and FDR, to borrow another of Levinson's phrasings, seem to be urging a "protestant" engagement with that faith, taking constitutional self-government, in the form of knowing and thinking about fundamental law, to be a task of citizens and government officials. Lincoln, for instance, insists that, "Reason, cold, calculating, unimpassioned reason, must furnish all the materials for our future support and defence," though he then calls for these materials to be molded into "a reverence for the constitution and laws."[52]

These urgings to know "the word" point us to the nature of the text and the presuppositions it rests upon. As FDR claimed, pointing to both its preamble and specific textual provisions, the Constitution "is an easy document to understand."[53] Lincoln's insistence that it be "taught in schools, in seminaries, and in colleges" and "preached from the pulpit," as well as "proclaimed in legislative halls," suggests a similar sort of appreciation and knowledge for the particulars of the Constitution.[54] On the one hand, these testimonials reveal the importance of constitutional forms. On the other, they point beyond them. After all, citizens taking such advice might be somewhat disappointed, or at least not moved toward political religion, to read: "The President shall, at stated Times, receive for his Services, a Compensation, which shall neither be increased nor diminished during the Period for which he shall have been elected, and he shall not receive within that Period any other Emolument from the United States, or any of them." Scanning the brief document, the earnest citizens would discover it to be full of like passages, perhaps leading one to think of Madison's Constitution, as did Patrick Henry, "as a crazy machine." Yet, the particular provision of Article II, Section 1, quoted here is part of the foundation of executive independence, which is central to the whole Constitution. In this manner, the particulars of constitutional form rest upon presuppositions about government and point toward ends beyond themselves. The Constitution forges a space in which the claims of political thought to govern and guide the polity might at least be heard. It is not a coincidence that Lincoln and FDR both invoked the Declaration as central to understanding the particulars of the Constitution. Interestingly, the Declaration itself referred to laws that have violated "our Constitution" before we had a formal written Constitution. In this way, the Constitution rests on an unwritten or, better still, small "c" constitution.

The interaction between the small "c" constitution and the large "C" written Constitution might be said to be the *whole* of our Constitution. This possibility does not reduce the written provisions, or the framework it brings to life, to mere means. The separation of powers, like the Constitution itself, is both a means and an end.[55] Indeed, the independent institutions of government, rooted in agonistic elements, have often conflicted over the proper ordering of constitutional values. The result, if I may steal a phrase, is a "living constitution," where constitutional meaning and authority are constructed with the Madisonian Constitution. This living constitution is not brought to life by facile views of judicial evolution, where an enlightened Court progressively brings the Constitution "up to date."[56] It is far better captured by President Lincoln's confrontation with Chief Justice Taney's *Dred Scott* decision, or FDR's attempt to turn to the language and intent of the Constitution against the Court, even if we think that these particular efforts were wrong in their understanding of constitutional meaning and authority. Within the Madisonian scheme, there is "no sovereign authority to settle our disputes."[57]

This potentially "disharmonic" gap between *constitutional* ideals and constitutional practice[58] is the inevitable result of making the *formal* constitution a *real* constitution. To see the Constitution through a Madisonian lens is to realize that the "Constitution does not always speak through the judiciary and does not always speak with one voice."[59] But, as Madison noted, this was the most reliable way to achieve constitutional ends. Simply put, what has been dubbed our "thick" Constitution is central to achieving the polity's higher constitutional aims, usually culled from the Constitution's preamble or the Declaration's second paragraph.

Departmentalism: Interpretation within the Constitutional Framework

Scholars have long promoted departmentalism or "interpretative plurality" in constitutional interpretation, and such an understanding flows from the nature of the Constitution I have sketched here. But the Madisonian vision runs deeper than "extrajudicial" interpretation—a phrase that itself remains too wedded to a legalist understanding—insofar as the diffusion of power inheres in the nature of the Constitution. It not only protects the Constitution in negative terms but, with conflicting interpretations, fosters our positive constitutional commitments as well. Executive and legislative interpretations are thus fundamental in bringing the Constitution to life and are different, in kind, from the Court's. The separation of powers, as I argue, creates different institutions that are suited to the different needs of the polity. These needs include balancing, for example, a powerful strand of democracy in the House, against a more moderate, indirect, and liberal form of democracy in the Senate. Each institution has its particular end, but the whole, even while foundationally republican, is emblematic of the mixed regime insofar as these elements represent aspects of the amalgam.

A glance at much of current constitutional law and theory might suggest that these elements are "mere surplusage."[60] Yet this is the essence of the written Constitution. Even those disposed to prefer the preamble should note that it "ordains and establishes *this* Constitution," that is, the "thick" Constitution.[61] Paying attention to the actual institutions the Constitution creates, and how they are constituted by way of balanced and countervailing constituencies and principles, will illuminate how institutional design was meant to maintain constitutional boundaries: rooted in countervailing power, the thick Constitution gives the political branches incentives to maintain their independence, which is seen as essential to constitutional government. It is interesting, in this light, that *The Federalist,* the great exegetical writing on the Constitution, refers to the true principles of republicanism and the institutional forms of the new Constitution but rarely to what we would today call constitutional law.[62] The "venerable Montesquieu" spoke of the separation of powers as being essential to political liberty, which was different from the liberty of the citizen (who also benefited from the separation of powers). Political liberty was more akin to self-government, which would best be maintained if sovereign authority—the authority to potentially end self-government, or what Madison called, nearly following Montesquieu, "public liberty"—was not vested in any one of these institutions.

Madison's most famous discussion of how these forms will maintain one another, and hence constitutional self-government, culminates in *Federalist* 51. He begins by asking how we are to maintain "in practice the necessary partition of power among the several departments as laid down in the Constitution." Madison says that the first reliance on maintaining constitutional boundaries is supplied by "exterior provisions." However, lest these devices fail, we must trust in auxiliary precautions—"by so contriving the interior structure of the government as that its several constituent parts may, by their mutual relations, be the means of keeping each other in their proper places."[63]

While power is separated, it must also be checked. To keep the legislature, Madison's first concern, from encroaching upon the powers of the executive or overstepping its constitutional bounds, the executive is fortified with a negative (the veto) against the legislature. The negative, however, is not absolute. Although the executive is the weaker branch, it too may overstep constitutional limits. What is needed is to order the Constitution so that the various parties under it have an interest in maintaining its boundaries: "But the great security against a gradual concentration of the several powers in the same department consists in giving those who administer each department the necessary constitutional means and personal motives to resist encroachments of the others." To drive home this point, Madison argued, "The interest of the man must be connected with the constitutional rights of the place."[64] Constitutional limits will be maintained in that those who hold office under it will have an interest in enforcing its written provisions—indeed, an institutionally structured self-serving interest. The branches of government themselves, balancing against one another, would police the Constitution's boundaries.

At the same time, Madison recognized the possibility that "in the ordinary course of things, the exposition of the laws and the constitution devolves upon the judicial branch." But, he cautioned, this did not mean that the Court was the final arbiter of constitutional meaning and authority: "But I beg to know, on what principle it can be contended that any one department derives from the constitution greater powers than another, in declaring what are the true limits of the constitution."[65]

Interestingly, Madison does not refer to judicial review in *Federalist* 51, his most prominent discussion of checks and balances. The nature of judicial review may fit within the institutional logic he spells out there. But, paradoxically, this check may elevate the judiciary above the legislature and executive if the judiciary is given "the unique power to enforce the Constitution," as the "Constitution structures politics and government."[66] As Jack Rakove argues, the power of judicial review "arises circumstantially, literally through the chronology of action—yet absent any conflicting vision, it expresses the latent intent of the document itself."[67] Thus, while judicial review begins within the context of the separation of power and the logic of checks and balances, it comes to be the final word on constitutional interpretation. In contrast, if we begin from the institutional diffusion of power as the essence of our Constitution, the judiciary is only one feature of constitutional government. To illuminate this Madisonian understanding, I turn to two early constitutional debates in the Congress where Madison had a prominent role.

Madisonian Constructions: Constitutional Politics

Early debates on the nature and meaning of the Constitution occur primarily between the executive and the legislature as well as within these branches. The debates over the president's removal power and the establishment of the national bank[68] touch on central issues of constitutional meaning and authority, but rarely cast a glance at the judiciary. In these pivotal "Madisonian moments" of constitutional development, the judiciary was essentially silent.

The President's Removal Power

In 1789 the First Congress, which included many delegates to the Constitutional Convention, debated whether officials in the executive branch—who had been appointed with the advice and consent of the Senate—could be removed by the president alone. Madison argued that the legislature must uphold its constitutional responsibility, and, in this case, he insisted, the Constitution gave the president the sole power of removal. Because the Constitution was not self-evident on this point, one could not simply interpret Article II's vesting clause as requiring this solution, so Madison's conclusion required the Congress to situate the clause within the underlying scheme of the separation of powers. At stake, according to Madison, was "whether the government shall retain that equilibrium which the constitution intended." He went so far as to say that Congress's decision may "affect the fundamental principles of the government under which we act, and liberty itself." Congress was therefore obligated to consider "the genius and character of the whole government" in its exposition of the Constitution. Thus, Madison did not see the legislation Congress drafted giving the executive the sole power of removal as merely advisory; rather, he put it forward as in accord with the "true meaning of the constitution" by which we must be guided.[69]

William Smith of South Carolina objected to this construction, claiming that the consent of the Senate was necessary to remove an appointee, as it was necessary to appoint him in the first place. In drawing out his argument, Smith pointed to the eminent *Federalist* 77, where Alexander Hamilton, Madison's great collaborator as Publius, argued that the Senate was necessary "to displace as well as appoint." Smith then pushed his argument a step further, insisting that the Congress—particularly the House—had no business in deciding the matter. Because constitutional meaning was in doubt, Smith suggested that this was preeminently a judicial question. Rather than illegitimately attempting to expound on the Constitution, Smith thought the Congress should wait until the question came before the judiciary to be settled.[70]

Against this line of thinking, Madison argued that the judiciary was not, nor could it have been meant to be, the primary expositor of the Constitution. "But the great objection drawn from the source to which the last arguments would lead us is, that the Legislature itself has no right to expound the constitution; that whenever its meaning is doubtful, you must leave it to take its course, until the Judiciary is called upon to declare its meaning." For Madison, the Congress had as much right to determine constitutional meaning as the judiciary; indeed, he doubted whether "this question could even come before the judges."[71] As Madison argued, "But, I beg to know, upon what principle it can be contended, that any one department draws from the constitution greater powers than another, in making out the limits of the powers *of the several departments*?" And again, "If the constitutional boundary of either be brought into question, I do not see that any one of these departments has more right than another to declare their sentiments on that point."[72]

In the course of this debate, Madison insisted on a "maxim which ought to direct us in expounding the constitution," a maxim that "is found in the political writings of the most celebrated civilians, and is everywhere held as essential to the preservation of liberty." It was this: "that the three great departments of government be kept separate and distinct; and if in any case they are blended, it is in order to admit a partial qualification in order more effectually to guard against an entire consolidation." If this case turned on a particular constitutional question, the sweep of Madison's analysis pointed to this maxim as central to the nature of our Constitution: "there is no one government that I know of, in which provision is made for a particular authority to determine the great constitutional limits, and the great division of power between the branches of government. In all systems there are points which must be adjusted by the departments themselves, to which no one of them is competent."[73]

Madison's argument is often taken as the great defense of departmentalism in constitutional interpretation. This may be so, but we must be clear on the term's meaning. In some guises, departmentalism signifies that each department is the primary interpreter of *its* constitutional power; that is, it interprets those provisions of the Constitution that apply to it specifically.[74] In this instance, the Court is not the final authority on Congress's power, although it may well be on issues of a judicial nature. This line of thinking is clearly not Madison's argument here. Instead, Madison insists that the Congress (or any branch) can touch on questions of constitutional meaning—that is, look to the "whole genius" of the Constitution—if these questions are properly before it.[75] In the case of the removal power, notice, Congress is largely defining *executive* power and authority under the Constitution. Yet the Congress was doing so to maintain executive independence, thereby squaring Article II concerns with the overarching constitutional scheme. Hence, Congress's interpretation should govern because it "expresses the meaning of the constitution as must be established by fair construction."[76]

The Bank of the United States

We see a reliance on congressional and executive interpretation and an under-standing of the whole constitutional enterprise from Madison as president when he signed the act establishing the Second Bank of the United States into law in 1816. Madison had argued against the establishment of the First Bank of the United States while serving in the First Congress. In this great debate over the nature of the Constitution and how to properly interpret it, Madison joined Jefferson against his one-time ally Hamilton. Madison claimed that the Constitution did not grant the national government the power of incorporation. Jefferson echoed this argu-ment from the executive branch as secretary of state, whereas Hamilton, also from the executive branch as secretary of the treasury, insisted that the national gov-ernment, relying on the "necessary and proper clause," had the power.[77] While the debate over constitutional interpretation is fascinating in and of itself, it is not my primary concern. The compelling point is the politically contested state of this constitutional question as it traces its way through the separation of powers.

Madison's and Jefferson's arguments are interesting in that members of Con-gress and the executive articulate constitutional meaning in a way that limits their power. This negative function—saying no to governmental power by drawing on the Constitution—is not just a judicial function. Even more revealing, however, is a point that is neglected by the proponents of judicial supremacy. To best under-stand the constitutional framework, the branches of government may be seen in relation to one another. This mode is particularly true of the Court, as, given its constitutional form, it may hear cases and controversies only when suit has been brought. Its actions, then, first depend on the preceding action of the Congress and president.[78] If the Congress and the president have a limited view of their consti-tutional power, many foundational constitutional questions, depending on the particular Congress and president, may never come before the Court.[79] For the Court to speak to constitutional meaning and authority, the president and Con-gress must act in ways that create a constitutional dispute; otherwise constitutional interpretation will persist without the Court. Tracing out this logic, the Court may be a defender of constitutional limits at a particular time, given a particular Con-gress and president, but it may not be at a later time, depending, again, on the other branches. This is precisely why, Madison argued, a diffusion of power is more likely to maintain constitutional government.[80]

Against Madison's and Jefferson's objections, the First Congress established the bank, which was signed into law by President Washington. Nevertheless, the constitutional issue was settled only over a period of decades (and was ultimately reopened and reconstructed in the Progressive and New Deal eras).[81] Its construction, Madison later said, "had undergone ample discussions in its passage through the several branches of the Government. It had carried into execution throughout a period of twenty years with annual legislative recognition . . . and with the entire acquiescence of all the local authorities, as well as of the nation at large; to all of which may be added, a decreasing prospect of any change in the public opinion adverse to the constitutionality of such an institution."[82]

Today Marshall's decision in *McCulloch v. Maryland* is seen as settling this question; a constitutional dispute is taken to be settled only if the Court has addressed it.[83] In an interesting way, though, the question of whether the national government could charter a bank was taken as settled when it came before Marshall and the Court. As Marshall himself recognized in his opinion, "It has truly been said that this can scarcely be considered as an open question, entirely unprejudiced by the former proceedings of the nation respecting it. The principle now contested was introduced at a very early period of our history, has been recognized by many successive legislatures, and has been acted upon by the judicial department, in cases of peculiar delicacy, as a law of undoubted obligation."[84] Even given this history, Spencer Roane and other republicans urged overturning the law as beyond Congress's power. In doing so, they illustrate the Madisonian position. The correct interpretation of the Constitution should govern—not any particular branch of government. This position embraces judicial review while rejecting judicial supremacy. What is perhaps most interesting about Marshall's opinion is its potential claim to judicial supremacy. Marshall advised that "the constitution of our country, in its most interesting and vital parts, is to be considered." But the question "must be decided peacefully, or remain a source of hostile legislation, perhaps of hostility of a still more serious nature; and if it is to be so decided, by this tribunal alone can the decision be made. On the Supreme Court of the United States has the constitution of our country devolved this important duty."[85] Marshall is too often taken at his word. Subsequent history belies his argument.

The Court's opinion did not cease constitutional argument on the question. Just over a decade later, the debate was rejoined when President Jackson rejected Marshall's *McCulloch* opinion and insisted the bank was unconstitutional.[86] Subsequent presidents, "articulating" Jackson's constitutional "reconstruction," vetoed a new bank on similar grounds. Thus, the constitutional issue was settled for a large portion of the nineteenth century *against* the bank—even if *McCulloch* was never overturned, allowing it to be resurrected (and reconstructed) by twentieth-century constitutional law while ignoring our actual constitutional history. "[President]

Tyler's vetoes prevented the dismantling of Jacksonian Democracy's major political achievements. Those same vetoes, however, blocked a case challenging the bank's constitutionality from reaching a Supreme Court packed with Jackson's anti-bank partisans. Thus, Tyler may have inadvertently saved *McCulloch* from the dustbin of history and denied Jackson's movement what would have been its greatest victory."[87] The opportunity never presented itself because the precondition of judicial review is legislative and executive action rooted in a broad understanding of their constitutional power.[88]

Yet, Madison's Constitution does not reject judicial interpretation; it rejects only the notion that the Court is the final interpreter of the Constitution.[89] Madison did worry that judicial interpretation might inexorably lead to judicial supremacy. In an oft-quoted letter to John Brown, he made evident this concern: "In the State Constitutions and indeed in the Federal one also, no provision is made for the case of a disagreement in expounding them; and as the Courts are generally the last in making ye decision, it results to them by refusing or not refusing to execute a law, to stamp it with its final character. This makes the Judiciary Department paramount in fact to the Legislature, which was never intended and can never be proper."[90] Judicial review and judicial supremacy may be kept distinct from one another by placing judicial review within the Madisonian Constitution.

Judicial Review, Judicial Supremacy, and the Nature of the Constitution

I begin, as so much of constitutional theory does, with Marshall's opinion in *Marbury*, as it is taken as the foundational argument for judicial supremacy. Both the Court and contemporary defenders of judicial supremacy turn to *Marbury* in justifying their positions. And they do so because Marshall is seen as articulating their central premise: the constitution is law.[91] Consequently, these proponents insist that judicial review is central to a written constitution and that judicial review requires judicial supremacy. Thus, although the conventional understanding of judicial review is mentioned in the context of Madison's separation of powers, it is not easily reconciled with the notion of checks and balances, as it places the Court "over the Constitution" rather than within it.

The Written Constitution

"The question, whether an act, repugnant to the constitution, can become the law of the land, is a question deeply interesting to the United States; but, happily, not of an intricacy proportioned to its interest. It seems only necessary to recognize certain principles, supposed to have been long established, to decide it."[92] The nature of a written Constitution means that an act repugnant to the Constitution is *unconstitutional.* All agree on this first principle of a written Constitution. The question is, Who decides that an act is repugnant to the Constitution? It is perfectly logical to claim that judicial review does not follow from this fundamental axiom of a written constitution. In his famous dissent in *Eakin v. Raub,* Judge John Bannister Gibson insisted that an act of the legislature contrary to the Constitution must be void. But Gibson then argued that, because the Constitution does not "come before the court," it is not for the Court to declare legislation void by exercising the power of judicial review.[93] Instead, the *people* were the primary enforcers of the Constitution's written limits acting through elections: "I am of the opinion that it rests with the people, in whom full and absolute sovereign power resides, to correct abuses in legislation, by instructing their representatives to repeal the obnoxious act."[94] Taking issue with the notion that judicial review stems from the nature of a written constitution, Gibson brought this lesson to bear:

> It has been said, that this construction would deprive the citizen of the advantages which are peculiar to a written constitution, by at once declaring the power of the legislature in practice to be illimitable. . . . But there is no magic or inherent power in parchment and ink, to command respect and protect principles from violation. In the business of government a recurrence to first principles answers the end of an observation at sea with a view to correct the dead reckoning; and for this purpose, a written constitution is an instrument of inestimable value. It is of inestimable value, also, in rendering its first principles familiar to the mass of the people; for, after all, there is no effectual guard against legislative usurpation by public opinion, the force of which, in this country, is inconceivably great.[95]

Yet, as I have argued, Madison does not trust in parchment and ink. And if he does trace power to the people themselves, they are, in the first place, bound by natural rights and, in the second, channeled through constitutional forms. If judicial review cannot be logically deduced from the nature of a written constitution, it might be called forth by Madison's institutional forms. In this context, however, judicial review is only one dimension of maintaining the written Constitution and exists within the contours of countervailing power. Drawing on revisionist scholarship, I argue that Marshall's *Marbury* opinion shares the Madisonian view of the Constitution in important respects.[96]

Marbury and the Madisonian Constitution

In *Marbury,* Marshall begins with the nature of a written Constitution: "Certainly all those who have framed written constitutions contemplate them as forming the fundamental and paramount law of the nation, and consequently the theory of every such government must be, that an act of the legislature, repugnant to the constitution, is void." This statement simply asserts the fundamental axiom of a written Constitution that I previously noted. But Marshall then goes on to bring the Constitution before the Court. "If an act of the legislature, repugnant to the constitution, is void, does it, notwithstanding its invalidity, bind the courts, and oblige them to give it effect?" To which Marshall says this cannot be. Otherwise a written constitution, "the great improvement of our 'political institutions,'" would be reduced to "an absurd attempt on the part of the people to limit a power that is illimitable." While this interpretation clearly seems to entail judicial review, Marshall is claiming only that, as the Constitution obligates the Court, the Court cannot be bound by an unconstitutional act of the legislature. Marshall goes on to cast this in more active terms: "It is emphatically the province and duty of the judicial department to say what the law is. Those who apply the rule to particular cases, must of necessity expand and interpret that rule. If two laws conflict with each other, the courts must decide on the operation of each." That is, the Court must determine which conflicting rule governs the case. In doing so, Marshall treats a conflict between a law and the Constitution as the same as a conflict between two ordinary laws. This determination, Marshall tells us, is "the very essence of judicial duty." And rather obviously, if we follow Marshall's formulation, the Court must prefer the Constitution—fundamental law—to an ordinary act of the legislature. If it were otherwise, "it would give the legislature a practical and real omnipotence."[97]

The modern Court and proponents of judicial supremacy have seized on this logic, arguing that the Court must be *the* institution that keeps the legislature within its constitutionally prescribed limits.[98] But Marshall's opinion does not claim so much. It insists only that the Court is bound by the Constitution. Being so bound, the Court cannot give voice to an unconstitutional act of the legislature: "Those who controvert the principle that the constitution is to be considered, in court, as a paramount law, are reduced to the necessity of maintaining that courts must close their eyes on the constitution, and see only the law. This doctrine would subvert the very foundation of all written constitutions."[99] True, Marshall does place inordinate emphasis on the power of judicial review. But that is because judicial review is the Court's primary method of upholding its constitutional obligations in the Madisonian framework.[100] Marshall is claiming an equal role for the Court in enforcing the Constitution, as is evident in the closing lines of *Marbury*, noting "that courts, as well as other departments, are bound by that instrument."[101] Judicial review is one dimension of policing constitutional boundaries within a framework of countervailing power. Marshall's insistence that institutional forms (such as judicial review) are central to maintaining a written constitution is very much akin to Madison's. And, like Madison, he notes that this requires independent interpretation of the Constitution by these different institutions.

This view is most evident in Marshall's insistence that the "constitution must be looked into by the judges," and open to them in its entirety, in deciding cases. "[I]f then the courts are to regard the constitution; and the constitution is superior to any ordinary act of the legislature; the constitution, and not such an ordinary act, must govern the case to which they both apply."[102] The Court, that is, must interpret the Constitution *if* the Constitution is implicated in the case before it. That does not imply that the Court's interpretation of the Constitution is binding on the other branches of government as a matter of law. Nor does it imply a special role for the Court in upholding the Constitution. On the contrary, the insistence is only that the Court, *like* the Congress and the president, is obligated by the Constitution as fundamental law. Such an understanding of judicial review is consistent with the notion that Court opinions would settle the case before it, not the broader constitutional question. Given institutional independence, each branch is obligated to interpret the Constitution. Moreover, each branch can read the whole of the Constitution when it is properly before it. So, for example, the Court cannot be obligated by the Congress's understanding of Congress's power. Nor can the president be obligated by such an understanding.

This understanding is particularly so if we consider that the Court's exercise of judicial review is not "last" in the process of checks and balances, as it is so frequently described. Again, many constitutional issues never come before the Court. More importantly, situated within a framework and across time, judicial review is only one dimension of the constitutional separation of powers; it is not an end in itself.[103]

Judicial Supremacy: Court over Constitution

Against this understanding of judicial review, the current Court has insisted that our understanding of constitutionalism is "not readily separable from [our] understanding of the Court invested with the authority to decide [our] constitutional cases and speak before all others for [our] constitutional ideals."[104] In doing so, the Court cites *Marbury.* Yet Marshall, as we have seen, claims no such role for the Court in *Marbury.*[105] Marshall does note "that the people have an original right to establish, for their future government, such principles as, in their opinion, shall most conduce to their own happiness, is the basis, on which the whole American fabric has been erected."[106] He goes on to insist that the judiciary, in order to maintain the constitution the people have established, must exercise the power of judicial review. But Marshall, unlike the current Court, does not claim that the Court's role is primary, that the Court speaks before all others in articulating constitutional meaning. Nor does Marshall suggest the people will be "tested" in their willingness to heed the Court's voice. Indeed, Marshall's argument for judicial review rests upon the fixed foundations of the Constitution legitimized by popular ratification. The Court's power stems from the people as it acts to preserve "the original and supreme will" that organizes the government. This argument echoes Madison's understanding: "the authority of constitutions over governments, and of the authority of the people over constitutions, are truths which are at all times necessary to be kept in mind; and at no time, perhaps, more necessary than at present."[107] This latter advice is perhaps apt in our own time, where the Court places itself over the Constitution in insisting that it alone is responsible for the Constitution.

Those who turn to Marshall to justify judicial supremacy reframe his argument for judicial review in this manner: (1) It is the Court's duty to say what the law is. (2) The Constitution is law. (3) Therefore, it is the Court's duty to say what the Constitution means. Judicial supremacy thus begins from the axiom that the Constitution is law (usually without puzzling over how fundamental law is profoundly different from ordinary law).[108] This formulation sweeps far wider than Marshall's argument in *Marbury.* Still, Sylvia Snowiss ventures that "Marshall transformed explicit fundamental law, different in kind from ordinary law, into supreme ordinary law, different only in degree."[109] Thus, even when claims to judicial supremacy are rooted in the institutional capacities of the various branches of government, these, too, turn on the notion that fundamental law is just a "higher" version of ordinary law.

Law, Politics, and the Separation of Powers

The claim that judicial supremacy is an incident of the Court's role within the separation of powers turns on the distinction between law and politics, which places the Constitution on the "law" side of this divide. As part of its power of saying what the law is, the Court must incidentally patrol the other branches of government; it may thereby "rule the political branches by defining the outlines of their duties," making it, in essence, first in "dignity and authority"[110] under the Constitution.[111] As Justice Anthony Kennedy argues, "Our national experience teaches that the Constitution is preserved best when each part of the government respects both the Constitution and the proper actions and determinations of the other branches. When the Court has interpreted the Constitution, it has acted within the province of the Judicial Branch, which embraces the duty to say what the law is."[112] Kennedy acknowledges that the political branches may interpret the Constitution when it implicates their own duties, but when they do so, they must interpret it in accord with the Court's opinions.[113] As an earlier Court put it, "deciding whether a matter has in any measure been committed by the Constitution to another branch of government, or whether the action of that branch exceeds whatever authority has been committed, is itself a delicate exercise in constitutional interpretation, and is a responsibility of this Court as ultimate interpreter of the Constitution."[114] Not surprisingly, both of these opinions cite *Marbury* and cast the Court's role as the authoritative interpreter of the Constitution as a part of its duty within the separation of powers to say what the law is.[115]

At first glance, this understanding of judicial review (which implies judicial supremacy) may intuitively coincide with the system of checks and balances: it is the Court's check on the legislative and executive branches. But the more famous arguments for judicial review, as articulated by the conventional understanding of *Marbury* and Alexander Hamilton's *Federalist* 78, do not contemplate judicial review as one check in the midst of many. It is seen, rather, as *the check that maintains the Constitution* because the Constitution is seen as law. Whether Marshall or Hamilton saw the Constitution in this light is another question.

"Those Tutored in the Law"

Following the general analysis of *The Federalist,* those dealing with the judiciary (numbers 78 to 83) "do not quite fit into the whole." Rather, the treatment of the judiciary "stands somewhat apart from the rest of the book, just as the judiciary stands somewhat apart from politics."[116] *The Federalist* rarely refers to the Constitution's legal status, focusing instead on its institutional arrangements as maintaining its primacy. Yet Hamilton's discussion of the judiciary in the last few papers, published, incidentally, in the second bound volume and not in the newspapers, does seem to treat the Constitution as akin to ordinary law, with the judiciary enforcing the law.[117]

The interpretation of the laws is the proper and peculiar province of the courts. A constitution is, in fact, and must be regarded by the judges as, a fundamental law. It therefore belongs to them to ascertain its meaning as well as the meaning of any particular act proceeding from the legislative body. If there should happen to be an irreconcilable variance between the two, that which has the superior obligation and validity ought, of course, to be preferred; or, in other words, the Constitution ought to be preferred to the statute, the intention of the people to the intention of their agents.[118]

The Constitution controls, but, as this passage is often interpreted, the Court says what the Constitution means. It is the Court's "proper and peculiar province" to do just this. *Federalist* 78 may best be read far less expansively. More consistent with the Madisonian Constitution, it may simply be claiming the power of judicial review and the Court's duty to interpret the Constitution in a case before it (much as *Marbury* does). Hamilton, for example, is quick to hedge an expansive view of judicial power, suggesting that the judiciary has "neither FORCE or WILL but merely judgment." Still, the judiciary is, in Hamilton's formulation, "the faithful guardian of the Constitution."[119] Whereas in the earlier *Federalist* papers the political dynamic of the Constitution is emphasized, when the judiciary is discussed the Constitution is seen in more legalistic terms. And even if the political branches may check the Court, it is given a special role in interpreting constitutional meaning and authority. In this regard, the Court's check against legislative and executive invasions becomes an instrument that enables it to take up primary responsibility for constitutional interpretation.[120]

This understanding of the Court's role draws on the separation of powers in a manner that gives weight to the peculiar relationship between the judiciary and the Constitution by insisting upon the Constitution's legality.[121] While the separation of powers brings to mind checks on governmental power, it was also instituted for effective governance: each branch is institutionally designed to meet the peculiar nature of its task. *The Federalist,* for example, speaks of a unitary executive designed to foster "energy" and a plural and bicameral legislature to foster "a jarring of parties" and democratic deliberation.[122] Hamilton also draws this point out in speaking of the institutional design of the judiciary—namely, its independence and learning in the law—pointing to its particular task within the operation of the government. So the executive partakes of "the executive power" and likewise for the judiciary. This is not to say that powers are rigidly separated between the branches, so that all "executive" power must be delegated to the executive. In giving us "checks and balances," the Constitution did not embrace such a rigid rule of separation.

But here I wish to emphasize the power of separation. If checks and balances make the government limited, separation of powers helps to make it competent.[123] Combined, they help maintain the Constitution.

Like the other branches, the judiciary is constructed in such a way as to call forth those virtues required for the art of judging. Judges, unlike all other high offices, serve by appointment and during good behavior, ensuring their independence, so as to enable them better to perform their peculiar task. The judiciary has a liberal and even aristocratic cast, balancing it against the more democratic elements of the legislative branch. For Hamilton, this means men of a particular character and learning; it is a small number of men "who unite the requisite integrity with the requisite knowledge"[124] to sit on the bench. Based on their learning in the law and their subtlety of mind, on their reasoning spirit and independence from political pressure, judges may justly claim to be uniquely suited to the task of legal interpretation. These traits become expansive when the Constitution itself is viewed wholly through a legal lens. Thus, in "construing the Constitution, the judge performs a political duty through the exercise of a technical duty." This exercise draws the Court closer to the Constitution than the other branches as "the judiciary acts as special guardian of the principles of the Constitution," making it a sort of republican schoolmaster in the constitutional scheme.[125] If the Constitution is law, by training and by institutional design the judiciary is uniquely positioned to lay down the intricacies of constitutional meaning. Moreover, it is the judiciary's task alone, as the other branches, constituted as they are, are not suitable for such delicate work.

Marshall himself relies heavily on the legal nature of the question in *Marbury* to justify the judiciary's authority in resolving the dispute. Marshall insists, again and again, that whether Marbury is entitled to his appointment is a question for the judiciary alone, as it is a question of law: "The question whether a right has vested or not, is, in its nature, judicial, and must be tried by the judicial authority."[126] Marshall draws on this distinction between law and politics and argues that legal questions are, by their nature, questions for the judiciary. He also notes the inverse: political questions, by their nature, have no place before the Court.[127] But Marshall's reasoning applies only to the narrow question of whether a right has been "vested" and not, as the Court's citations to *Marbury* suggest, to the sweeping claim that the Constitution itself is law and, therefore, the judiciary is its peculiar defender.[128] These two understandings emphasize a profound difference in the scope and power of the judiciary. In the first instance, judicial power is narrow and circumscribed. The Court may be the primary expositor of ordinary law, but this is different from the fundamental law of the Constitution. When it comes to constitutional questions, the Court has an equal role in interpreting the Constitution. As part of deciding cases and controversies, it may strike down acts of the Congress or the president that run contrary to its interpretation of the Constitution. But this result does not imply that the Court speaks for the Constitution, or that the other branches are obligated to follow its understanding once it has spoken.[129] This understanding of judicial review fits, albeit with some tension, within the idiom of Madison's checks and balances.

In the second understanding, however, the whole of the Constitution is law to be expounded on and enforced by the Court, which asserts what Madison said could never be intended; that is, it makes the judiciary superior to the legislature and executive by making it the guardian of the whole Constitution, placing it outside the separation of powers, if not above it.[130] Here the other branches may reach constitutional issues, so long as they are political and not legal, although the crucial point, surely, is who says what a "legal" question is.[131] If Marshall did not claim that constitutional questions were by their nature legal questions that the Court alone must determine, the current Court has.

Legalizing the Constitution

To be sure, claims for judicial supremacy are rooted in elements of the American regime. The Constitution does pronounce itself to be law, and the judiciary might, then, be uniquely positioned to speak to, say, Sixth Amendment issues that are rooted in common-law understandings of legal process. And its independence is a powerful liberal counterweight to popular democratic majorities. Contained within the Madisonian vision, the Court's learning in the law and its potentially "countermajoritarian" tendencies are virtues. Yet these virtues become vices when they are pushed as the exclusive principles of the constitutional order, eclipsing all other elements of the American amalgam. If the judiciary defines the separation of powers, it indirectly rules the other branches of government. But because elements of the Constitution cannot be reduced to legalities, it ends up narrowing and distorting the constitutional mind-set.

Laurence Tribe, for example, goes so far as to insist that the executive should not veto a law because he thinks it unconstitutional. In an extraordinary fit of hyperbole, Tribe has suggested that such an act is "an abuse of the fundamental structure of our system of government" in that it "unilaterally . . . deprives the court of their unique Constitutional function: to pass on legislation that is not obviously unconstitutional."[132] Put aside the fact that the veto was originally conceived precisely so that the president could veto legislation he thought went beyond constitutional limits.[133] Yet, as Tribe would have it, only the judiciary may speak to constitutional issues. Other proponents of judicial supremacy echo this sentiment: "[the] executive and legislative officials should do what *they* are assigned to do, and what t*hey* are assigned to do does not include constitutional interpretation."[134] The Court itself supports this line of reasoning, arguing that Congress, under Section 5 of the Fourteenth Amendment, "has been given the power 'to enforce,' not the power to determine what constitutes a constitutional violation. Were it not so, what Congress would be enforcing would no longer be, in any meaningful sense, the 'provisions of [the Fourteenth Amendment].'"[135] Here, as Edward Corwin has argued, the Court invokes a miracle: "It supposes a kind of transubstantiation whereby the Court's opinion of the Constitution . . . becomes [the] very body and blood of the Constitution."[136]

If we digest this legalist understanding, for the legislature and executive to see the Constitution with their own eyes threatens our constitutional fabric: "At stake . . . is the binding effect of the Constitution, as construed by the Court, upon those whom the people elect to public office—those whose oaths to uphold the Constitution as the supreme law of the land can be enforced in no other way than through Supreme Court review."[137] A formal constitutional oath to uphold the Constitution amounts, then, to an oath to follow the Court. This mirrors the subversion of the written Constitution: what began as written fundamental law visible to all is translated into the ancient equivalent of legal French for the schooled few.

Thinking in this manner encourages irresponsibility and perniciously distorts the whole of the Constitution. Consider that senators, following this logic, cannot ask judicial nominees about constitutional meaning and authority but must focus solely on their "legal qualifications." This restriction would seemingly be true of the executive as well. This outcome would be the legal Constitution with a vengeance: the Constitution is what the Court says it is. And yet, would-be (legal) philosophers are free to whisper in the ear of judges, correcting their possible errors, thereby helping them rule indirectly. Most stunningly, however, this is all put forward with nary a glance at constitutional practice and history, which is all the more remarkable as so many of the claims for judicial supremacy rest on empirical presuppositions.[138] Thus, such a truncated view of constitutional theory has led to an antiseptic constitutionalism altogether divorced from American constitutional practice; it is perhaps not a coincidence that one of the most famous defenders of judicial supremacy calls his *imaginary* judge Hercules.[139]

Dueling Constitutions

In asking how a written constitution was to be maintained, so that it was not a mere "parchment barrier," Madison rejected the notion that there could be a single sovereign enforcer. As fundamental law is rooted in the very basis of the political compact, to make any single body its highest authority is, effectively, to allow it to define the regime. Such a move was likely not only to make our constitutionalism less secure but also to undermine the "cause of republican government." In attempting to balance agonistic principles, which furnish the basis for a workable and contained political order, the Madisonian framework necessarily invites struggles over constitutional meaning and identity.[140] This process is illustrated in the chapters that follow, which turn to American constitutional practice, detailing the necessarily partial and incomplete articulations of constitutional authority and meaning within a framework of countervailing power.

Congress, the Supreme Court, and the Meaning of the Civil War Amendments

On the eve of the Civil War, Abraham Lincoln argued that states could not, as a matter of constitutional logic, secede from the Union. Yet the Constitution did not specifically address this question. And Lincoln himself insisted that much of the conflict threatening to tear the Union apart stemmed from questions that the Constitution did not explicitly answer: "no organic law can ever be framed with a provision specifically applicable to every question which may occur in practical administration. No foresight can anticipate, nor any document of reasonable length contain, express provisions for all possible questions."[1] Turning to the questions at hand, Lincoln illuminated this dilemma: "Shall fugitives from labor be surrendered by national or State authority? The Constitution does not expressly say. May Congress prohibit slavery in the Territories? The Constitution does not expressly say. MUST Congress protect slavery in the Territories? The Constitution does not expressly say."[2] Such vexing questions would turn on particular constructions of constitutional authority and meaning. Arguing that his interpretation of the Constitution was the only coherent interpretation of the constitutional order, Lincoln rejected secession as inconsistent with the terms of the constitutional Union. Still, the war came. And it came over conflicting constitutional understandings that could no longer be contained within the Madisonian framework.[3]

Many of these questions were answered in the bloodshed that followed—and they were answered on Lincoln's terms. If state secession was a disputed constitutional question prior to the Civil War,[4] it was resoundingly answered by way of Lincoln's first inaugural address and his Gettysburg Address, perhaps the two most important acts of constitutional interpretation in our history.[5] So, too, has Lincoln's constitutional vision framed the relationship between slavery and the Constitution of 1787, closing off earlier avenues of constitutional thought by pointing to the irreconcilable tension between slavery and the fundamental commitments of American constitutionalism as articulated in the Declaration of Independence.[6] This chapter examines Lincoln and the Republican Congress's attempt to construct constitutional authority in a manner that would make the Union they saved "forever worthy of the saving."[7] For the antislavery and free labor Republicans, this rested upon the Declaration of Independence's promise of liberty and equality, which ultimately entailed the passage of the Fourteenth Amendment. By amending the Constitution, the Republicans sought to settle a bundle of constitutional questions that had vexed the American polity, giving their vision permanent constitutional authority by rooting it in constitutional text.

This promise, however, was only partially realized. Viewed from the Madisonian lens, the Congress and the Court struggled over the Republicans' attempt to solidify constitutional meaning and authority by way of the Civil War amendments. This debate was, at root, about the identity of the Constitution: How did these new amendments cohere with the Constitution? Were they revolutionary or transformative, or did they complete the Constitution? The construction of constitutional meaning by the different branches was conflicted on this foundational question. Against the Republican vision, the Court and Democrats sought to confine the reach of the Civil War amendments, situating them within the strands of antebellum constitutional thought that the Republicans sought to overturn.[8] In this manner, the constitutional meaning of the Civil War amendments was limited. After an initial struggle, free labor ideas about liberty and equality triumphed in the latter half of the nineteenth century as applied to white males. These constitutional commitments were abandoned, however, when it came to the newly freed slaves.[9] Rather than a grand synthesis of Founding and Republican constitutionalism,[10] Republican constitutional thought was entrenched in some areas and narrowed in others. Tragically, this tension also reveals the disharmonic gap between American constitutional ideals and American constitutional practice. The constitutional text pointed to the aspirational qualities of liberty and equal protection, but the polity seemed determined to retreat from such a view as it applied to African Americans.[11]

The Civil War Amendments: The Centrality of Countervailing Power

The Civil War amendments offer a unique prism through which we may view the Madisonian logic of countervailing power. These amendments explicitly invite congressional enforcement of constitutional meaning. Section 5 of the Fourteenth Amendment reads: "The Congress shall have power to enforce, by appropriate legislation, the provisions of this article." For those who hold that the Court alone must interpret the Constitution, section 5 is a textual oddity.[12] Constitutional language that seemingly empowers Congress amounts, in truth, to a command to enforce the Court's interpretation of "this article" and not the provisions of the article itself.[13] Yet the Fourteenth Amendment was passed against the backdrop of the Supreme Court's *Dred Scott* decision and sought to constitutionalize the Republican understanding of citizenship and rights—completing Madison's imperfect Constitution.[14] Proponents of the amendment were deeply reluctant to rely on Court enforcement alone. After all, as a Republican candidate for Senate and then the presidency, Lincoln invoked Andrew Jackson's insistence that, even against Supreme Court precedent, each public functionary must support the Constitution "as he understands it."[15]

According to Republicans, the Court had willfully distorted the Constitution in *Dred Scott.* Reading blacks out of the Declaration of Independence by way of distorted history, the Court held that blacks—free as well as slave—were forever excluded from the terms of citizenship under the Constitution. The Court then went on to prohibit congressional regulation of slavery in the territories as (1) in violation of due process under the Fifth Amendment and (2) against constitutional language that seemed to clearly vest Congress with that authority.[16] While the due process argument advanced by Roger Taney came to be criticized in the twentieth century as an invention of substantive due process, it is telling to note that that was not the essence of the Republican criticism against Taney's due process argument.[17] Rather, Republicans rejected the notion that property in slaves was just the same as property in anything else—and particularly Taney's claim that "the right of property in a slave is distinctly and expressly affirmed in the Constitution."[18]

The crux of the matter, then, was not substantive due process—which found expression in free labor thought and which many Republicans embraced as prohibiting slavery in the territories—but the wrongness of holding property in men. As Lincoln argued against Judge Stephen Douglas, "upon the score of equality, the owners of slaves and owners of property—of horses and every other sort of property—should alike hold them alike in a new Territory. That is perfectly logical, if the two species of property are alike and are equally founded in right. But if you admit that one of them is wrong, you cannot institute any equality between right and wrong."[19] Lincoln and the Republicans, of course, insisted upon the wrongness of property in men, which is why the national government should ban slavery in the territories. Rejecting Judge Douglas's purely democratic vision, where slavery could be voted up or down by the people, the Republicans offered a liberal understanding grounded in rights as the precondition of and counterbalance to democracy. Thus, majorities could rule, so long as democracy was bounded by liberalism. Again, let me repair to Lincoln's words: "When the white man governs himself that is self-government; but when he governs himself, and also governs another man, that is more than self-government—that is despotism." Lincoln went on to argue that consent was the basis of self-government, the "sheet anchor of American republicanism."[20] Douglas's popular sovereignty threatened our "ancient faith" insofar as it rejected its substance—"all men are created equal"—for democratic process alone.

Lincoln sought to fight this perversion of "original principles" on the foundation of "original principles" in what he called a "Madisonian fashion."[21] Lincoln here might have quoted Madison's own words against the logic of Douglas's position: "There is no maxim in my opinion which is more liable to be misapplied, and which therefore more needs elucidation than the current one that the interest of the majority is the political standard of right and wrong."[22] Given Douglas's insistence on democracy as the measure of right and wrong, which must lead to studied neutrality on the question of slavery, there was an irony, Lincoln argued, in the "sacredness" that Douglas "throws around" *Dred Scott.* For Taney's decision prohibited a democratic vote in removing slavery; it was not something the people could reject for themselves, as one had a constitutional right to bring slaves into the territories. What drew these lines of thought together, according to Lincoln, was a "tendency, if not a conspiracy," to alter the foundations of American constitutionalism by rendering it, at best, indifferent to slavery or, at worst, "proslavery." This tendency was evident, for Lincoln, when a popular-sovereignty democrat such as Douglas could turn to complete faith in a Court decision—a decision that became for Douglas a "*Thus saith the Lord*"—that rejected popular sovereignty. This position was either a shirking of his constitutional responsibility or a pernicious means of silencing a debate on the essence of our constitutional identity. According to Lincoln, the foundational identity of the Declaration's natural rights and "all men are created equal" was being "adapted" as part of a "common plan" to "make slavery perpetual and universal in this nation."[23] Whether or not Taney and Douglas, along with President Buchanan, were part of a common plan in this effort, upon secession the Confederacy would explicitly reject the Declaration and its principles, embracing John Calhoun's insistence that "nothing can be more unfounded and false" than the axiom that "all men are born free and equal."[24] In his "Corner Stone Speech," Alexander Stephens, then vice-president of the Confederate States, would go so far as to claim, "Our new government is founded upon exactly the opposite idea; its foundations are laid, its corner-stone rests upon the great truth, that the negro is not equal to the white man; that slavery—subordination to the superior race—is his natural and normal-condition."[25]

To return the Constitution to its moorings in the wake of the Civil War, Republicans sought to make their understanding inescapable by rooting it in constitutional text by way of the Fourteenth Amendment. Not surprisingly, Republicans refused to simply trust that the judiciary would properly enforce the provisions of the Fourteenth Amendment as it was explicitly meant to reject an unconstitutional Supreme Court decision. Thus, the Fourteenth Amendment turned initially to congressional enforcement of constitutional rights. Accordingly, as William Nelson argues, the Fourteenth Amendment was put forward as a broad political principle based upon the Republicans' constitutional vision; it was not a legalistic document that gave detailed and codified guidance to the courts.[26]

The amendment mirrors the Madisonian Constitution it was meant to complete. As Judge Gibson noted, a written constitution articulates "first principles" for the people and the government. Embedding these principles in constitutional text makes them self-evident for all to see, obligating the government and edifying citizens by their terms. As one member of Congress put it in debating the language of the Fourteenth Amendment, "Constitutions should have their provisions so plain that it will be unnecessary for courts to give construction to them; they should be so plain that the common mind can understand them."[27] Yet, as Lincoln noted about the Constitution itself, as we descend from general principles to particular questions, the amendment does not explicitly answer all of our questions. The amendment thus initially relied on congressional enforcement. The dilemma, as one member of Congress noted, was that such language "proposes to leave it [the enforcement of the Fourteenth Amendment] to the caprice of Congress."[28] Mindful that subsequent Congresses may not be faithful to the terms of section 1, congressional power to enforce the amendment was added as a separate section (section 5), which, thereby, would *also* provide for judicial enforcement. Judicial enforcement might be implied insofar as Republicans accepted the notion, put forward by Marshall, that Court's too could interpret the Constitution. And if they could look to it, they could look to the whole of it in a case properly before them. Thus, Republicans followed Lincoln in rejecting judicial supremacy, while accepting judicial review. Much like Madison before them, congressional Republicans were reluctant to trust any one branch with maintaining the Constitution. The Civil War amendments were more likely to be realized over time if all of the branches were able to insist on their terms.

The result was to invite constitutional dispute on specifics, which is not necessarily at odds with achieving the Constitution's true meaning.[29] Just such a conflict occurred shortly after the ratification of the Fourteenth and Fifteenth amendments when Congress passed a series of acts to enforce these new amendments. In doing so, Congress necessarily relied on its understanding of the amendments' constitutional commitments. The acts themselves were attempts to ensure that the meaning of the amendments would not be subverted in the South, given the emerging violence and resistance to these newly formalized civil liberties.[30] The constitutionality of these acts, and by implication Congress's interpretation of the Civil War amendments, came before the Supreme Court under the newly appointed Chief Justice Morrison Waite. But the Court's initial opinions, given by Waite himself, hardly settled the matter.[31] On the contrary, constitutional meaning and principle were argued over within the Madisonian framework in the ordinary politics of 1870–83, not just in the momentous politics of the Civil War based on the "reconstructive" presidency of Lincoln, or the possibly transformative constitutional vision of the Republican Congress.[32]

The *Slaughterhouse Cases:* Preliminaries

The story begins with the *Slaughterhouse Cases* (1873).[33] Although at stake in these cases was a state law that granted a monopoly to the Crescent City Live-Stock Landing and Slaughter-House Company, it is a necessary beginning point because it is the first case in which the Court interpreted the Fourteenth Amendment. As such, I suggest it represents the beginning of conflict between the Congress and Court over the meaning of the amendment and not the judicial solidification of the amendment, as Bruce Ackerman argues.[34] The *Slaughterhouse Cases* may give Supreme Court approval to the Fourteenth Amendment's constitutional legitimacy, given its peculiar ratification, but this is only part of the story. And it is far from clear that the nation subsequently accepted the Fourteenth Amendment's legitimacy because the Supreme Court did.[35]

Ackerman sees the Court's decision in *Slaughterhouse* as the close of the extraordinary politics of the Civil War era insofar as it solidifies Lincoln's and the Republican Congress's constitutional "transformation." This understanding misses crucial constitutional developments about the nature and meaning of the Civil War amendments. Dispute about constitutional meaning and authority continued after the *Slaughterhouse Cases,* as the Congress (often with the support of the executive branch) articulated its construction of the Civil War amendments, which was met with skepticism from the Court. Ackerman's account is odd on another level as well. He sees the constitutional politics of Reconstruction as a constitutional "transformation" that is then enforced by the Court (until we get the next "constitutional transformation" in the constitutional politics of the New Deal era). But Justice Samuel Miller's majority opinion in the *Slaughterhouse Cases* (a 5–4 decision), which Ackerman sees as solidifying this constitutional transformation, hardly supports the constitutional construction that the Court later articulates. Indeed, this strand of Republican constitutional thought is articulated in the dissenting opinions of Stephen Field, Joseph Bradley, and Noah Swayne, which was rejected by Miller's opinion.[36] Miller does, however, recognize the force of the amendments when it comes to black equality. Even here, however, Miller's reading cuts against the Republican vision of national citizenship. In tracing out the constitutional politics of this era, I suggest the Republican vision was successfully entrenched in its "free labor" guise as applied to white men; yet "the unity of purpose" in the amendments, which was aimed at the freedmen, was rejected in the ordinary politics following the Civil War.

In *Slaughterhouse*, Miller upheld a monopoly granted to the Crescent City Live-Stock Landing and Slaughter-House Co. (which the Louisiana legislature bestowed after being bribed by the company), noting that it did not violate the terms of the Fourteenth Amendment's privileges and immunities clause, due process clause, or equal protection clause. Miller's opinion, in fact, eviscerated the "privileges and immunities clause," which read, "All persons born or naturalized in the United States and subject to the jurisdiction thereof, are citizens of the United States and the State wherein they reside. No State shall make or enforce any law which shall abridge the privileges and immunities of citizens of the United States[.]"[37] Reading this clause, Miller divided citizenship into two categories—state and national—and argued that the Fourteenth Amendment protected only those privileges and immunities which were bestowed by virtue of being a citizen of the United States (and not a state citizen). Against the Republican vision that sought to constitution-alize national citizenship, Miller argued that most privileges and immunities of citizenship (such as the right to choose your trade) were derived not from national citizenship but from state citizenship.[38] He rejected the notion that the Fourteenth Amendment was meant to clarify this contested issue by nationalizing the privileges and immunities of citizenship. Thus, while citing Justice Bushrod Washington's famous opinion in *Corfield v. Coryell*, which listed numerous "privileges and immunities" of citizenship, Miller acted as if it were wholly settled that these were protected by way of state citizenship and not national citizenship. He then insisted that the Fourteenth Amendment was not meant to rework (or clarify, depending on the argument) this relationship between state and national citizenship.

Prior to the Fourteenth Amendment, many Republicans had insisted on national citizenship (and the privileges and immunities therein, including rights such as free speech), which they argued were being violated by the states. Other Republicans saw the amendment as altering this relationship precisely to secure national rights. In Chief Justice John Marshall's famous opinion in *Barron v. Baltimore,* the Court itself had said that the Bill of Rights did not apply to the states.[39] However, this exclusion may not have applied to "the privileges and immunities" of citizenship—as these were distinct from those rights articulated in the Bill of Rights, which Congress could not abridge. Bushrod Washington's opinion in *Corfield,* for instance, insisted upon "privileges and immunities" of citizenship that went far beyond the Bill of Rights.[40] The question was whether these were attached to state or national citizenship. While Washington seems to insist upon national citizenship, his opinion may plausibly be read the other way. This issue, much like that of state secession, was a fundamentally contested question in antebellum constitutional thought.[41] What does seem clear, however, is that the Fourteenth Amendment sought to settle this issue in favor of national rights.[42] Indeed, for all of the division within the Republican Congress, Miller's *Slaughterhouse* opinion put forward an argument that no one had advanced during the debate over the framing and ratification of the Fourteenth Amendment.[43]

Having rejected the privileges and immunities argument, Miller quickly dismissed the claim that making butchers pay a fee to the Crescent City Live-Stock Landing and Slaughter-House Co. (given its monopoly) deprived them of property without due process. He then held that the equal protection clause was aimed primarily at the "newly emancipated negroes" and not butchers.[44] Thus, the Fourteenth Amendment did not apply to the butchers.

Justices Field, Bradley, and Swayne all wrote dissenting opinions (and Field's dissent was joined by Bradley, Swayne, and Chief Justice Salmon Chase). Each justice argued that the Court had badly misread the nature of citizenship under the Fourteenth Amendment, which vested all citizens with the fundamental rights and privileges of citizenship by making them United States citizens (thus, state citizenship was only incidental to U.S. citizenship). Following the Republican understanding, these fundamental rights were not contingent upon state citizenship (as Miller held). If this was a heavily disputed constitutional question prior to the Fourteenth Amendment, the proponents of the amendment sought to settle this issue (and here there are important differences among Field's, Bradley's, and Swayne's dissents).[45] In reframing the language of section 1 of the Fourteenth Amendment, John Bingham explained that he drew on Marshall's opinion in *Barron v. Baltimore* to make it clear that no state would *now* be able to deny the rights of citizenship.[46] As Field argued,

The first clause of the fourteenth amendment changes this whole subject, and removes it from the region of discussion and doubt. It recognizes in express terms, if it does not create, citizens of the United States, and it makes their citizenship dependent upon the place of their birth, or the fact of their adoption, and not upon the constitution or laws of any State or the condition of their ancestry. A citizen of a State is now only a citizen of the United States residing in that State. The fundamental rights, privileges, and immunities which belong to him as a free man and a free citizen, now belong to him as a citizen of the United States, and are not dependent upon his citizenship of any State.[47]

Mirroring Republican thought that connected the Fourteenth Amendment to the Declaration, Field went on, "the amendment was intended to give practical effect to the declaration of 1776 of inalienable rights, rights which are the gift of the Creator, which the law does not confer, but only recognizes."[48] Bradley, too, drew on this understanding:

[T]he Declaration of Independence, which was the first political act of the American people in their independent sovereign capacity, lays the foundation of our National existence upon this broad proposition: "That all men are created equal; that they are endowed by their Creator with certain inalienable rights; that among these are life, liberty, and the pursuit of happiness." Here again we have the great threefold division of the rights of freemen, asserted as the rights of man. Rights to life, liberty, and the pursuit of happiness are equivalent to the rights of life, liberty, and property. These are the fundamental rights which can only be taken away by due process of law, and which can only be interfered with, or the enjoyment of which can only be modified, by lawful regulations necessary or proper for the mutual good of all; and these rights, I contend, belong to the citizens of every free government.[49]

Bradley's insistence that the Declaration had long been the ground for such rights echoed Lincoln's understanding of the relationship between the Declaration and the Constitution. The Fourteenth Amendment, accordingly, was simply clarifying this relationship; "re-adopting," as it were, the logic of the Declaration of Independence as it inheres in the Constitution.[50]

In criticizing Taney's opinion in *Dred Scott,* which read blacks (free as well as slaves) out of the terms of citizenship, Lincoln claimed that the Declaration's clause that "all men are created equal" meant just that. In his debates with Douglas, as I noted earlier, Lincoln pointed out that "Chief Justice Taney in the Dred Scott case" was "the first man who ever said that, 'the Declaration did not include blacks.'"[51] While Lincoln was its most famous expositor, the idea that the Declaration's principles undergirded the American constitutional order was central to Republican constitutional thought prior to and after the Civil War. Prior to the War, these principles led Republicans to be free labor and antislavery.[52] After the war, Republicans moved to bring the freedmen into the terms of free labor. The first strand of this thought was articulated by Field in dissent: "There is no more sacred right of citizenship than the right to pursue unmolested a lawful employment in a lawful manner. It is nothing more nor less than the sacred right of labor."[53] Lincoln, again in his debate with Douglas, drew these strands together. First insisting that the Negro was "entitled to all the natural rights enumerated in the Declaration of Independence," he then put this in free labor terms: "But in the right to eat the bread, without the leave of anybody else, which his own hand earns, he [the Negro] is my equal and the equal of Judge Douglas, and the equal of every living man."[54]

For many Republicans, the Constitution properly understood already preserved the essential privileges and immunities of citizenship and, extending these to all persons, was incompatible with slavery. Making the formal Constitution live up to its implicit constitutional commitments would require eradicating slavery. Thus, these Republicans saw the Thirteenth, Fourteenth, and Fifteenth amendments as completing the Constitution rather than transforming it.[55] This is evident in Bradley's *Slaughterhouse* dissent: "But even if the Constitution were silent, the fundamental privileges and immunities of citizens, as such, would be no less real and no less inviolable than they now are." If these issues were more deeply contested than Republican constitutional thought suggested, the Fourteenth Amendment was put forward to settle these issues, indisputably grounding such rights in the Constitution. This transformative potential is clearly articulated in Swayne's dissent where he suggested the amendment rose to "the dignity of a new Magna Charta." The Civil War amendments, Swayne argued, were "a new departure and mark an important epoch in the constitutional history of the country. They trench directly upon the power of the State, and deeply affect those bodies."[56] Thus, even if Miller was right about the relationship between nation and state in regard to constitutional rights *prior* to the Fourteenth Amendment's ratification, according to Swayne, its ratification dramatically transformed this relationship.

Drawing on the free labor aspects of Republican constitutional thought, Field, Bradley, and Swayne all found the monopoly unconstitutional. Treating the privileges and immunities clause, the due process clause, and the equal protection clause as various parts of a whole, Field and Bradley in particular argued that the monopoly did not serve a legitimate *public* purpose. The granting of a monopoly in no way served as a genuine "health" regulation, but merely transferred public power to a private company.[57] Butchers could not be made to pay a *private* company as the cost of engaging in their trade. This brings to mind, once more, Lincoln's insistence that slavery denied the inherent rights of blacks by seizing the bread their own hand earns. Pushing the liberty of free labor as the means of achieving equality—and overcoming slavery by holding out hope even to the former slave—Lincoln pointed out: "There is no permanent class of hired laborers amongst us. Twenty-five years ago, I was a hired laborer. The hired laborer of yesterday, labors on his own account to-day; and will hire others to labor for him to-morrow. Advancement—improvement in condition—is the order of things in a society of equals."[58] This constitutional logic would be drawn out more deeply in the latter half of the nineteenth century and into the twentieth as symbolized by the redoubtable case of *Lochner v. New York.*

Thus, as Ackerman argues, "the Lochner Court was doing what most judges do most of the time: interpreting the Constitution, as handed down to them by the Republicans of Reconstruction."[59] Yet the constitutional vision Ackerman speaks of, which comes to represent late nineteenth-century police powers jurisprudence, is far better represented by the various dissents than Miller's majority opinion (a point Ackerman himself concedes). What is odd here is that Ackerman is arguing that an opinion of the Court solidifies a constitutional transformation based on the Republican Congress's constitutional construction, but does so in an opinion that seems to subvert the meaning of that vision. I suggest that Ackerman misses this contradiction because he ends the story too soon, neglecting the significant constitutional arguments that come after the *Slaughterhouse* decision.[60] And he does so, because he remains wedded to the notion that the Supreme Court "ratifies" and "legitimizes" the Republicans' constitutional "transformation."

The debate over the meaning of the Civil War amendments did not end in the extraordinary politics of 1860–68 but continued with the more ordinary politics of 1870–83. And here the Republican construction of constitutional meaning was only partially successful. Sadly, much as Lincoln insisted that the Declaration represented our best constitutional aspirations rather than the reality of their enforcement, the same could ultimately be said of the Fourteenth Amendment as applied to blacks.

The Court's (Indirect) Reconstruction of the Civil War Amendments

As violence erupted in the South (and in much of the North) against Reconstruction governments and the move to black equality, it became clear that the Civil War amendments would not be self-enforcing. In response to this, and with the strong approval of the Grant administration, Congress passed a series of enforcement acts from 1870 to 1872. The acts were an attempt to give sustenance to the newly ratified Fourteenth and Fifteenth amendments, the meanings of which were being evaded by black codes, intimidation, and outright rejection.[61] Congress established the machinery to implement the acts and bring enforcement of the amendments through both the newly created Department of Justice and the federal courts. To be sure, some of this stemmed from a determination to capitalize on black suffrage in the South, adding numbers and an important constituency to the Republican Party. Republicans, though, were also motivated by constitutional commitments: they were determined to see that the Union did not return to a variant of the pre–Civil War Constitution, which excluded blacks from the terms of citizenship. As William Nelson argues, for all of their differences "there was one point on which nearly all Republicans agreed. No Republican was prepared, as a matter of general principle, to defend as rational a distinction grounded in race."[62] Yet, a scant few years after these amendments' ratification, they were being ignored or interpreted so as to limit their power and allow for racial discrimination.

It is not going too far to suggest, along with Walter Murphy, that some members of the Court in this era seemed to view the Republican construction of the Fourteenth Amendment as an "unconstitutional" constitutional amendment.[63] Taken on Republicans terms, the Fourteenth Amendment would so alter the Constitution's identity that it would be incompatible with its fundamental structural division between nation and state. Thus, the Court interpreted the Civil War amendments in light of antebellum stands of constitutional meaning and authority to maintain continuity and coherence with foundational constitutional commitments (as it read them). That is, the Court reconstructed the meaning of the Civil War amendments—situating them within the contours of the pre–Civil War thought that the amendments were meant to reject by either "transformation" or "completion"—so they would cohere with its understanding of the Constitution of 1787. As I noted previously, Republicans saw the Fourteenth Amendment as either completing the Constitution of 1787, thus solidifying what it already did properly interpreted, or transforming specific aspects of the Constitution to bring it into line with its foundational commitments as manifest in the Declaration. Either way, Republicans (1) saw the fundamental privileges and immunities of citizenship as national and (2) saw blacks as citizens, thereby jettisoning the constitutional logic of both *Dred Scott* and the state-centered vision. Building on the *Slaughterhouse Cases,* the Court seemed determined to thwart Congress's understanding of the amendments.

Subverting Congress's Constitution by Indirection: *Reese* and *Cruikshank*

In *United States v. Reese* and *United States v. Cruikshank,*[64] the Court continued its reconstruction of Congress's constitutional understandings begun in the *Slaughterhouse Cases.* Both *Reese* and *Cruikshank* took up the constitutionality of provisions of the most important Enforcement Act, that of May 1870, which was generally aimed at protecting the right to vote. The act was entitled "An Act to enforce the Right of Citizens of the United States to vote in the Several States of the Union . . ." and set penalties for state officials who denied the right to vote on racial grounds, or for private persons who conspired to prevent the exercise of this right. While these parts of the act were aimed at implementing the Fifteenth Amendment, the act also made it a crime to conspire with the intent of hindering any citizen in the full exercise of any right or privilege granted by the Constitution or laws of the United States, which was aimed at protecting the "privileges and immunities of citizenship" in section 1 of the Fourteenth Amendment.

In *Reese,* the Supreme Court took up the constitutionality of sections 3 and 4 of the act, which made it a crime for any official or any person to act to deny the right to vote. Two Kentucky municipal elections inspectors were charged with refusing to receive or count the vote of a black man, William Garner. Chief Justice Waite's opinion for the Court is perhaps most memorable for asserting, "The Fifteenth Amendment does not confer the right of suffrage upon anyone." Rather, it simply "prevents the States, or the United States, . . . from giving preference, in this particular, to one citizen of the United States over another on account of race, color, or previous condition of servitude."[65] Waite then went on to find sections 3 and 4 of the Enforcement Act unconstitutional, as they were not confined to infringements of voting rights based on "race, color, or previous condition of servitude."[66] Recognizing the right not to be deprived of the vote based on race, Waite's opinion thereby recognized Congress's power under section 2 of the Fifteenth Amendment to enforce this more limited right (rather than the general right to vote). Yet that seemed to be exactly what Congress was doing in the Enforcement Act of 1870, as sections 1 and 2 of the act, which directly preceded sections 3 and 4, explicitly addressed the issue of race. As Justice Ward Hunt pointed out in a compelling dissent, if sections 3 and 4 are read in light of sections 1 and 2, then they are limited to denying the right to vote based on race and therefore are within the clear confines of section 2 of the Fifteenth Amendment.[67] Waite, though, read the section more broadly, therefore finding the statute not "appropriate legislation."[68]

Oddly, Waite's opinion did not specifically find sections 3 and 4 of the Enforcement Act unconstitutional; instead, it found them insufficient, or not "appropriate
legislation."[69] So they were no longer good law, but what was the constitutional
reason for rejecting them? Or, what constitutional guidance did this offer the Congress?[70] Waite's opinion cuts in two directions. It offers a clear understanding of
what the Fifteenth Amendment means and how Congress may enforce it by "appropriate legislation." The Fifteenth Amendment conferred the right not to be discriminated against based on race in the exercise of the franchise and nothing more.
His opinion spelled out very clearly the meaning and terms of the Fifteenth Amendment and how it would be applied in the future, even while offering a narrow view
of the constitutional right at stake (that is, it only bestowed a right *not* to be discriminated against). Congress could, then, by appropriate legislation, enforce this
right. Given this clear constitutional rule, Waite therefore found sections 3 and 4
wanting because they were not clearly hewed to the amendment's meaning—they
were based, that is, not on race (which came under the purview of the Fifteenth
Amendment) but on general discrimination (which did not).[71] Presumably, Congress could repass the legislation, making this issue clear by narrowing the terms
of the statute to racial discrimination, and the Court would find it constitutional.
Charles Fairman goes so far as to say that "it is not to be doubted that if Congress
had enacted the substance of sections 3 and 4 in apt language, the validity of the
legislation would have been affirmed."[72] If this assertion is so, we have an emerging "constitutional dialogue" between Congress and the Court wherein the Court
is asking Congress to clarify the constitutional basis of the statute and giving it
clear constitutional guidance in doing so.[73] This reading of Waite's opinion has
problems.

   According to the dissenting opinions, it may be doubted that this course of
action is what the Court was asking of Congress, as Congress had already limited
the statute to these very terms.[74] By way of statutory (mis)construction, the Court
attempted to hem in Congress's constitutional authority without explicitly denying that authority: it told Congress that it must do what it had already done. This
is, at root, the basis of Justice Hunt's dissent. Unlike the majority opinion, Hunt
found it necessary to clearly put forth his views on the constitutional points.[75]
Finding that the indictments fell under the terms of the statute, Hunt then found
the statue itself constitutional.

   That Waite's opinion obscured the constitutional issues is made evident by Justice Nathan Clifford's dissenting opinion, which is almost always seen as a concurring opinion because Clifford agreed with the Court that the lower court's judgment should be affirmed. Thus, he was in agreement with the specific holding of

the case. Yet Clifford's opinion is reported as a dissent in the United States Reports. If the central issue before the Court is the constitutionality of the sections of the Enforcement Act, Clifford is in dissent. While this case blended complex questions of jurisdiction and statutory construction with constitutional issues, Clifford thoroughly examined the indictments brought under the Enforcement Act. He concluded that none of those being tried fell under the terms of the Enforcement Act.[76] But he did not think the Court needed to touch the constitutional issues, which, even if obscurely, Waite's opinion did. Thus, no sections of the Enforcement Act needed to be struck down. That Waite's opinion did rule against the act is further confirmed by the fact that Clifford was initially assigned to write the opinion in *Reese.* As Waite wrote to Clifford in assigning him the opinion, "when I supposed the enforcement cases would be decided on constitutional grounds I felt it to be my duty to try and write the opinion myself." Because it would not take up the constitutional questions, though, Waite turned the opinion over to Clifford saying, "you are perfectly familiar with criminal law and I am not."[77] The subsequent change was not explained, but it seems evident that Waite felt compelled to write the opinion because the case was decided on constitutional grounds. In doing so, Waite's opinion rejected Congress's constitutional understanding (and authority) in an indirect way that did not bring it into explicit conflict with Congress, even while potentially undermining Congress's enforcement of the amendment.[78]

The question of constitutional clarity and meaning is even more prevalent in *Cruikshank.* The new chief justice again wrote the opinion of the Court, handed down the same day as *Reese,* but did so in a way that skirted the constitutionality of the Enforcement Act, even while expounding on the meaning of the Fourteenth and Fifteenth amendments. In the wake of one of the bloodiest events of Reconstruction, the Colfax Massacre, federal officials indicted nearly 100 whites for "conspiring" to deprive two black men of their constitutional rights. The Court's opinion ultimately turned on sections 6 and 7 of the act, which made it a crime for private citizens to conspire to deprive a citizen of rights protected by the Constitution or federal law. Waite's opinion rests squarely on the notion of "dual citizenship" recently articulated by the Court in *Slaughterhouse* (although the lower courts, which included Supreme Court justices, initially upheld these acts).

Following Miller's *Slaughterhouse* opinion, Waite divided the rights of citizenship—those recognized in the "privileges and immunities clause" and the "due process clause" of the Fourteenth Amendment—into state and federal rights.[79] Most rights, Miller had argued, are held by virtue of being a citizen of a state. Freedom of speech, the right to vote, and the like were all based upon state citizenship and therefore protected by the states. Such rights do not come under Fourteenth Amendment protection. A handful of rights—the right to protection on the high seas, for example—are conferred by virtue of being a citizen of the United States and do come under Fourteenth Amendment protection. These, accordingly, were the rights Congress could protect under section 5 of the Fourteenth Amendment. All other rights are protected by the state and beyond the reach of congressional power.[80] As with the *Slaughterhouse Cases*, the Court's reading of the Fourteenth Amendment (to paraphrase Field) made it much ado about nothing. It was read, that is, in light of the antebellum understandings of the Constitution that it was meant to overturn.[81] The only dramatic alteration, then, was that the Fourteenth Amendment now provided that blacks could be citizens of the United States (and were therefore protected in the rights of citizenship thereby bestowed).

Once Waite divided rights into federal and state protection, the question was: Were the rights allegedly violated here subject to Congress's power under section 5 of the Fourteenth and section 2 of the Fifteenth amendments? Here, Waite turned to an analysis of the indictments themselves and not section 6 of the Enforcement Act, on which the indictments were based. He then suggested that two of the rights (First and Second amendment rights) were protected against only the federal government and not the states, so they were beyond the reach of the statute in this case. Remarkably, Waite relied on Marshall's *Barron v. Baltimore* opinion of 1835, which held that the Bill of Rights did not apply to the states and ignored the question of whether section 1 of the Fourteenth Amendment had fundamentally altered this relationship (as many within Congress who had framed the amendment argued), leaving Marshall's opinion a historical relic of pre–Fourteenth Amendment jurisprudence. Instead, Waite rather cavalierly asserted that it was now "too late to question the correctness of this construction [*Barron v. Baltimore*]."[82] Waite thus ignored the possibility that the Fourteenth Amendment was meant to guarantee national rights and situated the amendment within the confines of a pre–Civil War Supreme Court precedent. This move is all the more remarkable in that John Bingham, in framing the Fourteenth Amendment, explicitly invoked the language of Marshall's *Barron* opinion as a guide. But he did so to be clear that states could *not* deprive citizens of rights they held by virtue of being United States' citizens. Waite, following *Slaughterhouse*, concluded that the Fourteenth and Fifteenth amendments protected one only from being deprived of rights based on race and then only against state neglect. The trouble with the indictments, Waite argued, was that the alleged deprivation of rights was not clearly based on race nor was it a direct result of state neglect.[83]

Waite's opinion, in this manner, reaches out broadly to expound on the nature and meaning of both the Fourteenth and Fifteenth amendments. In doing so, he rejected much of the congressional interpretation of these amendments as put forward in the Enforcement Act. But, much as he did in *Reese,* he does all of this indirectly. In fact, Waite does not even question the constitutionality of section 6 of the Enforcement Act.[84] He merely finds the indictments wanting. At a glance, the opinion seems to rest on the particular facts of the case—the inadequacy of the indictments—and does not address questions of constitutional meaning and authority. As with *Reese,* this reading is not so easily sustained.

The trouble is that the constitutional analysis Waite puts forward is not superfluous but central to the Court's narrow conclusion and, therefore, cannot simply be *dicta.* Waite can only find the indictments "wanting" and section 6 of the Enforcements Act overly broad based on his full reading of the amendments. This assessment is made more evident, again, by Justice Clifford's opinion. As with *Reese,* Clifford's opinion is treated as a concurring opinion because he finds the indictments "insufficient." As he did in *Reese,* he carefully goes through the indictments and finds that they do not fall under the terms of the Enforcement Act. In coming to this conclusion, he says, the Court does not have to "deny the constitutionality of the Enforcement Act."[85] While Waite did not explicitly say so, Clifford seems to be under the impression that Waite's opinion rejected the constitutionality of section 6 of the Enforcement Act. In this, Waite's opinion is a masterpiece of judicial sleight of hand—all the more so as the Court's broad constitutional understanding, not just the particular holding in each case, was celebrated and became the basis of future Supreme Court opinions that far more explicitly spoke to constitutional meaning.[86]

"Viewed in historical perspective," Charles Warren has declared, "there can be no question that the decisions in these cases were most fortunate. They largely eliminated from National politics the negro question which has so long embittered Congressional debates; they relegated the burden and the duty to protecting the negro to the States, to whom they properly belonged; and they served to restore confidence in the National Court in the Southern States."[87] Chief Justice Waite, in the tradition of Marshall and Taney, had taken it upon himself to deliver the Court's opinion in these highly visible and hotly contested constitutional cases, and he was rewarded, by and large, with praise. It is difficult to be as sanguine as Warren about the Court's constitutional reconstruction, but he does put his finger on the shifting political landscape. Waite's opinions are most celebrated because they signal a retreat from the constitutional commitments of the Civil War amendments.[88] Rogers Smith suggests that "Chief Justice Waite's opinions for the Supreme Court were redolent of the Northern Republican retreat from continued civil rights struggles.[89]

Reconstructed Constitutional Meaning and the Congressional Election of 1874

Perhaps the most important incident in the struggle over the constitutional meaning of the Civil War amendments came in the congressional elections of 1874. With civil rights and constitutional meaning the foremost campaign issue, Republicans suffered a stunning defeat, losing eighty-nine seats in the House. Thus, by the time *Reese* and *Cruikshank* were decided by the Court in 1876, there was little congressional opposition to the Court's opinions. Individual members of Congress, especially Republican holdovers who voted for the various Enforcement Acts and the Civil Rights Act of 1875, were alarmed at the Court's construction, but Congress as a whole seemed content to leave this matter with the Court. Even many Republicans who thought the Court was clearly wrong felt it most prudent not to make an issue of it.[90] This change in Congress represented a seismic shift in the political landscape that allowed the Court's reconstruction to persist.

From 1870 to 1874, the Republican-dominated Congress passed legislation, rooted in its understanding of the Civil War amendments, which a majority of the Court viewed as constitutionally suspect. The Court and the Congress thus offered conflicting interpretations of the Civil War amendments within the Madisonian framework. The precondition for this clash was Congress's insistence that the Enforcement Acts were within the confines of its constitutional authority—essential if the Civil War amendments were to be truly binding. The Court reconstructed the meaning of the Civil War amendments in a manner that rejected Congress's interpretation. But as the Court was doing so, the (new) Congress, with the Democrats in control of the House, no longer articulated this constitutional construction.[91] Simply put, the Congress retreated to constitutional indifference on the meaning of the Civil War amendments, which allowed the Court's reconstruction to stand.

Congress's Last Stand

The last great act of the Reconstruction Congress took place in the waning days of the Forty-third Congress, just before the official change in power. The Civil Rights Act of 1875, passed in honor of the recently deceased Senator Charles Sumner, who had been trying to pass such legislation for years, put forward constitutional commitments that the incoming Congress had little interest in defending—commitments, it was argued, that had been roundly defeated by the public in the elections of 1874.[92] This constitutional understanding would bring the transitory

Congress into conflict with the Court. Yet based on *Slaughterhouse*, the only Court case to speak to the relevant constitutional questions when the act was passed, this was not a foregone conclusion.

The most controversial sections of the Civil Rights Act outlawed racial discrimination in public accommodations. The congressional debates on the Civil Rights Act, much like the earlier debates, reveal wide-ranging discussion of constitutional authority and meaning, with the members engaging in constitutional interpretation on their own, as well as referring to *Slaughterhouse*. In making reference to this Court opinion, some members refused to be bound by it, arguing that "Congress is called upon to legislate, and when it comes to legislation it must legislate . . . in conformity with [its reading] of the Constitution."[93] These members of Congress thought that Congress should act in conformity with its interpretation of the Constitution *no matter what the Court had or had not said*. In this vein, a number of senators and representatives insisted that Congress must go forward despite the *Slaughterhouse Cases*, some viewing the opinion as constitutionally wrong, others viewing it as indeterminate but agreeing that Congress should be bound by the authority of the Constitution, not the Supreme Court.[94]

Other congressmen argued that the Congress was bound by the Court's opinion.[95] Yet there was debate over just what being bound by the Court's opinion entailed: how did the prior opinion speak to the particular constitutional issue that Congress was debating? In answering this question, Congress was compelled to interpret the Court's opinion, weighing it, at times, against the Constitution and against its own past actions. This Congress was perhaps unique in that many of its members had acted as framers of the Thirteenth, Fourteenth, and Fifteenth amendments. Some congressmen claimed that the *Slaughterhouse Cases* presumptively made the Civil Rights Act unconstitutional.[96] Still others cited the *Slaughterhouse Cases* to support the act, arguing that even this case recognized that the primary motivation of the Fourteenth Amendment was black equality, which is what the Civil Rights Act, targeting public accommodations, was trying to achieve.[97] In an earlier debate about Sumner's bill, a senator objected that the *Slaughterhouse* decision seemingly rendered the bill "a violation of the Constitution[.]" Sumner himself responded, arguing that "the opinion did not 'by a hair's breadth' interfere with his bill."[98]

Even for those members of Congress looking to be bound to the Constitution by way of Supreme Court opinions, *Slaughterhouse* did not give Congress clear guidance on this score. While placing most rights under the prerogative of the states, Miller's opinion had clearly stated that the "one pervading purpose found [in the Civil War Amendments, was] the freedom of the slave race, the security and firm establishment of that freedom, and the protection of the newly-made freeman and citizen from *the oppression of those who had formerly exercised unlimited dominion over him.*" Would this last part be enough to justify, for the Court, a congressional exercise of power that admittedly intruded into the domain of the states (under pre–Civil War terms)? This was, after all, "the evil to be remedied by [the amendment]."[99] The Court's opinion on this score is ambiguous, not because it is an undertheorized opinion—quite the contrary—but because it did not specifically take up this constitutional question. Court opinions, no less than the Constitution, lend themselves to legitimate interpretive debate. Opinions are not infinitely interpretable. But insofar as constitutional debates are often about particular acts, there may be multiple plausible readings of just how a past opinion applies to particular circumstances. Even if the Congress wanted to defer to the Court's judgment, given the nature of the Supreme Court's decision, the result is a constitutional dialogue about the fundamental meaning of the Constitution.[100] For those who rejected the binding authority of the Court's opinion, the result was a debate and clash over the fundamental meaning of the Constitution. In either scenario, the Madisonian separation of powers is both means and ends.

The Court and the Emerging Constitutional Construction

It is tempting to say that these questions of constitutional meaning and authority, which had convulsed the body politic for more than a decade, were finally settled in Justice Joseph Bradley's opinion in the *Civil Rights Cases* (1883), which struck down sections 1 and 2 of the Civil Rights Act of 1875 and brought an end to this public debate about constitutional fundamentals. Charles Warren suggests something like this: "The meaning and effect of that Amendment [the Fourteenth], however, so far as it concerned the negro race for whose protection it had been primarily adopted, were fully and definitively settled by Waite and his Court, in a series of eight cases between 1876 and 1884."[101] But this suggestion does not quite capture the dynamic.

The change in Congress (combined with a change in the presidency with the famous "compromise of 1876") paved the way for a constitutional "settlement" on the "Negro question."[102] This shift in mind-set was captured perfectly in the debate over the Civil Rights Act itself. In voting against the Civil Rights Act of 1875, one Republican senator admitted its "justice" and "conformity with the late constitutional amendments." But, he added, "I do not want to go down with my party quite so deep as the bill will sink it if it becomes law."[103] It is this mind-set that was on display in the "compromise of 1876." If the country was in need of elementary constitutional instruction, it got it by way of the separation of powers. But the country did not want elementary instruction, as the senator's comments illustrate. As Madison argued even while defending constitutional forms, and their "aptitude and tendency" to honor constitutional commitments, such forms would be of limited utility against "overbearing majorities."[104] Lincoln might more accurately capture the particulars of this situation, when he insisted that "public sentiment is everything. With public sentiment, nothing can fail; without it nothing can succeed."[105] For "public sentiment" was precisely what was required here. Because of southern recalcitrance against the Republican construction of the Civil War amendments, for their meaning to be realized, public opinion would have to demand it. The resolve was not there.[106]

Still, we should not be so quick to simply accept that the Court's reconstruction settled the matter. Yes, the Republicans failed to entrench their understanding of the Fourteenth Amendment as it applied to race. And, with tragic irony, Alexander Stephens, former vice-president of the confederacy and an opponent of both the Fourteenth and Fifteenth amendments, was more successful in entrenching a vision of these amendments as they applied to race. Echoing the Court's earlier reconstruction, Stephens argued that the Republican understanding of the Fourteenth Amendment "would entirely upset the whole fabric of the Government, the maintenance of which in its integrity was the avowed object of the war."[107] Stephens, who earlier had seen slavery at the war's root in his "Corner Stone Speech," and thus understood the Constitution of 1787 to be antislavery at its core, now attempted to situate the Fourteenth Amendment within the confines of a nearly confederate understanding of the constitutional order.[108] Yet, while the Court embraced aspects of this understanding, it did not necessarily mirror the congressional retreat on all fronts. And there would be the lingering sense that this reconstruction had retreated from the constitutional commitments of the Civil War amendments.

This tension is reflected in the *Civil Rights Cases*.[109] The first case reached the Court in 1876, but for reasons that remain unclear, the Court did not hand down its opinion until 1883. Arguing that the Fourteenth Amendment protected rights only from state invasion or failure, not from private discrimination, Bradley's opinion for eight members of the bench struck down sections 1 and 2 of the Civil Rights Act of 1875. Under section 5 of the Fourteenth Amendment, Bradley argued, Congress could act only to preserve rights against explicit state abridgment or to address a failure on the part of the states to protect such rights.[110] Thus, Congress's power under section 5 was wholly remedial, giving it the ability to protect rights only if the states were first involved in their denial.[111] The *Civil Rights Cases* further spun out the logic the Court had offered earlier that year in *United States v. Harris*.[112] These cases persisted in narrowing the Republican understanding of the Fourteenth Amendment. In this, "the Supreme Court was more royalist than the king, more devoted to a restricted states rights interpretation of the Constitution than even some southern Democrats."[113]

If this understanding persisted within official channels, it was due as much to indifference as to affirmation. There was a deep sense from the moment the *Slaughterhouse Cases* were decided that this constitutional reconstruction had distorted, if not subverted, the meaning of the Civil War amendments. And the formal constitutional text, as well as the debates about its meaning, remained. There was, in fact, no insistence that the Civil War amendments had been *transformed* by popular understanding as manifest in elections during and after Reconstruction or by congressional acquiescence. On the contrary, there was often recognition of a *political* retreat from *constitutional* commitments, as with Fredrick Douglass's remark that "the fourteenth and fifteenth amendments are virtually nullified. The rights which they were intended to guarantee are denied and held in contempt. The citizenship granted in the fourteenth amendment is practically a mockery, and the right to vote, provided for in the fifteenth amendment, is literally stamped out in face of government."[114] His insistence that our official acts were at odds with foundational constitutional principles echoed, all too readily, the sort of arguments that he and Lincoln had made prior to the Civil War.

Interestingly, this fact was openly acknowledged at the time.[115] The *New York Times*, for example, claimed that Justice John Marshall Harlan's famous dissent in the *Civil Rights Cases* was "a learned, candid, and able paper." But it went on to say, "the tendency during the war period was toward the construction he favors. Since then a *reaction* has set in, which, so far, is beneficial[.]" The Court's opinion "has satisfied public judgment, and Justice HARLAN's will hardly unsettle it."[116] Harlan's dissent drew on Republican constitutional thought. Pointing to the retreat from the original understanding, Harlan argued that "Constitutional provisions, adopted in the interest of liberty, and for the purpose of securing, through national legislation, if need be, rights inhering in a state of freedom, and belonging to American citizenship, have been so construed as to defeat the ends the people desired to accomplish, which they attempted to accomplish, and which they supposed they had accomplished by changes in their fundamental law."[117] Harlan proceeded to detail Congress's power to protect rights—including the rights of slave owners in passing the fugitive slave acts—prior to the passage of the Civil War amendments. He then proceeded to explicate how the Thirteenth and Fourteenth amendments secured new rights, rejecting antebellum constitutional understandings in regard to free blacks and slaves. Congress, then, had the clear power and authority to secure these newly constitutionalized rights by way of primary legislation.

Harlan's opinion, anchored as it was in Republican constitutional understandings, was affirmed by Frederick Douglass, who insisted that the Court "has construed the Constitution in defiant disregard of what was the object and intention of the adoption of the Fourteenth Amendment. It has made no account whatever of the intention and purpose of Congress and the President in putting the Civil Rights' Bill upon the Statute Book of the Nation."[118] Douglass even pointed to the "sudden and causeless reversal of all the great rules of legal interpretation by which this Court was governed in other days, in the construction of the Constitution and of laws respecting colored people," which was most reflected by Justice Bradley himself.[119] In his dissent in the *Slaughterhouse Cases,* Bradley had spoken of the Fourteenth Amendment as rooting in constitutional text the foundational commitments of the Declaration of Independence. He went so far as to claim that, properly understood, even without the Fourteenth Amendment the Constitution would protect such rights, as it could only truly be understood against the foundational logic of the Declaration. This logic had been put forward perhaps most passionately by Douglass himself, asserting that the Declaration was the polity's "sheet anchor."[120] The Civil War amendments, as Bradley argued in his *Slaughterhouse* dissent, formalized and ratified this understanding. But this understanding was silenced in the *Civil Rights Cases,* so much so that even Charles Fairman wonders about Bradley's consistency: "But when a decade later [in the *Civil Rights Cases*] it was a question, not of butchers, but of blacks, Bradley could find in the Constitution no such large significance. The colored citizen's freedom to go where he chose was constricted: he must be content with such accommodations as were provided for blacks, or pray to the white citizen for an act of grace."[121]

Yet, simultaneous with this retreat from the logic of Bradley's *Slaughterhouse* dissent as it applied to blacks was its validation as it applied to whites. The Republican constitutional understanding took root in liberty of contract and due process cases against Miller's *Slaughterhouse* opinion. Indeed, embracing the dissenting opinions in that case, the Court became a "censor upon all legislation of the States, on the civil rights of their own citizens"[122]—the very thing that Miller in *Slaughterhouse* said could not be so. Articulating the Republican vision of liberty, Justice Rufus Peckham's opinion in the 1897 case of *Allgeyer v. Louisiana* could have been penned by Bradley. In drawing out the logic of the liberty protected by Fourteenth

Amendment due process, Peckham repeatedly quoted *Butchers' Union Company v. Crescent City Company:* "The right to follow any of the common occupations of life is an inalienable right. It was formulated as such under the phrase 'pursuit of happiness' in the Declaration of Independence, which commenced with the fundamental proposition that 'all men are created equal[.]'" Peckham then proceeded to quote further: "the learned justice said: 'I hold that the liberty of pursuit—the right to follow any of the ordinary callings of life—is one of the privileges of a citizen of the United States.'"[123] The learned justice was none other than Bradley.

The year before, the Court handed down *Plessy v. Ferguson*—the case that provided for "equal, but separate"—traveling some distance even from Bradley's opinion in the *Civil Rights Cases*.[124] The *Civil Rights Cases* held out the possibility that state-mandated distinctions on the basis of race might be unconstitutional. For it is the states, not individuals, Bradley insisted, that come under the terms of the Fourteenth Amendment.[125] At stake in *Plessy* was *state-mandated* segregation. Thus, *Plessy* does not inexorably flow from the *Civil Rights Cases* and may be in tension with Bradley's decision there as well as with the Court's opinion in *Slaughterhouse*. In *Plessy*, however, the Court ruled that laws "permitting, and even requiring, their [the races] separation in places where they are liable to be brought into contact do not necessarily imply the inferiority of either race to the other, and have been generally, if not universally, recognized as within the competency of the state legislatures in the exercise of their police power." In elaborating on this reconstruction, the Court turned to pre–Civil War cases that had upheld segregation. Thus, the Court's construction of the amendment had a far great debt to Alexander Stephens and opponents of the amendment than to the Republican understanding.[126] If this outcome was recognized in some quarters, the opinion as a whole was met with silence. *Plessy,* unlike the *Civil Rights Cases,* was an uneventful opinion, revealing how far the country had traveled from 1883, let alone 1868–75. The Civil War amendments failed to bond the polity to the word of the Constitution at least insofar as it applied to blacks. If Harlan's dissent represented the spirit of Republican constitutionalism, it found only partial expression in practice.[127]

Coda: The Subtle Vices of "Settlement"

The Civil War amendments during this era would shape our understandings as the nation revisited questions of race and the Fourteenth Amendment. In time, the president and the Congress would challenge the terms of this past "settlement." But, at least at times, rather than directly confronting this inherited understanding, the president and the Congress negotiated around these cases, as did the Court.

Even the Court's much-vaunted opinion in the *Brown v. the Board of Education,* which has contributed much to the mythology of judicial supremacy, did not overturn *Plessy.*[128] This fact should help illuminate how adhering to Court opinions may give us a distorted view of constitutional meaning, as well as of the reconstruction and evasion of past "settlements."[129]

Such adherence is evident in the congressional debate over the passage of the Civil Rights Act of 1964, as well as the Court's upholding that act in *Heart of Atlanta Motel* and *Katzenbach v. McClung.*[130] And it is the *Civil Rights Cases* of 1883 that loom so large in this debate. As we have seen, the *Civil Rights Cases* held that Congress may not reach private discrimination under section 5, unless the state first *fails to act.*[131] Although the Court had limited the reach of the *Civil Rights Cases,* and some members had clearly rejected it,[132] many in Congress and the Kennedy (later Johnson) administration were reluctant to rest Title II of the Civil Rights Act of 1964 on Congress's section 5 power, given that the *Civil Rights Cases* had not been explicitly overturned. Title II prohibited racial discrimination in public accommodations, much as the Civil Rights Act of 1875 had done. If the *Civil Rights Cases* had properly constructed constitutional meaning on this issue, Title II was unconstitutional if it rested on the Fourteenth Amendment. To get around this understanding, Congress and the administration advanced the argument that Congress could reach private discrimination in public accommodations by way of the commerce clause rather than by way of the Fourteenth Amendment. This move was all politics: Congress rested the Civil Rights legislation on the commerce clause because it thought the Court would uphold it, not because it thought it was regulating interstate commerce.

The ironies abound. Everyone knew Congress was regulating civil rights but insisted that it was regulating interstate commerce because of a past Supreme Court opinion that many thought had been wrongly decided.[133] Many members of Congress, in fact, were willing to return to what they deemed a proper constitutional understanding, but were precluded from doing so in order to "adhere" to a Supreme Court precedent. Yet, Title II of the Civil Rights Act and the Supreme Court opinions that upheld it were not consistent with the *Civil Rights Cases.* While they managed to get around the Supreme Court's view of section 5 in the *Civil Rights Cases,* rather than drawing on the Republican understanding to challenge it, the commerce clause argument that Title II ultimately rested on was indirectly rejected by Bradley's 1883 opinion. There Bradley argued that "no one will contend that the power to pass . . . [the Civil Rights Act of 1875] was contained in the Constitution before the adoption of the last three Amendments [the Thirteenth, Fourteenth, and Fifteenth amendments]."[134] As the commerce clause was part of the original Constitution of 1787, Bradley rejected any notion that it gave Congress the power to reach civil rights. Now, we might think Bradley was wrong on this score, or we might say that the commerce clause has evolved in such a manner as to outrun the past decision, but either way we are evading the logic of the *Civil Rights Cases* even while engaging in the pretense of upholding it. Once more, we see that Court opinions, even if we desire to follow them, require Congress and the president to puzzle out their constitutional logic and, in so doing, engage in constitutional judgments.

In a rare moment of lucidity, counsel for the Heart of Atlanta Motel said what everybody knew: "the argument of counsel [Archibald Cox] and of the government that this is done to relieve a burden on interstate commerce is so much hogwash; that the purpose of Congress was to pass a law [by] which some way or another they could control discrimination by individuals in the United States."[135] Archibald Cox, as solicitor general arguing the government's case, refused to touch the section 5 argument, insisting that Title II was nothing but a regulation of interstate commerce. In its opinions upholding the act, the Court indulged this fiction: it felt it unnecessary to reach the Fourteenth Amendment argument as the commerce clause provided solid constitutional footing. Out of a feigned respect for Court precedent, the Court and the solicitor general perpetuated a constitutional fiction. This course gives us a distorted view of constitutional meaning and authority that is not even in line with a past "settlement." This distortion is compounded by the fact that the *Civil Rights Cases* were interpreted in line with the "state action" doctrine. As I noted previously, however, Bradley's opinion may plausibly be read as insisting upon "state failure" to protect rights before Congress could intervene with legislation; and it may well rule out *state-mandated* segregation of the sort the Court accepted in *Plessy.*[136] Thus, the pretense of maintaining the *Civil Rights Cases* may well be based on a *misinterpretation* of those very cases.[137]

These discontinuities have been deepened by the Court's most recent opinions in regard to section 5, which rested in part on the *Civil Rights Cases* of 1883 in a putative effort to maintain "constitutional stability."[138] These discontinuities grow even sharper when we turn to the Rehnquist Court's commerce clause opinions, which have rejected the reach of the New Deal and the Warren Court constructions of "interstate commerce" that provided the constitutional foundation for upholding the Civil Rights Act of 1964.[139] I explore these tensions more fully in chapters 4 and 5. But first, in chapter 3, I consider the origin of this expansive view of the commerce clause, put forward as part of the progressive effort to reconstruct aspects of Lincoln's and the Republicans' constitutionalism.

CHAPTER THREE

The Progressive Reconstruction of American Constitutionalism

You cannot compound a successful government out of antagonisms.

Woodrow Wilson

In the spring of 1895, the Supreme Court struck down the newly passed national income tax,[1] held that the Sherman Antitrust Act did not apply to a virtual monopoly of sugar manufacturing,[2] and, critics insisted, used this same act to uphold an injunction against a labor strike.[3] The public explosion in reaction to these cases sparked a great debate about the nature of judicial power in a democratic society. This reaction was in marked contrast to the Court's decision a year later in *Plessy v. Ferguson,* which was met with silence, as the Court went with the current of popular thought in retreating from the constitutional commitments of Reconstruction.[4] But in 1895 the Court was accused of defending "the propertied class" against labor,[5] of injecting its personal preferences into law, and of illegitimately usurping democratic power. Against populist views of democracy and emerging progressive thought, the nature of judicial review was suspect, leading to distinctly "countermajoritarian" criticisms of the Court.[6] In the 1912 election, Teddy Roosevelt captured this sentiment in his "Confession of Faith," noting that "the first essential of the Progressive program is the right of the people to rule."[7]

The Court's exercise of judicial review was a manifestation of the central problem of countervailing power for progressives. As Herbert Croly explained, "Now that a plain tendency exists to emancipate legislation from judicial control, the serious practical weakness with which this aspect of the traditional system was afflicted should not escape scrutiny."[8] Roosevelt went so far as to say, "It is the people, and not the judges, who are entitled to say what their constitution means, for the constitution is theirs, it belongs to them and not to their servants in office—any other theory is incompatible with the foundation principles of our government."[9] Even

Woodrow Wilson, who in *Constitutional Government in the United States* praises the Court in whiggish terms as "the balance-wheel of our whole constitutional system," did so because the Court had, according to Wilson, seen fit to "adapt" the "Darwinian constitution" to the "opinion of the age."[10] Where judges were concerned with "fine-spun constitutional argument" rather than democratic adaptation, they should be led "to a back seat" where they might "pass unnoticed from the stage."[11] Sidney Milkis goes so far as to suggest that progressives sought to bring about direct democracy and thus were altogether suspicious of constitutional limitations and forms.[12] At the same time, however, progressives drew on earlier stands of constitutional thought, reconstructing the nationalism of Alexander Hamilton and Abraham Lincoln to justify the expansion of national power as rooted in constitutional foundations, rendering the "state-building" project a natural extension of our constitutional ends.

In *The Promise of American Life,* Croly singled Lincoln out as the only exceptional political figure of the latter half of the nineteenth century. Interestingly, Croly dwelled on Lincoln's "generous spirit" and not on his constitutional thought. Like most progressives, Croly had little interest in questions of race, symbolizing the nation's tragic retreat from the promise of Reconstruction.[13] He also had little patience for Lincoln's invocation of the Declaration of Independence and natural rights, or his insistence that they were the "sheet anchor" of American constitutionalism. Thus, Croly sought to rework Lincoln, drawing exclusively on his "nationalist" spirit, as part of reconstructing American constitutionalism. For all the differences among various progressives, and for all of their praise of Lincoln and Hamilton, they were united by a common criticism of the Madisonian Constitution and its "whig mechanics" of countervailing power.[14] Carefully drawing upon Lincoln's refusal to be bound by the *Dred Scott* case, Teddy Roosevelt sought "to make legislature and court alike responsible to the sober and deliberate judgment of the people," insisting that it was "for the people and not the courts to determine the principles and policies in accordance with which our constitution was to be interpreted and our government administered." In rejecting judicial supremacy, however, Roosevelt seemed to cast doubt on all constitutional forms that might thwart popular will: "Our prime concern is to get justice. When the spirit of legalism, the spirit of hair-splitting technicality, interferes with justice, then it is our highest duty to war against this spirit, whether it shows itself in the court or anywhere else."[15]

Wilson's *Constitutional Government,* reading as an extended quarrel with James Madison, evinces this furnishing of mind at nearly every turn. Again and again, Wilson notes that the Constitution was constructed on a "theory of checks and balances" that drew "upon the Whig theory of political dynamics, which was a sort of unconscious copy of the Newtonian theory of the universe."[16] The problem with this theory, Wilson argued, is that government is a living thing: "no living thing can have its organs offset against each other as checks, and live. On the contrary, its life is dependent upon their quick cooperation, their ready response to the commands of instinct or intelligence, their amicable community of purpose."[17] Wilson was a shrewd enough political thinker to note that this deliberate fostering of antagonisms owed a debt to Montesquieu, going so far as to say that "the admirable expositions of the Federalist read like thoughtful applications of Montesquieu to the political needs and circumstances of America."[18] Wilson, however, thought that such antagonisms were inimical to efficient and effective governance. Under the sway of Darwin, far more so, one is tempted to say, than Madison was ever under the sway of Newton, Wilson did not consider that such tensions could help foster the virtues of constitutional government. Indeed, Wilson praised the Constitution precisely because it was broad enough to transcend any notion of countervailing power. As a living organism, it could be adapted to the needs of the day, bringing all of the branches together to insist upon the will of the people.[19]

Here, progressives like Wilson, Croly, and Roosevelt came together.[20] Seeing democracy as the foundational element of the American regime, they rejected the Constitution's embrace of liberal forms, which channeled democracy by way of countervailing power. This rejection led progressives both to attack the Constitution directly—particularly its distinctly liberal elements—and to reconstruct it to fit the "needs of the day." Thus, progressives sought to reconstruct constitutional meaning and authority to accord with a mixture of "pure democracy" and, in James Ceaser's characterization, History.[21] Croly and TR, for example, drew on Hamilton's nationalist vision in a manner that dissolved constitutional formalities for a national democracy, reconstructing constitutional authority to favor a unified people led by the president who promoted their will.[22] This approach is most famously illuminated by Croly's claim that progressives were using "Hamiltonian means to Jeffersonian ends." Wilson, too, came to view the presidency in these terms and even argued that the "Whig theory" of the Constitution prevailed over "the very different theory of Hamilton." Hamilton's theory, according to Wilson, coincided with the progressive vision: "that government was not a thing which you could afford to tie up in a nice poise, as if it were to be held in inactive equilibrium, but a thing which must act every day with straightforward and unquestionable power, with definite purpose and consistent force, choosing its policies and making good its authority, like a single organism[.]"[23]

If progressives drew on Hamilton and Lincoln (among others) to justify their reconstruction of constitutional authority to accord with a "pure" version of democracy, this reconstruction, just as surely, required jettisoning earlier strands of constitutional thought in a "deconstructive" process, including, for instance, Lincoln's free labor vision.[24] Similarly, in the hands of Wilson, the "stewardship theory of the presidency" was essentially a means to overcome the now archaic Madisonian separation of powers and administer the "will of the people."

This chapter focuses on the progressive attempt to transform and reconstruct the Constitution based on the twin imperatives of democracy and evolution. I focus in particular on the progressive reconstruction of the national government's power and authority to regulate economic life and, as a corollary, on the progressive reconstruction of liberty, which was seen as a barrier to democratic regulation. I focus on these issues of constitutional authority and meaning as the progressive effort to reconstruct them played out within the Madisonian separation of powers in an often conflicted and antagonistic process. Progressives did not, of course, overturn the constitutional framework. But their ideas—particularly about the place of democracy in the American amalgam—have subsequently shaped how we think about the Constitution. If Abraham Lincoln's first inaugural address was the most important act of constitutional interpretation for the nineteenth century, Woodrow Wilson's interpretation of the presidency in the constitutional order may well be the most important act of the twentieth century.[25]

Yet, like the Republicans of Reconstruction, the progressive effort to reconstruct constitutional meaning and authority was partial and incomplete.[26] This struggle over our constitutional identity, a national "debate over the content of our most fundamental commitments,"[27] would last for nearly a half a century. In this chapter, I first examines how progressives were able to lay the foundations of the administrative state, even while conflicted views of the national government's power under the commerce clause sat uneasily alongside one another for decades. Progressives were aided by defenders of the constitutional order, like William Howard Taft, who thought that such regulation was in accord with constitutional ends. Taft, however, defended constitutional forms, rejecting the notion that "pure democracy" should be the governing principle of the American regime, or that constitutional evolution required that we overcome the separation of powers. Then, I turn to the progressive reconstruction of liberty, particularly in regard to due process and liberty of contract. Here the progressive reconstruction was not solidified until the middle years of the New Deal—and then, as I argue in the next chapter, in a "deconstructive" rather than "reconstructive" form. Indeed, the progressive insistence on evolutionary change, the flow of History, raised fundamental question about the nature and essence of the Constitution. Elements of the progressive understanding would overlay and conflict with the Madisonian Constitution. Chapters 4 and 5 trace this trajectory, examining how such understandings of "what" the Constitution is played out in quarrels over constitutional interpretation as the essence of maintaining the Constitution.

The Reach of the Commerce Clause: Merging Antitrust with the Commerce Power

Not only do the Sherman Antitrust Act and the Court cases around it provide the initial arena in which clashes over the reach of the commerce power would be contested, but the initial clashes they caused were central to the progressive construction of national democracy and national power. In 1890 Congress passed the act, which made "contracts, combinations or conspiracies in restraint of trade" illegal. The meaning of the act would be contested over the next few decades as the constitutional issues were given various constructions by the Court, the Congress, and the president. While there was interaction and "dialogue" between the branches over the meaning of the Sherman Act and the reach of the commerce power, there was also independent construction of the constitutional issues by each branch of government that often paid little heed to the other branches, or squarely blamed them for inaccurate understandings of the issues. Moreover, antitrust sat uneasily alongside other commerce clause issues symbolizing the tensions and uncertainties over the constitutional authority of the national government within this period.

Against fears of a growing concentration in industrial relations, the Sherman Act has been seen as a way of protecting the market and fostering competition, as a statutory embodiment of the common law, and, perhaps most prominently, a symbolic act aimed to satiate public desires for action against the "trusts." The act was passed with virtually no opposition (one vote against it in the Senate and none in the House), casting some doubt on the act as a clear outline of antitrust policy, and it depended on executive and judicial enforcement.[28] These cases, fleshed out over two decades, were among the high-profile cases of the day, with prosecutions under the act brought by the executive branch—much to the attention of the public and the media. While the executive had primary responsibility for bringing prosecutions, the Court was called upon to interpret the reach of the act and its constitutional application. As the sponsor of the act himself put it, the application "must be left open for the Courts to determine in each particular case."[29] Such "patchwork" attempts at regulation were, on occasion, an invitation to judicial supremacy, as when one senator debating the Sherman Act argued: "I do not see how we are ever going to know whether this bill is constitutional or not until it has been referred to the Supreme Court."[30] Thus, when Edward Corwin refers to the "judicial legislation" surrounding antitrust, he is not far off the mark. It is Congress, though, that seemingly invited such "policy making" from the bench.[31] William Howard Taft favored this understanding in *The Anti-Trust Act and the Supreme Court,* arguing that critics of the Court often failed to understand that Congress passed the Sherman Act against the backdrop of the common law, which called on judicial construction.[32] Even if one does not accept Taft's common-law view, which does find significant support in the legislative debates, the act did call on executive and judicial construction foreshadowing the entrenchment of the administrative state. As Corwin himself notes, when Roosevelt and Taft breathed life into the government's antitrust policy, the Court upheld such prosecutions (even if it did not always go along with the logic put forward by the executive branch).

In what was popularly known as the "Sugar Trust Case," the Court's first foray into the field, the government sought an injunction under the Sherman Act to prevent the American Sugar Refining Company from acquiring four competing sugar producers in Pennsylvania, which would give it control of 98 percent of the sugar market in the United States. The Court's opinion in *E. C. Knight* was the first time it touched on the Sherman Act. In an opinion for the Court with only Justice John Harlan dissenting, Chief Justice Melville Fuller found the Sugar Trust beyond the reach of the Sherman Act. Fuller's opinion upheld the Sherman Act as constitutional by essentially merging it with his reading of Congress's commerce power, which led him to conclude that the act did not apply to the case at hand. Fuller distinguished "commerce" from "manufacturing," an area that was traditionally reserved for the states, and reasoned that the commerce power, and by extension the Sherman Act, did not apply to manufacturing or those things that had only an "indirect" effect on commerce. Congress, Fuller argued, did not intend the act to touch on such areas, a reading that found some support in Senator Sherman's view: the act goes "as far as the Constitution permits Congress to go, because it only deals with two classes of matters: contracts which affect the importation of goods into the United States, which is foreign commerce, and contracts which affect the transportation and passage of goods from one State to another. The Congress of the United States can go no farther than that. It is claimed by no one that it can."[33] Moreover, President Cleveland's attorney general, Richard Olney, who argued the case before the Court, noted "any literal application of the provisions of the statute is out of the question."[34]

Justice Harlan, in the familiar position of lone dissenter, forcefully objected to this reading of both the commerce power and the Sherman Act. Yet, as Taft cautions, Harlan also noted in his dissent that the government's case was not well prepared.

That is, the government did not bring proof that the Sugar Trust was *contracting* to put a restraint on trade or commerce, an action that would clearly fall under the Sherman Act.[35] Harlan, as we will see in later cases, sought to get at the reality underlying such forms as part of applying fixed constitutional principles to changing social conditions.[36]

Constitutional Authority and Constitutional History in Antitrust

Progressives would later seize on *Knight,* suggesting the Court, bent on curbing congressional power against any kind of national economic regulation, deliberately subverted the meaning of the Sherman Act.[37] But antitrust does not end with *Knight.* The Court almost immediately clarified its construction of the commerce clause in upholding antitrust prosecutions.[38] The reach of the commerce clause in *Knight* was the subject of a five-decades-long debate over national constitutional authority within the separation of powers. This record suggests a far more complex relationship between the Court, the Congress, and the executive than the progressive lore of *Knight* would suggest.[39]

The Court's opinions that immediately followed *Knight* in the spring of 1895, however, lent some credence to progressive claims that it was manipulating constitutional meaning to protect the propertied class against the democratic majority. The Democratic Platform in 1896 went so far as to say that one of the Court's opinions was not only wrong "but that it departed from previous rulings issued 'by the ablest judges who have ever sat on that bench.'"[40] In stark contrast to *Knight,* the Court in *Debs* upheld an injunction against the Pullman strike. Under the leadership of Eugene V. Debs, the American Railway Union staged a strike against any train carrying a Pullman car. The strike crippled rail transportation and United States Attorney General Olney sought an injunction under the terms of the Sherman Antitrust Act, calling the strike a "conspiracy" and "combination" to hinder trade. The Supreme Court upheld the injunction, leading progressives to note, with superb irony, that this was the government's "first successful *criminal* prosecution based upon the Sherman Act. The Supreme Court thus struck down not the oil trust, or the sugar or beef or steel trusts, but the *union trust*[.]"[41] This overstates the case, as Justice David Brewer's opinion for the Court upheld the injunction not on the basis of the Sherman Act—even though the Court did not distance itself from the lower court, which did—but on the constitutional grounds that the state must be able to preserve order.[42] Progressives, though, were surely right in noting the uneasy notion of national power within the Court's opinions. In *Knight,* the commerce power could not intrude into the realm of manufacturing, which was constitutionally reserved for the states, while in *Debs* national power to put down a labor strike was seen to be extensive.[43]

Yet in three cases shortly after *Knight*, the Court upheld prosecutions under the Sherman Act—although they were not easily squared with the popular perception of *Knight*. In his *Anti-Trust and the Supreme Court*, Taft argued that these cases essentially "eliminated" the *Knight* decision. Writing in 1914, Taft went so far as to say that "the dissenting opinion of Mr. Justice Harlan was a very strong statement, and I don't think it is too much to say that it represents much more fully the present view of the Court as to what may constitute a direct restraint upon interstate commerce than does the opinion of Chief Justice Fuller."[44] But these cases, as Taft noted, often turned on particular facts rather than broad constitutional principles. In *Knight* itself—the opinion that progressives continually invoked—Fuller insisted on the plenary authority of Congress's commerce power. In fact, all of these opinions would assume the plenary authority of the commerce power and, in doing so, turn to Chief Justice Marshall's opinion in *Gibbons v. Ogden:* Congress's power to regulate interstate commerce "is complete in itself, may be exercised to its utmost extent, and acknowledges no limitations, other than are prescribed in the Constitution."[45] Progressives would later seize on this sentiment, constructing "plenary" to mean both unlimited and not subject to judicial review. This interpretation was the real root of disagreement.

For most members of the Court, as well as Taft, the question was whether any putative regulation of interstate commerce was, in truth, a regulation of interstate commerce. The Court, being bound by the Constitution, could not simply take Congress's word that it was regulating interstate commerce (as progressives would later advocate). Even Harlan's famous *Knight* dissent spoke of regulations that "would be in excess of any power granted to Congress."[46] Where such regulations seemed excessive, justices were prone to quote Marshall's reading in *McCulloch*, that "should Congress, under the pretext of executing its powers pass laws for the accomplishment of objects not intrusted to the government, it would become the painful duty of this tribunal" to strike down such laws.[47] We see strikingly similar constitutional constructions, even while disagreeing on particulars, from Roosevelt and Taft, who led the charge in exercising national power.

The Constitutional Foundations of National Power in Roosevelt and Taft

In a 1902 message to Congress, Teddy Roosevelt insisted that Congress's power to regulate interstate commerce was "an absolute and unqualified grant, and without limitations other than those prescribed by the Constitution." He continued, "this power has not been exhausted by any legislation now on the statue books." Roosevelt did not reference the Court's opinions. And while nothing he said explicitly contradicted them—in fact, some of his language, "directly upon such commerce," for example, seemed consistent with them—he rejected the notion that the Sherman Act simply embraced the common law. Such an understanding suggested that the act broke with traditional regulation, potentially calling forth far more expansive national administration. Most importantly, Roosevelt called for Congress to make appropriations "for the better enforcement of the anti-trust law as it now stands."[48] In doing so, Roosevelt called forth a Hamiltonian understanding of the Constitution, which would potentially cut against aspects of Fuller's opinion in *Knight*. As Croly argued in regard to Roosevelt, "the whole tendency of his program is to give a democratic meaning and purpose to the Hamiltonian tradition and method." According to Croly, Roosevelt was a "Hamiltonian with a difference," insofar as he sought to overcome the "antagonism" between efficient "national organization" and "radical democratic institutions and ideals."[49] Witness Roosevelt's position on executive enforcement, which drew on Hamilton's notion of "energy," even if altering it, and pointed to the primacy of executive action and discretion in regulating national life. This is vividly illustrated in Roosevelt's promotion of executive action against the trusts, which would also come to mean the executive's ability—not the legislature's or the courts'—to distinguish between good and bad trusts. Such an understanding underpinned Croly's claim that "a thoroughly representative government is essentially government by men rather than by Law."[50]

Jeffrey Tulis helpfully qualifies this view. Even while Roosevelt was engaged in a reconstruction of Hamilton, it was to preserve the constitutional order rather than undo it. As Tulis argues, "Roosevelt expressed a bi-level, Lincolnian approach to constitutional interpretation and statecraft. If the essential objects and most general principles of the Constitution could be adumbrated, specific constitutional prescriptions could be altered or abandoned as a matter of constitutional fidelity."[51] To be true to the essentials of the constitutional order, Roosevelt might need to break with some inherited constitutional understandings, a position in contrast to that of Croly and other progressives, who insisted that constitutional fundamentals would themselves have to be abandoned as the flow of History had made them a hindrance.[52]

In his 1905 inaugural address, Roosevelt invoked Lincoln as the great preserver of the republic, suggesting that, while the specific tasks before us where unknown to the past, "the spirit in which these tasks must be undertaken . . . remains essentially unchanged."[53] In a highly public campaign to increase the administrative capacity of the Interstate Commerce Commission (ICC), Roosevelt cast himself as preserving the Constitution: this republic "will and shall remain as its founders intended it to be, and as its rescuers under Abraham Lincoln intended it to be, a government where everyman, rich or poor . . . is given his full rights[.]"[54] After a contentious battle, with Roosevelt breaking with members of his own party, Congress gave the ICC the power to regulate railway rates in the Hepburn Act of 1906.[55] A leading scholar of American political development has suggested that in upholding the Hepburn Act, the Court helped entrench the constitutional foundations of the administrative state and provided Roosevelt with a lasting victory.[56] For TR, as well as defenders of the traditional constitutional order like Taft and Senator Henry Cabot Lodge, these developments were rooted in foundational constitutional commitments. In making constitutional arguments for the national regulation of a rapidly expanding national economy, these statesmen turned to *The Federalist*. If circumstances were changing, then altering the application of fixed principles in a manner that would preserve the essentials of constitutional structure and identity was necessary. But this "monarchy of the Word," as Croly called the Constitution, could not be radically transformed based on appeals to democracy or History.

As Roosevelt went on to recommend in his inaugural, *if* it was impossible to secure the vigorous enforcement of antitrust under the Constitution, then we ought to amend the Constitution to secure such a power.[57] Roosevelt drew further on Hamilton and the redoubtable John Marshall to insist on the continuity of his policies with the fundamentals of the Constitution: vigorous enforcement of the Sherman Act was consistent with constitutional meaning. Still, we want to notice the fact that he held out the possibility that such action might not be constitutional and, then, proper recourse would be constitutional amendment. The implicit message was that the Constitution could not be radically transformed or abandoned based on our democratic desires.[58]

Interestingly, Croly, who prominently defended Roosevelt's and Taft's views of antitrust against the Court's, thought that "in the end the American Federal Constitution, like all Federal Constitutions framed during the past century, will have to dispense with the distinction between state and inter-state commerce[.]" Croly thought this the one aspect of the Constitution that would have to be formally amended rather than "reconstructed."[59] But as a tireless advocate for the "emancipation of popular political power and responsibility from the overruling authority of the Law and the courts," Croly's criticism of the Court's Sherman Act opinions primarily focused on its failure to allow for enough *executive discretion.*[60] The executive ought to be able to distinguish, as Roosevelt was, from "good" and "bad" trusts as "huge corporations have contributed to American economic efficiency. They constitute an important step in the direction of the better organization of industry and commerce."[61] Croly sought to amend the Sherman Act to recognize this distinction—one that was not clear from the statute itself and one that the Court did not recognize at the time, even while it *upheld* executive action against the trusts under the act. Notice, though, that Croly would prefer to make sovereign the executive, acting on popular will, rather than the Constitution. Coming from a very different angle, Taft claimed that the Roosevelt administration had proceeded to bring prosecutions under the act and, in conjunction with Congress and the courts, was fleshing out the reach of national power by carefully calibrating constitutional principles against changing circumstances. Consequently, an amendment was unnecessary.[62] As Taft would later insist, "It is not that the Court varies or amends the Constitution or a statute, but that, there being possible several interpretations of its language, the Court adopts that which confirms to prevailing morality and predominant public opinion."[63] But all of this must be consistent with constitutional fundamentals.

Roosevelt, Taft, and the Court: Fleshing Out the Reach of National Power

In *Northern Securities* the Roosevelt administration brought forth its Hamiltonian understanding of the Constitution. The crux of the argument was that under the commerce power, "Congress can regulate anything and everything in the sense that it can prohibit and prevent its use in a way that will defeat the law that Congress may constitutionally enact." The administration, then, citing *Champion v. Ames,* went on to argue that "the 'penetrating and all-embracing' nature of this power has often been stated, explained, and emphasized by this Court. *Gibbons v. Ogden.*"[64] While it is tempting to read this argument, as progressives would later do, as suggesting there were no constitutional limits on the reach of the commerce power, it need not be construed in that manner. In light of TR's constitutional understandings during this period, it is more consistent to see the argument as an articulation of the national government's power derived from a clear constitutional end—the power to regulate interstate commerce. But this interpretation did not render the power limitless, as TR included actions that the national government *could not* take under the commerce power. Nor did such a construction render the power beyond the realm of the separation of powers and checks and balances.

This, at any rate, was Harlan's argument for the Court in *Champion,* which the government relied upon so heavily. Harlan, as was his wont, quoted not only *Gibbons* in terms of laying out the reach of the commerce power but also *McCulloch,* insisting that while Congress might choose the *means* to regulate interstate commerce, such means must be "plainly adapted to that end."[65] In *Northern Securities,*

Justin Harlan again wrote for the Court, upholding the government's position in a 5–4 opinion. The various opinions, four in all, reflected persistent tensions, with Harlan upholding the act as a valid regulation of interstate commerce, even while recognizing limits to that power, and White conceding the plenary authority of the power, even while rejecting this application as beyond the national government's reach.[66] This debate replayed the argument between Harlan and Fuller not just in *Champion* but also, at root, in *Knight*. It was a debate that would be played out for another three decades both on and off the Court.

I must pause for a moment on Justice Holmes's dissent in *Northern Securities* as he occupies a central place in the progressive reconstruction of constitutional meaning and authority. Holmes focused on the statutory interpretation of the Sherman Act—"to read English intelligently"—but his reading of the law rests on constitutional understandings. Holmes's insistence that all we need do is read English intelligently was a swipe at Justice Harlan's reading of the statute who, as the last of the "tobacco-spittin' judges," presumably had difficulty reading English intelligently.[67] If Harlan's reading of the statute were correct, Holmes argued, the Sherman Act would be unconstitutional. Holmes cited the *Knight* opinion favorably twice in dissent and insisted on judicially enforceable limits to Congress's commerce power. At one point, he even claimed that if the logic of the government's position were correct then there is "no part of the conduct of life with which on similar principles Congress might not interfere."[68] As this was not a tenable constitutional position, Holmes construed the statute in such a way as to limit its reach and preserve its constitutionality (although his reading does not readily square with the plain language of the statute).

Holmes's opinion is deeply interesting for two reasons. First, Holmes's jurisprudence was drawn on by progressives in their reconstruction of the commerce power in a manner that rejected judicially enforceable limits to that very power (which I take up more extensively in the next chapter). But Holmes rejects this position. Second, and more immediately relevant, Holmes became most famous during this period for his celebrated *Lochner* dissent a year later, in which he insisted that "the word liberty in the Fourteenth Amendment is perverted when it is held to prevent the natural outcome of a dominant opinion[.]"[69] This language, with its claim that democratic will trumps constitutional forms, became a rallying point for progressive criticism of the Court. Yet Holmes's simplistic reading ought to give us pause against the backdrop of his dissent in *Northern Securities*.

Drawing these two cases against one another—and *Northern Securities* was more visible at the time—illustrates how difficult it is to speak of judicial deference to a democratic majority within a system of countervailing power that deliberately fosters differing and competing democratic majorities. It is not just a question of legislative intent, which scholars have emphasized in speaking to this dilemma.[70] We also have competing democratic majorities that do not necessarily overlap— indeed, they are deliberately in conflict with one another in an effort to balance and channel democracy by way of liberal constitutional forms. If Holmes's reading of the Sherman Act is correct—and that is far from clear—then *Northern Securities* would seem to pose the executive against the legislature. Why is it more democratic to go with the legislature against a popular president enacting a popular program? If this is precisely the reason for the Court to act against the executive, as Holmes suggested in private correspondence, then judicial independence against demo-cratic action is far more important than Holmes made it out to be in his *Lochner* dissent (or at least the progressive and New Deal understanding of his dissent). In fact, it would point to the importance of judicial review within the separation of powers, which progressives rejected. This complex interplay, blending elements of liberalism and democracy, cannot be captured by aphoristic slogans about "the right of a majority to embody their opinions in law."[71]

In his *Swift* opinion of the same year, Holmes would further illustrate the ten-sions within the Court's construction of the commerce power, as well as the ten-sions within the progressive reconstruction of constitutional authority under the commerce clause. In *Swift,* Holmes emphasized "the stream of commerce," arguing that Congress's power to regulate interstate commerce was a question of "proxim-ity and degree."[72] In some ways, Holmes's opinion seemed to endorse Harlan's long-standing insistence that it was the *impact* on commerce that was central to national regulative authority. Yet Holmes cited *Knight* favorably, distinguishing "direct" and "indirect" effects from the "stream of commerce."[73] Barry Cushman argues that this distinction was perfectly coherent, as only "those 'local' enterprises 'affected with a public interest' could be located in a stream of interstate commerce and thereby subject to federal regulation."[74] In these cases, the commerce clause was read in light of the due process clause's "public purpose." If true, this may suggests that Holmes's *Lochner* dissent was not the stinging critique of due process that pro-gressives made it out to be.[75]

As a Yale Law professor, Taft attempted to retrospectively bring order to the Court's various constructions of the commerce power (and of the Antitrust Act). Turning in particular to *Standard Oil* and *American Tobacco,* opinions by Chief Justice Edward White, elevated to the center seat by Taft himself, Taft argued that the Court finally adopted the distinction between "reasonable" and "unreasonable" restraints on trade, which, as Roosevelt had argued, should be determined on a case-by-case basis by the executive branch.[76] The road had not been quite so

smooth. But these struggles did underlie agreement on the constitutional foundations of the administrative state. Still, the conflict over the reach of the commerce
power would continue, and the election of 1912 would be played out as a profound
argument about the place of constitutionalism and democracy within the American amalgam.

The Current of Constitutional Drift: Progressive Reconstruction and the Election of 1912

Despite Taft's efforts in antitrust, he was challenged by Roosevelt for his party's
nomination in the election of 1912. While Taft held onto the Republican nomination, he was trounced in the general election, winning the electoral votes of only
Vermont and Utah. The 1912 election has thus aptly been described as a smashing
victory for progressives unified by Roosevelt's and Wilson's deep criticism of the
Constitution and its self-appointed "high-priests."[77] Sidney Milkis has persuasively
suggested that the election represented the birth of "modern politics," laying the
foundations for the rhetorical and plebiscitary presidency. Such understandings of
democracy and "popular will" shaped our view of American institutions through
the twentieth century—giving birth, for instance, to the notion of a countermajoritarian dilemma, which became an "academic obsession" framing constitutional
law for much of the twentieth century.[78] In 1912, however, the progressive victory
was incomplete.[79] If Wilson played the role of a constitutional prophet, he did not
live to see the promised land. Rather, Wilson had partial victories, many of which
were fostered and sustained by defenders of the Court and Constitution like Taft—
the bête noire of the 1912 election.

Critical of particular Court decisions, Taft nevertheless offered a robust defense
of the Court's institutional role within the Madisonian system. For Taft, the Court
was simply doing its job, which was not to settle the larger constitutional issues but
to decide the cases brought before it.[80] This description applied even when Taft
invoked the language of judicial supremacy. While Taft shared a view of antitrust
that often moved in stride with progressives like Croly, he was an adamant defender
of the constitutional framework against such critics. Croly, like many progressives,
had no patience for legalisms or constitutional forms that might thwart bold governmental action: in a word, "democracy and legalism are incompatible." The creation of national spirit and reform thus required overcoming such legalism, trans-
posing Madison's insistence that the government is subordinate to the Constitution:
"And how will the individual and the national spirit have to be transformed, in case
the Law is to be subordinated to the government instead of the government to the

Law?"[81] Croly persisted as a tireless advocate of "the emancipation of popular political power and responsibility from the overruling authority of the Law and the courts[.]"[82] While this seems a clear indictment of constitutionalism, Croly drew on aspects of American constitutional thought that, reconstructed, might dissolve the Law of the Constitution. Against this criticism, Taft, and fellow travelers like Henry Cabot Lodge and Elihu Root, turned to Hamilton and Lincoln to defend the Constitution; indeed, as Milkis argues, they saw this as a "struggle for the soul of the Constitution."[83] This struggle, however, was not aimed at prohibiting national economic regulation. For Taft and Lodge, like TR before 1912, regulation could be achieved within the Madisonian Constitution. Such regulation might even flow from our constitutional commitments as expounded by *The Federalist.*

Roosevelt came to symbolize the fragmented constitutional divide, which would preoccupy the country into the New Deal years. Like Taft and Lodge, TR initially proposed that, properly constructed, the Constitution's foundational principles could be applied to changing circumstances: "I am not pleading for an extension of constitutional power. I am pleading that the constitutional power which already exists shall be applied to new conditions which did not exist when the Constitution went into being." Putting forward this nationalist vision, Roosevelt drew on James Wilson, insisting that, like Lincoln, he had a faith in the people and the ability of their representatives in the national government to be "given full and complete power to work on [the peoples'] behalf." Roosevelt also drew on John Marshall's notion of "inherent power" beyond those enumerated powers "conferred by the Constitution," arguing that the Constitution "must be interpreted not as a straight jacket, not as laying the hand of death upon our development, but as an instrument designed for the life and healthy growth of the Nation." For TR, "If the theory of the Marshall school prevails, then an immense field of national power, now unused, will be developed, which will be adequate for dealing with many, if not all, of the economic problems which vex us." Yet even when invoking the language of the Constitution as a "living organism," Roosevelt believed that "the Constitution is now and must remain what it always has been," which included its limits on national power. The national government, for example, "can do little in the matter of child labor." And here, "courts must determine what is national and what is State commerce."[84] But they should do so with Marshall's vision in mind. None of this was in necessary contradiction to the general outlook of the Fuller Court, even if it cut against particular opinions.

Yet, in the 1912 election, Roosevelt would draw on progressive criticism of the Constitution as outdated, undemocratic, and inefficient. In *The New Nationalism,* which was released as a precursor to his 1912 bid for the presidency, there was a subtle, though profound, shift in Roosevelt's emphasis. In both the opening and closing chapters of the book, Roosevelt harshly criticized the Court's decisions in *Knight* and *Lochner*. Just as he had in the past, he drew on Lincoln in defense of such criticism. "I continue to uphold the doctrine enunciated fifty-three years ago by Abraham Lincoln as regards criticism of the actions of the courts. I feel most strongly that the decisions to which I object, and which I hope will be reversed, are wrong, for the reasons set forth so admirably and with such convincing clearness by Justices Harlan, White, Day, and Holmes."[85] But these justices' reasons, as I elaborate below, were quite different—and the differences were important in constitutional terms. Unlike Harlan's, White's, or Day's, Roosevelt's own reasons seemed to turn on the notion of "popular rights." Reference to Wilson, Marshall, or Hamilton, which had littered Roosevelt's early discussions, was absent as well. There was no claim that these Court opinions altered constitutional meaning, thwarting the government from doing things the Constitution allowed it to do. Rather, sounding like Holmes in *Lochner*, Roosevelt insisted that these decisions, though "nominally against national" or "states rights," are really decisions "against popular rights—against the democratic principle of government by the people."[86]

Such an understanding supports Milkis's contention that Roosevelt began to favor a form of direct democracy, which aligned him more fully with progressive attempts to fundamentally reconstruct, if not dissolve, the Madisonian Constitution by making it conform to "pure democracy." Roosevelt seemed to suggest that the people could transform the Constitution in any manner they saw fit—that democracy was the overriding value and, hence, trumped constitutional forms. Allies and friends of Roosevelt, including Lodge and Root, refused to support him in 1912 and even took to rescuing Hamilton, Lincoln, and the Constitution from his reconstructions.

One of the first recipients of a Ph.D. from Harvard, Lodge had edited *The Federalist* and written a biography of Hamilton. His biography even praised Hamilton's policies as having "converted the system of the Constitution into a living, vigorous organism."[87] He was, then, not so much critical of national regulation as skeptical of undoing the logic of the Constitution, with its blend of liberalism and democracy, in a fit of direct democracy. In a lecture at Princeton University in 1913, Lodge offered a corrective to Roosevelt's and Croly's reconstruction of Lincoln. In "The Democracy of Abraham Lincoln," Lodge drew on Lincoln to challenge the pure views of democracy that rejected constitutional limitations, as manifest in the referendum, judicial recall, and other progressive criticisms of constitutionalism. Lodge called back the notion of countervailing power, claiming that "the framers were well aware that a majority of the voters at any given moment did not necessarily represent the enduring will of the people."[88] Whereas Roosevelt turned to Lincoln's first inaugural address to criticize the courts and insist on popular democracy, Lodge quoted Lincoln's words to flesh out the context of his thought: "A majority held in restraint by constitutional checks and limitations, and always changing easily with deliberate changes of popular opinions and sentiments, is the only true sovereign of a free people."[89] Lincoln situated the people within the confines of constitutional limits according to Lodge: democracy was thus balanced, and contained, by the Constitution's liberal forms. Here Lodge argued that the separation of powers was, as I have said throughout, both means and ends. As Lodge would later illustrate in defeating Wilson's Versailles Treaty, the Constitution could foster deliberation precisely because it fostered antagonisms.[90] In thwarting pure democracy, the separation of powers would require the nation to engage in "reflection and choice" before acting. This approach was in profound contrast to the progressives' call for expressions of immediate popular will through the referendum and the recall. The democracy of the Constitution, because it was counterbalanced by liberalism, was a superior form of democracy. This form was also, according to Lodge, Lincoln's democracy, as his refusal to be bound by *Dred Scott* was grounded in constitutionalism, not an insistence on popular will. Taney's opinion was not wrong because it went against popular opinion; indeed, it found solid democratic support insofar as it reflected the unsavory compromise of 1854. It was wrong as a matter of constitutional logic. Lodge suggested the same sort of logic was at play in Lincoln's criticism of slavery, casting Douglas's popular sovereignty as an unacceptable form of pure democracy. Pure democracy, though, was the rallying cry in the 1912 election.

Woodrow Wilson's *The New Freedom* shared much in common with TR's *The New Nationalism,* and both bore a heavy debt to Croly's *The Promise of American Life* (a debt Roosevelt openly acknowledged). Wilson called for the emancipation of the people's generous energies and insisted that "our government has been for the past few years under the control of heads of great allied corporations with special interests." In the more scholarly *Constitutional Government,* Wilson called for adaptation of the Constitution to accord with the imperatives of History. Aspects of this argument were readily evident in Wilson's *The New Freedom:* "all that progressives ask or desire is permission . . . to interpret the Constitution according to the Darwinian principle."[91] In a move reminiscent of Lincoln, a man Wilson had little praise for, he even drew on the Declaration of Independence to properly understand the Constitution: "It is an eminently practical document, meant for the use of practical men; not a thesis for philosophers, but a whip for tyrants; not a theory of government, but a program of action. Unless we can translate it into the questions of our own day, we are not worthy of it, we are not the sons of the sires who acted in response to its challenge."[92] The tyranny we now face came from concentrations of "capital" against the people. Such concentrations of selfish businesses dominated the governments, which "cease to be governments representative of the people."[93]

This conflict would continue to play out most centrally in regard to Congress's power under the commerce clause and with regard to the meaning of due process and liberty of contract. As I discuss more thoroughly in the next section, Wilson called for recognition of the fundamentally altered relations between employee and employer, to bring a great economic system that was "heartless" under the control of popular will. Thus, he would call for a more rigorous enforcement of antitrust laws and cast himself against big corporations as such, although, like TR, he would also insist that "in the new order government and business must be associated closely."[94] Wilson adviser and later Supreme Court Justice Louis Brandeis claimed that the difference between TR and Wilson on this question was central: TR wanted to distinguish between good and bad trusts by way of executive discretion. Wilson and the Democrats, Brandeis argued, wanted to altogether break "the menace inherent in private monopoly and overwhelming commercial power."[95] Thus, Brandeis suggested not only a more rigorous enforcement of the Sherman Act but also rulings that would prevent trusts from emerging in the first place, rejecting TR and Taft's policies, as well as the Court's recent opinions.

The Current of Constitutional Drift

The Wilson administration would ultimately get Congress to pass the Clayton Antitrust Act and the Child Labor Act and continue the entrenchment of the administrative state with the Federal Trade Commission in 1914 and the Tariff Commission in 1916 (both of which depended on judicial decision making as a primary regulatory mechanism).[96] This legislation set the stage for a replication of the early debates over the commerce power. When the Court, for example, clearly applied the Sherman Act to labor in the Danbury Hatters Case,[97] Congress responded with the Clayton Act in 1914. The act partly exempted labor from antitrust, stating that "labor . . . is not a commodity or article of commerce." How far-reaching this exemption was meant to be is not immediately evident. Congress partly invited the courts to sort this out, as it did not specify what "lawful" activity was under the act. Moreover, the act specifically permitted courts to issue injunctions if necessary to "prevent irreparable injury to property, or to a property right."[98] When the Court upheld a labor injunction under the terms of the act in *Duplex Printing*, both

Mahlon Pitney's opinion allowing an injunction in this particular case and Brandeis's dissent, denying the injunction's validity, were plausible readings of the act.[99] Ken Kersch persuasively argues that Pitney's opinion was in line with traditional constitutional understandings, while Brandeis was engaged in a reconstructive effort to cast employees and employers in sweeping group terms (which is how he read the Clayton Act).[100]

Even while calling for an evolutionary Constitution, prior to becoming president, Wilson embraced a reading of the Congress's commerce power that was at odds with the Keating-Owen child labor act passed under his administration. He noted that "the real difficulty has been to draw the line where the process of expansion and adaptation ceases to be legitimate and becomes a mere act of will on the part of the government, served by the courts." Turning to the specifics of Congress's power to regulate interstate commerce to illustrate his point, Wilson asked, "May [Congress] also regulate the conditions under which the merchandise is produced which is presently to become the subject-matter of interstate commerce? May it regulate the conditions of labor in the field and factory? Clearly not, I should say; and I should think that any thoughtful lawyer who felt himself at liberty to be frank would agree with me."[101] Yet in 1916 Wilson not only signed the child labor act into law, which, albeit ambivalently, did just this, but also forced it through the Senate. That very year Wilson was criticizing "judges who seemed to think that the Constitution was a strait jacket into which the life of the nation must be forced, whether it could be with a true regard to the law of life or not."[102]

In *Hammer v. Dagenhart,* the Court adhered to Wilson's earlier understanding and struck down the Child Labor Act of 1916, citing the formal distinction between commerce and manufacturing articulated most fully in *Knight.*[103] Congress then repassed a child labor law under its power to tax, which the Court struck down as well.[104] In doing so, Chief Justice Taft first drew on *Hammer* and Marshall's opinion in *McCulloch,* arguing that Congress could not, by indirection, reach beyond its enumerated powers and seize those powers that were reserved to the states. Taft then distinguished this tax from the oleomargarine tax that the Court had upheld. Congress could prohibit the movement of goods in interstate commerce by way of a heavy tax if the goods themselves might be deemed "unhealthy," but if the products themselves were safe—the evil here was child labor—then Congress could not use its power in such a fashion.[105] Oddly, even Holmes joined Taft's opinion, though in his dissent in *Hammer* Holmes took issue with the Tenth Amendment argument and even cited the oleomargarine case as justifying the congressional regulation of child labor.

Yet, given Taft's endorsement of the "current of commerce" line of thought, it is difficult to say that he was trying to place the Constitution in a "strait jacket." In endorsing Holmes's *Swift* opinion, Taft said that its application of the commerce clause "was the result of the natural development of interstate commerce under modern conditions." He even praised the Court for declining to engage in a "nice and technical inquiry into the non-interstate character" of some of the "incidents and facilities" that would inevitably be bound up with such a movement of goods.[106] The reach of the commerce power continued to be contested as these strands of commerce clause thinking remained in tension until the late years of the New Deal, when a far more sweeping vision ultimately took root. Taft spoke similarly of the due process line of cases, which often informed commerce clause thinking. The tensions and discontinuities in this line of constitutional thought—and how they ought to be reconciled within the constitutional framework—would persist in tension into the New Deal years. Indeed, far beyond, as I argue in the next chapter.

The Ebb and Flow of Due Process

The year 1908 was, in many ways, as an explosive a year for the Court as 1895. Again handing down a troika of opinions that set off political debate, the Court invalidated Congress's prohibition of "yellow dog contracts,"[107] applied the Sherman Antitrust Act to labor,[108] and invalidated a congressional attempt to hold employers responsible for employee injury as beyond the reach of Congress's commerce power.[109] In reaction to this trio of opinions, the Court was accused of manifesting a strong bias against labor. The fact that the Sherman Act was applied to labor in constraining trade was cynically viewed as evidence of the Court's anti-labor animus. Compounding this view, *Adair* struck down a section of the Erdman Act of 1898, which itself was passed by Congress "in response to the Pullman strike of 1894 and was defended by its supporters as a measure to secure labor peace."[110]

Liberty of Contract and Free Labor

In many minds, this link between the Court's 1908 opinions and its 1895 opinions was a testament to the fact that no matter what Congress and the president tried, the Court would side with business against labor and the people. At the time, these opinions were given far more play than *Lochner,* the case that came to symbolize the era. The connection to *Lochner,* though, is important in *Adair. Lochner* represents the articulation of "free labor" thinking that is also at the heart of *Adair* and "liberty of contract." As I argued in the preceding chapter, this line of constitutional thought was connected with Lincoln and developed by the likes of Justice

Stephen Field, a Lincoln appointee, in the latter half of the nineteenth century. Discussing the issue of "capital" and "labor," Lincoln rejected the notion that they composed separate classes: "there is no such relation between capital and labor as assumed; nor is there any such thing as a free man being fixed for life in the condition of a hired laborer. Both these assumptions are false, and all inferences from there are groundless."[111] He went on to insist that "capital" and property are the legitimate fruits of labor. If Lincoln saw property rights—and the right to treat labor as property—as essential to liberty, which was essential to equality, this position was deemed untenable in the early years of the twentieth century.

Teddy Roosevelt argued that courts had favored "property rights" over "human rights" and drew on Lincoln to prefer "human rights" over property, which, of itself, could have no "rights" or "vote." Roosevelt was careful to give property and capital its due, particularly in the years before 1912. He cautioned that we must be fair to employer and laborer and distinguish between the good corporation and the bad corporation. In drawing such distinctions, Roosevelt argued that the public need must be maintained, opposing traditional practices of individual contract and federalism in calling for national involvement. Even while recognizing that "wages and other most important conditions of employment must . . . be left for adjustment by free contract between employers and wage earners," this prerogative must be "subject—and here I call your attention to the proviso—to [national] legislation which will prevent conditions which compel men or women to accept wages representing less than will insure decent living."[112] The government was now essential to securing the rights of the laborer and the "Constitution of the United States must be administered, if it is to be administered wisely, by men who sympathize with, and understand, the needs of the wage worker, just as they sympathize with, and understand, the needs of all other American citizens."[113] It is worth recalling that Roosevelt singled out *Lochner* in *The New Nationalism* as indicative of "ill-defined limits in which neither the nation nor any state should be able to exercise effective control, especially over big corporations" and their relations with the public and their employees.[114] Roosevelt even quoted generously from Harlan's *Lochner* dissent to illuminate his case. Yet Harlan's logic pointed in a different direction, as exemplified by his *Adair* opinion.

In *Adair* Harlan struck down section 10 of the Erdman Act, where Congress prohibited railroad companies from blacklisting members of railroad unions or requiring employees to sign a "yellow dog" contract, in which the employee promised not to join a labor union.[115] In doing so, Harlan relied on the presumption of liberty of contract and cited Peckham's opinion in *Lochner*. At root, Harlan shared the constitutional construction developed by Field's and Bradley's *Slaughterhouse* dissents, even while he thought the regulation at issue in *Lochner* was a legitimate regulation. Recall that Harlan's dissent in *Plessy* drew on this logic, treating "race" as an arbitrary and therefore illegitimate categorization.[116] Harlan, as in the commerce clause cases, thought the Court could consider altered circumstances and facts in applying constitutional principles, which, like the arguments of Taft and Lodge, provided flexibility in applying fundamental principles. Still, his logic called for fixed constitutional principles that would bind, and thereby limit, democratically enacted legislation. Thus, in *Lochner* Harlan thought the maximum-hours law *was* a legitimate health regulation, clearly aimed at preserving the health of the bakers engaged in a potentially hazardous trade, and thus was not tampering with one's liberty of contract for arbitrary reasons.[117] According to Harlan, Congress's attempt to prohibit "yellow dog" contracts served no legitimate public interest: it was a mere prohibition against both the employee and employer. "In all such particulars the employer and the employe [*sic*] have equality of right, and any legislation that disturbs that equality is an arbitrary interference with the liberty of contract which no government can legally justify in a free land."[118]

Harlan went on to argue that Congress's power to regulate interstate commerce, while extensive, could not violate a constitutional right. "It results, on the whole case, that the provision of the statute under which the defendant was convicted must be held to be repugnant to the Fifth Amendment and as not embraced by nor within the power of Congress to regulate interstate commerce, but under the guise of regulating interstate commerce and as applied to this case it arbitrarily sanctions an illegal invasion of the personal liberty as well as the right of property of the defendant Adair." Precisely because there was no legitimate public purpose in prohibiting "yellow dog" contracts, Congress could not tie this regulation to a legitimate regulation of interstate commerce.[119] Harlan momentarily entertained that Congress might be attempting "to accord to one class of wage-earners privileges withheld from another class of wage-earners engaged, it may be, in the same kind of labor and serving the same employer"—that is, that Congress was siding with union laborers over non-union wage earners. The Court could not indulge such a reading, with "due respect to a coordinate branch of government," as such a reading cut against Harlan's constitutional logic.[120] Progressives insisted that this was exactly what was needed—and what Congress had in fact done.

The Progressive Reconstruction of Liberty of Contract

Writing immediately after the *Adair* decision in the *Yale Law Journal*, Roscoe Pound, dean of Harvard Law School, asked, "Why do we find a great and learned court in 1908 taking the long step into the past of dealing with the relation between employer and employee in railway transportation, as if the parties were individuals—as if they were farmers haggling over the sale of a horse."[121] Pound's sociological jurisprudence began to recast the law in ways that rejected the old constitutionalism, not simply by taking into account social conditions, for Harlan's constitutional jurisprudence provided for that, but by letting social change dictate the essence of the law. Applied to the Constitution as fundamental law, the Constitution should accord with the imperatives of historical change. This line of thought found some support in Justice Holmes's *Adair* dissent. Whereas Harlan thought Congress could not use its power to foster unionization in railways, Holmes saw this application as perfectly acceptable: "I could not pronounce it unwarranted if Congress should decide that to foster a strong union was for the best interest, not only of the men, but of the railroads and the country at large."[122] Progressives had already seized on Holmes's *Lochner* dissent as a rallying cry of the people's right to rule against a "laissez-faire" Supreme Court. Indeed, the myth of *Lochner* was born in Holmes's famous and stunningly off-the-mark quip, "The Fourteenth Amendment does not enact Mr. Herbert Spencer's Social Statics."[123] Whether Holmes was wholly breaking with the constitutional thought of the day and his comments served as a harbinger, or only indulging a penchant for elegant rhetoric, which would retrospectively make his dissent appear innovative, is the subject of much debate.[124] Whatever the intricacies of this debate, the *Lochner* case and Holmes's dissent therein became central to constitutional debate over the next several decades. As with earlier legislation, congressional intent and "democratic will" were far more complex then Holmes intimated.

As George Lovell argues in regard to section 10 of the Erdman Act, "even though the Act was ostensibly a legislative alternative to the system of judicial control of railroad strikes that had been expanded in connection with the Pullman Strike, the law was not . . . an attempt by Congress to 'assault' judicial power or to place the courts 'under siege.' Rather, Congress included provisions that expanded the powers of the courts by giving judges important but vaguely defined oversight and enforcement responsibilities."[125] Focusing our eye more closely on congressional intent, we get a better understanding of the Court, revealing a dynamic where constitutional meaning is being negotiated by both sides in a conflicted and fragmented manner. As Lovell illustrates, the Erdman Act was not as prolabor and thus not as at odds with the Court's ruling in *Adair,* as it is usually made out to be. In fact, the bill was drafted by Attorney General Richard Olney, who had vigorously argued for the government's power to put down the Pullman strike, and the Erdman Act was passed in reaction to the strike. At multiple points, Congress rejected provisions that would have been much more clearly "prolabor," especially in explicitly removing the labor injunction from courts, which was labor's most frequent demand.[126] But the Act did not do this. Neither, though, were supporters of the act happy with the Court's reading. Even Olney wrote, "the inability of the Supreme Court to find any connection between the membership of a labor union and the carrying on of interstate commerce seems inexplicable."[127] Defenders of the traditional order, like Olney or Taft, were often perplexed and frustrated by particular Court opinions. Considering the *Lochner* line of decisions, Taft was critical but hopeful that the Court had found the proper balance: "the truth is that the Court as at present constituted has shown itself as appreciative of the change of conditions and the necessity for a liberal construction of the restrictions of the Constitution, with a view to such changes of conditions, as any court could be."[128] When the Court seemed to stray from this course, Taft would issue a stinging dissent as chief justice. Just as surely, Taft was deeply critical of reconstructive projects like Croly's that were explicitly hostile to the liberal elements of American constitutionalism.

In *The Promise of American Life,* Croly insisted that the government must take sides on behalf of the unions. "The labor unions deserve to be favored, because they are the most effective machinery which has as yet been forged for the economic and social amelioration of the laboring class." And just as Croly rejected the "small producer" in antitrust, he rejected the "non-union labor as a species of industrial derelict. He is the laborer who has gone astray and who either from apathy, unintelligence, incompetence, or some immediately pressing need prefers his own individual interest to the joint interests of himself and his fellow-laborers." The laborer's right to contract that Justice Harlan sought to protect was, "from the point of view of a constructive national policy," not entitled to recognition. "In fact," Croly insisted, "I am willing to go farther and assert that the non-union industrial laborer should, in the interest of a genuinely democratic organization of labor, be rejected; and he should be rejected as emphatically, if not as ruthlessly, as the gardener rejects the weeds in his gardener for the benefit of fruit- and flower-bearing plants."[129]

Croly was explicit about the reconstructive nature of this project and its reworking or elimination of rights, which "must be justified by their actual or presumable functional adequacy." As I illustrated earlier, Croly's reconstruction would mean radical constitutional change; indeed, Croly viewed "superstitious awe" of the Constitution as "the great bondage of the American spirit."[130] Roosevelt enthusiastically praised Croly's *Promise,* which was sent to him by the jurist Learned Hand, a close friend of Justice Holmes, and a stalwart critic of judicial "interference" with "democratic will." In the more radically democratic *Progressive Democracy,* Croly would go so far as to say that, "whether reasonable or not, the insertion of the bill

of rights in the Constitution contributed more than any other feature to convert it
into a monarchy of the Law superior in right to the monarchy of the people."[131]
Judge Learned Hand, more than four decades later in his Holmes lectures at Harvard Law School, would take this sentiment as the central lesson of the Progressive
Era[132]—a lesson that he advanced as early as 1908 in a *Harvard Law Review* article
that reinforces the traditional understanding of Holmes's dissent.[133]

In *The New Freedom,* Wilson echoed the need for a change in our views between
employer and employee, where our "wholly antiquated and impossible" laws "were
framed for another age." "Why is it that we have a labor question at all?" Wilson
asked. "It is for the simple and very sufficient reason that the laboring man and the
employer are not intimate associates now as they used to be in time past"—an age
where an employer and an employee could bargain with "each other as man with
man." Now, "we are all caught in a great economic system which is heartless," where
the employee is an individual and the employer a powerful group. For Wilson it
was necessary to adjust the "law to the facts of the new order."[134] This reconstructive project would require the rejection of constitutional rights and limits.

It is interesting to note that Wilson's description of employer and employee did
not capture the factual situation in *Lochner,* the case so often used as an example.
Ironically, Lochner himself is far more illustrative of Lincoln's notion that today's
employee may be tomorrow's employer than the progressive claim that the "wage-
earner" would always be distinct from the "property owner."[135] Joseph Lochner was
an immigrant from Bavaria who worked as a "wage-earning" baker for eight years
before opening up a bakeshop where he continued to work side by side with his
employees.[136] In fact, the legislation aimed at bakers was, very likely, the result of
larger bakeries' attempts to drive smaller bakers, as competitors, out of business.
For Wilson, however, such specifics interfered with the larger point, as America was
prone to overemphasize liberty: "Our peculiar American difficulty in organizing
administration is not the danger of losing liberty, but the danger of not being able
or willing to separate its essentials from its accidents."[137] He would go so far as to
insist that a "great deal of nonsense has been talked about the inalienable rights of
the individual, and a great deal that was mere vague sentiment and pleasing speculation has been put forward as fundamental principle."[138] If Lochner was driven
out of business, or the non-union labor was denied "choice," those were the terms
of progress: "The object of constitutional government is to bring the active, planning will of each part of the government into accord with the prevailing popular
thought and need, and thus make it an impartial instrument of symmetrical national development."[139] The essentials of liberty could be determined by government itself with executive agencies working out the necessities of governing de-

pending on the ever-changing demands of History. Liberty, then, could be fit to changing facts to accord with the stages of constitutional development. If this limited liberty, or cast off constitutional limits, so be it. For Wilson, "Political liberty consists in the best practical adjustment between the power of the government and the privilege of the individual; and the freedom to alter the adjustment is as important as the adjustment itself for the ease and progress of affairs and the contentment of the citizen."[140]

Brandeis would pioneer this necessary adjustment of adapting constitutional meaning and rights to ever-changing facts in his famous brief. While facts were compiled to demonstrate the necessity of governmental regulation, at a deeper level the facts were meant to reveal that such regulation would have to break with inherited constitutional limits. As Kersch describes it, Brandeis was engaged in an effort to defeat traditional constitutional understandings with "the displacement of courts as the institutional guardians" of liberty.[141] It did not matter if the Court was reasonably logical and consistent in demanding that the legislature connect regulations to a genuine public purpose.[142] Nor did it matter if the Court upheld the vast majority of governmental regulation—at the state and national level. In two articles in the *Columbia Law Review* in 1913, the progressive lawyer, legal historian, and soon-to-be assistant attorney general in the Wilson Administration, Charles Warren pointed to both of these facts.[143] Presaging revisionist criticism by well over half a century, Warren noted that nearly every governmental regulation under the state's police powers that came before the Court was upheld: "The reformers who claim that the Court stands as an obstacle to 'social justice' legislation, if asked to specify where they find the evil of which they complain and for which they propose radical remedies, always take refuge in the single case of *Lochner v. New York.*"[144]

More interestingly, Warren argued that fixing the proper line "beyond which the legislature cannot go without infringing the constitutional rights of the individual is, today, one of the most difficult tasks of a court." Warren then proceeded to quote a current member of the Court to illustrate the difficulty: "Any distinction, no matter how sensible and how plain, leads at least to a line which is worked out by the contact of decisions clustering around the opposite poles, and which may seem arbitrary if we attend to it alone and not to the nature of the groups which it divides."[145] The justice was Oliver Wendell Holmes. Even if Holmes may be drawn on to illuminate the general consistency and logic of this line of constitutional thought, he can also be cited in the effort to deconstruct this view. That is, even if there were only a few decisions rejecting "progressive" legislation, progressives rejected the foundations of this line of constitutional thought—often the very notion of judges protecting individual rights. "A judge whose essential function is the application of legal rules impartially to specific cases . . . cannot become a satisfactory or a sufficient servant of a genuinely social policy." The common-law judge thus represented a system "found on the protection of individual rights," a system now outmoded for achieving "social policy based upon a collective social ideal."[146]

Persistent Conflicts

Such sentiments, no doubt, drove Taft to what was later perceived as overwrought concern about creeping socialism and the "Bolshevki." But as a supporter of much "progressive" legislation, he could hardly be described as "reactionary." Moreover, if we turn to Felix Frankfurter's coterminous writings on the Constitution and its notion of liberty that appeared in the *New Republic,* it is not clear that Taft's concerns, while overstated, were wholly off the mark.[147] After all, Frankfurter repeatedly attacked the Old Court's "eighteenth century view of liberty" in cases like *Meyer v. Nebraska* and *Pierce v. Society of Sisters,* where it had, respectively, struck down a law prohibiting the teaching of the German language and a law prohibiting private secondary schools.[148] Progressives were ultimately successful in dismantling this logic of due process and liberty of contract, although it took four decades.[149] The reconstructive project, however, was not firmly entrenched. Its incomplete foundations would dominate constitutional discourse on liberty and the role of the Court for the second half of the twentieth century, given its inability to explain why such Lochnerian cases like *Meyer* and *Pierce* should remain part of a reconstructed constitutional order, which I detail in the next two chapters. In the meantime, Taft staked out a position that might best be described as moderately Lochnerian, as exemplified by his dissent in *Adkins v. Children's Hospital.* There, he insisted on a flexible balance between changed conditions and constitutional principle, while wholly rejecting the notion of simple democracy and judicial deference, as offered in Holmes's dissent.[150]

The year that *Adkins* was handed down, Elihu Root, the former secretary of state and New York senator, said in an address at the American Law Institute that "the confusion, the uncertainty" that beset constitutional law "was growing from year to year" and making it mere "guess work."[151] Root noted this vexed state of affairs while presenting the institute's far-flung project of giving the law a coherent structure, the particular report of which was aptly titled, "The Law's Uncertainty and Complexity." This sentiment came from a stalwart defender of traditional constitutional understandings. Root had delivered the Stafford Little Lectures at Princeton University in 1913 on "Experiments in Government and the Essentials of the

Constitution," where he praised the essentials of the Constitution against the transient experiments of the progressives that denied such essentials. Root not only defended the rights of the individual and the foundation of private property in the constitutional order but insisted that the Court had often acted wisely in striking down "carelessly or ignorantly drawn statutes" that have "failed to exhibit the true relation between the regulation proposed and the object sought, or have gone farther than the attainment of the legitimate object justified." Root went on to note the virtues of the separation of powers: "A very good illustration of this is to be found in the Federal Employer's Liability Act which was carelessly drawn and passed by Congress in 1906 and was declared unconstitutional by the Supreme Court, but which was carefully drawn and passed by Congress in 1908 and was declared constitutional by the same court."[152] But even this erstwhile defender of the Constitution against progressive reconstructions was troubled by the uncertainty and complexity of balancing constitutional limits against legitimate, if increasingly complex, regulation. If the mid- to late 1920s brought a respite from such conflict and drift, it was short-lived.

In *Constitutional Government in the United States,* Woodrow Wilson wrote that "each generation of statesmen looks to the Supreme Court to supply the interpretation which will serve the needs of the day." Yet Wilson did not call for freewheeling adaptation: "the safety and the purity of our system depend on the wisdom and the good conscience of the Supreme Court. Expanded and adapted by interpretation the powers granted in the Constitution must be; but the manner and the motive of their expansion involve the integrity, and therefore the permanence, or our entire system of government." Wilson's rhetoric would often carry him away from such sober judgments to calls for the dismantling of constitutionalism altogether, as when he drew out the power of the presidency in overcoming the notion of countervailing power: "Let him once win the admiration and confidence of the county, and no other single force can withstand him . . . he is irresistible."[153] But as president, Wilson was resisted—and most stunningly so by Henry Cabot Lodge, the ambitious and self-interested defender of the Senate's constitutional prerogatives, who insisted on his view of the Constitution against Wilson's in their struggle over the Treaty of Versailles, in a nearly perfect illustration of Madison's "living" Constitution.[154]

Franklin Delano Roosevelt would adopt these strands of Wilson's thought, connecting the "evolving constitution" with the founding in an effort to reconstruct constitutional authority and justify the New Deal by way of executive energy. The "Constitutional Revolution of 1937" entrenched an expansive view of the national government's power to regulate the economy under the commerce power—at least until President Ronald Reagan's attempt to unsettle these elements of the New Deal. This entrenchment, however, furthered a fragmented understanding of liberty that remains the subject of constitutional contestation.

CHAPTER FOUR

Discontinuities in the "Constitutional Revolution of 1937"

The people by their Constitution created three separate, distinct,
independent, and coequal departments of government. The government structure rests, and was intended to rest, not upon any one or
upon any two, but upon all three of these fundamental pillars. It
seems unnecessary to repeat, what so often has been said, that the
powers of these departments are different and are to be exercised
independently. The differences clearly and definitely appear in the
Constitution. Each of the departments is an agent of its creator; and
one department is not and cannot be the agent of another. Each is
answerable to its creator for what it does, and not to another agent.

Justice George Sutherland

I described the American form of government as a three-horse
team provided by the Constitution to the American people so that
their field might be plowed. The three horses are, of course, the
three branches of government—the Congress, the executive, and the
courts. Two of the horses are pulling in unison today; the third is not.

Franklin Delano Roosevelt

After the Supreme Court struck down the National Recovery Administration
(NRA) in *Schechter Poultry Corporation v. the United States,* Franklin Delano Roosevelt delivered an extraordinary radio address in which he called *Schechter* the most
important decision "of my lifetime . . . more important than any decision probably
since the Dred Scott case."[1] The Court would soon hand FDR a series of defeats,
finding much of the legislation at the heart of the New Deal unconstitutional.

Roosevelt, however, generally opposed amending the Constitution to clearly grant the national government power he thought it already had. To amend the Constitution, for Roosevelt, would concede that the Court's interpretation was right. The problem for FDR was not the Constitution, but the Court's interpretation of it, a point he emphasized in his battle with the Court: "And remember one more thing. Even if an amendment were passed, and even if in the years to come it were to be ratified, its meaning would depend upon the kind of Justices who would be sitting on the Supreme Court bench. An amendment, like the rest of the Constitution, is what the Justices say it is rather than what its framers or you might hope it is."[2]

Roosevelt was only partly being sly: he refused to believe that the Constitution was really what the justices say it is, but he put his finger squarely on the problem. For FDR, what was needed was a fundamental shift in our constitutional understandings, not a formal amendment to the Constitution. As Roosevelt's attorney general, Robert Jackson, later elevated to the Court, explained, "it may be possible by more words to clarify more words, but it is not possible by words to change a state of mind."[3] FDR's reconstruction of constitutional meaning and authority sought to change this state of mind, drawing heavily on progressive understandings, to insist that the Constitution must adapt to the times: "They [the opponents of the New Deal] do not know or realize that the Constitution has changed with the times. . . . We revere it and have an affection for it because of the principles which it reflects, but in its material applications it of necessity has changed in keeping with the changing times and conditions."[4]

FDR insisted, as Wilson and TR before him had, that the national government's power must be broadly adapted to regulate a modern economy. But unlike dominant strands of progressive thought, FDR attempted to situate his view within the original Constitution. In attempting to reconstruct our constitutional understandings, FDR linked the progressive notion of an evolutionary Constitution to the Founders' original constitutional understandings. If he was expanding government beyond traditional understandings, this expansion was necessary to preserve the constitutional order itself, and thus was consistent with it. As Robert Jackson argued, it was necessary to retreat "to the Constitution," away from the Court's illegitimate interpretations, "back to the original sweep and vigor of those clauses which confer power on the Federal Government," and to see that "those which limit it are reduced, if not to their original meaning, at least to tolerable approximations."[5] Yet, even while invoking the Founder's intentions and the traditional understandings of sweeping national power that he traced back to Chief Justice John Marshall and Alexander Hamilton, Jackson also pushed for expansive governmental power to deal with emergency conditions and changed economic circumstances. This view suggested a more open-ended and evolving Constitution that changed with history.

This uneasy merger of evolution with original understandings was often evident in FDR's invocation of the language of the Declaration of Independence: "We hold this truth to be self-evident—that government in a modern civilization has certain inescapable obligations to its citizens."[6] FDR would ultimately even call for a Second Bill of Rights, a necessary complement, he argued, to the Bill of Rights. Yet Roosevelt's notion of governmental power and rights—"the development of an economic declaration of rights, an economic constitutional order"—possibly called for a fundamental reconstruction of elements of the American constitutional order. Following progressives like Herbert Croly and Felix Frankfurter, whom he would later appoint to the Court, Roosevelt rejected traditional views of liberty and limitations on government. These would have to be jettisoned to make way for governmental regulation and control. Economic security, FDR insisted, was essential to meaningful liberty: "we must accept the restriction [of liberty] as needful, not to hamper individualism but to protect it." In his 1932 Commonwealth Club Address, which would become foundational to his view of American constitutionalism, Roosevelt explicitly drew on TR and Wilson as demanding and recognizing "the new terms of the old social contract." Roosevelt saw himself as completing this project, a project whose origins ran to Jefferson's Declaration: "We shall fulfill them, as we fulfilled the obligation of the apparent utopia which Jefferson imagined for us in 1776, and which Jefferson, Roosevelt, and Wilson sought to bring to realization."[7]

Like these figures, FDR was only partly successful in reordering our constitutional understandings. While his reconstruction of national constitutional authority was entrenched for decades and he solidified the executive as head of a vast administrative state, FDR did not succeed in reconstructing the separation of powers as part of his reconstruction of American constitutionalism.[8] Nor did he succeed in bringing about a new constitutional understanding of liberty (even while giving birth to new "constitutional" commitments). Indeed, the notion of an evolutionary Constitution that adapted to the accords of History raised fundamental questions about the Constitution's identity that remain with us. While FDR often linked evolution to constitutional ends rooted in original understandings, at other times evolution seemed to reject the notion of foundations. This rejection was most evident in the "deconstruction" of traditional due process nurtured in the Progressive Era, which came to be entrenched by the end of the New Deal years. But rather than firmly situating the Court at the center of a New Deal Constitution where it would protect "civil liberties," the Court would remain deeply fragmented in this area insofar as it was rooted in negative foundations. That is, the New Deal reconstruction of liberty was rooted in a "deconstructive" understanding rather than a positive foundation. This deconstruction is symbolized by the Court's various opinions in *Griswold v. Connecticut.* As I argue more fully in the next chapter, the return of "original intent" in the wake of *Griswold,* rooted in a critique of "judicial activism and lawmaking"[9] and preoccupied by cabining judicial will, is a viable strand of the New Deal's constitutional trajectory.[10]

After first considering the persistent conflict within the separation of powers over the national government's power under the commerce clause, including FDR's attempt to reconstruct the judiciary in the face of these persistent conflicts, the chapter turns to the discontinuities that result from the New Deal "breakthrough,"[11] as evidenced by conflicts over the role of the Court in the "new" constitutional scheme and the "deconstructive" view of liberty under due process. In situating the New Deal within the contours of long-standing progressive thought and tracing the trajectory of these persistent conflicts long after the core of the New Deal years, I also seek to show how the New Deal was less a unique constitutional moment than part of the ordinary flow of American constitutional development.[12]

The Court as Catalyst: Provoking Constitutional Conflicts

On May 27, 1935, what became known as Black Monday, the Court unanimously invalidated the National Recovery Administration and the Frazier-Lemke Act on mortgage moratoria.[13] Attention focused immediately on the *Schechter* decision, striking down the NRA in its entirety, as the Court's construction of the delegation of powers and the commerce power would have profound implications for future New Deal legislation.[14] Writing for the Court, Chief Justice Charles Evans Hughes first found that the congressional delegation of power to the president, allowing him to establish fair trade codes for a trade or industry, was an unconstitutional delegation of power. In a concurring opinion, Benjamin Cardozo even went so far as to call it "delegation running riot."[15] The opinion was not an immediate threat to congressional delegation, which was central to many New Deal agencies, because the Court focused on the lack of guidelines in this particular delegation of power, which, presumably, could be overcome in future legislation that was more carefully drafted. And the act itself was set to expire.[16] The opinion's true importance was found in its construction of the commerce clause—particularly because the Court was not compelled to reach this constitutional question. The act could have been held unconstitutional on delegation-of-power grounds alone.

Rather than stop there, Hughes found that the Schechter Poultry Corporation was a local operation engaged in production and therefore beyond the reach of the commerce power. The regulation of wages, hours, and working conditions was part of the NRA regulatory scheme, according to the corporatism of the NRA, in its attempt to bring order to industrial competition. To evade the regulatory scheme, as the Schechter brothers had, would affect interstate commerce as it would undercut the price of poultry in the national market and, thereby, undercut the income of farmers. Hughes, however, found that the Schechter Corporation was not engaged in interstate commerce: "Neither the slaughtering nor the sales by defendants were transactions in interstate commerce." Hughes then suggested that the particulars of this case could not be situated in the "stream of commerce" line of cases that Hughes himself had had a hand in developing: "The undisputed facts thus afford no warrant for the argument that the poultry handled by defendants at their slaughterhouse markets was in a 'current' or 'flow' of interstate commerce, and was thus subject to congressional regulation."[17] Establishing this, Hughes turned to the *Knight* line of decisions that continued to inform constitutional understandings.[18] "If the commerce clause were constructed to reach all enterprises and transactions which would be said to have an indirect effect upon interstate commerce, the federal authority would embrace practically all the activities of the people, and the authority of the state over its domestic concerns would exist only by sufferance of the federal government."[19]

The first wave of New Deal legislation challenged this line of constitutional thought even more than progressive legislation had. But it did so, in part, by drawing on the "current of commerce" strand of thought. As Robert Jackson put it, the New Dealers "knew that the constitutional doctrine on which they were relying had theretofore won adherence from only a minority of the Court. But they acted on it from conviction as well as necessity."[20] In widening the sweep of the "current of commerce" cases, Jackson argued that the New Dealers were seeking to entrench a more "centralized government" and altogether displace earlier understandings that limited the reach of the commerce power. While pointing to the possible tension between the "current of commerce" line of thought and the *Knight* line of cases, Jackson and others sought to reconstruct the former so as to make the Congress the sole judge of its commerce power.[21] In making its case before the Court, the administration was attempting to situate the Schechter Poultry business within the "current" of interstate commerce. As Chief Justice Taft had argued in *Stafford v. Wallace,* "This court will certainly not substitute its judgment for that of Congress in such a matter unless the relation of the subject to interstate commerce and its effects upon it are clearly non-existent."[22]

This is precisely what the Court found in *Schechter:* "It is not the province of the

Court to consider the economic advantages or disadvantages of such a centralized system. It is sufficient to say that the Federal Constitution does not provide for it."[23] Cardozo's concurring opinion, joined by Stone, is suggestive in this light. Although he did not embrace the conceptual distinction between "direct" and "indirect" effects, he did reason that "There is a view of causation that would obliterate the distinction between what is national and what is local in the activities of commerce." And, while noting that the law is "not indifferent to considerations of degree," he insisted that "To find immediacy or directness here is to find it almost everywhere. If centripetal forces are to be isolated to the exclusion of the forces that oppose and counteract them, there will be an end to our federal system."[24] Cardozo's opinion echoed Judge Learned Hand's concurrence for the lower Court, suggesting that while the New Dealers were attempting to situate their understandings within the "current of commerce," they were in fact pushing it far beyond anything the Court had in the past embraced.

FDR's Constitutional (Re)Construction

After the *Schechter* decision, FDR delivered an impassioned address to the nation, the peroration of which claimed that in the wake of the Court's opinion "we have been relegated to the horse-and-buggy definition of interstate commerce."[25] In a 1932 campaign speech, he had similarly chastised courts for "thinking in terms of the Seventeenth Century."[26] FDR seized on the notion of an adaptable and evolving Constitution drawn out by progressives like Croly and, especially, Wilson. Thus, FDR continued a dispute that had been vexing the polity for more than three decades. FDR, like Wilson, would insist on a Constitution that must adapt to history—indeed, as James Ceaser characterizes it: History.[27] This sentiment was put forward in more refined constitutional terms by Felix Frankfurter in his short book *The Commerce Clause*, published two years before FDR elevated him to the Court. Nurturing three decades of progressive thought, Frankfurter insisted that the "Constitution of the United States is most significantly not a document but a stream of history."[28] By way of the New Deal, FDR was simply trying to further the "organic" development of the Constitution, making his effort at one and the same moment a profound constitutional reconstruction and a constitutional restoration.[29] This ambivalence was reflected in the New Dealers drawing on past constitutional constructions to illuminate the commerce power.

In criticizing *Schechter*, Robert Jackson argued that the doctrine forbidding such a sweeping delegation of power was "a doctrine not based on any express words of the Constitution itself." He went on to criticize the Court for taking up the commerce clause issue at all, saying not only that it was unnecessary but that doing so "drew into doubt the capacity of the Federal Government by use of the commerce power to accomplish many other things that the emergency seemed to require." Thus, Jackson insisted, on the one hand, on returning to an earlier constitutional understanding of "federal power in the broad terms of Marshall and Hughes,"[30] while, on the other, on instituting emergency power that swept far wider than any notion of interstate commerce in Marshall's or Hughes's opinions. Pointing to Hughes's *Blaisdell* opinion, Jackson claimed that the Constitution must be adapted rather than confined to the interpretation of its Framers.[31] In *The Commerce Clause,* Frankfurter argued that Marshall had an organic conception of commerce much like Oliver Wendell Holmes's *Swift* opinion (though we should recall that *Swift* favorably cited *Knight,* much as Hughes had in *Shreveport,* both of which embraced the sort of logic that FDR unequivocally sought to tear down). Even while Marshall's thinking might impose "artificial patterns" on the "play of economic life," as evidenced in his *Gibbons* opinion, according to Frankfurter he laid the foundations for sweeping congressional authority "when the time did come for its more aggressive employment." Yet, in lesser hands, Frankfurter insisted, judges "rendered mechanical decisions in Marshall's name."[32]

It is difficult to see that this was afoot here. *Schechter,* after all, was authored by Hughes and included credentialed "liberals" like Brandeis, Cardozo, and Stone. As Jackson himself noted, Hughes was the author of the *Blaisdell* decision, in which he had allowed for a dramatic exercise of state power to preserve, as he put it, the nature of contract. It was an opinion, like Hughes's "current of commerce" opinions, that the New Dealers sought to draw on. Yet in *Blaisdell* Hughes specifically rejected the notion that emergency could create power. Moreover, his *Blaisdell* opinion might best be read as supporting a fixed understanding of the Constitution. Although the opinion did allow the state flexibility in the means of preserving the obligation of contract, it arguably did so based on the letter and spirit of a fixed constitutional end.[33] It should not, then, have come as a surprise in *Schechter* that Hughes rejected the notion that extraordinary conditions might allow for extraordinary measures: "such assertions of extra-constitutional authority were anticipated and precluded by the explicit terms of the Tenth Amendment."[34] In this way, the Tenth Amendment was a textual reminder of the enumerated powers of Congress.[35]

From FDR's perspective, the New Dealers were not truly claiming extraconstitutional power; rather, they were claiming that the Constitution must be read in a flexible manner, which had potentially grave implications for the traditional distinction between the police powers of the states and the commerce power of the national government[36]—a distinction, they insisted, that was no longer tenable. At the same time, as we saw with Jackson and Frankfurter, there was an effort to root this claim in original understandings—the constitutionalism of Alexander Hamilton and John Marshall. Croly's insistence that TR was attempting to use Hamiltonian means to achieve Jeffersonian ends is equally applicable to FDR. In his Commonwealth Club address, FDR argued that Hamilton "believed the safety of the republic lay in the autocratic strength of its government, that the destiny of individuals was to serve that government, and that fundamentally a great and strong group of central institutions, guided by a small group of able and public spirited citizens, could best direct the government of all." While FDR went on to praise Jefferson's more democratic sensibility, he also insisted that he "did not deceive himself with outward forms. Government to him [Jefferson] was a means to an end, not an end in itself; it might be either a refuge and a help or a threat and a danger, depending on the circumstances." Jeffersonian individualism had had its day and place. Now, "the day of enlightened administration has come"—a day better captured by Hamilton than Jefferson.[37]

In this spirit, FDR may be understood as adhering to the substantive ends of the Constitution, while viewing constitutional forms as instrumental and, therefore, adaptable in the pursuit of foundational ends.[38] This concept is quite different from a living constitution that rejects foundations in favor of historical evolution. Yet FDR drew deeply on historical adaptation as well, drawing on the constitutional past to reconstruct—perhaps even reject—foundational ends. Thus, while Bruce Ackerman has argued that in the wake of the *Schechter* opinion Roosevelt "put the country on notice that the New Deal was seeking to dismantle the framework of traditional constitutionalism,"[39] this is far from clear. FDR and erstwhile New Dealers like Jackson and Frankfurter, as we can see from their arguments, often insisted that the New Deal flowed from the Founder's constitutional commitments, which would make the New Deal a constitutional "restoration" rather than a constitutional transformation.[40]

In this way, FDR was somewhat different from earlier progressives. As Sidney Milkis argues, "Roosevelt gave legitimacy to progressive principles by embedding them in the language of constitutionalism and interpreting them as an *expansion* rather than a *subversion* of the natural rights tradition."[41] This required a profound reconstruction of traditional constitutional understandings in regard to the enumerated powers of the national government, the traditional division of federalism, and the traditional notion of individual rights as prior to government. Like the progressives, FDR sought to deconstruct much of this constitutional inheritance. But he then sought to reconstruct it as part of a new social compact, completed by a second bill of rights.[42] Elements of this reconstruction, however, were not as easily placed within the terms of original commitments as Roosevelt insisted. As Cass Sunstein argues, Roosevelt also drew deeply on the legal realists, rejecting any notion that there was a "natural" baseline that the Constitution could be built around. Rights, for example, were not things that one naturally had, but things that the government secured—the result of "legal rules," not nature.[43] Thus, there was no "natural" place to mark off rights and the limits of governmental power. They were, rather, things to be determined by the democratic process given a particular set of historical circumstances.

At root, this understanding drew on Woodrow Wilson's insistence that constitutional "development" would require that the people define individual liberty to accord with their needs and interests based on their place in the historical process. The restructuring of liberty—by "the freest right and opportunity of adjustment"—was the task of statesmanship.[44] As FDR put it, "The task of statesmanship has always been the re-definition of these rights in terms of a changing and growing social order."[45] Thus, "Roosevelt believed the real questions were pragmatic ones: What form of intervention best promotes human interests? What form of regulation makes human lives better?" Our Constitution should be flexibly reconstructed to meet our evolving understandings. As Sunstein explains, "Considered in this light, minimum wage legislation, which Roosevelt strongly supported, should not be seen as superimposing regulation on a realm of purely voluntary interactions. On the contrary, such legislation merely substituted one form of regulation for another."[46]

The New Deal legislative programs sought to do just this, justifying new regulations based on reconstructed constitutional understandings and the demands of history and democracy rather than a "natural" beginning point. It was not simply that natural rights were constructed—for that would hardly surprise the natural-rights thinking of the Founders, who insisted on precisely this point. It was that they were constructed to comport with the fundamental nature of human beings and that government, then, was constituted to protect such rights. The legal realist concept was not novel in suggesting that such rights were constructs. Rather, it was novel for its antifoundational relativism in insisting that, because rights were constructed, we could simply reconstruct them in a pragmatic rather than a principled manner: thus rights could be fit to the needs of government, rather than being antecedent to it.[47]

This pragmatic cast of mind was evident, at times, in battles with the Court over constitutional meaning. In pushing the Guffey Coal Act through Congress, for example, Roosevelt sent a letter to the committee urging it to resolve any doubts about the bill's constitutionality in its favor, "leaving to the courts, in an orderly fashion, the ultimate question of constitutionality."[48] When the Court found the act unconstitutional, FDR would reverse himself. Referring to the separation of powers as a three-horse team, he insisted: "If three well-matched horses are put to the task of ploughing up a field where the going is heavy, and the team of three pulls as one, the field will be ploughed. If one horse lies down in the traces or plunges off in another direction, the field will not be ploughed."[49] Roosevelt then situated his arguments in the flow of history, insisting that such legislative efforts did not originate with "what I call the principles of the New Deal." Rather he traced these efforts—"to raise wages, to reduce hours, to abolish child labor, to eliminate unfair trade practices . . . to establish machinery to adjust the relations between the employer and employee"—to past social demands and the Progressive Era.

Roosevelt's construction of constitutional meaning as part of an evolving consensus drew deeply on progressives like Wilson and Croly. His view of the three branches of government seemed to embrace Wilson's effort to overcome the notion of a separation of powers—all the branches must work together taking their cue from the executive. But the Court was not going along: just as with child labor under Wilson, Roosevelt noted, "you know who assumed the power to veto, and did veto that program." Roosevelt even reiterated the progressive trope first suggested in Holmes's *Lochner* dissent that the justice's opinions were rooted in personal preferences rather than constitutional logic, claiming that it "pleased the 'personal economic predilections' of the majority of the Court that we live in a Nation where there is no legal power anywhere to deal with its most difficult practical problems—a No Man's Land of final futility."[50] A few days later, he would even quote Justice Harlan Stone's dissent in *United States v. Butler* to this effect.[51]

The Judicial Role in the Separation of Powers

Stone's famous dissent is remembered most vividly for its discussion of judicial power, which is appropriate insofar as Stone, too, played the progressive trope of arguing that the Court should only be "concerned with the power to enact statutes, not with their wisdom." The insinuation was that the Court was striking down the Agricultural Adjustment Act because it did not think it wise, but nothing in Owen Robert's opinion, like so many other opinions of the Court that had been subject to this accusation in the preceding decades, suggested disagreement on this point. Justice George Sutherland, in fact, would later turn this accusation on its head, taking aim at Stone's insistence in *Butler* that "the only check upon our own [the Court's] exercise of power is our own sense of self-restraint."[52] But this restraint,

Sutherland would argue, was its own form of "law-making." Any notion of "restraint" was an act of will, an insistence on the wisdom of judicial action that was beyond the power of a Court obligated by the Constitution. This concept was central, Sutherland argued, to the separation of powers. Yet Stone's claim that courts must be reconciled to the democratic process was consistent with legal realism. Stone, however, also went on to quote, as had Roberts, from Marshall's *McCulloch* opinion situating New Deal legislation not as a constitutional transformation, but as consistent with long-standing constitutional ends.[53] But Stone, unlike Roberts, did not quote Marshall's argument that if Congress, under the guise of a legitimate end, sought to do things that it could not directly do, then the Court would be bound by the Constitution to hold such legislation unconstitutional. If, to meet the needs of the nation, we must write "a new chapter in our book of self-government" as Roosevelt insisted, recognizing modern social and economic conditions, Stone seemed to suggest that the Court should acquiesce to the judgments of the democratically elected branches.[54]

In *Carter v. Carter Coal,* handed down a few months after *Butler,* Justice Sutherland's opinion struck down the Guffey Coal Act rejecting the notion that the Court could interpret the Constitution for the sake of "efficiencies," whether economic or political, or defer to the democratic judgment of the legislature, given its constitutional obligations within the separation of powers. Sutherland insisted that while the government had the choice of means, the end had to be clearly derived from the Constitution's enumerated powers: "Thus, it may be said that to a constitutional end many ways are open; but to an end not within the terms of the Constitution, all ways are closed."[55] The end the government was trying to reach under the Guffey Act was not interstate commerce but production. Here, again, Sutherland turned to John Marshall, citing *Gibbons* to argue that commerce was "intercourse" between "parts of the nation."[56] The logic that Sutherland drew on had been articulated not just in cases such as *Knight* and *Hammer;* it had also been put forward in the current of commerce cases by the likes of Justices Harlan and Holmes. Thus, in *Carter,* Sutherland drew on deeply entrenched strands of constitutional thought. The economic crisis the country was facing, a point noted again and again in the Guffey Act, did not, in any way, change the principles underlying the government's power. Sutherland had noted just this in a vigorous dissent against the chief justice's opinion in *Blaisdell* two years before: "A provision of the Constitution, it is hardly necessary to say, does not admit of two distinctly opposite interpretations. It does not mean one thing at one time and an entirely different thing at another time."[57] Because the Constitution must be applied to ever-changing circumstances, its application may change. But this imperative does not allow the political branches, the

Court, or the people themselves to reconstruct constitutional meaning to accord with altered economic circumstances. The underlying principles remain fixed: The fact that Congress was attempting to regulate a small industry of little national consequence in *Schechter* and was now, in *Carter,* attempting to regulate a large-scale national industry did not alter the fact that in each case Congress was attempting to reach an area constitutionally anchored within the local sphere, to wit—production. Because of the constitutional nature of the Union, such regulation was properly the province of the states and not the national government.[58]

Even Chief Justice Hughes, whom FDR had drawn on to support his construction of the Constitution, insisted on this point:

> But Congress may not use this protective authority as a pretext for the exertion of power to regulate activities and relations within the States which affect interstate commerce only indirectly. Otherwise, in view of the multitude of indirect effects, Congress in its discretion could assume control of virtually all the activities of the people to the subversion of the fundamental principle of the Constitution. If the people desire to give Congress the power to regulate industries within the State, and the relations of employers and employees in those industries, they are at liberty to declare their will in the appropriate manner, but it is not for the Court to amend the Constitution by judicial decision.[59]

This decision dashed the hopes of some New Dealers that the reach of *Schechter* would prove limited. Sutherland's opinion, moreover, distinguished *Carter* and *Schechter* from the "current of commerce" doctrine as put forward in *Swift.* "In the Schechter case the flow had ceased. Here [*Carter*] it had not yet begun. The difference is not one of substance. The applicable principle is the same."[60]

Yet Cardozo seized on this logic, insisting the Court should uphold the price-fixing provisions as within the reach of Congress's commerce power: "The underlying thought is merely this, that the 'law is not indifferent to considerations of degree.'"[61] For Cardozo circumstances mattered, and they may, *pace* Sutherland, influence our reading of the Constitution. He argued that this approach was based on past readings of the Constitution as he, too, drew on the Court's "current of commerce" cases: "A survey of the cases shows that the words have been interpreted with suppleness of adaptation and flexibility of meaning. The power is as broad as the need that invokes it[.]"[62] Cardozo's opinion is redolent of the uneasy state of constitutional thought over the preceding four decades. As much as Sutherland, he is drawing on past Court opinions—"rulings the most orthodox"—even while offering an alternative construction of the Constitution. In trying to foster constitutional change, the proponents of the New Deal were entering a long-standing conflict. And the Court had already engineered elements of change in opinions like *Blaisdell* and *Nebbia* before the full emergence of the New Deal and long before FDR's court-packing plan.[63] At the same time, even justices sympathetic to FDR's evolving constitutional understandings, such as Cardozo, recognized limits to the national government's power and the obligations of the Court within the separation of powers. This is true, as well, of justices as diverse as Harlan, Holmes, and Taft. These justices gave the commerce power a sweep that might push beyond the "direct" and "indirect" effects rule, but this sweep remained balanced by the notion that the national government was a government of enumerated powers. If the Court should respect the judgments of a coequal branch, as a coequal branch, it was obligated by the Constitution and thus could not simply defer to Congress's judgments about constitutionality. Following progressives, FDR seemed to insist that the Court should defer to the judgment of the "people themselves" as expressed by the other members of the three-horse team.[64] In this sense, the constitutional divide was widening.

Constructing Constitutional Revolution as Evolution

In FDR's second inaugural address, in the wake of the Supreme Court's 1936 term, he again insisted that the New Deal was based on the fundamentals of the Constitution of 1787: "A century and a half ago they [our forefathers] established the Federal Government in order to promote the general welfare and secure the blessings of liberty to the American people. Today we invoke those same powers of government to achieve the same objectives." He went on to claim that the expansion of national power was central to preserving the Constitution, but in a manner that also suggested profound change: "By using the new materials of social justice we have undertaken to erect on the old foundations a more enduring structure for the better use of future generations."[65] At a Democratic victory dinner on March 4, five days before he announced what would become known as the "court-packing bill," FDR opened the terms of the conflict, revealing that even if the second round of New Deal legislation was more carefully crafted than the first round, he was not engaged in a constitutional dialogue with the Court, or attempting to construct his constitutional vision so that the "nine old men" would find it constitutional. FDR argued, "neither individually nor as a party can we postpone and run from that fight on the advice of defeatist lawyers."[66] Rather, he was engaged in open conflict with the Court and insisted on his constitutional construction, whether or not the Court found it acceptable.

Turning to the cases I discussed in the preceding section, FDR defied "anyone to read the opinions concerning the A.A.A., the Railroad Retirement Act, the National Recovery Act, the Guffey Coal Act and the New York Minimum Wage law, and tell us exactly what, if anything, we can do for the industrial worker in this session of Congress with any reasonable certainty that what we do will not be nullified as unconstitutional."[67] In the fireside chat introducing his plan, FDR argued that the Constitution must be constructed in a manner that would allow the nation to meet "squarely our modern social and economic conditions." This, he insisted, was easy to do when one grasped the intent of those who framed the Constitution, as made evident in the great outlines of the preamble. Roosevelt then claimed that the Framers did not stop with such general sentiments, but went further, giving Congress ample powers "to levy taxes . . . provide for the common defense and general welfare of the United States," which provided the basis for reaching national problems "undreamed" of in 1788. Referring, once more, to the separation of powers as a three-horse team driven by the people themselves, Roosevelt insisted that the nation "must take action to save the Constitution from the Court and the Court from itself." He offered his plan, then, as a way of maintaining an independent judiciary, but not one so "independent that it can deny the existence of facts which are universally recognized."[68]

Despite such provisos, court packing was seen as a way of overcoming the separation of powers. As Kevin McMahon argues, FDR's court-packing plan was not simply a way to constitutionalize the New Deal but part of a larger reconstructive effort. FDR sought to "revolutionize the judiciary" by infusing it with legal realism. The Court could then keep the Constitution up-to-date with modern demands, "restoring it to its rightful and historic place in our system of constitutional government and to have it resume its high task of building anew on the Constitution 'a system of living law.'"[69] Infused with legal realism, FDR's judges would "bring to the Court a present day sense of the Constitution" providing deference to the executive—judicial restraint was an act of "legal politics" as exemplified by realist thinking—and, thereby, the reconstruction of constitutional rights. These features were inextricably bound up as part of the historical adaptation of constitutionalism, which would require a profound shift in constitutional structure and rights—and, in fact, would birth the modern separation of these two deeply intertwined constitutional components.[70]

In rejecting natural rights—or the notion that the protection of rights could have a natural beginning point—FDR sought to jettison traditional understandings of individual liberty. By casting rights as the creation of government, they could be reconstructed and even dissolved depending on the current of history and the needs of democracy. As FDR put it in his plea for a second bill of rights, "The republic had its beginning and grew to its present strength under the protection of certain unalienable political rights—among them the right of free speech, free press, free worship, trial by jury, freedom from unreasonable searches and seizures. They were our rights to life and liberty. As our nation has grown in size and stature, however—as our industrial economy has expanded—these political rights proved inadequate to assure us equality in the pursuit of happiness. We have come to the realization of the fact that true individual freedom cannot exist with economic security and independence."[71]

Thus, some traditional rights, like liberty of contract, must be erased to accord with history, while other liberties could be reconstructed to fit modern conditions. At the same time, FDR distanced himself from progressivism's inherent hostility to rights by, first, insisting on traditional rights like freedom of speech and religion and, second, by invoking new "programmatic rights" that were bound up with expansive government. In his Four Freedoms speech FDR would go so far as to insist on the "positive" rights of "freedom from want" and "freedom from fear," which would be articulated in a more clearly enumerated form in his proposed second bill of rights.

FDR's more far-reaching attempts to overcome the Madisonian Constitution with the court-packing bill and with the "constitutional purge campaign of 1938" where both rejected by the polity—and rejected in Madisonian terms. The court-packing bill was seen not so much as an attempt to bring the Court "up-to-date" but to subordinate it to the executive. As Senator Burton Wheeler, a New Freedom progressive argued, "to give the Executive the power to control the judiciary is not giving the law-making power back to that branch of the Government to which it rightfully belongs but rather is increasing the dangers inherent in the concentration of power in any one branch of our Government."[72] Even those like Wheeler, who rejected the Court's interpretation of the Constitution, insisted on judicial independence against the executive. This sentiment was echoed throughout the battle and virtually insured the plan would fail.[73]

The same force, and the same suspicions, drove FDR's purge campaign in 1938. In the midterm elections of 1938, FDR entered the political thicket against southern Democrats and appealed to the people to elect ideologically "pure" New Dealers. The purge campaign, much like court packing, was an essentially Wilsonian attempt to create "pure" ideological parties—in this case a liberal party—that would provide a coherent way of overcoming the separation of powers.[74] The Congress and the Courts could be organized as supporters of a coherent political vision directed, as FDR's three-horse team, by the president and thereby overcome the framework of countervailing power. But the purge campaign was also a failure.

Parties persisted in Madisonian rather than Wilsonian terms, and they did so in a constitutional framework that provided for the independence of the branches, making conflict a reality and comprise a necessity. Interestingly, much of FDR's success came by way of the separation of powers in the form of congressional legislation of which he was skeptical.

Grounding the Revolution

In many ways, the Wagner Act was the culmination of the progressive struggle to reconstruct the rights of labor—moving them from a constitutionalism of individuals bargaining about work to a group-oriented understanding where the national government could actively promote "labor" as a class.[75] And the Wagner Act has often been seen as the heart of the New Deal insofar as it reconstructed the rights of individual workers and reached into the traditional domain of state power. Yet FDR was a late supporter of the act, skeptical, in part, of the carefully calibrated views of its lawyerly defenders.[76] He seemed to prefer a direct fight with the Court, insisting on "political and economic democracy" whether or not the Court thought it constitutionally permissible.[77] Thus, while the government would attempt to argue in carefully crafted legal terms, allowing the Court to maintain its most recent decisions, Roosevelt would continue to push for a reconstructed judiciary and, then, a reconstructed party system even after the Court began upholding New Deal legislation. Upholding legislation was not enough. Turning to his metaphor of the "three-horse team," FDR noted that the horses must pull together.

The continued push against the Court also allows us to see that the opinions upholding New Deal legislation were not the reversal they were retrospectively made out to be. Depending on how *NLRB v. Jones & Laughlin Steel Corp* and *West Coast Hotel Company v. Parrish* were constructed, they might sit within the contours of earlier constitutional thought.[78] They surely were not a wholehearted endorsement of FDR's far-reaching reconstructive effort, nor were they an announcement that the Court would abdicate its constitutional responsibilities when it came to so-called economic affairs.

In *Parrish,* Chief Justice Hughes explicitly overturned *Adkins,* which has come to be seen as the official beginning of the New Deal "revolution" in constitutionalism. Yet, as Barry Cushman has argued, some of the important changes had occurred more gradually through the progressive years. And it is not just that *Parrish* was decided prior to FDR's court-packing plan, which poses problems for the claim that the Court switched in the face of FDR's plan. Far more tellingly, in insisting first that "Liberty under the Constitution is thus necessarily subject to the restraints of due process, and regulation which is reasonable in relation to its subject and is adopted in the interests of the community is due process," and, second, that this had long ago been recognized by the Court, Hughes's opinion seemed to favorably cite *Lochner*.[79] Given *Lochner*'s symbolic importance to progressives, it would be remarkable if Hughes was rejecting such an understanding of liberty. Nothing, however, in Hughes's formulation is inconsistent with *Lochner*. Recall that Peckham's opinion, too, argued that liberty of contract could be regulated, that it was not absolute. Hughes thus suggested that *Adkins* was an aberration from this line of thought (although we find the insistence there, too, that liberty of contract can be regulated). At the same time, Hughes pointed to criticisms that would play powerfully in the future: "The Constitution does not speak of freedom of contract"; rather, it speaks of liberty, which "in each of its phases has its history and connotation. But the liberty safeguarded is liberty in a social organization which requires the protection of law against the evils which menace the health, safety, morals and welfare of the people."[80] Suggestions that liberty might be adapted to present circumstances would allow for alterations in the meaning of liberty in accord with FDR's Wilsonian vision. Hughes gave this more bite in his closing lines, where he argued that the Court must take judicial notice of "changing economic circumstances."

Much like *Parrish*, Hughes's opinion two weeks later in *Jones & Laughlin* might be situated within the constitutional debates of the past forty years. While it has been dubbed revolutionary, it may well have more in common with the contentious thinking about the commerce clause of the early twentieth century than the complete judicial retreat from policing Congress's commerce power that came to be associated with the Revolution of 1937. Hughes found that the activities of Jones & Laughlin clearly fell under the scope of the Wagner Act, insisting that "it is a familiar principle that acts which directly burden or obstruct interstate or foreign commerce, or its free flow, are within the reach of congressional power."[81] Even the casual reader of Hughes's opinion can see the reliance on the "current of commerce theory."[82] Hughes then continued, in what has too often been seen as a rejection of *Schechter* and *Carter Coal:* "The fundamental principle is that the power to regulate commerce is the power to enact 'all appropriate legislation' for 'its protection and advancement.'" And that power "is plenary and may be exerted to protect interstate commerce 'no matter what the source of the dangers which threaten it.'"[83] But as we have seen throughout this chapter, as well as in the preceding chapter, the same thing was said again and again in opinions such as *E. C. Knight*, which, like *Lochner*, had been a rallying cry for progressive critics of the Court.[84] And even while upholding the legislation, Hughes made clear that the commerce clause had judicially enforceable limits: "the scope of this power must be considered in the light of our dual system of government and may not be extended so as to embrace effects upon interstate commerce so indirect and remote that to embrace them, in view of our complex society, would effectually obliterate the distinction between what is national and what is local and create a completely centralized government."[85]

Hughes's opinion was thus far more consistent with the constitutional logic put forward, at different times, by a Justice Harlan or a William Howard Taft, rather than the sweeping national power claimed by the advocates of the New Deal.[86] Indeed, Felix Frankfurter, a leading member of FDR's "brain trust" in thinking about the Constitution, would ridicule, in an unbecoming manner, these very men, casting their thought at odds with a "forward"-looking Constitution. FDR would push for this more forward-looking vision.

Revolutionary Change as Evolutionary Adaptation

The solidification of one element of FDR's constitutional reconstruction and the emerging scope of national power became much clearer in Justice Stone's opinion in *United States v. Darby* and Justice Jackson's opinion in *Wickard v. Filburn.* Amid the Court's opinions in 1937, Congress and the administration passed laws that were of questionable constitutional validity if the early New Deal cases were still good law—and they had not been explicitly repudiated in 1937. While in some cases Congress was careful to tailor the law so as to distinguish it from earlier laws that were struck down, in other instances, such as the Agricultural Adjustment Act of 1938[87] and the Bituminous Coal Act of 1937,[88] it virtually repassed the existing legislation.

The real revolution, then, took place after 1937, drawing heavily on one line of past constitutional cases, fissured though it was, but reconstructing these cases in such a way as to dramatically increase the scope of national power and outline the contours of New Deal constitutionalism. For Roosevelt, this change was consistent with our flexible Constitution, which would allow for a great deal of institutional innovation, based on the thinking of Hamilton and Marshall. FDR would further expand this vision by recasting the nature of rights and attaching them to an expansive national government. The Court developed FDR's first line of thought as it reworked, *sotto voce,* prior decisions in such a way as to present revolutionary change as the restoration of our (living) Constitution.

In *Darby,* the Court upheld the Fair Labor Standards Act of 1938, which directly regulated working conditions in the form of hours and wages and prohibited the shipment of products in interstate commerce that violated the set standards. This act was clearly a sweeping regulation of production, giving Congress the power to regulate production directly as part of its power to regulate interstate commerce. Stone's opinion drew in part on Hughes's in *Jones & Laughlin,* arguing that Congress's power over commerce was plenary.[89] The plenary nature of Congress's commerce power was not, however, disputed. Rather, the question was what role the Court should have in policing Congress's power. *Darby* was unique insofar as it seemed to embrace FDR's view that the Court should defer to the executive's and legislature's understandings of the Constitution, rather than relying on its own. Such a move rejected the notion of countervailing power when it came to national economic regulation.

Stone played this abdication as if in accord with deeply rooted understandings of the Constitution, traced back to Marshall. These "principles of constitutional interpretation have been so long and repeatedly recognized by this Court as applicable to the Commerce Clause, that there would be little occasion for repeating them now were it not for the decision of this Court twenty-two years ago in *Hammer v. Dagenhart.*" Here Stone dismissed this logic, asserting that the Tenth Amendment was "but a truism" and not a substantive limitation on national power. To say that the Tenth Amendment was "but a truism," much like Stone's insistence that Congress's power to regulate interstate commerce was plenary, was not fundamentally disputed. Could Congress, though, under the guise of its enumerated powers to regulate interstate commerce regulate activities that were not part of commerce and that had been, as the Tenth Amendment reminded us, reserved to the states? Stone's opinion here pointed to judicial retreat. He even claimed that the logic of *Hammer,* which had been relied on even in the 1937 commerce clause cases, "has long since been abandoned."[90] But this logic was truly abandoned only in this case.[91] The judicial abdication to the political branches, endorsing FDR's constitutional reconstruction, was made exquisitely clear in *Wickard.*[92] There Justice Jackson, Roosevelt's former solicitor general and the author of *The Struggle for Judicial Supremacy,* insisted that the Court did not have a role to play in limiting national power to regulate the economy under the Constitution. This retreat raised a profound question about judicial review: was the Court any longer part of the separation of powers?

An Unsettled Inheritance: The Court and the Living Constitution

> The fault with the American system in this respect consists not
> in the independence of the Federal judiciary, but in the practical
> immutability of the Constitution. If the instrument which the
> Supreme Court expounds could be altered whenever a sufficiently
> large body of public opinion has demanded change for a sufficiently
> long time, the American democracy would have much more to
> gain than to fear from the independence of the Federal judiciary.
>
> *Herbert Croly*

Prior to the Court's *Wickard* opinion, FDR delivered a speech on the "Four Freedoms" that highlighted his expansive constitutional reconstruction while speaking the language of rights. There he spoke of "freedom from want" and "freedom from fear," which might require limitless action on the part of the national government. Even when he spoke of "freedom of speech and expression" and the "freedom of every person to worship God in his own way," he spoke of securing such rights in expansive terms—that is, "everywhere in the world."[93] FDR had previously spoken of such rights in his Commonwealth Club speech as part of a new "economic constitutional order," which was put forward in very particular terms in his Second Bill of Rights calling for the guarantee of a host of "economic" rights—such as the "right to a useful and remunerative job" and the "right of every family to a decent home."[94] Such rights could not be seen in "negative" terms, or something held "against government." Nor were they natural in the sense of being rooted in human nature and the foundation of constituting government. Rather they were "positive" because they were bequests from the government, or "programmatic" because they depended on vast governmental programs to nurture and support them.[95] "In other words, unlike the original conception of individual rights in America, which sought to limit federal power, the rights-centered second New Deal endeavored to employ an energetic centralized state to empower individuals by enlarging and protecting their rights in the pursuit of a more democratic society."[96] It is not clear, however, that the Court was to have a serious role in protecting such rights. Its role is even more ambivalent if we take seriously the notion that the Court should defer to the executive branch, which should be given wide flexibility in modern governance. The Court might, then, be a protector of those "civil liberties" the executive branch sought to defend. Even though the Roosevelt administration took action in prohibiting discrimination based on race and creed, rights were still dependent on government, and the proper stance of the Court was deference.[97]

This dilemma was compounded, first, by the language of judicial restraint, if not abdication, nurtured over the past four decades: and, second, by the legal realist and progressive rejection of a reasonably fixed constitutional meaning that might be judicially discerned. The defense of this constitutional change took two forms. At times, FDR seemed to insist that the original constitution sought to protect certain substantive ends, but as a "layman's instrument of government," these substantive ends must come before the particular constitutional forms. To be true to these ends, we must reorder constitutional particulars—including both structure and rights (as they would come to be seen).[98] At other times, FDR viewed the Constitution as a flexible instrument, the *meaning* of which could be altered with changing circumstances, rendering it a living constitution with no real essence or identity; it was, rather, all about the process of evolving.[99] There is a deep tension in these different views. Both, however, provided for change that threatened to drain the Constitution of core meaning, paving the way, as one constitutional theorist has put it, for the "transvaluation of liberal constitutionalism." If rights, like other facets of constitutional meaning, were "to vary with the adaptation of law to changing" needs, how was the judiciary to protect them without falling prey to the long-standing progressive–New Deal criticism?[100]

This tension became, as has long been noted, the central dilemma for the post–New Deal Court. The progressive and New Deal critique of the Court came to be entrenched, but largely in its deconstructive aspects. As Sotirios Barber, a leading theorist of welfare constitutionalism, puts it, "Today's view of constitutional functions . . . fails to reflect the constitutionalism of the Progressive Era and the New Deal."[101] This is certainly true insofar as a positive view of rights was not entrenched as part of the constitutional change of this era. Rather, constitutional thought would be plagued by skepticism about constitutional foundations as manifest in the insistence on judicial deference and restraint. Gary Jacobsohn draws our eyes to the central problem: "A situation may demand self-restraint or it may demand activism—the actual choice is to be determined by whatever appears necessary to affirm constitutional principle and purpose." Thus, any "particular approach to judicial power ought to be derived from a constitutional principle (which, more than the approach, requires defense), and the approach must therefore vary according to the circumstances surrounding the application of such principles."[102]

A central inheritance of the constitutional change wrought by the Progressive and New Deal eras was the insistence on restraint without regard to principle—or to the abstract principles of democracy and evolution. This insistence is perfectly captured by Stone's famous *Butler* dissent, where he called for judicial "self-restraint" as "the only check" on the Court and argued that for "the removal of unwise laws from the statute books appeal lies not to the courts but to the ballot and to the process of democratic government."[103] If I might play on Stone's language drawn from another opinion, this latter point was to state but a truism, as there was no disagreement on this latter point. Such words could have been penned by nearly any of the pre–New Deal justices who were now caricatured and demonized. Yet the criticism that the Old Court had indulged its "policy preferences" and not deferred to the other branches became a central tenet of New Deal constitutionalism.[104]

This criticism is evident in the conflicted lines of constitutional thought that emerge based on the experience of this era. It is often suggested that, "from the debate over FDR's [court-packing] plan came a new vision of the role of the courts. Tremendous power having been ceded to the national government, the plan was the point at which the country balked. The accretion of government power threatened judicial independence, which at the time referred to the emergent role of the Court as the defender of individual liberty."[105] This is far from clear. The Court had protected civil liberties long before the New Deal—including civil liberties such as "the freedom of speech" that were important to FDR. Moreover, FDR's reconstruction of civil liberties would read some liberties out of the tradition. Nor did it necessarily call for judicial protection for those that were now "in." But, more to the point, there was a profound disagreement on *what* liberties where to be protected and *how* they were to be protected. Indeed, skepticism that there were permanent principles underlying the Constitution essential to interpreting it was one dimension of constitutional change, calling forth discontinuous development.

Searching for Solid Ground

It is not a coincidence that the most vexing constitutional question in the wake of the so-called Constitutional Revolution of 1937 was how to legitimately ground judicial power—"how objective judicial decisions should be reached."[106] It was a "quest for uncertainty."[107] In the formative years after 1937–41, there were three clear alternatives to grounding judicial power that were rooted in the New Deal reconstruction. These three central attempts to recast judicial power in light of the progressive criticism of courts and the New Deal reconstruction might be described as "democracy-reinforcing," identified with Justice Stone; "jural reasoning," identi-fied with Justice Frankfurter; and, "rights-based textualism," identified with Justice

Hugo Black.[108] I offer but a sketch of these familiar lines of thought, but want to draw out how each set out to resolve the "judicial problem" against the backdrop of the New Deal reconstruction.

Harlan Stone: Reinforcing Democracy

Although obliquely tucked away, Stone's footnote 4 in *United States v. Carolene Products* would become the most famous statement auguring a recasting of judicial power.[109] There Stone, soon to be elevated by FDR to the center seat, followed Roosevelt's insistence that the Court should follow the lead of the other two branches. As Stone put it in the body of the opinion, "the existence of facts supporting the legislative judgment is to be presumed" in most instances.[110] Stone then inserted footnote 4 to potentially qualify the Court's deferential attitude and its presumption of constitutionality. At root, Stone's logic developed a two-tier theory to guide and ground the use of judicial power. In most circumstances, the Court would defer to the legislature, applying what came to be known as the rationality test, allowing for a flexible understanding of large swaths of the Constitution. This judicial deference perfectly coincided with the progressive and New Deal understanding of national power, although it was also put forward as a restoration of John Marshall's Constitution. In a much smaller group of cases, the Court would subject the legislation to "a more exacting judicial scrutiny." Stone marked out these areas in footnote 4, suggesting them as possible areas where the Court might more rigorously patrol the legislature, such areas that might interfere with the democratic process or directly implicate the Bill of Rights.

The critical basis of *Carolene Products* was that it recast judicial power as supplementing the democratic process: the Court's role was not to "second-guess" the legislature in its constitutional understandings but to police the system in such a way that kept the democratic process open. Thus, the judiciary might legitimately act to ensure that the democratic process remained open and fair or if a "discrete and insular minority" could not trust the protection of its rights to the democratic process. This move was rooted in the progressive criticism of the Court as a "countermajoritarian" institution and the insistence from Wilson to FDR that the Constitution must be adaptable. As John Hart Ely argued, the Court's taking on the maintenance of the democratic process fit neatly with the rejection of a substantive or fixed Constitution, making democracy the primary value in the American regime and the role of the Court consistent with that ordering of values.[111] Yet, part of preserving the democratic process would also entail the preservation of constitutional rights intimately connected to the democratic process, what would become known as the "preferred freedoms." These freedoms—free speech in particular—occupied a preferred position because, unlike other rights, they were intimately connected to the "core of free government," which now meant democracy. In an ordering of constitutional values, they required special judicial solicitude. This move, too, furthered FDR's understanding of freedom of speech and expression as central to democratic government—even if the Court had protected such rights prior to the New Deal breakthrough.[112]

Felix Frankfurter: The Jural Mind

> Never write a constitution. What you need are independent judges, not a written constitution.
>
> *Felix Frankfurter*

Frankfurter rejected both Stone's footnote 4 and Black's textualism (especially as it applied to incorporation). Yet Frankfurter's own attempt to ground judicial discretion is elusive.[113] Frankfurter's plea for judicial restraint at times seemed to call for a complete judicial retreat in the face of democratically enacted legislation; it was very much consistent with the progressive understanding of Justice Holmes and the general skepticism of the legitimacy of judicial review as an undemocratic institution. The essential rejection of judicial review was articulated by Frankfurter's good friend Judge Learned Hand and drew deeply on elements of progressive thought that Frankfurter shared.[114] Yet Frankfurter would insist that restraint was best grounded in a peculiar judicial temperament that was necessary to protect those values that are central to our conception of "ordered liberty."[115] Frankfurter was ever aware that justices would inevitably exercise discretion as part of their judicial duty. Indeed, Frankfurter was fully aware that "judicial restraint" was, in legal realist terms, an act of will. But because axiomatic foundations did not inhere in the Constitution, the answer to limiting such discretion must be found in just this conscious recognition—a recognition cultivated by the proper judicial temperament.[116] This led Frankfurter to be exceedingly deferential to the democratic process, suggesting that, so long as that process was open, the Court should stay its hand.[117] "In no instance is this Court the primary protector of the particular liberty that is invoked."[118] Whether legislation impinged on rights that were fundamental to the democratic process or rights that were textually enumerated made no difference.[119]

Here Frankfurter rejected both Stone's and Black's insistence that certain rights are entitled to more judicial protection than other rights. The deeper point is that Frankfurter rejected the notion of "preferred freedoms" as a sort of mechanical jurisprudence.[120] For Frankfurter, the solution to the problem of judicial will was based primarily on the proper judicial temperament. It was the justice's proper furnishing of mind that would overcome the dilemma of the Progressive and New Deal eras.[121] This approach required self-restraint in most instances, but also the flexible articulation of fundamental values, the drawing out of which was part of Frankfurter's notion of the jural mind, when necessary. Thus, Frankfurter would often claim to be "disinterested."[122]

For Frankfurter, the flexible discovery and articulation of fundamental values, balanced against the needs of society, was the very art of judging, central to the notion of a flexible and living constitution. Unlike Stone and Black, Frankfurter, sought to overcome the "lessons of 1937" not by recasting the role of the Court but by recasting the jural mind. Whereas the Old Court "referred to natural right," Frankfurter "spoke of 'notions of justice,' of 'civilized canon of decency,' and of the 'concept of ordered liberty.' But in point of fact, their perspective standards were not too dissimilar."[123] And so Frankfurter would overcome his restraint if, given standards of due process, the state's action "shocks the conscience."[124] At other times, though, Frankfurter would insist that the justices must defer: "relief must come through an aroused popular conscience that sears the conscience of the people's representatives."[125] Knowing when to invoke a particular mode was part of the proper furnishings of a jural mind, making the Court a reliable partner in FDR's "three-horse team."

Hugo Black: Textualism

> Make a constitution immediately, and make it so stringent that no Supreme Court can evade it.
>
> *Hugo Black*

Carolene Products was handed down in Black's first year on the Court, and while Black joined the opinion, he wrote a brief concurrence for the sole purpose of rejecting Stone's footnote 4.[126] This move helps illuminate Black's subsequent attempt to ground the judicial protection of constitutional rights. It also illustrates the constitutional consensus in terms of the national government's power to regulate the national economy without limit under the commerce clause. If Black speaks the language of textualism, his focus is exclusively on the Bill of Rights, which swallows up the Constitution and altogether eclipses the earlier view that rights were protected by enumerating governmental powers. Thus, he quietly accepts elements of the living constitution, but rejects the notion that the Court has any role to play in its adaptation. His position embraces the New Deal as restoration with its severe criticism of "natural rights judicial law-making."

Although Black is often associated with the short-lived era of preferred freedoms as articulated by Stone, this description does not quite capture his thinking and threatens to obscure his fundamental disagreement with Stone. For Black, the search for preferred freedoms that should be robustly protected by the Court was not so elusive: the Court was obligated to robustly protect those rights that had been marked off for protection when they were clearly enumerated in the Bill of Rights. These were preferred freedoms, not because they were central to the democratic process, not because they were fundamental to a conception of ordered liberty, but because they were singled out for protection by a democratically ratified constitutional text.[127] As Black put it in a later concurring opinion, taking particular aim at Frankfurter's jurisprudence, "I believe that faithful adherence to the specific guarantees in the Bill of Rights insures a more permanent protection of individual liberty than that which can be afforded by the nebulous standards stated by the majority. What the majority hold is that the Due Process Clause empowers this Court to nullify any state law if its application 'shocks the conscience,' offends 'a sense of justice' or runs counter to the 'decencies of civilized conduct.'"[128]

For Black, this gloss on due process, much like the Court's special solicitude for the democratic process, was no different from earlier attempts to protect liberty of contract; it risked equating the values of the justices with the Constitution.[129] When Frankfurter found that certain conduct offended notions of due process because it "shocked the conscience," Black claimed that such pleas were there equivalent of natural-law reasoning. And Black's insistence that anything that smacked of "natural law" was the equivalent of judicial lawmaking was firmly rooted in progressive and New Deal understandings of the Constitution. Having fully digested Professor Frankfurter's legal realist critique of the Old Court and constitutional formalism, Black argued that the only way to ground judicial discretion, to get around the personal preferences of the justices, was to root judicial decision making in constitutional text.[130] This drove Black's insistence that the Fourteenth Amendment incorporated the Bill of Rights.[131] Thus, liberty in the Fourteenth Amendment was neatly defined by the Bill of Rights itself, which grounded notions of due process by tethering judicial discretion to constitutional text and not the "vague contours of due process" that allowed justices to roam at large and engage in "natural law" thinking.

To turn to the democratic process or fundamental notions of ordered liberty, as Stone and Frankfurter did, was to open oneself to the same criticism that these justices had leveled against "substantive due process" that was tainted as "natural law" thinking. It was a criticism that Black himself would level against his fellow justices in *Griswold v. Connecticut*, the contraception case that evoked memories of "substantive due process."[132] Allowing justices to gloss notions of due process and fundamental fairness was of a piece with allowing justices to determine the reasonableness of state or congressional regulation of textual rights: both put us at the mercy of justices.[133]

Negative Foundations in the Progressive–New Deal Reconstruction

Criticism of the judiciary, and skepticism of its role in the constitutional framework, has a long-standing history within American constitutionalism. Brutus's famous criticism that the courts were "empowered to explain the constitution according to the reasoning spirit of it, without being confined to the words or letter," after all, occurs prior to the Constitution's ratification.[134] The progressive–New Deal criticism of the Court was unique insofar as a consensus emerged on what was illegitimate, not what was legitimate. Even if there was some consensus on articulating "fundamental rights" against an expansive state, there was no clear consensus on how this was to be done. The consensus at the heart of this constitutional change seemed to be on what not to do. Digesting the progressive understanding of Holmes's *Lochner* dissent did not yield a new foundation, as is evident in the Black-Frankfurter debate over incorporation. The debate between these justices over incorporation was a debate about how best to cabin judicial will, which led both of them to slight and mischaracterize earlier constitutional thought, whether for its "natural rights" foundations or its "formalistic" reasoning.

Black reconstructed the Court's earlier precedents as explicitly engaged in incorporation, even though some of the most forceful advocates of what would become dubbed "incorporation" were the "natural law" jurists Black rejected: Field, Bradley, Peckham, Brewer, and Harlan.[135] In *Twining*, for example, a case that Black dismissed for its foundation in "natural law," Harlan argued in dissent that the Fifth Amendment applied to the states (or its principles did, if not the actual amendment), but he did not limit liberty under the Fourteenth Amendment to the provisions of the Bill of Rights. Much as Field and Bradley had argued in their *Slaughterhouse* dissents, these were simply some of the liberties protected by way of the privileges and immunities clause and the due process clause, but they were not the whole of them. Defining incorporation as the alpha and omega of Fourteenth Amendment due process, Black was reconstructing the earlier cases to situate them as precedents for "incorporation." In pointing out Black's unfounded position on incorporation, Frankfurter even noted that only one "eccentric" justice had ever insisted upon this position in the past—Justice Harlan.[136] But Frankfurter was also engaged in a reconstructive effort. While Harlan thought the rights in the Bill of Rights were part of Fourteenth Amendment liberty, he did not argue that this was the whole of liberty under the amendment. Nor did he insist that these rights were included within the contours of due process *because* they were textually enumerated. On the contrary, Harlan thought that these rights—as well as unenumerated rights like liberty of contract—were "fundamental in Anglo-American liberty."[137] Here Harlan drew on a definition of "due process" that Frankfurter himself would be at home with. For in the very opinion in which Frankfurter dismissed Harlan as an "eccentric," he also referred to the liberty protected under due process as part of the "notions of justice of the English-speaking peoples[.]"[138] This, of course, was the sort of phrase that Black thought reeked of "natural law." For all of their differences, both Black and Frankfurter sought to reconstruct past lines of constitutional thought so as to limit judicial will, rather than letting the judicial role follow from constitutional precepts in a system of countervailing power. The Court, as Justice Sutherland insisted, should not be "active" or "restrained" but concerned with constitutional fidelity—making its role dependent on constitutional foundations. The New Deal justices reversed this order.

This reversal makes it difficult to speak of the New Deal Constitution as a coherent constitutional regime. Elements of the New Deal reconstruction, such as the national government's power to regulate the economy, certainly take hold. Arguably, this effect is true of social security, if it is seen as a nonenforceable "constitutional commitment."[139] And it is certainly true of freedom of speech and religion, although these rights were accorded protection prior to the constitutional changes of the New Deal years, so they do not flow from a New Deal regime even if they are endorsed by it.[140] At the same time, Herbert Wechsler's deep misgiving about the judicial protection of rights, as well as Learned Hand's argument that judicial review should play almost no role within our constitutional framework, were both squarely rooted in our New Deal inheritance. At the heart of the New Deal reconstruction lie deep discontinuities that were never reconciled.[141] While these tensions were evident in the conflicting lines of thought that emerged from the Court, and numerous other cases illustrate these difficulties, the unraveling of any semblance of a coherent New Deal constitutionalism became obvious in *Griswold v. Connecticut*—a case that became a symbol for judicial lawmaking, much as *Lochner* had been before.[142]

Coda: *Griswold* and the Symbolic Unraveling of New Deal Constitutionalism

In his opinion for the Court in *Griswold v. Connecticut*, Justice William Douglas posited a right to privacy against governmental intrusion but attempted to ground that right in the "penumbras, formed by emanations from those guarantees" in the Bill of Rights. Douglas's move is symbolic of the New Deal's constitutional change: rather than placing the burden on state regulation—What is the basis for the state's prohibition of contraception between married couples?—he assumes the legitimacy of regulation unless it violates a specific right. Douglas, thus, engaged in a tortured construction of "penumbral" rights to meet this challenge. His refusal to draw on the due process clause is a direct result of the progressive and New Deal criticism of *Lochner:* he is all too aware that any move in that direction will be open to the challenge that he is glossing the word liberty in the Fourteenth Amendment to align with his own political preferences. Thus, he seeks—albeit unpersuasively—to ground privacy in the emanations from the text of the Bill of Rights, insulating him from the charge of Lochnerizing or reasoning from "natural rights." Douglas opened his opinion with just this in mind: "We are met with a wide range of questions that implicate the Due Process Clause of the Fourteenth Amendment. Overtones of some arguments suggest that Lochner v. New York should be our guide. But we decline that invitation as we did in West Coast Hotel v. Parrish."[143]

It is not a coincidence that Justice Black's scathing dissent touches briefly on Douglas's opinion but saves its ire for the concurring opinions of Goldberg, White, and Harlan, who draw on the Ninth Amendment notion of unenumerated rights (Goldberg) and the due process clause of the Fourteenth Amendment (White and Harlan) to find the law unconstitutional. For Black, Douglas's opinion might be a poor interpretation of the Bill of Rights, but at least it had the virtue of attempting to ground the right to privacy in constitutional text. The concurring opinions, on the other hand, let judicial will roam at large: "If these formulas based on 'natural justice,' or others which mean the same thing are to prevail, they require judges to determine what is or is not constitutional on the basis of their own appraisal of what laws are unwise or unnecessary."[144] Black, drawing on a central teaching of the progressive and New Deal criticism of the Court, explicitly accuses these justices of Lochnerizing:

The Due Process Clause with an "arbitrary and capricious" or "shocking the con-science" formula was liberally used by this Court to strike down economic legislation in the early decades of this century, threatening, many people thought, the tranquility and stability of the Nation. See, e.g. Lochner. That formula, based on subjective con-siderations of "natural justice," is no less dangerous when used to enforce this Court's views about personal rights than those about economic rights. I had thought that we had laid that formula, as a means for striking down state legislation, to rest once and for all in cases like West Coast Hotel Co.[145]

Notice that *West Coast Hotel,* which not only did not overturn *Lochner* but at one point leaned on it, was now reconstructed by all sides as fundamentally reject-ing this earlier line of constitutional thought. Notice, too, that the Court is united in rejecting this earlier line of thought as enabling "judicial lawmaking." For Justice Harlan levels a similar charge, if more subtly and indirectly, at Douglas and Black. Harlan notes that the common link between Douglas's majority opinion and Black's dissent is a belief that by limiting the due process clause's meaning to the Bill of Rights,

> judges will thus be confined to "interpretation" of specific constitutional provisions, and will thereby be restrained from introducing their own notions of constitutional right and wrong into the "vague" contours of the Due Process Clause. While I could not more heartily agree that judicial "self-restraint" is an indispensable ingredient of sound constitutional adjudication, I do submit that the formula for achieving it is more hollow than real. "Specific" provisions of the Constitution, no less than "due process," lend themselves as readily to "personal" interpretations[.][146]

Need one look further than Douglas's opinion to confirm this point?

For Harlan, as for Frankfurter, judicial will is more likely to be disciplined by judicial temperament than by textual interpretation, which gives his approach a gloss of "substantive due process."[147] If *Griswold* could be situated within any strand of constitutional thought that stems from the New Deal, it would have to be Frankfurter's. It is plausible, as we see from Harlan's concurrence, that Frank-furter's flexible view of history and tradition might allow for this sort of play. Yet it is doubtful, given Frankfurter's absolute rejection of the so-called Progressive Era "privacy" cases—*Meyer* and *Pierce* that Douglas actually cites as precedent for the right to "privacy." But neither case, as I noted in the previous chapter, is a privacy case. In this earlier line of constitutional thought, it would make no sense to speak of a "right to privacy." Rather, these "substantive due process" cases examined the substance of the law against its purported end. In doing so, the Court was not content that the law had been passed in a formally correct manner; it turned to the law's substance to ensure that the law was indeed aimed at a legitimate governmental interest. The government, after all, might regulate privacy in all manner of legitimate ways, but it could not, under the pretext of legitimate end, lay down a merely arbitrary rule even if it had been passed by the correct procedures. Yet this was the logic that Douglas rejected in refusing to follow *Lochner,* even while recasting these cases as precedent for the long-standing right of "privacy."

Even Goldberg, who turns to the Ninth Amendment, is preoccupied by the need to discipline judicial will in light of this critique and "establish" a "fundamental right."[148] His understanding of the Ninth Amendment also serves to illustrate the profound changes wrought by progressive and New Deal thought, illuminating the shadow cast by its negative foundations. As Goldberg argued, "Although the Constitution does not speak in so many words of the right of privacy in marriage, I cannot believe that it offers these fundamental rights no protection. The fact that no particular provision of the Constitution explicitly forbids the State from disrupting the traditional relation of the family—a relation as old and as fundamental as our entire civilization—surely does not show that the Government was meant to have the power to do so. Rather, as the Ninth Amendment expressly recognizes, there are fundamental personal rights such as this one, which are protected from abridgment by the Government though not specifically mentioned in the Constitution."[149] This Ninth Amendment argument, however, is awkward, considering the central changes of the New Deal.

The Ninth Amendment is best understood as an instruction on how to read the Constitution. That is, rights, including natural rights, are protected by way of limiting power.[150] Thus, the Ninth Amendment reminds us of the government's *limited* grant of power: government laws, then, must be clearly aimed at a legitimate end and not treat individuals in an arbitrary manner.[151] This logic also reveals how natural rights were protected by the form of a written constitution, inhering in the underpinnings of the Constitution itself, rather than being some "brooding omnipresence in the sky." Rights were protected not by enumerating them, but by enumerating and thereby limiting governmental powers.[152] Profoundly increasing the scope of governmental power—and placing the burden on the individual rather than the government—the New Deal displaced this framework. If we must name rights before they can be protected, as we now presume that governmental action is constitutional unless it impinges on a "fundamental right," then it very much looks like we are reading our preferred rights, based on some abstract conceptions of "natural justice," into the Constitution.[153] This was precisely Black's charge against Goldberg—and it rang true, given that there was a consensus on sweeping governmental power but not on which rights must then be protected against such power.[154] Indeed, in some ways the reconstruction of constitutional powers under the New Deal rendered the Ninth Amendment an "inkblot." This was Judge Robert Bork's famous description of the amendment in his criticism of *Griswold*. And, as I argue in the next chapter, the reemergence of original intent in the wake of *Griswold* is deeply informed by the putative lessons of 1937.

Facing backward, the New Deal may well be seen as the culmination of decades of constitutional struggle over national power to regulate the economy. But at the heart of this "breakthrough" were deep discontinuities. On the one hand, FDR drew on the Founders to argue that original constitutional ends, embedded in the identity of the union, required us to adapt and reconstruct some features of the constitutional order to meet these ends in dramatically altered modern conditions. On the other hand, FDR spoke of a living and evolving Constitution that would have to be reconstructed to accord with History and the imperatives of democracy. Such an understanding seemed to reject any notion of a core constitutional identity in favor of an ever-evolving process.[155] Facing forward, the New Deal breakthrough left the role of the Court and the meaning of liberty adrift.

These tensions were made evident with the return of "substantive due process" in *Griswold* (if not long before). The persistent struggle over these questions has been shaped by the progressive thought that was at the foundation of the New Deal breakthrough. The return of original intent is deeply connected to this trajectory in its understanding of liberty protected by the Court. In the Court's most recent substantive due process case, the Court's leading advocate of original intent, when he turned to the judicial protection of fundamental rights, argued that the only rights protected beyond those clearly enumerated in the Bill of Rights were "rights which are deeply rooted in this nation's history and tradition."[156] We hear not just the faint echoes of the New Deal inheritance in Justice Antonin Scalia's reasoning but, as I argue more fully in the next chapter, a hearty synthesis of Justices Black and Frankfurter fundamentally preoccupied by tethering judicial will to text and tradition. In this, original intent draws deeply on the "Constitutional Revolution of 1937."

Unsettling the New Deal and the Return of Originalism

Ronald Reagan consciously drew parallels between himself and Franklin Delano Roosevelt—so much so, in fact, that after his acceptance speech at the 1980 Republican Convention, the *New York Times* lead editorial ran under the headline: "Franklin Delano Reagan."[1] But, as William Leuchtenburg writes, "Reagan presented himself as Rooseveltian . . . not in order to perpetuate FDR's political tradition but for exactly the opposite purpose: to dismantle the Roosevelt coalition."[2] Utilizing FDR's view of executive leadership, Reagan, far more ambitiously than breaking the already strained New Deal coalition, sought to dismantle elements of the New Deal constitutional reconstruction that remained entrenched.[3] As Reagan himself put it, he sought a return to constitutional first principles, which the New Deal had altered and the Supreme Court had sorely distorted by turning to a mutable and "living constitution."

In his first inaugural address, Reagan turned FDR on his head, declaring that "in the current crisis, government is not the solution to our problem; government is the problem." Against the sweeping power and political mentality of the New American State forged, if incompletely, by progressives and New Dealers, Reagan sought to return to "self-government," which he rooted squarely in constitutional foundations. As he continued in his first inaugural, "we have been tempted to believe that society has become too complex to be managed by self-rule, that government by an elite group is superior to government for, by, and of all the people. Well, if no one among us is capable of governing himself, then who among us has the capacity to govern someone else?" Reagan then linked this concept to an explicit effort to reconstruct constitutional authority: "Our government has no power except that granted it by the people. It is time to check and reverse the growth of government which shows signs of having grown beyond the consent of the governed. It is my intention to curb the size and influence of the Federal establishment and to demand recognition of the distinction between powers granted to the Federal Government and those reserved to the States or to the people."[4] Much as FDR's attempt before him, this would require the nation to shift its constitutional understandings—to alter, borrowing Robert Jackson's phrase, our state of mind. Here the parallel between Reagan and FDR is striking: Reagan was the first president since FDR to insist that he had the authority to interpret the Constitution in his own right. Much like FDR, Reagan was prepared to articulate his view of constitutional meaning and authority, flatly rejecting the notion that he was bound by the Supreme Court's interpretation of the Constitution as handed down in its opinions.

Insisting on the Founders' original intent in reconstructing constitutional authority and meaning, Reagan saw himself as restoring original understandings, particularly in regard to the notion of limited government. Although FDR had also turned to the Founders, Reagan's view of original intent, unlike FDR's, insisted on the primacy of natural rights as prior to government. Reagan promoted the foundational logic of limited government, whereas FDR had sought to recast liberalism by claiming that liberty depended on positive government.[5] Accepting elements of positive constitutionalism, Reagan rejected the notion of evolving constitutional meaning and the judicial balancing that had grown up around it.[6] In its place, he called for a return to fixed constitutional meaning, which was put forward as historical original intent.[7] Ironically, here is precisely where elements of Reagan's constitutional reconstruction were rooted in the contours of the New Deal breakthrough.[8] While Reagan himself often made principled arguments on behalf of originalism, many of the judges he sought to appoint, as well as many of the lawyers working within his administration, insisted on originalism as the only mechanism capable of binding the judiciary to the Constitution. Digesting a central problem of legal realism—how to ground judicial will in a democracy—as the organizing principle of American constitutionalism, Reagan's originalist judges viewed the "what" of the Constitution through the lens of the judiciary, rather than situating the judiciary within the Madisonian separation of powers in accord with Reagan's departmentalism.

Here Reagan shared further similarities with FDR in his effort to work constitutional change through a reconstructed judiciary.[9] The evidence is at least suggestive that Reagan's determination to return the Supreme Court to the separation of powers by enforcing federalism and limits on national power was partly accomplished by his Rehnquist Court appointees. And yet such an understanding helps sustain the notion of judicial supremacy and a legalistic Constitution; it may even foster irresponsibility on the part of the Congress and executive in sustaining constitutional government.[10] It is not without irony that the Reagan justices have insisted on judicial supremacy as the essence of constitutional government, despite the fact that the resident who appointed them rejected this notion as corrosive to our constitutionalism.[11] Yet Reagan's effort in reconstructing our constitutionalism was broader than judicial appointments and necessarily included shaping our constitutional culture in much the manner that Woodrow Wilson and FDR had before him. Here Reagan's success has been less well understood, largely because we remain fixated by Court opinions. Reagan's insistence on originalism and, stemming from this, his insistence that the president is a coequal interpreter of constitutional meaning have had a profound influence on our larger constitutional culture. At the time, having wholly digested the Warren Court's claims to judicial supremacy and a living constitution, many in the legal academy acted as if Reagan was out to subvert constitutional government. But in the nearly two decades that have passed since Reagan advocated originalism and the president's place as a coequal expositor of constitutional meaning, these tenets of Reagan's constitutional reconstruction have found, once more, a lasting place within our constitutional discourse. Indeed, they have appeared even in the realm of academic constitutional theory, where they find expression on the left as often as on the right.

This development is central insofar as Reagan's constitutional reconstruction was not, in contrast to the progressives and New Dealers, attempting to justify governmental action or a particular legislative agenda. On the contrary, Reagan was trying to foster a constitutional mentality; it was a shift in mind-set rather than a detailed agenda that he put forward.[12] This shift would require forbearance on the part of the national government, returning constitutional authority to the states and the people on a number of issues that since the New Deal reconstruction had been taken up by the national government, exceeding, according to Reagan, its constitutional authority. Reagan not only sought to return to an understanding that rights were held antecedent to government, rather than dispensed by it, but that, at root, liberty depended primarily on forces outside of government. Self-government was not possible if, in a Rousseauian mold, individuals were independent of one another and yet "in absolute dependence on the State."[13] Reagan's understanding might aptly be called Tocquevillean—he even went so far as to refer to Alexis de Tocqueville "at least 58 times in public addresses"—insofar as he insisted on a return to decentralization under the Constitution.[14] For Reagan, decentralization was inextricably bound up with liberty and self-government.

This mentality, and a renewed sense of the importance of federalism, has taken root as a vibrant strand of thought in our constitutional discourse. One legal scholar has aptly suggested that the Rehnquist Court's jurisprudence finds a theoretical foundation in Tocqueville's understanding of democracy in America, arguing that the "Rehnquist Court is tending toward [reviving Tocqueville's America] through reviving federalism, protecting and facilitating rights of civil and religious association, and empowering juries at the expense of judges."[15] Here Reagan's originalism sought to return to pre–New Deal understandings, viewing federalism as a constitutional principle, as well as a virtue of government, and not just a matter of convenience.

Yet, as I noted, aspects of Reagan's originalism, particularly as expressed by some within his administration and his court appointees, were deeply rooted in the New Deal's "deconstructive" or negative foundation. This is particularly true in understanding unenumerated rights as the flip side of enumerated power in the Constitution's overarching logic. If Reagan attempted to return to an understanding of enumerated and limited national powers, which followed from natural rights antecedent to government, his administration often rejected the Ninth Amendment as a reminder of this constitutional logic. This tendency is particularly true of Reagan appointee Judge Robert Bork who, having digested the New Deal erasure, described the amendment as an "inkblot," even while insisting on the centrality of its neighbor, the Tenth Amendment.[16] For Bork, as well as for Chief Justice William Rehnquist and Justice Antonin Scalia, only enumerated rights could be judicially protected; otherwise, judges might simply read their personal inclinations into the Constitution.[17] Digesting the New Deal reconstruction, these jurists fostered it insofar as they rejected earlier originalist lines of constitutional thought as based in "natural law." Originalism, then, was put forward as the antidote to judicial lawmaking, not as a principled understanding of constitutional meaning. This was true, as well, of the insistence on "strict construction" and "judicial restraint." And here is precisely where these jurists, like their New Deal counterparts, reduce the whole of American constitutionalism to the dilemma of the judicial role.

Reagan's Reconstruction and the New Deal

Reagan was the first president living in the shadow of FDR who cast himself in opposition to the New Deal on constitutional grounds. In doing so, Reagan sparked a debate about constitutional fundamentals that continues to shape constitutional discourse. The election of 1980 was the most important since 1936 in terms of constitutional import.[18] Reagan's victory brought federalism and the notion of a limited government of enumerated powers back as constitutional issues in a way that challenged the validity of the New Deal state. It is not simply that the election looked like the long-awaited political realignment but that it cast the issues in constitutional terms against the New Deal's expansive national government, which had been entrenched, according to some, as the equivalent of a "new" Constitution.[19]

The first full year of the Reagan administration seemed to fulfill this promise as Reagan pushed through sizable tax cuts and a reduction in government expenditures, aiming specifically at rolling back the New Deal state and recasting our constitutional mentality. Comparisons to FDR and the 100 Days Congress were inevitable. Yet the Reagan Revolution seemed to stall in the election of 1984. Reagan won a landslide victory, but the Republicans failed to gain control of the House of Representatives. Reagan's personal victory was thus not translated into a constitutional rejection of the New Deal. In 1986 Democrats won back control of the Senate and the Reagan Revolution fizzled out in the scandal of Iran-Contra. Thus, the Reagan Revolution has been seen as a failed constitutional revolution. "For all that the New Beginning changed the terms and conditions of national politics, it proved far less successful than the New Deal in reconstructing American government."[20] As Mark Landy and Sidney Milkis put it, "Reagan's emphasis on presidential politics and executive administration relegated his administration to the task of managing—even reinforcing—the state apparatus it was committed to dismantling."[21] Bruce Ackerman even speaks specifically of Reagan's "failed" constitutional transformation.[22]

These various analyses are unified in their understanding of "reconstructive presidents" who "engage the nation in a struggle for its constitutional soul" and thereby "reset the very terms and conditions of constitutional government,"[23] teaching "the citizenry about the need for great change but also about how to reconcile such change with American constitutional traditions and purposes."[24] Casting an eye at our constitutional history, it is hard to deny Keith Whittington's claim that "reconstructive" presidents have a unique capacity to challenge judicial supremacy and "play the role of constitutional prophet."[25] Situated against this understanding, and particularly against the New Deal, Reagan is seen to come up short. Yet concurrent with pronouncements of Reagan's failed constitutional reconstruction, scholars began speaking of the "Rehnquist Court's federalism revolution" as auguring a post–New Deal constitutionalism. Some accused the Court of "unconstitutionally" rejecting the New Deal's constitutional "settlement."[26] These successes, which go beyond the Court, challenged elements of the New Deal that had largely been unquestioned for four decades. In other areas, as I argued in the preceding chapter, the New Deal had only ever taken root in deconstructive terms and always had an uneasy relationship to the Warren Court. Here Reagan's reconstruction of constitutional meaning and authority was not so much challenging the New Deal, but the Warren Court, which not only ran far beyond the fundamental strands of thought within the New Deal but, in its way, was antagonistic to the central understandings of New Deal constitutional change in regard to liberty.

The New Deal constitutional order was perplexed by deep incongruities at its heart. It remained reasonably coherent in terms of governmental power but was beset by tensions from the outset in the realm of "civil liberties."[27] In this way, it is difficult to merge the Warren Court with the New Deal order; rather, the Warren Court brought out the tensions in the various strands of New Deal constitutionalism, breaking with all of them on some issues. Lyndon Johnson's Great Society followed the path of the New Deal in one area (national regulation), even while it inherited the discontinuities and deconstructive elements of it in another (the role of the Court in relation to civil liberties). Yet scholars have attempted to merge the Great Society and the Warren Court as natural developments of the New Deal order.[28] These scholarly efforts might be seen as attempts to prop up a fractured constitutional order, uneasily pushing it in new directions, while holding Reagan's call for a return to originalism at bay.

Against this backdrop of a fractured New Deal order, Reagan's constitutional construction required recognizing governmental limits. Accomplishing this alteration in constitutional authority and meaning required an alteration in public expectations and constitutional culture: the people must demand less of the national government; they must be weaned away from national administrative programs and entitlements. Dependence on the state threatened what Tocqueville called a "soft-despotism" antithetical to self-government (and potentially degrading to human beings).[29] In an early television address, Reagan looked to our past to illuminate this notion, quoting Tocqueville as an unnamed Frenchmen: "'in America when a citizen saw a problem that needed solving he would cross the street and talk to a neighbor about it and the first thing you know a committee would be formed and before long the problem would be solved.' And then he added, 'you might not believe this, but not a single bureaucrat would have been involved.'"[30] Reagan sought to recapture this spirit and energy that, he argued, had been stifled by centralization. This was not so much at odds with FDR's insistence that "necessitous men cannot be free men," as an insistence that in the current order the New American State had transitioned itself from solution to problem.[31] In his second inaugural address, Reagan made this explicit: our "system has never failed us, but for a time we failed the system. We asked things of government that government was not equipped to give. We yielded authority to the National Government that properly belonged to states or to local governments or to the people themselves."[32]

Such a project seemed well suited to Reagan's rhetorical leadership, itself an outgrowth of the modern presidency, rather than the earlier style of Calvin Coolidge whom Reagan often trumpeted as an ideal president. And, to a degree, Reagan succeeded. It was the Democratic president Bill Clinton, after all, who pronounced that "the era of big government is over" and ended New Deal–style welfare, while his greatest failure as president was the New Deal–style attempt at government-mandated universal healthcare.[33] At the same time, partly using the tools of the New Deal state—a reliance on administration and the courts to bring about constitutional change—Reagan seemed trapped by the old order and unable to reconstitute our fundamental *constitutional* commitments.[34] And if Reagan insisted that we recognize limits as inherent in the nature of constitutional government, his administration often did not act on this principle. While Reagan spoke about constitutional limits as part of the inherent limits of what government can do, he did not force such choices on the American people.[35] Here, Reagan failed to bring about his whole constitutional reconstruction.

Still, Reagan's constitutional thought has itself constituted subsequent political developments. Rather than tracing out electoral politics, important as they are, I want to illustrate how Reagan's thought has shaped the constitutional landscape and our institutions therein. The Reagan Revolution succeeded in reopening a debate about the nature of our constitutionalism and placed the legitimacy of the New Deal breakthrough squarely at the center of this debate—a debate that is very much alive.[36] Indeed, in the mid-1970s, Martin Diamond could note, at a conference on authority and responsibility within our federal system, that there was not a single reference to the Constitution's enumeration of national powers. These questions were considered in pragmatic and not constitutional terms.[37] In the wake of Reagan's reconstruction, it is difficult to imagine that the constitutional import of such questions could be neglected. Some of the most careful textual exegeses of the Constitution now come from left-of-center scholars who earnestly insist on discovering and adhering to original constitutional meaning.[38] This is the sort of "interpretivism" that was deemed "arrogant" and "impossible" by Justice William Brennan when Reagan was insisting upon it.[39] If debates about constitutional meaning were once waged between "interpretivists" and "noninterpretivists," as John Hart Ely suggested, in light of Reagan's reconstruction one might venture that we are all interpretivists now.[40] And, in fact, subsequent thinking about constitutional interpretation situates itself more carefully, and more capaciously, in the constitutional enterprise.

Reagan and Contemporary Constitutional Theory

When Reagan's attorney general Edwin Meese announced that the president could interpret the Constitution in his own right and was not, therefore, bound by judicial opinions in the broad sense of adhering to them as a matter of constitutional principle,[41] many in the legal academy acted as if Meese was out to subvert—rather than maintain—constitutional government.[42] Since Reagan, this position has again gained prominence. Still, the wider debates about constitutional meaning that Reagan provoked tend to be measured against the backdrop of the New Deal, so debates about the legitimacy of the Court's new federalism and other departures from the Warren and Burger Courts serve as a proxy, in some ways, for debates about the legitimacy of the New Deal Constitution and Reagan's attempt to reconstruct it. Oddly, though, this treats the constitutional change that came after the New Deal—and very often against its fundamentals—as if they were simply part of this order. As I have argued throughout this book, it is difficult to speak of such coherent orders, as the Constitution itself has rarely come to life as a coherent and continuous whole. The Warren Court not only departed from progressive and New Deal understandings but, according to many proponents of these earlier views, went against them.[43] We should recall that many of the earliest critics of the Warren Court were ardent supporters of the New Deal and critical of the Warren Court long before opinions such as *Griswold,* where the replacement of New Deal legal stalwart Felix Frankfurter with Justice Arthur Goldberg led to the emergence of "history's Warren Court."[44]

Scholars and justices have labored to provide a constitutional foundation to the Warren Court based on the understandings wrought in the New Deal years in terms of "reinforcing democracy," providing for "active liberty," defending "fundamental rights," or simply situating these profoundly different Courts in the flow of History. The last does bring together the New Deal years and the Warren Court, uniting them in terms of a living constitution. It was, after all, the progressive Herbert Croly who first suggested that the Court might become a powerful expositor of the living constitution, making it an asset to democratic change rather than a hindrance to it. Given this, Croly has aptly been described as the founder of modern constitutional theory.[45] Yet there were subtle, but important, differences in these versions of the living constitution. For New Dealers and progressives, it was the democratic branches that were to adapt the Constitution to modern needs.[46] The Court was to exercise "judicial restraint," thereby allowing for such adaptation by deferring to the democratic branches. For the Warren Court and later thinkers, it

was the Court that was the primary instrument of adaptation.[47] Justice Brennan
even went so far as to insist that a living constitution was the necessary result of
judicial supremacy: "Because we [the Supreme Court] are the last word on the
meaning of the Constitution, our views must be subject to revision over time, or
the Constitution falls captive, again, to the anachronistic views of long-gone
generations."[48] Even putting aside these differences, to merge these different understandings as all part of an evolving and living constitution undermines the notion
of coherent constitutional orders, unless such orders simply refer to constitutional
change in the flow of history.[49] If so, then the question is why the changes brought
about by Reagan are not simply the newest manifestation of constitutional "development." But constitutional thinkers, many wedded to midcentury constitutional
thought, have actively sought to reject this proposition, at times proffering a sort
of "New Deal Originalism,"[50] or treating the New Deal as "the end of history."[51]

In some sense, these scholars recall progressive efforts, turning to "popular constitutionalism" and "democratic deliberation," to realign the judicial role with
national democratic aspirations. And they are united in their criticism of the Rehnquist Court's decisions on federalism. This scholarship is linked insofar as, first, it
melds the New Deal and Warren Court together and, second, its pleads for judicial
restraint, or a rejection of judicial review altogether, to preserve the fundamentals
of New Deal and Warren Court. Thus, I treat these works of constitutional scholarship as endogenous aspects of the project of maintaining the legitimacy of the
Warren Court and elements of the New Deal against Reagan's reconstructive
efforts.[52]

It is perhaps not a coincidence that many of these scholars sought to "take the
Constitution away from the courts" at the very moment that the courts began to
articulate elements of Reagan's constitutional reconstruction. In the wake of the
1995 case of *United States v. Lopez,* in which the Court rejected a congressional act
as beyond the scope of the commerce power for the first time since the New Deal,[53]
Mark Tushnet asked if we were living in a constitutional moment.[54] Three years
later, he argued at great length that judicial review was unnecessary and potentially
harmful in *Taking the Constitution Away from the Courts.* Tushnet sought to return
to elements of progressivism, rejecting judicial review, which would allow the people to adapt the Constitution to their needs: "It would make populist constitutional law the only constitutional law there is." Taking his bearings from the Constitution's "thin" principles, Tushnet argued that "thick" constitutional formalities
could be altered to accord with our more democratic aspirations. While Tushnet
begins with the inalienable rights of human beings, he then insists that "the Declaration's principles, the values that constitute the American people, are always

subject to change as the people change," which seems to reject foundations beyond "the people."[55] As he explained popular constitutionalism, "we can start telling a different story about ourselves precisely because we constitute *ourselves*. We can, in short, change who we are." And, in the process, change the Constitution to accord with our understandings of who we are.

Tushnet played this out in his *The New Constitutional Order,* where he argued that we are not living in a constitutional moment with grand constitutional ambitions. Rather, we are living in a new constitutional order that is characterized by "chastened constitutional ambitions" and symbolized by "the end of big government." This is not the victory for Reagan that it might seem, for his efforts, consolidated by President Clinton, halted the growth of the old order, but did not reconstruct it. Thus, the grand constitutional ambitions of the Warren Court and the New Deal, merged together, have more or less been preserved.

This preservationist turn, and the easy merger of the New Deal with the Warren Court, is most prominent in Ackerman's *We the People.* In the second volume of *We the People,* Ackerman insisted that "we the people" had already spoken. And in speaking, we rejected Reagan's transformative constitutional ambitions in an affirmation of our New Deal Constitution. So while "we the people," in acts of Rousseauian popular sovereignty, can transform the Constitution in whatever manner we see fit, and wholly outside of Article V's specific procedures for amendment, as a people we decided not to alter it from its New Deal–Warren Court path. This occurred, according to Ackerman, when the Court handed down its decision in *Planned Parenthood v. Casey* upholding *Roe v. Wade.* Thus, Ackerman argues that "we the people" rejected Reagan's constitutional reconstruction, and, therefore, the New Deal Constitution stands because *the Court* upheld a precedent that was at odds with the central lines of New Deal constitutional thought.[56]

We see a similar sort of reasoning in Cass Sunstein's argument for "judicial minimalism." Sunstein argues that the Court should move "one case at a time," handing down opinions on the narrowest possible ground. According to Sunstein, the Court ought to be "minimalist" so as to allow for "democratic deliberation" as we the people work out our constitutional aspirations.[57] Sunstein himself has called for us, as a polity, to complete FDR's unfinished revolution by creating a second bill of rights—including sweeping positive constitutional rights.[58] Thus, Sunstein is most skeptical of judicial power—what he calls judicial "activism"— when it might prohibit such "popular constitutional self-government." While not a popular constitutionalist himself, Sunstein situates popular constitutionalists like Tushnet and Kramer as "minimalists," whom he contrasts with "fundamentalists," who are largely conservatives like Justices Scalia and Thomas. In thwarting democratic deliberation, conservatives are "radicals in robes" who seek to adhere to "history's dead hand" by bringing back "a constitution-in-exile."[59]

Sunstein's argument for judicial minimalism serves the dual function in a putatively conservative era of preserving the inheritance of the New Deal and Warren Courts, while preventing conservative judicial appointees from writing their constitutional understandings into constitutional law. This is evident in Sunstein's choice of cases. Sunstein prefers "minimalist" constitutional law that forgoes deep theorizing of a "fundamentalist" variety, but the cases accord neatly with preserving the old order far more than they do with minimalism per se. Not surprisingly, *United States v. Lopez* is cast as a fundamentalist opinion that nods toward returning the "constitution-in-exile."[60] And yet *Casey,* of all cases, manifests the virtues of minimalism.[61]

Larry Kramer's *The People Themselves* shares these concerns. Following FDR, Kramer argues that the Constitution is a laymen's instrument of governance, not a lawyer's document. In Kramer's hands, this laymen's instrument can seemingly be whatever the people want it to be—there is no constitutional foundation inherent in its written nature. Not surprisingly, Kramer turns to the progressive efforts to "reconstruct the nation's constitutions, root and branch," as an inspiration to recover our sense of popular constitutionalism. But Kramer ultimately merges the New Deal and the Warren Court, without a word of criticism for the latter, and insists upon this reading of history: "While making their presence felt on questions of individual rights, these Courts carefully respected the space carved out for popular constitutionalism at the time of the New Deal and left questions respecting the scope of national powers to the political process."[62] In rejecting this accommodation, striking down laws on the basis of federalism, the Rehnquist Court thwarted popular constitutional understandings. Kramer, though, ducks the hard questions of why the judicial protection of some liberties is consistent with popular constitutionalism, while the judicial limitation of national power, or the protection of other liberties, is not.[63] Nor does he explain how liberties that were rejected by the New Deal are deserving of judicial protection within the contours of the "New Deal accommodation" or why Reagan's rejection of elements of the New Deal reconstruction is not the most recent manifestation of popular constitutionalism.

This is all the more pressing as Reagan frequently invoked the phrase "We the people," long before it was fashionable for law professors to do so, insisting that "Our Constitution is a document in which 'We the people' tell the government what it is allowed to do."[64] But, as Reagan put it, quoting James Madison, if "the sense in which the Constitution was accepted and ratified by the nation is not the guide to expounding it, there can be no security for a faithful exercise of its powers."[65] This criticism was leveled most forcefully at the Warren Court, which Reagan saw as engaged in *writing* a Constitution rather than interpreting one and, thereby, preventing the people from doing things it was constitutionally allowed to do. In these scholars' hands, however, the Warren Court is *writing* a Constitution in accord with popular aspirations. This is most evident in Ackerman's thought, which, with some irony, defends the New Deal as a constitutional transformation by neglecting many of the constitutional arguments put forward by the New Dealers themselves.[66]

Ackerman explicitly draws connections between FDR and Reagan, arguing that Reagan attempted to reconstruct constitutional authority in a peculiarly New Deal style: by way of transformative judicial appointments. Ackerman argues that one of the fundamental changes wrought by the New Deal was the "self-conscious use of *transformative judicial appointments* as a central tool for constitutional change."[67] Yet Ackerman paints Reagan's attempted constitutional transformation as a failure. Unlike Roosevelt, Reagan did not win a solid Republican majority in the Congress in the 1984 election, and in 1986 the Republicans lost the Senate, which very likely resulted in the defeat of Reagan's nomination of Judge Robert Bork to the Supreme Court. Bork's confirmation, for Ackerman, combined with Reagan's earlier elevation of William Rehnquist to the Chief Justiceship and the appointment of Antonin Scalia to the Court, may well have culminated in a series of transformative constitutional opinions—namely the overruling of *Roe*.[68] Instead, failing to win widespread support for his constitutional reconstruction, Reagan was forced to appoint the more moderate Anthony Kennedy to the Court, who brought Reagan's transformative ambitions to a halt when he joined Justice Sandra Day O'Connor, another Reagan appointee, and Justice David Souter, a Bush appointee, in a plurality opinion upholding *Roe* in *Casey*.[69]

But what if Kennedy had voted to overturn *Roe*? Even if presidents and political coalitions might attempt to produce constitutional change—or stasis—through the judiciary, in a framework of countervailing power, given judicial independence, this is hardly a guarantee. To say that Kennedy's upholding of *Roe* is a reflection of popular constitutionalism runs the risk of tautology: whatever constitutional decisions are reached are the ones the people wanted.[70] The Madisonian framework is meant to thwart, or break up, just such popular majorities. This is evident when we turn to the constitutional foundations at the root of these developments. In appointing Bork, Reagan surely sought to overturn *Roe* (though that was hardly all he sought to do).[71] But he was able to appoint him because of the constitutional foundations of his office. The Senate, a combination of Democrats and some moderate Republicans, was able to reject Bork because of its constitutional foundations. And, turning to Kennedy, it was his judicial independence, rooted in the

Constitution, which allowed him to join a decision like *Casey.* While electoral politics are important and certainly have an impact on constitutional development, they take place within the constitutional framework that inevitably shapes and constrains various democratic majorities.[72] This is true of constitutional thought as well. Put another way, the focus on electoral politics as the primary mover fails to take constitutional thought seriously in its own right—to acknowledge that constitutional meaning exists independently of electoral outcomes. But, even within the context of electoral politics, it fails to see how constitutional thought constitutes the political landscape that actors act within.

We see this in Ackerman's odd argument that the New Deal Constitution stands, and hence Reagan's reconstructive efforts failed, because the Court failed to overturn *Roe.* This argument reduces Reagan's constitutional reconstruction to a single issue. Odder, it is the issue where his thinking was at one with New Deal understandings. The Court's opinion in *Roe* was utterly at odds with the various stands of New Deal constitutional thought, serving to highlight the Warren, and then Burger, Court's departure from the core elements of the New Deal. As I argued in the preceding chapter, the fundamental agreement in the area of due process was a rejection of the notion of unenumerated rights, or what came to be dubbed dismissively as "substantive due process."[73] At the center of the New Deal was a need to tether judicial power against this kind of reasoning, against the Court's articulation of the substantive principles of the Constitution.[74] While there was not a solid foundation or reconstruction on what constitutional rights were protected, there was a solid core that rejected earlier views of due process, congealing around the progressive understanding of Holmes's *Lochner* dissent.

Dissenting in *Roe,* then Justice Rehnquist drew attention to this fact: "while the Court's opinion quotes from the dissent of Mr. Justice Holmes in *Lochner,* the result it reaches is more closely attuned to the majority opinion of Mr. Justice Peckham in that case."[75] Rehnquist's dissent echoed Justice Hugo Black's *Griswold* dissent that I discussed in the preceding chapter. Let me return to Black's words:

> The Due Process Clause with an "arbitrary and capricious" or "shocking the conscience" formula was liberally used by this Court to strike down economic legislation in the early decades of this century, threatening, many people thought, the tranquility and stability of the Nation. See, e.g. Lochner. That formula, based on subjective considerations of "natural justice," is no less dangerous when used to enforce this Court's views about personal rights than those about economic rights. I had thought that we had laid that formula, as a means for striking down state legislation, to rest once and for all in cases like West Coast Hotel Co.[76]

The return of substantive due process highlighted the fractured state of New Deal jurisprudence and provoked many legal scholars who had been weaned on the progressive critique of the old court—on the ghost of *Lochner*—to cry foul.[77] Even John Hart Ely, who attempted to defend the Warren Court's jurisprudence as an extension of Harlan Fiske Stone's famous footnote 4 in *Carolene Products,* objected to *Roe* as out of accord with the New Deal accommodation. For progressives, substantive due process was synonymous with judicial lawmaking.[78] Reagan's call for a return to a jurisprudence of "original intent" highlighted the tension between rejecting *Lochner* and embracing *Roe*. In this, originalism (or at least its first wave) was partly rooted in the contours of the progressive–New Deal reconstruction.

Originalism and the Incongruities of Constitutional Development

The first wave of originalists, jurists like Bork and scholars like Raoul Berger, took the progressive and New Deal critique of judicial lawmaking as their organizing principle, digesting central tenets and lessons from the New Deal breakthrough.[79] In doing so, they reject the concept that the Constitution rests on substantive principles and, therefore, they cast efforts to extract these principles by way of interpretation—"the nature and reason of the thing"—as a futile quest: all such paths lead inward to a judge's subjective sense of morality. Following "the modern heresy," they insist that the judicial protection of unenumerated rights is the equivalent of judicial will.[80] They accept the progressive view that unenumerated rights must necessarily float as a sort of "higher law,"[81] rather than being embedded in constitutional text by way of enumerated power. Thus, they would come to invert constitutional foundations as articulated by *The Federalist* and James Wilson. As Wilson taught, "in a government consisting of enumerated powers, such as is proposed for the United States, a bill of rights would not only be unnecessary, but, in my humble judgment, highly imprudent." Wilson claimed that such a move would invert the fundamentals of constitutionalism, for with a written constitution, the people give only powers therein enumerated. Reversing this order, if we attempt an enumeration of rights, "every thing not enumerated is presumed to be given."[82] Despite the Ninth Amendment's textually explicit reminder against this logic, this sentiment finds expression in the legal positivism of Berger and Bork who, in this, hue the line of the great New Deal jurist, Justice Black.[83]

Thus, while a leading legal scholar finds it odd that a conservative like Bork would expresses concern about the countermajoritarian nature of judicial review,[84] this is not particularly perplexing. The preoccupation of reconciling judicial review with democracy—as if democracy was the foundation of American constitutionalism—was a central inheritance of the Progressive Era.[85] Like all legal scholars after the New Deal breakthrough, Bork was weaned on the progressive critique of the *Lochner* Court and the New Deal telling of history. The lessons from this era were digested by "conservatives" as readily as by "legal liberals." This is typified by the scholarship of Herbert Wechsler, a one-time law clerk to Stone, and his search for "Neutral Principles" in constitutional adjudication. Wechsler captured the central dilemma rooted in the New Deal breakthrough: "The problem for all of us became: How can we defend a judicial veto in areas where we thought it helpful in American life—civil liberties area, personal freedom, First Amendment, and at the same time condemn it in the areas where we considered it unhelpful?"[86] Taking this critique seriously, Wechsler raised criticism of the Warren Court's *Brown* decision, prior to anything like *Griswold,* in his Holmes Lecture at the Harvard Law School on "Neutral Principles."[87] As Wechsler argued, neutral principles were necessary in constitutional adjudication so that judges were not simply using judicial review in areas where they happened to like the political result.

It is not surprising that Bork took the search for "neutral principles" to be central to justifying judicial review in a democracy. He took it to be, in fact, the organizing feature of one of his most famous law review articles, "Neutral Principles and First Amendment Adjudication," prior to his turn to originalism. As I argue in the next section, legal liberals faced the same dilemma. And, as I suggest, with some irony, the legal liberal defense of *Griswold* and then *Roe* in the wake of the New Deal breakthrough is far more of a departure from the New Deal inheritance than the first wave of originalists whom they attack.

Bork's originalism, his preoccupation with the legitimacy of judicial review—and his attempt to ground judicial will in "original intent"—draws squarely on the New Deal inheritance. Bork, thus, speaks of the "Madisonian dilemma," that is, how to reconcile judicial review with the principle of majority rule.[88] This was, after all, the central constitutional theme in the scholarship of Bork's Yale Law School colleague and friend, and former law clerk to Frankfurter, Alexander Bickel.[89] True, the dilemma Bork speaks to is not quite Madison's. Bork notes that the Constitution thwarts some forms of democracy by way of the Bill of Rights. But, otherwise, the right of majorities to rule, and "simply because they are majorities," is taken as the backdrop against which the Bill of Rights preserves the liberties of minorities. Not only does the Constitution not rest upon substantive principles such as natural rights, but any attempt to articulate these from the bench is to engage in "minority tyranny" precisely because there are no principles underlying the Constitution that are essential to its interpretation other than majority rule.[90] Democracy is thus the highest feature of our constitutionalism, which is tempered in the few places where the Constitution explicitly enumerates rights against it. Justice Scalia, too, seems to embrace just such a view: "the whole theory of democracy . . . is that the majority rules; that is the whole theory of it. You protect minorities only because the majority determines that there are certain minority positions that deserve protection."[91]

The primary defense of original intent, from this perspective, is that it grounds judicial discretion in the historical intent of the positive law, which is rooted in a democratic majority.[92] Originalism is the best theory of interpretation not because it captures the ends of the Constitution, or its fundamental identity as it underlies the words in the text, but because it is the only theory that provides the judge with a neutral basis for constitutional interpretation.[93] The construction of constitutional meaning, here, is being driven by the dilemma of judicial will: the whole of the Constitution is reduced to obviating judicial lawmaking.[94] Consider that Justice Scalia, the current Court's most powerful articulator of originalism, defends it in precisely these terms: "Now the main danger in judicial interpretation of the Constitution—or, for that matter, in judicial interpretation of any law—is that the judges will mistake their own predilections for the law. Avoiding this error is the hardest part of being a conscientious judge; perhaps no conscientious judge ever succeeds entirely."[95] Originalism, while not perfect—Scalia calls it "the lesser evil"—is the best method of interpretation because it "does not aggravate the principal weakness of the system [judicial discretion], for it establishes a historical criterion that is conceptually quite separate from the preferences of the judge himself."[96] For Scalia, constitutional text and historical original intent combine to limit judicial discretion.

This is evident in Scalia's "substantive due process" dissents where he has insisted that only rights that were explicitly enumerated in constitutional text or had been accorded long-standing historical protection in American society would qualify for the Court's most exacting level of review, strict scrutiny. As Scalia has put it, drawing on the progressive understanding of *Lochner,* "In my history-book, the Court was covered with dishonor and deprived of legitimacy by Dred Scott v. Sandford (1857), an erroneous (and widely opposed) opinion that it did not abandon, rather than by West Coast Hotel (1937), which produced the famous 'switch in time' from the Court's erroneous (and widely opposed) constitutional opposition to the social measures of the New Deal."[97]

That this version of originalism may well owe more to legal positivism than the Founders' constitutionalism only reaffirms the notion that it is rooted in the New Deal breakthrough.[98] Given this, it is perhaps not surprising that Bork is ambivalent about John Marshall, calling him the "divided" John Marshall for his occasional lapses in expounding upon the nature and spirit of the Constitution.[99] Bork's dismissal of unenumerated rights and his insistence that the Ninth Amendment is an inkblot essentially accepts the New Deal "erasure" of its original meaning, which is a principled means of overcoming the Federalist critique of a bill of rights. Judge Bork's original intent, however, finds common cause with Justice Black's denunciation of natural rights "as an incongruous excrescence on our Constitution."[100] If these originalists draw on the ghost of *Lochner* to criticize "judicial activism" and "natural law," it is because they have digested the deconstructive tenets of the New Deal reconstruction.[101]

Legal Liberalism's Break with the New Deal

If unenumerated rights have a deep foundation in American constitutionalism, the New Deal, drawing on the Progressive Era, was a rejection of this earlier constitutional thought: liberty would have to be altered to accord with modern democracy.[102] If the New Deal wrought legitimate constitutional change, providing for the protection of some "civil liberties," it is, indeed, foundational to ask which rights are included within the contours of this change. The first wave of originalists is merely echoing the various New Deal strands of constitutional thought on the issue of "civil liberties." It is the defenders of the New Deal "transformation" who obscure these earlier arguments.[103]

If the New Deal breakthrough was truly the collapse of constitutional originalism, rejecting the judicial protection of unenumerated rights, then the jurisprudence of a Bork is one plausible outcome of this change. Efforts to rescue *Griswold* and *Roe* by linking them to the "New Deal constitutional synthesis" or the path of constitutional development tend to neglect the arguments put forward by progressives and New Dealers in arguing for these changes. The difficulty is that very little that was settled in this constitutional shift justifies either opinion, while there is much at the heart of the New Deal's deconstruction of traditional due process that squarely rejects such thinking. At least these were the sort of arguments made by ardent advocates of the New Deal like Wechsler, Bickel, and Hand, not to mention New Deal justices like Frankfurter, Black, and Stone (as well as Holmes, Brandeis, and Cardozo preceding them).[104] This was the legal liberal's dilemma as exemplified by Wechsler's "Neutral Principles."

Drawing on the logic of constitutional development, Stephen Griffin explicitly rejects Wechsler's dilemma. "Although the approach of the majority in *Lochner* was abandoned after the New Deal, this does not mean that the return of substantive due process in *Griswold* and *Roe* was the return of *Lochner*. The new substantive due process doctrine was used for different purposes and operated in fundamentally different political, legal, and social contexts. To ask how *Roe* can be justified if *Lochner* was unjustified thus makes the anachronistic assumption that the normative standards and relevant background did not change between 1905 and 1973."[105] Griffin does not explain, though, how the "normative standards and relevant background" changed. Nor does he suggest why such changes would justify the exercise of this sort of judicial reasoning in some areas but not others—that is, why they are a legitimate part of constitutional development, rather than simply what has occurred.[106] Moreover, the first wave of originalists explained very clearly why, as a matter of constitutional logic, they reject both *Lochner* and *Roe*. And in doing so, they highlighted how the earlier arguments against substantive due process at the heart of the New Deal breakthrough rejected it in all its manifestations. It was not embraced in some areas and rejected in others.

Ackerman too focuses on constitutional change to unravel the traditional legal liberal dilemma. For Ackerman, *Lochner* was rejected in the Constitutional Revolution of 1937 whereby the people ultimately ratified a new Constitution. This New Deal Constitution, according to Ackerman's synthesis, is broad enough to encompass *Griswold* and *Roe*. So simply put: *Roe* is grounded in the Constitution, *Lochner* is not. This is made evident in Ackerman's curious discussion of *Casey* that I touched on earlier. Yet, Ackerman says very little about how the New Deal reconstruction justifies *Roe*. Rather, Ackerman argues that *Griswold* (and thus presumably *Roe*) was a synthesis of the Founders' concern with personal liberty in a "post–New Deal world of economic and social regulation."[107] To arrive seamlessly at this conclusion, Ackerman ignores the reasoning put forward in Justice Douglas's *Griswold* opinion, which I discussed in the preceding chapter, which was preoccupied by the dilemma Ackerman seeks to dissolve.[108]

This dilemma is vividly evident in *Bolling v. Sharpe,* the companion case to *Brown v. Board of Education*. While *Brown* has been situated within the shape of the New Deal, it is interesting that many of these efforts are altogether silent on *Bolling*.[109] I suggest that *Bolling* recaptures the dilemma of judicial review as the post–New Deal order saw it, which subsequent developmental scholarship has attempted to undo. *Bolling* dealt with segregated schools in Washington, D.C., and so it did not implicate the Fourteenth Amendment's equal protection clause— which applies only to the states—but was a Fifth Amendment due process case. In striking down segregation in the District of Columbia, Chief Justice Warren noted that "discrimination may be so unjustifiable as to be violative of due process." The Court then cast its argument in terms that could have been penned by the now discredited Old Court: "Although the Court has not assumed to define 'liberty' with any great precision, that term is not confined to mere freedom from bodily restraint. Liberty under law extends to the full range of conduct which the individual is free to pursue, and it cannot be restricted except for a proper governmental objective. Segregation in public education is not reasonably related to any proper governmental objective, and thus it imposes on Negro children of the District of Columbia a burden that constitutes an arbitrary deprivation of their liberty in violation of the Due Process Clause."[110]

But rather than grounding its argument in terms of substantive due process, the Court insisted that if the states were prohibited from engaging in racial discrimination, then it was "unthinkable" that the Constitution would impose a lesser duty on the national government. Chief Justice Warren did not explain why this was so. And because "due process" was at stake in both cases, the reasoning of *Bolling* should subsume the Court's argument in *Brown*. Indeed, if correct, this logic would explain why segregation was constitutionally impermissible beyond the realm of education (where *Brown* did not venture and which the Court never bothered to explain). The Court did not do this, we might deduce, because this line of constitutional thought had been roundly discredited in the wake of the New Deal breakthrough. As Bork points out, *Bolling* is substantive due process, however much one likes the result. Whether it is also a "clear rewriting of the Constitution"[111] is far less clear. It is, though, a clear attempt to negotiate around this discredited understanding rather than an "interpretive synthesis."[112]

These attempts to root the judicial defense of "civil liberties"—particularly "privacy"—in constitutional change amount to "a sophisticated refinement" of the "progressive model of constitutional development."[113] While legal liberals attempted to weave these different modes of thought into a coherent order, these attempts reveal that the Warren Court had already instituted constitutional change that fell away from the New Deal—unless, that is, the New Deal is simply taken to have brought forth a "living constitution" grounded in legal realism. If so, it is not clear why this understanding of a living constitution could not turn in a conservative direction.[114] Yet Reagan's originalism was an attempt to recover constitutional foundations of a very different sort.

Federalism and Liberty: Retreat from New Deal Centralization

If Reagan's originalism traveled easily with the New Deal's rejection of substantive due process, it posed a challenge to the changes brought about by the New Deal when it came to federalism and limits on national power. When the New Deal Court abandoned substantive due process, it also embraced a far-reaching view of Congress's power to regulate interstate commerce, not simply rejecting arguments that federalism or the Tenth Amendment should be reminders of the limitations of national power, but insisting that the Court had no role to play in policing these boundaries.[115] On these issues, Reagan's constitutional vision squarely challenged elements of the New Deal that had been securely entrenched. As Bork described it, "The [New Deal] Court's refusal to enforce limits of any kind simply abandoned this aspect of the Constitution. That worked a revolution in the relationship of the federal government to the state governments and to the people, and the revolution did not have to await a constitutional amendment."[116]

For Reagan, the Constitution had a meaning that could not be interpreted out of existence, or ignored, as had occurred with the enumerated powers of the national government.[117] But, in Tocquevillean terms, he also saw centralization as harmful to constitutional self-government—that is, as harmful to our constitutional soul as much as to the written Constitution. He was fond of quoting Thomas Jefferson's claim that the states are "the most competent administrations for our domestic concerns and the surest bulwarks against antirepublican tendencies."[118] He insisted not only that the Tenth Amendment had formalized this relationship but that "federalism is rooted in the knowledge that our political liberties are best assured by limiting the size and scope of the national government."[119] Thus, Reagan often drew upon Jeffersonian "strict construction" as part of restoring a decentralized constitutional order.[120]

In doing so, he returned to the vexing debate about the foundations of the Union, going so far as to argue, following Jefferson, that "the states created the national government, not the other way around." Thus, Reagan spoke often of "states' rights" and "state sovereignty," at times seeming to draw on Anti-Federalist thought in reconstructing constitutional authority against centralization. While invoking such freighted language, Reagan did not reject the essentials of the national union—particularly the insistence that the national government acted directly on the people—but, rather, argued that the reach of the national government was limited. To some degree, like the progressives before him, Reagan uneasily wove together Jeffersonian and Hamiltonian thought.[121] He drew on Hamilton's understanding of a vigorous executive as central to the separation of powers, even while following the Jeffersonian notion of "strict construction" and "states' rights." Reagan, for instance, turned to Hamilton's insistence on "a unitary executive" to revive the separation of powers within the administrative state.[122] At other times, Reagan seemed to follow Jefferson's insistence (against Hamilton) that "I consider the foundation of the Constitution as laid on this ground that 'all powers not delegated to the U.S. by the Constitution, not prohibited by it to the states, are reserved to the states or to the people.' To take a single step beyond the boundaries thus specially drawn around the powers of Congress, is to take possession of a boundless field of power, no longer susceptible of any definition."[123] Reagan did not hue so closely to the Jeffersonian line. His attorney general even followed the Hamiltonian logic of Marshall in *McCulloch v. Maryland* against Jefferson, even while claiming that a Hamiltonian understanding could not be read, as some were apt to read it, in support of "the idea that the Constitution is a protean, changeable thing[.]"[124] Yet the sentiment that latitudinarian constructions of the Constitution had swallowed up powers reserved to the states and the people rooted Reagan's constitutional understandings.

What was most egregious about decisions like *Roe,* according to Reagan, was not that they allowed abortion; it was the fact that they removed such decisions from where they constitutionally belonged: in the hands of the states and the people. The states themselves might choose to allow abortion, but constitutional principles of federalism commanded that the issue be decided by the states and not by the Supreme Court.[125] This was not a matter of constitutional formalism alone, but central to the art of self-government. The habits of mind fostered by individual initiative and local government were essential to maintaining a healthy constitutional democracy against "administrative tyranny." Decentralization might even be prudentially mandated by the national government as part of fostering a healthy constitutional culture (which raises curious questions about the proper division of power). In calling for a return to limited national powers and some forms of decentralization as fundamental to liberty, Reagan was not exquisitely clear on just what the *constitutional* balance was. Still, Reagan did instigate the return of such constitutional questions, which had been eclipsed since the New Deal.

The return of federalism suggests that Reagan's challenge to the New Deal was at least partly successful. The same year that *Casey* was handed down, the Court reopened a debate on the meaning of the Tenth Amendment for the first time since the late New Deal years.[126] Three years later, the Court, in *Lopez,* struck down a law as beyond the scope of Congress's commerce power for the first time since 1936. Since that time, the Court has shown that it is willing to police the boundaries between the states and the national government: limiting Congress's power under the commerce clause,[127] breathing life into the Tenth Amendment,[128] and putting forward the sovereign immunity of the states.[129] The Court has also endorsed Reagan's Tocquevillean vision in other areas—particularly in recognizing the free exercise of religion and freedom of political and civic association.[130] Whether this line of federalism decisions will be solidified over time is an open question. But it will not turn on judicial appointments alone. Rather, it must take root at a much deeper level. As Tocqueville put it, capturing the flavor of Reagan's constitutional reconstruction, "political societies are created not by their laws but by the feelings, beliefs, ideas, the habits of the heart and mind of the men who compose those societies, by that which nature and education have made them, have prepared them to be."[131] It is unmistakable that this long-neglected aspect of American constitutionalism is a potent force in contemporary constitutional thought—in government, on the bench, within the academy, and with the public.

Reagan's Transformative Appointments?

Much like Roosevelt before him, Reagan "self-consciously attempted to use the power of judicial appointments to place on the bench judges who shared [his] general philosophy."[132] This tactic is confirmed by those within the administration, who not only spoke of potential judges and justices in constitutional terms but also sought to entrench the return of originalism in the judiciary.[133] Reagan saw a transformation of the judiciary as key to his constitutionalism, and this drove his judicial appointments. The administration even started vetting candidates for the Supreme Court before there were vacancies.[134] But, unlike Roosevelt, the Court did not play spoiler to Reagan directly. To return to a more limited vision of government, the administration could cut government spending, programs, and taxes, allowing (and encouraging) the states and local governments to take up their more traditional roles. As long as the government acted in such a fashion, it could bring about significant change on its own. Yet absent a significant change in our constitutional culture—including fundamental changes on the Court—Reagan's constitutional construction threatened to be transitory rather than foundational. To help solidify his constitutional construction, he turned to judicial appointments.[135] Attorney General Meese explained this move as an effort "to institutionalize the Reagan revolution so it can't be set aside no matter what happens in future presidential elections."[136]

Reagan's quarrel with the Court was partly rhetorical, insisting that it let states and local governments return to their traditional constitutional functions.[137] The Supreme Court opinions he was most critical of—those forcing school busing, forbidding prayer in public schools, and nationalizing abortion and criminal rights—prevented the states from making choices he thought they were constitutionally vested with the power to make. In speaking of the Court, Reagan, much like FDR, called for judicial restraint: the Constitution vested these decisions in state legislatures, communities, and the people. In prohibiting these decisions by calling on a "living constitution," the federal courts were engaged in unfounded judicial "activism." Here, many advocates of Reagan's constitutionalism easily drew on the progressive and New Deal criticism of the Old Court, even while rejecting the notion of a living constitution. This language of restraint, however, was only part of the picture, and it exemplified how parts of Reagan's call for originalism remained framed by the legal realism of progressive and New Deal thought. Restraint, after all, was originally put forward as a means of allowing constitutional adaptation on the part of the political branches. This constitutional adaptation is precisely what Reagan sought to prevent by returning to originalism. The return of originalism, however, could call on the Court to preserve the constitutional logic of federalism in a way that had not occurred since the pre–New Deal years.[138]

Here, Reagan and conservative jurists, like progressives before them, did not attend carefully to what they meant by "activism." Nor did they explain why "restraint" or "strict construction" would be constitutionally founded. Rather than speaking to foundational constitutional principles and allowing the judicial role to unfold from the nature of the Constitution, "restraint" and "strict construction" were invoked as limiting judicial lawmaking. Neglecting when the Court should legitimately enforce constitutional meaning and limits threatened to "conservatize" the judiciary, much as FDR had "liberalized" it, rather than speaking clearly to its constitutional task.[139] This left the Rehnquist Court, just as the New Deal Court before it, open to embarrassing charges of hypocrisy and a double standard.[140] The Rehnquist Court has even been labeled "the most activist Court in history."[141] Mirroring the neglect of constitutional substance in the old and tired debates about activism and restraint, judicial "activism" has been redefined in banal social scientific terms, divorced from normative commitments, as simply the *act* of striking down legislation. The Court is thus "active" whenever it exercises the power of judicial review.[142] The result, in accord with neutral social science, makes judicial enforcement of constitutional meaning no different from judicial alterations of constitutional meaning.

And yet Reagan did not impart a contrary lesson insofar as his rhetoric put forward "judicial restraint" as "a guiding principle."[143] Nor did he develop the logic behind the rhetoric, which would require a deeper unfolding of our constitutionalism than he gave.[144] Still, if Reagan embraced the rhetorical presidency, unlike many modern presidents, his rhetoric raised "important constitutional concerns" and attempted a broader shift in constitutional thinking.[145] Reagan's rhetoric provoked a debate about the nature of the Constitution that ran far beyond his own immediate concerns. This is true of both his call for originalism and his rejection of judicial supremacy, which merged together in rejecting the Court's logic in *Cooper v. Aaron*, as it insisted that "the federal judiciary is supreme in the exposition of the law of the Constitution, and that principle has ever since been respected by this Court and the Country as a permanent and indispensable feature of our constitutional system."[146] Reagan, to the contrary, took it as a constitutional obligation to adhere to and interpret the Constitution independently of Supreme Court opinions.

Meese insisted that *Cooper* "was, and is, at war with the Constitution, at war with the basic principles of democratic government, and at war with the very meaning of the rule of law."[147] At times, the rhetoric of originalism suggested that the Court had fallen away from the Constitution and that the president was thereby better positioned to "rediscover" constitutional meaning.[148] At the center of this "rediscovery" was the insistence that the Constitution be interpreted to accord with the principles of federalism: "Washington, ignoring the principles of the Constitution, was trying to turn the states into nothing more than administrative districts of the federal government."[149] Meese echoed this thinking in taking direct aim at the Supreme Court's opinion in *Garcia v. San Antonio Metropolitan Transit Authority,* in which the Tenth Amendment was rejected as a limitation on national power. In an affirmation of the New Deal reconstruction, the Court insisted that the judiciary was ill-equipped to police the boundaries of state and national power.[150]

Meese rejected this understanding and argued that in *Garcia* "the Court displayed—in the view of the administration—an inaccurate reading of the text of the Constitution and a disregard for the Framers' intention that state and local governments be a buffer against the centralizing tendencies of the national leviathan." Pushing this further, Meese noted that "the administration's view is that Federalism is one of the most basic principles of our Constitution," and he added, "we hope for a day when the Court returns to the basic principles of the Constitution as expressed in *Usery*" (a return that calls for judicial *enforcement* rooted in *substantive* constitutional principles).[151] In *National League of Cities v. Usery,* a case out of line with the New Deal reconstruction of federalism, Justice Rehnquist had returned to the view that the Tenth Amendment limited congressional power. The year that *Garcia* overturned *Usery,* Reagan elevated Rehnquist to the chief justiceship. And dissenting in *Garcia,* Rehnquist turgidly noted that "I do not think it incumbent on those of us in dissent to spell out further the fine points of a principle that will, I am confident, in time again command the support of a majority of this Court."[152] Rehnquist has led just such a resurgence that has its roots in Reagan's constitutional reconstruction.

Federalism and the New Deal on the Court

The Court's contentious federalism decisions are often a debate about the New Deal between the majority and dissenting justices. In *Lopez,* when the Court struck down the Gun-Free School Zone Act of 1990, Justice Souter, writing in dissent, raised the specter that the Court may be returning to a pre-1937 reading of the commerce clause. He even accused the majority of "ignoring the painful lesson learned in 1937."[153] And Justice Stephen Breyer's dissenting opinion insisted that Court's opinion "runs contrary to modern Supreme Court cases," with particular emphasis on *Wickard v. Filburn,* which solidified the New Deal understanding of the commerce power by allowing Congress to regulate purely local matters.[154] It is appropriate that *Wickard* was written by Justice Robert Jackson, who as Roosevelt's solicitor general had articulated the New Deal constitutional reconstruction to a usually hostile Court. Now on the bench, Jackson solidified this constitutional reconstruction without a single dissenting opinion. Writing about the opinion to a lower-court judge, Jackson explained it thus: "in any case where Congress thinks there is an effect on interstate commerce, the Court will accept that judgment."[155]

Rehnquist's opinion slyly evades the logic of *Wickard,* noting that the regulation at issue there at least purported to regulate *commercial activity,* while in *Lopez* it was not regulating commercial activity at all. But, as Justice Breyer pointed out, "the Wickard Court expressly held that Wickard's consumption of home grown wheat, '*though it may not be regarded as commerce,*' could nevertheless be regulated—'whatever its nature'—so long as 'it exerts a substantial effect on interstate commerce.'"[156] *Lopez* does not sit easily with *Wickard.* That is surely why Rehnquist rested *Lopez* on the logic of an earlier New Deal case: *Jones & Laughlin Steel.* As I noted in the preceding chapter, this watershed case upheld the Wagner Act against a commerce clause challenge, thus allowing a key piece of New Deal legislation to go forward, even while reminding the Congress that "the scope of this power must be considered in the light of our dual system of government and may not be extended so [as to] obliterate the distinction between what is national and what is local and create a completely centralized government."[157] This is just what *Wickard* did four years later. In returning to the logic of *Jones & Laughlin Steel,* the Rehnquist Court turned to pre-1937 understandings of the commerce power and rejected the full reach of the New Deal reconstruction as put forward in *Wickard.*[158]

The Court opened up another such departure in *New York v. the United States,* where it held that the Congress may not "commandeer" the states by forcing them to take action to implement a federal program. For our purposes, *New York* is significant in that the Court's reading of the Tenth Amendment revived the amendment as a textually explicit reminder that the national government's powers are enumerated, a notion all but buried in the New Deal reconstruction. As O'Connor explained,

The Tenth Amendment . . . restrains the power of Congress, but this limit is not derived from the text of the Tenth Amendment itself, which, as we have discussed, is essentially a tautology. Instead, the Tenth Amendment confirms that the power of the Federal Government is subject to limits that may, in any given instance, reserve power to the States. The Tenth Amendment thus directs us to determine, as in this case, whether an incident of state sovereignty is protected by a limitation on an Article I power.[159]

Much like Chief Justice Rehnquist in *Lopez,* O'Connor held that this interpretation was consistent with New Deal precedent, even quoting Stone's opinion in *United States v. Darby:* "The Tenth Amendment 'states but a truism that all is retained which has not been surrendered.'"[160] O'Connor uses this truism, though, to breathe life into the Tenth Amendment as reminder that the national government's powers are limited under the federal scheme. This is exactly what Stone rejected: *Darby* was meant to bury the notion that the Court should enforce limits on Congress's enumerated powers by reading the Tenth Amendment as a reminder of these limits. For Stone, the balance between the states and the national government was a question of policy, not constitutionality. These Rehnquist Court decisions were a clear departure from such an understanding.

The Court's break became evident in *United States v. Morrison* when it struck down the Violence against Women Act, even though Congress had offered substantial findings "that gender-motivated violence affects interstate commerce." This was something Congress had not done in *Lopez.* The Court made apparent the meaning of *Lopez* when Rehnquist insisted that "whether particular operations affect interstate commerce sufficiently to come under the constitutional power of Congress to regulate them is ultimately a judicial rather than a legislative question."[161] In its commerce clause opinions since *Wickard,* the Court had—even if it was theoretically possible to suggest limits to the commerce power—suggested that Congress's power was not subject to a judicial check. By itself, *Lopez* may have been a simple recognition of such outer limits—but, even so, it was a break with New Deal understandings. But *Morrison* made clear that the Court would police the "distinction between what is truly national and what is truly local." This reading gave the doctrine of enumerated powers a bite that, even if theoretically plausible in the Court's earlier opinions, was simply not there in practice, a point Rehnquist made explicit:

Although JUSTICE BREYER argues that acceptance of the government's rationales would not authorize a general federal police power, he is unable to identify any activity that the States may regulate but Congress may not. JUSTICE BREYER posits that there might be some limitations on Congress' commerce power . . . [but] these suggested limitations, when viewed in light of the dissent's expansive analysis, are devoid of substance.[162]

Rehnquist made clear that the Court would give substance to these constitutional limitations on congressional power and, in doing so, broke from the core of the New Deal's constitutional reconstruction. As I argued in the preceding chapter, Chief Justice Hughes's opinion in *Jones & Laughlin Steel* might be best situated within the contours of pre–New Deal commerce power thinking, insofar as it insists upon judicially enforceable limits within the federal scheme. And this is precisely what the Rehnquist Court has proposed.

Morrison solidified the reconstruction of federalism on another front as well. In addition to the commerce clause analysis, Rehnquist's opinion rejected the idea that Congress may federalize traditional state matters, such as violence against women, under section 5 of the Fourteenth Amendment. Federalism was held to limit Congress's power to enforce the terms of the Fourteenth Amendment. Here federalism bled into the Court's claim of judicial supremacy in *City of Boerne v. Flores,* which *Morrison* rested squarely upon. In *Boerne,* Justice Kennedy, appointed by a president who insisted that he must interpret the Constitution independently of what the Court had said, insisted that the Court's interpretation of constitutional meaning and authority was final: "Congress," Justice Kennedy lectured, "has been given the power 'to enforce,' not the power to determine what constitutes a constitutional violation. Were it not so, what Congress would be enforcing would no longer be, in any meaningful sense, the "provisions of [the Fourteenth Amendment]."[163] Kennedy wedded Court and Constitution as one and the same: Congress, then, can interpret constitutional meaning only in accord with Court decisions, which are the Constitution incarnate. Despite the fact the Meese had such a heavy hand in appointing Kennedy, this understanding is surely at odds with Meese's insistence that judicial supremacy is "at war with the Constitution." As Meese argued, "once we understand the distinction between constitutional law and the Constitution, once we see that constitutional decisions need not be seen as the last words in constitutional construction . . . we can grasp a correlative point: constitutional interpretation is not the business of the Court alone, but also properly the business of all branches of government."[164] Kennedy denied that there was a distinction between constitutional law and the Constitution, or, at least, it was not a distinction of which *the polity* could be cognizant: the Court is the institutional embodiment of the Constitution. Might this suggest a return to judicial supremacy, solidifying a departmentalist president's constitutional reconstruction?

Congress, the Court, and the Separation of Powers

We might better understand these developments as a feature of reconstruction through the Madisonian Constitution. The Congress has not simply accepted the Court's opinions or, for that matter, Reagan's reconstruction. Nor has the Court simply followed Reagan's reconstruction. To be sure, the Court has not so much led a "'federalism revolution'" as "followed national political trends."[165] But, at the same time, the Court has not followed Reagan's insistence on departmentalism. In fact, every single justice Reagan appointed to the Court, as well as every justice appointed by George H. W. Bush, "faithful son of the Reagan revolution," insists on judicial supremacy. The focus on electoral politics treats Reagan's departmentalism as ancillary to his call for federalism; it is seen, put another way, as mere means because such approaches do not take constitutional thought as primary. Yet, for Reagan, departmentalism was foundational to our constitutionalism and has ramifications for the separation of powers: it calls for all of the branches to accept their constitutional responsibilities as central to the form of constitutional government.

We see a glimmer of this sense of responsibility in Congress's reluctance to simply accept the Court's recent decisions. After the Court struck down the Gun-Free School Zones Act in *Lopez* and Religious Freedom Restoration Act in *Boerne*, Congress refused to let the Court settle the constitutional issue. In passing the Violence against Women Act in 1999, the Congress touched on both of these cases. The act rested on both Congress's commerce power and its power under section 5 of the Fourteenth Amendment. In *Lopez,* the Court had rejected the federal regulation of guns in a school zone as far too tenuously linked to the regulation of interstate commerce. So in passing the Violence against Women Act, Congress compiled a "mountain of data" to show "the effects of violence against women on interstate commerce." Here, Congress was engaging the Court and attempting to work within the contours of its opinion. The Court, as we have seen, rejected Congress's attempt to do this. In the same act, though, Congress did challenge the Court's opinion in *Boerne.* By also resting the Violence against Women Act on its section 5 power, Congress was attempting to define substantive rights under the amendment, which the Court, in *Boerne,* insisted Congress could not do. But even here Congress attempted to engage the Court: it tried to show that these rights were not being preserved in the states, which therefore justified congressional action (something it did not clearly show in the Religious Freedom Restoration Act).

In this, Congress has been ambivalent about the Court's power, at times deferring to the Court or the president, neglecting its role as an independent interpreter of the Constitution. Casting an eye on the contemporary Congress as it confronts constitutional issues, Keith Whittington has suggested that "James Madison has left the building."[166] Congress asserts its power on occasion and refuses to simply follow Court opinions (often flatly ignoring them), but it does not flatly reject the Court's claims to judicial supremacy. At times, Congress even indulges it. This congressional attitude has lead many scholars to argue that the Rehnquist Court, in contrast to earlier courts, has not yet prevented political actors from achieving significant political goals. Rather than acting against the political branches, the Court is following their lead. There is truth to this understanding. But, at the same time, the Rehnquist Court has struck down significant pieces of legislation—not just the Violence against Women Act and Religious Freedom Restoration Act, but the line-item veto and sections of the American's with Disabilities Act. It has also declared actions by the George W. Bush administration unconstitutional or not authorized by congressional statute in a time of war.[167]

The trouble may be the persistent and romantic view of the Court as the lone guardian of the Constitution. Its role has been far more modest, much as the vaunted *Lochner* Court's was, but important nevertheless. Judicial review, as we see here, plays an important part in the separation of powers, often forcing the Congress to confront constitutional issues in a more forthright manner. But it alone does not determine our constitutional fate. Here, the dissenting justices have proved just as overwrought as the Court has in its insistence on judicial supremacy. As Justice Breyer warned,

> An overly restrictive judicial interpretation of the Constitution's structural constraints (unlike its protections of certain basic liberties) will undermine the Constitution's own efforts to achieve its far more basic structural aim, the creation of a representative form of government capable of translating the people's will into effective public action. This understanding, underlying constitutional interpretation since the New Deal, reflects the Constitution's demands for structural flexibility sufficient to adapt substantive laws and institutions to rapidly changing social, economic, and technological conditions.[168]

Yet we may instead leave the putative lessons of 1937 a remnant of the New Deal era. With gay marriage looming as a central issue within the federal scheme, federalism may take on a whole new relevance, beyond even Reagan's imagination. We are, in the meantime, in a state of contentious constitutional debate, but such a state is a familiar one in the American polity.

"In 1937 the Supreme Court began a revolution in jurisprudence that ended, it appeared forever, the reign of laissez-faire and legitimated the arrival of the Leviathan State."[169] Finality, though, is not the language of American constitutionalism. A return to laissez-faire seems unlikely—particularly as it never existed—but we are again drawing a line between national and state authority and, thereby, rejecting the Leviathan state.[170] Reagan, like Tocqueville, saw decentralization as an element that helped maintain constitutional self-government. And Reagan has succeeded in shaping our constitutional culture and discourse to this end. His constitutional reconstruction of the New Deal—playing FDR in reverse—reflects the ebb and flow of constitutional change, rather than the dramatic politics of constitutional transformation. Here we see Reagan's break with the New Deal as well as his affirmation of much of its legacy.[171]

Conclusion

I say that to me it appears that those who damn the tumults
between the nobles and the plebs blame those things that were
the first cause of keeping Rome free, and that they consider
the noises and the cries that would arise in such tumults more
than the good effects that they engendered.

Niccolò Machiavelli

The separations at the heart of the American constitutional order, while bringing to mind the tensions of the mixed polity, are wholly republican. And if the
tumult in America has largely been characterized by discordant constitutional understandings, rather than violence, these tensions can still be seen as complementary to constitutional liberty and self-government. Writing in *Democracy in America,* Alexis de Tocqueville observed, "Scarcely have you descended on the soil of
America when you find yourself in the midst of a sort of tumult; a confused clamor
is raised on all sides; a thousand voices come to your ear at the same time, each of
them expressing some social needs." He then continued in a manner that brings to
mind our constitutional discourse: "Citizens assemble with the sole goal of declaring that they disapprove of the course of government, whereas others gather to
proclaim that the men in place are the fathers of their country."[1] The Madisonian
Constitution seeks to channel such conflict, even foster it; it does not seek to abolish it. To attempt do away with conflict by way of a constitution, rather than insti-
tutionalizing it, would reach beyond the limits of what a constitution could do. The
lesson at the heart of modern constitutionalism recognizes the limits of politics
and, thus, the existence of conflict as an inescapable feature of politics.[2]

The notion that the Constitution was a harmonious machine comes to us
largely from progressives like Woodrow Wilson, who wrote about it as Newton's
mechanical theory of the universe applied to politics.[3] Although Wilson spoke of
frictions in the Newtonian scheme—frictions, however, that were part of "politics
turned into mechanics"—he also insisted that government "is not a body of blind

forces; it is a body of men."[4] Despite Wilson's views, this is precisely what under-pins Madison's willingness to utilize conflict. With some irony, the progressive fostering of democratic tumult was, in fact, a way of overcoming the Madisonian Constitution: it was tumult to forge democratic and evolutionary unity.[5] The progressives' insistence on democracy, in this manner, bears a striking resemblance to Rousseau's emphasis on the sovereign will of the people that challenged the earlier progenitors of modern constitutionalism like Montesquieu.[6] While Wilson himself owed a significant debt to Rousseau's great critic, Edmund Burke, the progressive insistence on democracy unbound by constitutional forms reads like an application of Rousseau's theory of the general will, much as *The Federalist* reads like an application of Montesquieu's theory of the separation of powers. Even Wilson's critique of the separation of powers finds expression in *The Social Contract,* in which Rousseau rejected the notion that sovereignty itself could be divided, taking aim at "separations" in politics altogether: "But our politicians, being unable to divide sovereignty in its principle, divide it in its object. They divide it into force and will, into legislative power and executive power; into rights of taxation, or justice, and of war; into internal administration and foreign relations—sometimes conflating all these branches into a fantastic being, formed of disparate parts; it is as if they created a man from several different bodies, one with eyes, another with arms, another with feet, and nothing else."[7]

If sovereignty cannot be divided according to Rousseau, neither can it be bound: "If, then, the people simply promises to obey, it dissolves itself by that act and loses its character as a people; the moment there is a master, there is no longer a sovereign, and forthwith the body politic is destroyed."[8] What is more, Rousseau presumed a natural harmony between democracy and the good: "the general will is always right and always tends toward the public good."[9] This supposition, too, finds expression in the progressive insistence that constitutional forms cannot legitimately bind the people's will: constitutional development naturally follows the historical development of our national consciousness as it moves in a progressive direction.[10] The sentiment that the Constitution does not bind the people (as opposed to the government) also underlies the efforts of popular constitutionalists.[11] In the hands of popular constitutionalists, democracy becomes primary, as other formal institutions should yield to the people's judgments about constitutional meaning.[12] Larry Kramer explains that constitutionalism is too often seen as working within a particular constitutional order rather than working out that order.[13] There is surely some truth to this. But even in Kramer's able hands, working out the constitutional order seems to become a mere matter of popular expression.

Here we return to Rousseau's general will in a twofold manner. How do we know an authentic expression of popular sovereignty, such that it can alter the written constitution, when we see it?[14] For just as Rousseau's general will is not quite the same as a majority vote, so it is with the people's sovereignty in the hands of progressive and popular constitutionalists.[15] Yet, are there limits to popular sovereignty, in terms of both the formal constitution and the philosophical principles that underlie constitutionalism? These questions cut to the heart of modern constitutionalism: such vexing questions are at the root of *formalizing* politics in a written Constitution. And this constitutional effort does not presuppose a natural harmony in the demos.[16]

Even if we assume that the people are the source of all legitimate constitutional authority, and that we can discern a potentially inscrutable popular will, the Constitution limits how the people may act within the confines of the Constitution they brought to life. As William Harris puts it, "This people may be the author of the text, but it [is] also a textually bounded creature of its own constituent act." To draw this out, Harris offers an illuminating distinction between "The Constitutional People" and the "Sovereign People." The constitutional people, no less than the institutions they call to life, are bound by this constitution. The sovereign people remain "outside" the constitutional order, where they might, in a revolutionary act, alter or abolish this constitutional order.[17] Popular constitutionalists blur this distinction—placing transformative or revolutionary acts of the people within the confines of remaking the existent constitutional order. Thus, the Constitution's meaning can be amended, for them, by "extraordinary" popular acts outside of Article V, or even in the ordinary course of "the people themselves" acting in elections. Popular constitutionalists blur the line not only between constitutional interpretation and constitutional amendment but between interpretation and revolution.[18]

The fact that the Constitution "could say something that it does not now say," indicates the limits and constraints on constitutional meaning and interpretation.[19] If we can change the Constitution's meaning, it has a meaning, or identity, to be changed. By placing democracy by way of popular sovereignty as the essential value, popular constitutionalists dissolve meaningful constitutional limits.[20] At root, they deny that there is a constitutional identity independent of popular sovereignty—or, if there is, it can be remade by the people, effectively making democracy primary to constitutionalism. Thus, popular constitutionalists tend to undo the constitutional—or liberal—elements of our regime.

We might best understand this logic by turning to Walter Murphy's puzzle of an "unconstitutional constitutional amendment." While it is conventional wisdom that the constitutional people, acting within the formal structures of Article V, can alter the Constitution in any manner they wish, this does not so readily follow. As Murphy explains, an amendment that alters the Constitution's identity would not be "amending" it, but, in essence, creating a new Constitution. If we can do this by way of Article V, then the constitutional order can be swallowed whole by popular sovereignty. Even if one accepts popular sovereignty in this vein, and there is good reason to pause before doing so, *within* our constitutional order we still want to distinguish between the people acting in a revolutionary capacity and the people acting in a constitutional capacity. Article V, then, need not create the formal pretext by which the people destroy the Constitution in the guise of amending it.[21] As Murphy argues, "the purpose of the charter and its amendments is to transubstantiate those norms into the political reality of a constitutional order." In this manner, the principles that the Constitution rests upon "limit and control the constitutional text and the entire constitutional order."[22] Viewed in this light, amendments cannot take place outside of Article V, but even within Article V there are limits to constitutional change. Revolutionary change comes outside of the constitutional order in the form of a revolutionary people.

Yet, even when speaking of the revolutionary people, we should note substantive limits on their ability to act legitimately. Recall that the Declaration itself, that great act of a revolutionary people, spoke of our Constitution.[23] Popular sovereignty is one facet of the American amalgam, but unlike Rousseau's version, which "is nothing but the exercise of the general will," it has bounds. The revolution was justified not simply because American sovereignty was being denied—"altering fundamentally the Forms of our Governments"—but because "whenever any Form of Government" becomes destructive of its ends, the people have a right to alter or abolish it. In the Declaration, this revolutionary right is rooted in the natural rights of human beings: to "secure these Rights, Governments are instituted among Men." If the Declaration is America's small "c" constitution, or its constitutional soul, it shapes and potentially limits our large "C" Constitution: there is a limit to what consent, by way of popular sovereignty, can legitimately achieve.[24] Such a limit is evident in the thought of James Wilson, Thomas Jefferson, and James Madison— three of the Founders most frequently turned to in order to justify popular sovereignty as trumping, in various ways, constitutional forms.[25] Interestingly, however, these thinkers argue that even outside of the Constitution, in revolutionary rather than constitutional terms, the people are bound. If consent is necessary to the procedures of government, such procedures are substantively bound by natural rights.

In his first lecture on jurisprudence, Wilson proposed that the "revolutionary principle" ought to be taught "as a principle for the constitution of the United

States," and, during the ratifying conventions, he added that "the truth is, that the supreme absolute and uncontrollable authority, *remains* with the people." Yet Wilson insisted on this point as legitimizing the act of creating a *new* constitution based on the popular authority of the people and not the states. At the end of his speech, he even argued that this unalienable right of the people was illustrated by the Declaration.[26] He then proceeded to quote the second paragraph, where consent legitimizes power because it obligates government to recognize unalienable rights. These unalienable individual rights are the basis of self-government by way of consent.

In a similar manner, Jefferson insisted, again and again, that "the earth belongs to the living" and, thus, that each generation has "a right to choose for itself the form of government it believes most promotive of its own happiness."[27] Jefferson, though, also spoke of natural right as limiting what any generation acting as popular sovereign can do. It was Jefferson's Declaration, after all, that Abraham Lincoln appealed to in arguing that slavery was not something that could legitimately be decided on the grounds of popular sovereignty.[28] And even when Madison claimed that the people are the best protectors of their rights, he denied the "majority is the standard of right and wrong." Rather, Madison spoke of rights as prior to and binding upon civil society.[29] I do not wish to labor over the intricacies of these thinkers, so much as to suggest that even in *creating* a constitutional order, they tended to draw on a combination of popular sovereignty and natural rights, with the latter, at the very least, tempering and limiting the reach of the former, which would ineluctably shape the form our written constitution could take. Thus, popular sovereignty, even outside the formal Constitution, existed within a foundation and was distinct from popular will.

We have, as I have endeavored to show, conflicted over the proper balance between liberalism and democracy within our constitutional order. Yet, in canvassing such disputes, which have inevitably shaped how we see the Constitution, I have attempted to maintain a distinction between the Constitution in thought and the Constitution on the ground.[30] Key to this distinction, banal as it may sound, is that constitutional meaning is distinct and separate from whatever expression it is actually given in the politics of the day.[31] This distinction is, admittedly, one that can be difficult to puzzle out.[32] Still, the Constitution does not mean whatever happens to come out of the separation of powers or elections. The president, the Congress, and the people themselves—even if they do come together—can be wrong about constitutional meaning in the same manner that the Court can be. The constitution as it exists on the ground may well be at odds with the Constitution. This distinction is worth keeping in mind lest the Constitution be seen as whatever happens to exist at a particular time—captured by the "live hand of the present"—which would be an ever-changing constitution devoid of meaning or identity.[33]

And yet it may be that constitutional meaning is forged in the interaction between general constitutional principles and particular political and historical circumstances. This is not to say that whatever comes out of our historical debates is constitutional meaning—that is, the Constitution as history.[34] Nor, though, is it to say that whatever meaning comes out of these great debates is constitutional *development*—that is, the Constitution as History.[35] Rather, it is to offer a far more tentative suggestion. The Constitution was meant to create an order that would endure for ages to come. Inevitably, sustaining this order would require the application of its principles to changing, and unforeseen, historical circumstances. As Edmund Burke said, in looking to the form of a commonwealth, "it may be obliged to pass, as one of our poets says, 'through great varieties of untried being,' and in all its transmigrations to be purified by fire and blood."[36] The poet was Joseph Addison, and it happens that Burke was quoting from *Cato: A Tragedy,* about the failure of preserving the Roman Republic. It also happens that *Cato* was a favorite of George Washington. Perhaps not surprisingly, we find a similar sentiment expressed in Washington's Farewell Address, which is preoccupied with preserving the American experiment, "In all the changes to which you may be invited, remember that time and habit are at least as necessary to fix the true character of Governments, as of other human institutions; that experience is the surest standard, by which to test the real tendency of the existing Constitution of a country[.]"[37]

As I have argued throughout this book, conflicts over constitutional meaning and authority, rooted in the separation of powers, may well lead us to reflect more seriously about the Constitution. In this manner, the Constitution might truly be said to be dialogic rather than agonistic. Historical changes force us to unfold the implications of the Constitution's fixed principles if it is to endure for ages to come without opening itself to "perpetual change."[38] If so, we must hold out the corollary. If constitutional judgment and reflection are essential to maintaining and realizing the Constitution—precisely so that it does not become whatever the people, courts, or political branches say it is—this inevitably opens us up to various forms of constitutional failure.[39]

As a polity, we might drift from constitutional meaning, which also raises the central question of how binding the Madisonian Constitution is. There is often, as I have argued, a disharmonic gap between constitutional ends and constitutional enforcement. Words are not always translated into deeds. This gap is most evident in our failure to realize the commitment of the Civil War amendments as they applied to blacks for nearly a century after their ratification. But this is surely not the only failure to translate constitutional meaning into constitutional deeds, or lapse from foundational constitutional understandings, as the erasure of the Ninth Amendment and its underlying logic illustrates. At the same time, the contentious struggles over constitutional meaning and authority that we have witnessed are about what the Constitution is and how, then, we are obligated by it. The Constitution is not coterminous with justice or the good—even if, in Noah Webster's phrase, it invented an "empire of reasons."[40] Nor, of course, is it an oracle. To insist upon its autonomy, so to speak, is to take the constitutional enterprise seriously. The Constitution creates a space between the people and the government, and then within the government itself, where constitutional principles can be taken seriously. It creates a space for constitutional statesmanship even if the Constitution does not depend on it.[41] But this space is created by a diffusion of power that refuses to repose trust in any "one center."[42] And this space between thought and practice gives us a critical perspective on practice itself that may help sustain the written Constitution. Thus, even if we accepted the claims of judicial supremacy, a precondition to thinking, arguing, and making sense of the Court is understanding the Constitution independently of Court decisions. To begin to make sense of how the Court has acted, we need to have a sense of constitutional meaning—we need to render, that is, constitutional judgment.[43]

Consider the case of *Brown v. the Board of Education*, a case that is frequently called to the bar as evidence that judicial supremacy is essential to constitutionalism. Intriguingly, *Brown* has become a touchstone for questions of constitutional interpretation, despite the fact that Chief Justice Warren's reasoning has few defenders.[44] To the contrary, there is a wide consensus that the reasoning put forward in *Brown* was unpersuasive on the constitutional issues, even if the result it reached was constitutionally justified—indeed, mandated. As a polity we have come to reason that state-mandated racial segregation is inconsistent with constitutional principle. In doing so, we have essentially rewritten the constitutional logic of *Brown*, discarding the opinion's narrow focus on education in relation to equal protection and its foundations in psychological feelings of inferiority.[45] Traveling a great distance from the historical *Brown*, we have refashioned the opinion, rooting it in constitutional principles, to speak to racial segregation per se. As the *New York Times* put it in the wake of *Brown:* Justice Harlan's lone dissent in *Plessy* has effectively become "the law of the land." In fact, this revision speaks to a general sense of the harmful and arbitrary nature of racial segregation, which resonates much more with *Bolling v. Sharpe*, which I discussed in the preceding chapter, and of which scholars have been conspicuously silent, than it does with *Brown*. After all, *Brown* has been taken by the polity to have overturned *Plessy v. Ferguson* and the doctrine of "separate but equal" when it did not.[46] Needless to say, we did not arrive at such an understanding overnight. Rather, *Brown* ultimately provoked a profound debate about the meaning and application of constitutional principle far beyond segregation in state schools.

A number of state legislatures went so far as to formally nullify the Court's decision as unconstitutional. Many southern representative and senators signed on to the "The Southern Manifesto: A Declaration of Constitutional Principles," which rejected *Brown* as an "unwarranted decision" that was "contrary to the Constitution."[47] Resistance to the Court's opinion, particularly as it moved beyond schools without explanation, was widespread in the South. This atavistic reaction, as it has been dubbed, pushed the constitutional question on the country. Such resistance moved President Eisenhower, who had quietly signed off on the government's brief urging the Court to overturn *Plessy,* to publicly enforce the decision by mobilizing force against southern resistance. It is not overreaching to suggest that this conflict, which called forth passionate defenses of racial segregation, moved much of the country to the conclusion that state-mandated racial segregation was at odds with the Constitution.[48] We can also trace the passage of the Civil Rights Act of 1964 and the Voting Rights Act of 1965, breathing life into the Civil War amendments, to this constitutional conflict, which revisited the conflicts of the post–Civil War era.[49] Fifty years after *Brown,* the reach of these debates persists within the contours of the Madisonian Constitution in regard to affirmative action, to take but a single example.[50] This sketch belies the Court's insistence, in the midst of this conflict, that judicial supremacy is "a permanent and indispensable feature of our constitutional system."[51]

And yet it is on just this issue that Congress equivocates, as I noted in the close of chapter 2. This equivocation is evident in the Senate confirmation hearings of John Roberts to be chief justice. In his opening statement, now Chief Justice Roberts likened his role to that of an umpire. This metaphor recast, in a manner, the dilemma we see in Chief Justice Marshall's famous *Marbury* opinion, illuminating how the judiciary sits somewhat uneasily within the constitutional scheme. On the one hand, this description comported well with the modest role of a judge as not having will. On the other, playing umpire for the entire constitutional order situates the judge outside of the constitutional order. Judges thereby rule the constitutional order indirectly by determining and guiding its meaning. In Madison's language, this role makes one of the centers of power sovereign. In a move that does not easily comport with constitutional language, Congress—one of the participants in the constitutional order—is allowed to alter, in the vast majority of cases, what sort of issues the Court may hear. If we use Chief Justice Roberts's metaphor, this is the equivalent of allowing a "player" in the game to determine the sort of calls an "umpire" can make. Such clear constitutional language would seem, at the very least, to call into question the insistence that the Court is the umpire of the constitutional order. Roberts was pushed on this very issue:

SENATOR BROWNBACK: There is also another area that you wrote about when you were working within the Reagan administration. That was the ability of Congress to limit the authority and the review of the courts, of what you would have. And I want to look at that in particular. It's the power to define jurisdiction that we would have. It's in Article III, Section 2. And I just want to read this because I don't think it's well understood as the check and balance, and I want to get your reaction to it.

This is Article III, Section 2. "In all cases affecting ambassadors, other public ministers, councils and those in which a state may be a party, the Supreme Court shall have original jurisdiction." No question there. It goes on: "In all the other cases before mentioned, the Supreme Court shall have appellate jurisdiction both as to law and fact, with such exceptions and under such regulations as the Congress shall make."

This last phrase, as you know, is known as the exceptions clause. You wrote about this when you were in the Reagan White House, about this exception clause, and you stated this: "It stands as a plenary grant of power to Congress to make exceptions to the appellate jurisdiction of the Supreme Court. The clause by its terms contains no limit"—these are your words—and, quote, "this clear and unequivocal language is the strongest argument in favor of congressional power, and the inevitable stumbling block for those who would read the clause in a more restrictive fashion." Now, I understand that you also argued on policy grounds this is not a good idea for the Congress to do, but would you agree with those earlier statements that you made about the nature of this power being a plenary power of the Congress and stands as a clear standard in favor of the Congress to be able to limit the jurisdiction of the courts?

JUDGE ROBERTS: Well, you know, Senator, that that writing was done at the request of the attorney general, and he asked me specifically to present the arguments in favor of that power. He was receiving from elsewhere in the department a memorandum saying that this was unconstitutional, the exercise of that authority. He wanted to see the other view before making up his mind for the department.

So I was tasked to present the arguments in favor of constitutionality. And as you say, they focused and start with the language in the Constitution, the exceptions clause, which is as you read it. And I went on to explain that it had been interpreted in the famous case of Ex Parte McCardle around the time of the Civil War, which seemed to suggest that the Framers meant what that language says on its face. Also, though, a later case, United States against Klein, suggested that there were limits on the power of Congress in this area. It is a central debate among legal scholars, the scope of that authority.

The argument on the other side, the one that the attorney general adopted rather than the argument he asked me to present, is that it is the essential function of the Supreme Court to provide uniformity and consistency in federal law, and that if you carve out exceptions in its core constitutional area, that you deprive it of that ability, and that that itself violates the constitutional scheme.

It's an area in which most distinguished scholars line up on either side because it does call into question basic relationships between the Congress and the courts. But now the—

SEN. BROWNBACK: Could that language be any clearer, though, in the exceptions clause?

JUDGE ROBERTS: Well—

SEN. BROWNBACK: I mean, I understand how legal scholars maybe can debate what a single word means, but that language is pretty clear, isn't it?

JUDGE ROBERTS: The argument on the other side says that it's intended to apply to—well, for example, we have clear situations in the lower federal courts like the amount in controversy; those cases are excluded. You can have rules about timing, you know. The question is whether it was intended to address core constitutional areas or simply more administrative matters. The argument on the other side says if you get into the core constitutional areas, that undermines the Supreme Court's authority; that the Framers didn't intend that.

SEN. BROWNBACK: Then what check is there on the court's power?

JUDGE ROBERTS: Well, I think the primary check is the same one that Alexander Hamilton talked about in "The Federalist Papers," because the exact argument was raised in the debates about the Constitution. People were concerned about a new judiciary; what was it going to do. They were concerned that it might deprive them of their rights. And of course, Hamilton's famous answer was the judiciary was going to be the "least dangerous" branch because it had no power; it didn't have the sword, it didn't have the purse, and the judges were not going to be able to deprive people of their liberty because they were going to be bound down by rules and precedents; they were going to just interpret the law, and if judges just interpreted the law, there was no threat to liberty from the judicial branch.

So I would say the primary check on the courts has always been judicial self-restraint and a recognition on the part of judges that they have a limited task; that they are insulated from the people. They're given life tenure, as you mentioned, precisely because they're not shaping policy; they're not supposed to be responsive, they're supposed to just interpret the law.[52]

The senators did not push Chief Justice Roberts further on this pressing question, but rather, in accord with Roberts's own understanding, searched for legal means to bind and tether judicial will: the check on judicial will comes largely from the judge. We search, then, for ways to get the judge to tether himself or herself to the mast, as a would-be Odysseus. If we find just the right solution—the proper theory of precedent, judicial restraint, a judge sympathetic to the flight of ordinary people, or the proper theory of constitutional interpretation—then we will succeed in binding the judge. All of these issues are important and ought, properly, to be discussed in Senate hearings and beyond. But they are not foundational insofar as they require judges to bind themselves—something the Constitution refuses to do for all other constitutional actors—and thus leave them outside, if not above, the Constitution. The modest and impartial role of the judge becomes the means whereby he or she rules the constitutional order by defining it; it is, in fact, impartiality that underlies the claim to rule. Yet they cannot tell us how they would define the constitutional order, because doing so would negate their impartiality and hence their claim to "umpire" the order.[53]

This perplexity is a result of reducing the whole constitutional order to "law" explicated by the Court. If a legal mind-set is proper for the judiciary within the constitutional scheme, the scheme itself cannot be captured as "higher" ordinary law. The diffusion of powers constitutionalizes conflicts and tensions, providing the space within which constitutional arguments—including constitutional law— take shape. To take a prominent issue that persistently recurs, we might turn to disputes between the executive and legislature over issues of war and peace that have aptly been characterized as an invitation to struggle.[54] It is also an area in which the Court has not seen fit to play "umpire," despite invitations to do so.[55] Rather, the Constitution has given rise to debates about the reach of executive power in necessitous circumstances against the lawmaking authority of Congress. Rival claims have been staked out since nearly the inception of the Constitution. In 1792 President Washington's Neutrality Proclamation found Alexander Hamilton and James Madison, collaborators as Publius in *The Federalist*, at odds with one another on the reach of executive power in the constitutional order. Hamilton, from the executive branch, insisted as Pacificus that the declaration of neutrality was properly part of "the executive power," even as it nullified a section of a treaty with France that had been approved by the Senate, noting a "concurrent" right to expound on the Constitution.[56] Madison, then a representative in Congress, claimed that Hamilton's argument, "under colour of vindicating an important public act," advanced principles of executive prerogative "which strike at the vitals of [our] constitution."[57] Even while denying that the executive could reach a power *vested solely* with the legislature, Madison insisted that the independent departments, in "the exercise of their functions, interpret the constitution differently, and thence lay claim each to the same power. This difference of opinion," Madison continued, "is an inconvenience not entirely to be avoided. It results from what may be called, if it be thought fit, a *concurrent* right to expound the constitution."[58]

In this manner, the Constitution may be said to constitutionalize this debate. While Madison insisted that the constitutional question was clear, that Hamilton's reading imported an alien understanding of prerogative into the Constitution, recourse was to come from congressional resistance to the executive: the separation of power provides for an independent executive but also provides for limits and checks on the executive by way of Congress.[59] The Constitution watches over and nourishes this dynamic.[60] The constitutional separation of powers—the form of each institution—may also shape the outlook of the actors. Fast-forward to the modern incarnation of this debate: the War Powers Act of 1973, which by congressional statute provides the executive with authority to act in an emergency, while insisting on congressional approval within a short period of time to stay the executive's hand. It is perhaps not a coincidence that every president since the passage of the War Powers Act, following Hamilton from the executive branch, has rejected it as an unconstitutional intrusion on the executive power. And its many defenders in Congress, following Madison from that same branch, insist on its constitutionality, even while authorizing particular executive actions.[61] And such defenses persist, despite the fact that the Supreme Court has declared the legislative mechanism by which Congress would invoke the War Powers Act unconstitutional.[62]

In Madisonian terms, such conflicts are never-ending: they have persisted since the founding and will remain with us long into the twenty-first century.[63] This fact does not absolve us of constitutional judgment. It points, rather, to the importance of thought in fostering and sustaining a constitutional mind-set. Return to the Pacificus-Helvidius exchange between Hamilton and Madison where this mind-set is on display, much as it was in *The Federalist*.[64] Both Hamilton and Madison rooted their arguments in the Constitution and brought them forward in a manner so as to defend and justify their particular actions, reaching out to persuade others of their constitutional logic. In so doing, both saw fit to flex their wit on the whole of the Constitution: this debate sought to instruct the polity as both Hamilton and Madison rooted their particular interpretations within the overarching logic of the whole constitutional order. We might draw this lesson: how we think about the

Constitution matters, as it may shape whether or not we think constitutionally. Is it a coincidence that neither Hamilton nor Madison saw fit to refer to the judiciary in the midst of this constitutional quarrel?[65]

In discussing the political foundations of judicial supremacy, a leading scholar of American constitutional development has illustrated how the "Court has not taken the Constitution away from the people. The Constitution has often been entrusted to the hands of the judges, if not by the people themselves, then at least by their elected representatives."[66] While Keith Whittington acknowledges that this delegation raises possible normative concerns, which he has written on to great effect, he also suggests that it "is not obvious, however, that our democratic politics would be better absent the temptation to judicial supremacy."[67] This conclusion is less clear. Insofar as it reminds us that democracy is bound and tempered by liberal elements, it could be of great value, even if in largely symbolic terms. But judicial review alone provides for this effect. In contrast, judicial supremacy fosters a mind-set that distorts our constitutionalism, even if it is partly rooted in the practical political choices of the representative branches. Lord Keynes claimed that practical statesmen, driven only by real-world concerns and not the higher reaches of the intellect, are usually the slaves of some now defunct academic scribbler.[68] In this manner, digesting the idea of judicial supremacy indulges the Court's distorted view of the constitutional order, indulges Congress and the president in irresponsibly neglecting their duty of forthright constitutional judgment, and distorts the people's understanding of American constitutionalism. The result flattens our constitutionalism.

How we think about the Constitution ineluctably frames the landscape within which we operate. Recovering a sense that the president and the Congress, no less than judges, have a duty and an obligation to reach constitutional judgments could help cultivate this state of mind. To do so entails a responsibility on the part of the president and Congress to justify their actions in constitutional terms (and not merely take refuge in the Court). Such constitutional judgments can also be a healthy reminder that judges are not the peculiar custodians of the Constitution.

Drawing out the implications of this lesson might also inform our seemingly endless attempts to limit the Court. It would be far better to contain the judiciary—just as we do the other branches—within the confines of the Madisonian system by refusing to be bound by it, if we think it has misinterpreted or distorted the Constitution. After all, when Alexander Hamilton claimed in *Federalist* 78 that the judiciary had neither force nor will, he was speaking of the fact that its authority depends on its judgment, which depends on the will and force of the executive. Refusing to follow in broad terms what amounts to unsound judgment, or refusing to follow it in passing future legislation, is to act within the constitutional scheme. In just this manner, neither of these branches could instruct the Court on how to render decisions before it. The Court is obligated by the Constitution, just as the other branches are. The obligation to the Constitution is also where the other branches have, at the ready, ways of resisting judicial supremacy (even while insisting on an independent judiciary). Let me repair to the words Edmund Burke put forward to the British Colonists of North America, offering a sort of symmetry as I come near the close, as this book began with his words: "But we are well assured from experience, that even if all were true that were contended for, and in the extent, too, in which it is argued, yet as long as the solid and well-disposed forms of this constitution remain, there ever is within . . . itself the power of renovating its principles, and effecting a self-reformation[.]"[69]

If the result is a constitutional conflict, such conflict may indeed be a virtue in sustaining the Constitution.[70] It is certainly at the heart of American constitutionalism. Seeing the Constitution in a more political light should not denigrate it or reduce constitutionalism to politics in a crass sense. Rather, recognizing that contests over constitutional meaning are, at root, about deep political choices should restore to politics—in all of its complexity and tension—the dignity it deserves. To see the Constitution in a more political light is to recover a more traditional understanding of constitution; it is to see how our Constitution constitutes our political life. Recovering such a view may even give us a deeper sense of ourselves as a polity, illuminating the ways in which the Constitution shapes our politics and, in turn, is shaped by them.

Introduction

1. Gordon Wood, *Creation of the American Republic* (Chapel Hill: University of North Carolina Press, 1998 [1969]), 281, and Sylvia Snowiss, *Judicial Review and the Law of the Constitution* (New Haven: Yale University Press, 1990).

2. Edward S. Corwin, "Marbury v. Madison and the Doctrine of Judicial Review," *Michigan Law Review* 12 (1914): 538–72.

3. Charles McIlwain, *Constitutionalism: Ancient and Modern* (Ithaca: Cornell University Press, 1947), 140.

4. *Planned Parenthood v. Casey,* 505 U.S. 833, 868 (1992). See also *City of Boerne v. Flores,* 521 U.S. 507, 529 (1997); *United States v. Nixon,* 418 U.S. 683 (1974); *Powell v. McCormack,* 395 U.S. 486 (1969); *Baker v. Carr,* 369 U.S. 186 (1962); *Cooper v. Aaron,* 358 U.S. 1, 18 (1958).

5. See especially Larry Alexander and Frederick Schauer, "On Extrajudicial Constitutional Interpretation," *Harvard Law Review* 110, no. 7 (1997): 1359–87, and "Defending Judicial Supremacy: A Reply," *Constitutional Commentary* 17 (2000): 455–82. In contrast, see especially the scholarship of the "Princeton School" taking its bearings from Walter F. Murphy. Essays by some of the leading scholars in this group are gathered in Robert P. George and Sotirios A. Barber, eds., *Constitutional Politics: Essays on Constitution Making, Maintenance, and Change* (Princeton: Princeton University Press, 2001). But this tendency is true beyond American constitutionalism. Comparative constitutional theorists even search for a moment where constitutionalism itself is solidified with the articulation, exercise, and entrenchment of judicial review. See Gordon Silverstein, "Globalization and the Rule of Law: A Machine That Runs of Itself?" *I-Con* 1, no. 3 (2003): 427–45. In a similar vein, we have begun to hear about the emergence of global constitutionalism, the defining feature of which is a transnational judiciary with universal jurisdiction capable of overcoming the inconvenient attachments of particular constitutions and enforcing "global constitutional norms." For a constitutional critique of this view, see Jeremy A. Rabkin, *Law without Nations? Why Constitutional Government Requires Sovereign States* (Princeton: Princeton University Press, 2005).

6. This view also takes root in the work of prominent and empirically grounded political scientists. Leading political scientist Gregory Caldaria, for example, lists judicial supremacy

as the correct answer to "Who is the final interpreter of the Constitution?" in a public opinion survey. Caldaria, "Courts and Public Opinion," in John B. Gates and Charles A. Johnson, eds., *The American Courts: A Critical Assessment* (Washington, DC: Congressional Quarterly Press, 1990). H. W. Perry Jr. and L. A. Powe Jr., "The Political Battle for the Constitution," *Constitutional Commentary* 21 (2004): 641–96; H. W. Perry, *Deciding to Decide: Agenda Setting in the United States Supreme Court* (Cambridge: Harvard University Press, 1991); Michael Comiskey, *Seeking Justices: The Judging of Supreme Court Nominees* (Lawrence: University Press of Kansas, 2004) (all rest on the assumption, made explicit, that judicial confirmation battles are so contested because the Court is the final interpreter of the Constitution).

7. See Scott Gordon, *Controlling the State: Constitutionalism from Ancient Athens to Today* (Cambridge: Harvard University Press, 1999), and Mark Blitz, *Duty Bound: Responsibility and American Public Life* (Lanham, MD: Rowman and Littlefield, 2005), 32–36, on the diffusion of the separation of powers as characteristic of liberal democracy. See also David Brian Robertson, *The Constitution and America's Destiny* (New York: Cambridge University Press, 2005), who persuasively argues that Roger Sherman has equal title to this claim.

8. Stanley C. Brubaker, "The Court as Astigmatic Schoolmarm: A Case for the Clear-Sighted Citizen," in Bradford P. Wilson and Ken Masugi, eds., *The Supreme Court and American Constitutionalism* (Lanham, MD: Rowman and Littlefield, 1999), offers the wonderful metaphor of the view from the Court as astigmatic.

9. Walter Murphy, "Who Shall Interpret? The Quest for the Ultimate Constitutional Interpreter," *Review of Politics* 48, no. 3 (1986): 401–23, and *Constitutional Democracy: Creating and Maintaining a Just Political Order* (Baltimore: Johns Hopkins University Press, 2007), 463–71. I do not think that the diffusion of powers in the federal government captures the whole of constitutional maintenance; indeed, insofar as the Constitution rests upon the compound of liberal democracy, much of what is required to sustain the constitutional enterprise takes places wholly outside of official constitutional channels. See especially Charles R. Kesler, "Federalist 10 and American Republicanism," in Kesler, ed., *Saving the Revolution: The Federalist Papers and the American Founding* (New York: Free Press, 1986), 13–39, and Thomas L. Pangle, *The Ennobling of Democracy: The Challenge of the Postmodern Age* (Baltimore: Johns Hopkins University Press, 1992), on how liberal democracy might benefit from features of classic republicanism in sustaining itself. See also Wayne Moore, *Constitutional Rights and Powers of the People* (Princeton: Princeton University Press, 1996), and John E. Finn, "The Civic Constitution: Some Preliminaries," in Barber and George, *Constitutional Politics,* on civic constitutionalism beyond official governmental channels.

10. I follow Murphy's formulation of "what" the Constitution is in speaking to its nature. *Constitutional Democracy,* 185–240.

11. William F. Harris II, *The Interpretable Constitution* (Baltimore: Johns Hopkins University Press, 1993), 46–83.

12. John Agresto, *The Supreme Court and Constitutional Democracy* (Ithaca: Cornell University Press, 1984).

13. Alexander Hamilton, James Madison, and John Jay, *The Federalist Papers,* introduction and notes by Charles R. Kesler, ed. Clinton Rossiter (New York: Signet Classics, 1999), 281.

14. On departmentalism, see Murphy, "Who Shall Interpret?"; Agresto, *The Supreme*

Court and Constitutional Democracy; Gary J. Jacobsohn, *The Supreme Court and the Decline of Constitutional Aspiration* (Lanham, MD: Rowman and Littlefield, 1986); Sanford Levinson, *Constitutional Faith* (Princeton: Princeton University Press, 1989); Keith E. Whittington, *Constitutional Construction: Divided Powers and Constitutional Meaning* (Cambridge: Harvard University Press, 1999), and "Extrajudicial Constitutional Interpretation: Three Objections and Responses," *North Carolina Law Review* 80, no. 3 (March 2002): 773–851; Susan Burgess, *Contest for Constitutional Authority* (Lawrence: University Press of Kansas, 1992); Finn, "The Civic Constitution." Keith Whittington has also referred to the political Constitution, but he draws a distinction between interpretation and construction that, partly, tends to reinforce the Court's connection with the (legal) Constitution; see *Constitutional Interpretation: Textual Meaning, Original Intent, and Judicial Review* (Lawrence: University Press of Kansas, 1999). This is perhaps most evident in Whittington's *The Political Foundations of Judicial Supremacy: The Presidency, the Supreme Court, and Constitutional Leadership in U.S. History* (Princeton: Princeton University Press, 2007). There Whittington gives tacit approval to some version of judicial supremacy insofar as it is rooted in the political choices of the more "democratic" branches of government.

15. Neal Devins, *Shaping Constitutional Values: Elected Government, the Supreme Court and the Abortion Debate* (Baltimore: Johns Hopkins University Press, 1996); Neal Devins and Louis Fisher, *The Democratic Constitution* (New York: Oxford University Press, 2004); and Louis Fisher, *Constitutional Dialogues: Interpretation as Political Process* (Princeton: Princeton University Press, 1988).

16. Madison would have put this as a "preface" to the Constitution along with the Bill of Rights woven throughout the text, making this sentiment textually explicit, though even here the people, arguably, would be bound by natural rights and reason and thus not sovereign in a Rousseauian sense. Jean-Jacques Rousseau, *The Social Contract and the First and Second Discourses* (New Haven: Yale University Press, 2002), 170.

17. See Fisher and Devins, *The Democratic Constitution,* and Sanford Levinson, *Our Undemocratic Constitution* (New York: Oxford University Press, 2006). On the character of liberal democracy and the separation of powers, see Blitz, *Duty Bound,* 25–51.

18. Hamilton et al., *The Federalist Papers,* Nos. 49 and 55, 312, 340. See also James W. Ceaser, *Liberal Democracy and Political Science* (Baltimore: Johns Hopkins University Press, 1990), and Walter F. Murphy, "Constitutions, Constitutionalism, and Democracy," in Douglas Greenberg, Stanley Katz, et al., eds., *Constitutionalism and Democracy* (New York: Oxford University Press, 1993), 3–25, discussing liberal democracy or constitutional democracy as a compound form of government.

19. Ceaser, *Liberal Democracy and Political Science,* 18.

20. Sotirios A. Barber, *On What the Constitution Means* (Baltimore: Johns Hopkins University Press, 1984), 180. See also Pierre Manent, *A World beyond Politics? A Defense of the Nation-State* (Princeton: Princeton University Press, 2006) (on the various "organization of separations" as key to liberal democracy), and Sheldon Wolin, *The Presence of the Past: Essays on the State and the Constitution* (Baltimore: Johns Hopkins University Press, 1990), 100–119 (for a critique of reason in *The Federalist*). Daryl J. Levinson and Richard H. Pildes, "Separation of Parties, Not Powers," *Harvard Law Review* 119 (2006): 2311, argue that the separation of powers has never really worked in this manner. For a compelling argument that it has, see

Joseph M. Bessette, *The Mild Voice of Reason: Deliberative Democracy and American National Government* (Chicago: University of Chicago Press, 1994).

21. Joseph Story, *Commentaries on the Constitution* (Durham: Carolina Academic Press, 1987 [1833]), 128.

22. See especially, Mark Tushnet, *Taking the Constitution Away from the Court* (Princeton: Princeton University Press, 1999), 191. Bruce Ackerman, *We the People: Transformations* (Cambridge: Harvard University Press, 1998), argues for "dualist democracy," which is explicitly antifoundationalist and allows the people, in unconventional acts, to transform the Constitution in unlimited ways. Larry Kramer, *The People Themselves: Popular Constitutionalism and Judicial Review* (New York: Oxford University Press, 2004), also urges the people to follow FDR and make the Constitution, once again, "a layman's instrument of government," where the Court should yield to the people's judgments about what the Constitution means. All of these scholars have written, often brilliantly, on constitutional development and the problems of constitutional enforcement. But, in the end, they all advocate some form of popular sovereignty which can easily trump the written Constitution. For a more extensive critique of popular constitutionalism, see George Thomas, "Popular Constitutionalism: The New Living Constitutionalism," *Studies in Law, Politics, and Society* 44 (2008): 75–107.

23. Hamilton et al., *The Federalist Papers,* No. 47, 269. See also Niccolò Machiavelli, *Discourses on Livy,* trans. Harvey C. Mansfield and Nathan Tarcov (Chicago: University of Chicago Press, 1996), I, preface.

24. Bryan Garsten, *Saving Persuasion: A Defense of Rhetoric and Judgment* (Cambridge: Harvard University Press, 2006), 208. See also Moore, *Constitutional Rights and Powers of the People,* arguing that multiple perspectives may exist outside of "official" constitutional channels. This point is vividly brought home by Madison in a letter to Jefferson, when he insisted that these political devices for maintaining the Constitution might fail: these mechanisms "are neither the sole nor the chief palladium of constitutional liberty. The people, who are the authors of this blessing, must also be its guardians." Quoted in Lance Banning, *Jefferson and Madison: Three Conversations from the Founding* (Madison, WI: Madison House, 1995), 21.

25. See Robert F. Nagel, *Constitutional Cultures: The Mentality and Consequences of Judicial Review* (Berkeley: University Press of California, 1989), 12–17, and Barber, *On What the Constitution Means,* 15–16.

26. Gary Jeffrey Jacobsohn, *Apple of Gold: Constitutionalism in Israel and the United States* (Princeton: Princeton University Press, 1993), 115. For the tensions within this framework, often played out in party politics rather than Court decisions, see Ken Kersch, *Constructing Civil Liberties: Discontinuities in American Constitutional Law* (New York: Cambridge University Press, 2004); Rogan Kersh, *Dreams of a More Perfect Union* (Ithaca: Cornell University Press, 2001); and Sidney Milkis, *Political Parties and Constitutional Government: Remaking American Democracy* (Baltimore: Johns Hopkins University Press, 1999). See also Robert A. Burt, *The Constitution in Conflict* (Cambridge: Harvard University Press, 1992).

27. Hamilton et al., *The Federalist Papers,* 282. Such a faith, or prejudice, is not necessarily incompatible with reason and may, if properly balanced, help sustain liberal democracy.

See Alexis de Tocqueville, *Democracy in America*, trans. Harvey C. Mansfield and Delba Winthrop (Chicago: University of Chicago Press, 2000) vol. 2, i, ch. 2.

28. Randy Barnett, *Restoring the Lost Constitution: The Presumption of Liberty* (Princeton: Princeton University Press, 2004), 105. As Sanford Levinson puts it, "To reject the ultimate authority of the Supreme Court is not in the least to reject the binding authority of the Constitution, but only to argue that the Court is to be judged by the Constitution itself rather than the other way around." Levinson, *Constitutional Faith,* 43. See also Barber, *On What the Constitution Means,* 13.

29. Thomas Hobbes, *A Dialogue between a Philosopher and a Student of the Common Laws of England* (Chicago: University of Chicago Press, 1971). See especially James R. Stoner Jr., *Common Law and Liberal Theory: Coke, Hobbes, and the Origins of American Constitutionalism* (Lawrence: University of Kansas Press, 1994). See also Gary McDowell, "The Language of Law and the Foundations of American Constitutionalism," *William and Mary Quarterly* 55, no. 3 (1998): 375–98, and "Coke, Corwin and the Constitution: The 'Higher Law Background' Reconsidered," *Review of Politics* 55, no. 3 (1993) 393–420; and Walter Berns, "Judicial Review and the Rights and Laws of Nature," *The Supreme Court Review, 1982* (Chicago: University of Chicago Press, 1983). Justice Hugo Black inverted this position, insisting that a written constitution was necessary for judges to bind themselves.

30. *Eakin v. Raub,* 12 Sergeant & Rawle 330 (1825), 62.

31. *Eakin* at 356.

32. Ackerman argues that the Constitution is a "dualist-democracy" rather than "rights-foundationalist," so the "hyper" formalist Article V does not apply to constitutional transformation when the people themselves speak. *We the People: Transformations,* 15–17. In Walter Murphy's formulation, popular constitutionalists might be best described as pushing for representative democracy, not constitutional democracy. The former, Murphy suggests, is all about procedure, whereas the later rests on substance limits that cannot be altered. "Who Shall Interpret?" 402–3.

33. Hamilton et al., *The Federalist Papers,* No. 51, 290.

34. Abraham Lincoln, "First Inaugural Address," in Gore Vidal, ed., *Lincoln: Selected Speeches and Writings* (New York: Vintage Books, 1992), 291. See also John E. Finn, "Transformation or Transmogrification? Ackerman, Hobbes (as in Calvin and Hobbes), and the Puzzle of Changing Constitutional Identity," *Constitutional Political Economy* 10 (1999): 355–65.

35. James Madison to Daniel Webster (1833), in Philip B. Kurland and Ralph Lerner, eds., *The Founders' Constitution,* vol. 1 (Indianapolis: Liberty Fund, 1987), 94. We should also note that reason and nature in the form of natural rights were seen to be limits on the sovereign authority of the people, giving it a Lockean foundation, rather than one in Rousseau's "General Will." See also Stanley C. Brubaker, "The Countermajoritarian Difficulty: Tradition versus Original Meaning," in Kenneth D. Ward and Cecilia R. Castillo, eds., *The Judiciary and American Democracy: Alexander Bickel, the Countermajoritarian Difficulty, and Contemporary Constitutional Theory* (Albany: SUNY Press, 2005), 105–22.

36. Gary Jeffrey Jacobsohn, "Constitutional Identity," *Review of Politics* 68 (2006): 361–97.

37. Jeffrey K. Tulis, *The Rhetorical Presidency* (Princeton: Princeton University Press,

1987), 17. See also Ken I. Kersch and Ronald Kahn, introduction to Kersch and Kahn, eds., *The Supreme Court and American Political Development* (Lawrence: University Press of Kansas, 2006), 1–30.

38. Harvey C. Mansfield, *America's Constitutional Soul* (Baltimore: Johns Hopkins University Press, 1990).

39. Keith E. Whittington, "James Madison Has Left the Building," *University of Chicago Law Review* 72, no. 3 (2005): 1137–58. Whittington draws this out more fully in examining how presidents have been central to constructing judicial authority in *Political Foundations of Judicial Supremacy.*

40. Hamilton et al., *The Federalist Papers,* No. 51, 292.

41. Barber, *On What the Constitution Means,* 178.

42. Donald Lutz, *The Origins of American Constitutionalism* (Baton Rouge: Louisiana State University Press, 1988). James Madison, "Of Ancient and Modern Confederacies," in *The Writings of James Madison,* ed. Gaillard Hunt (New York: G. P. Putnam's Sons, 1900), 2:369–90. See Machiavelli, *Discourses,* I, 4, and Montesquieu, *The Spirit of the Laws* (New York: Cambridge University Press, 1989), book III, 1–10, on tensions within the political regime.

43. Hamilton et al., *The Federalist Papers,* No. 44, 266. Garrett Ward Sheldon, *The Political Philosophy of James Madison* (Baltimore: Johns Hopkins University Press, 2001), argues that this suspicion of perfection in government and the motives of men stems from Madison's Calvinist education, 1–26.

44. Mansfield, *America's Constitutional Soul,* 148.

45. Harvey C. Mansfield Jr., *Taming the Prince: The Ambivalence of Modern Executive Power* (Baltimore: Johns Hopkins University Press, 1993).

46. Stoner, *Common Law and Liberal Theory,* 211. See also James R. Stoner Jr., *Common-Law Liberty: Rethinking American Constitutionalism* (Lawrence: University Press of Kansas, 2003).

47. On "intercurring" orders, see Karen Orren and Stephen Skowronek, *The Search for American Political Development* (New York: Cambridge University Press, 2004).

48. See especially Mark Brandon, *Free in the World: American Slavery and Constitutional Failure* (Princeton: Princeton University Press, 1998) (who draws on Sanford Levinson's *Constitutional Faith* in noting this tendency is American constitutionalism).

49. Brandon, *Free in the World.* As Brandon notes, there is nothing inherently problematic about multiple constitutional perspectives coexisting; although a breakdown of constitutional dialogue where nothing is shared in common could lead to a constitutional "failure" as during the Civil War. This points to the importance of what Robert Nagel calls a shared "constitutional culture" within which these institutions function. See Nagel, *Constitutional Cultures,* and Stoner, *Common-Law Liberty.*

50. Hamilton et al., *The Federalist Papers,* No. 10.

51. Harry V. Jaffa, "The Nature and Origin of the American Party System," in Robert Goldwin, ed., *Political Parties U.S.A.* (Chicago: Rand McNally, 1965), 59–83.

52. Tulis, *The Rhetorical Presidency,* 17, on the notion of "two Constitutions" and a layered "text-polity."

53. Mark Graber, "Constitutional Politics and Constitutional Theory: A Misunderstood

and Neglected Relationship" (Review of Lucas A. Powe Jr., *The Warren Court in American Politics*), *Law & Social Inquiry* 27 (2002): 309–38.

54. Robert Dahl, "Decision-Making in a Democracy: The Supreme Court as a National Policy-Maker," *Journal of Public Law* 6 (1958): 279–95. See especially J. Mitchell Pickerill and Cornel Clayton, "The Rehnquist Court and the Political Dynamics of Federalism," *Perspectives on Politics* 2, no. 2 (2004): 233–48, and "Guess What Happened on the Way to Revolution? Precursors to the Supreme Court's Federalism Revolution," *Publius* 34, no. 3 (2004): 85–114; Kevin McMahon, *Reconsidering Roosevelt on Race: How the Presidency Paved the Road to Brown* (Chicago: University of Chicago Press, 2004).

55. For a critique of this emerging literature, see Thomas M. Keck, "Party Politics or Judicial Independence? The Regime Politics Literature Hits the Law Schools," *Law & Social Inquiry* 32, no. 2 (2007): 511–44.

56. How is it that the president might resist the demands of his governing coalition? What about when the Court does not follow the election returns? Is it so easy to speak of governing coalitions given divided power? Why governing coalitions rather than democratic majorities? These questions all point to the Constitution.

57. Stephen M. Griffin, *American Constitutionalism: From Theory to Politics* (Princeton: Princeton University Press, 1996), seeks to remove normative questions from constitutional theory, which tends to eclipse a constitutional perspective as we move from "theory" to "politics" in a manner that not only neglects the possible autonomy of thought, but often rationalizes the actual.

58. Hamilton et al., *The Federalist Papers*, No. 16, 85.

59. Abraham Lincoln, "The Dred Scott Decision," in Roy P. Basler, ed., *Abraham Lincoln: His Speeches and Writings* (New York: Da Capo Press, 2001), 352–65. Scholars coming from a constitutional angle also raised this criticism prior to the emergence of the regimes literature. See Charles R. Kesler, "Separation of Powers and the Administrative State," in Gordon S. Jones and John Marini, eds., *The Imperial Congress: Crisis in the Separation of Powers* (New York: Pharos Books, 1988), 22.

60. Bruce Ackerman, *We the People: Foundations* (Cambridge: Harvard University Press, 1991) and *Transformations*, vol. 2. See also Gerard N. Magliocca, *Andrew Jackson and the Constitution: The Rise and Fall of Generational Regimes* (Lawrence: University Press of Kansas, 2007), which insists on a clockwork-like cycle of generational constitutional regimes.

61. Whittington, *Political Foundations of Judicial Supremacy;* "The Political Foundations of Judicial Supremacy," in Barber and George, *Constitutional Politics,* 261–97; and "Presidential Challenges to Judicial Supremacy and the Politics of Constitutional Meaning," *Polity* 33, no. 3 (2001): 365–95. Whittington's work focuses on the political construction of judicial power and is thus more open to regimes being fluid, as he is often deeply critical of Dahl and Ackerman as not fully capturing the intricate and subtle construction of judicial power led by the political branches.

I see *The Madisonian Constitution* not so much in conflict with Whittington's *The Political Foundations of Judicial Supremacy*—it is often, in fact, complementary—but as operating at a different level. Whittington seeks to illuminate the political motivations that have led presidents to construct judicial supremacy—that is, how does judicial supremacy further the president's political ambitions? In this, Whittington tends to follow scholarship in American Political Development (APD) that focuses on electoral outcomes as shaping institutions. Constitutional thought, as thought, is not at all central to Whittington's project. The Madisonian Constitution, while engaging APD scholarship, seeks to root its understanding more clearly in constitutional foundations, which, I argue, are a mix of thought and institutions. The Madisonian Constitution begins by examining how the Constitution is structured to preserve itself as fundamental law, which includes creating a space in which autonomous thought has a chance to guide the polity. It then traces out constitutional conflicts that illustrate the importance of this foundational framework for American constitutional development.

American constitutionalism, I suggest, is an "amalgamation" that cannot be reduced or captured by any one element. In partial contrast, Whittington concludes by offering a qualified defense of judicial supremacy insofar as it is rooted in the choices of the political branches rendering it "democratic." In contrast, I argue that our constitutional foundations are more complex as they are rooted in the very tension between liberalism and democracy. This tension is captured by our agonistic institutions, which do not always move together. Even presidents who attempt to provide the political foundations of judicial power do not easily reconstruct the Court. Rather, conflicted episodes are continuous in our constitutional history and do not lead to a neat packaging of presidents that provides the political foundations of judicial supremacy. (Whittington himself notes this dilemma, which, I think, could be strengthened by speaking of the Constitution in Madisonian terms.) Judicial independence often remains because it has become an important element within our constitutional understandings. In this sense, constitutional thought might operate autonomously, shaping our actual politics and providing the horizon in which it operates. Thus, unlike many APD approaches, I want to suggest the possible harm that accepting judicial supremacy as a matter of thought can do—precisely because I take thought itself seriously. How we think about the Constitution matters. Such an understanding is absent in APD approaches, which have not only been neglectful of thought but, like behavioral political science, tend to reduce the Constitution to actual outcomes (that is, to political *behavior*).

62. Here I follow Wayne Moore's insistence that "creating and maintaining constitutional meaning and authority are ongoing and normal processes, not periodic or extraordinary." *Constitutional Rights and Powers of the People*, 3. Louis Seidman, *Our Unsettled Constitution: A New Defense of Constitutionalism and Judicial Review* (New Haven: Yale University Press, 2001), examines how judicial review may work to unsettle politics, but the argument on the whole is a normative justification for a particular view of the Court and judicial review.

One · Madison's Complex Constitutionalism

1. Gordon Wood, *Creation of the American Republic* (Chapel Hill: University of North Carolina Press, 1998), 281.

2. As Gordon Wood says, "There was therefore no logical or necessary reason why the notion of fundamental law, so common to Englishman for over a century, should lead to the American invocation of it in the ordinary courts of law. Indeed, in an important sense the idea of fundamental law actually worked to prohibit any such development, for it was

dependent on such a distinct conception of public law in contrast to private law as to be hardly enforceable in the regular court system." Ibid., 292. See also Robert Burt, *The Constitution in Conflict* (Cambridge: Harvard University Press, 1992), 59–76.

3. William F. Harris II, *The Interpretable Constitution* (Baltimore: Johns Hopkins University Press, 1993).

4. Edward Corwin, "Marbury v. Madison and the Establishment of Judicial Review," *Michigan Law Review* 12 (1914): 555. See also Charles Grove Haines, *The American Doctrine of Judicial Supremacy* (Berkeley: University of California Press, 1932), and Charles McIlwain, *Constitutionalism: Ancient and Modern* (Ithaca: Cornell University Press, 1948).

5. Wood, *Creation of the American Republic*, 291.

6. See, for example, Michael Comiskey, *Seeking Justices: The Judging of Supreme Court Nominees* (Lawrence: University Press of Kansas, 2004), which suggests that the stakes over Supreme Court nominees are so high because they are rightly seen as the final interpreters of the Constitution. Similarly, H. W. Perry Jr., *Deciding to Decide: Agenda Setting in the United States Supreme Court* (Cambridge: Harvard University Press, 1991), 231, notes that the Supreme Court is the final interpreter of the Constitution.

7. See *City of Boerne v. Flores,* 521 U.S. 507, 529 (1997); *Planned Parenthood v. Casey,* 505 U.S. 833, 868 (1992); *Cooper v. Aaron,* 358 U.S. 1, 18 (1958).

8. See especially Larry Alexander and Frederick Schauer, "On Extrajudicial Constitutional Interpretation," *Harvard Law Review* 110, no. 7 (1997): 1359–87. It is useful, here, to distinguish between two forms of judicial supremacy. The strong form of judicial supremacy suggests that the judiciary is the exclusive interpreter as well as the authoritative interpreter of constitutional meaning (exclusive, after all, implies authoritative). A modified version of judicial supremacy suggests that the Supreme Court is not the exclusive interpreter of the Constitution but that its interpretations are final. On both normative and empirical grounds, the distinction between a strong form of judicial supremacy and a modified version is important, but it is not central to the question I wish to raise. Whether judicial interpretation is held to be exclusive or final, each view insists that authoritative *judicial* settlement is necessary to constitutional governance. See Scott Gant, "Judicial Supremacy and Nonjudicial Interpretation of the Constitution," *Hastings Constitutional Law Quarterly* 24 (1997): 359–440. For a general discussion, see also Bruce Peabody, "Nonjudicial Constitutional Interpretation, Authoritative Settlement, and a New Agenda for Research," *Constitutional Commentary* 16 (1999): 63–90. For a historical analysis, see Barry Friedman, "The History of the Countermajoritarian Difficulty, Part One: The Road to Judicial Supremacy," *New York University Law Review* 73, no. 2 (1998): 333–433.

9. McIlwain, *Constitutionalism: Ancient and Modern*, 141.

10. John Agresto, *The Supreme Court and Constitutional Democracy* (Ithaca: Cornell University Press, 1984).

11. When I refer to the Madisonian Constitution or the Madisonian solution to maintaining constitutional government, I do not mean to suggest that it has developed exactly as Madison himself would want it to, or that it is "proper" because Madison saw it this way. Nor is this an exegesis of his constitutional thought. Rather, I argue that the system can be described as Madisonian because it operates broadly as he suggested even if many of the particulars go against his own vision. For an excellent discussion of Madison's political thought,

see Gary Rosen, *American Compact: James Madison and the Problem of Founding* (Lawrence: University Press of Kansas, 1999).

12. Edward S. Corwin, "The Constitution as Instrument and Symbol," *American Political Science Review* 30, no. 6 (1936): 1071–85. Unlike Corwin, who prefers the Constitution as an adaptable instrument, I argue it is both instrument and symbol.

13. Alexander Hamilton, James Madison, and John Jay, *The Federalist Papers,* introduction and notes by Charles R. Kesler, ed. Clinton Rossiter (New York: Signet Classics, 1999), No. 37, 198.

14. James Madison, Helvidius, No. II, in Morton J. Frisch, ed., *The Pacificus-Helvidius Debates of 1793–1794* (Indianapolis: Liberty Fund, 2007), 68–69. See also Sylvia Snowiss, *Judicial Review and the Law of the Constitution* (New Haven: Yale University Press, 1990), 98, and Wayne Moore, *Constitutional Rights and Powers of the People* (Princeton: Princeton University Press, 1996), 239–74.

15. Hamilton et al., *The Federalist Papers,* Nos. 10 and 37.

16. Michael Zuckert, *The Natural Rights Republic* (Notre Dame: University of Notre Dame Press, 1996), 4.

17. Madison, "Letters of Helvidius," in Frisch, *The Pacificus-Helvidius Debates of 1793– 1794,* 55–98. See also James Madison, "Of Ancient and Modern Confederacies," in Marvin Meyers, ed., *The Mind of the Founder: Sources of the Political Thought of James Madison* (Indianapolis: Bobbs-Merrill Company, 1973), 69–81, and Hamilton et al., *The Federalist Papers,* No. 31. On nature as a foundation, see James W. Ceaser, *Nature and History in American Political Development* (Cambridge: Harvard University Press, 2006), and Leo Strauss, *Natural Right and History* (Chicago: University of Chicago Press, 1954).

18. Hamilton et al., *The Federalist Papers,* No. 37.

19. Sotirios Barber, *On What the Constitution Means* (Baltimore: Johns Hopkins University Press, 1984), 8.

20. *Marbury v. Madison,* 1 Cranch 137 (1803), 178.

21. Wood, *Creation of the American Republic,* 281.

22. St. George Tucker, *View of the Constitution of the United States* (Indianapolis: Liberty Fund, 1999), 105. See also Wood, *Creation of the American Republic,* 275, and Gary McDowell, "Coke, Corwin, and the Constitution: The 'Higher Law' Background Reconsidered," *Review of Politics* 55, no. 3 (1993): 393–420, and "The Language of Law and the Foundations of American Constitutionalism," *William and Mary Quarterly* 55, no. 3 (1998): 375–98.

23. Harris, *The Interpretable Constitution,* 2.

24. Hamilton et al., *The Federalist Papers,* No. 48, 281.

25. *Marbury* at 177.

26. Hamilton et al., *The Federalist Papers,* No. 51, 290–91. See also Michael Zuckert, "Epistemology and Hermeneutics in the Constitutional Jurisprudence of John Marshall," in Thomas Shevory, ed., *John Marshall's Achievement: Law, Politics and Constitutional Interpretations* (Westport, CT: Greenwood Press, 1989), 193–215.

27. Hamilton et al., *The Federalist Papers,* No. 10, 75. On *The Federalist,* see especially Martin Diamond, "The Federalist," in William A. Schambra, ed., *As Far as Republican Principles Will Admit: Essays by Martin Diamond* (Washington, DC: AEI Press, 1992), 37–57, and Charles R. Kesler, "Federalist 10 and American Republicanism," in Kesler, ed., *Saving the*

Revolution: The Federalist Papers and the American Founding (New York: Free Press, 1987), 13–39.

28. Madison to Jefferson, October 17, 1788, in Myers, *The Mind of the Founder,* 206.

29. Colleen Sheehan, "The Politics of Public Opinion: James Madison's 'Notes on Government,'" *William and Mary Quarterly* 49, no. 4 (October 1992): 625.

30. Drew R. McCoy, *The Last of the Fathers: James Madison and the Legacy of Republican Government* (New York: Cambridge University Press, 1989). See also Samuel H. Beer, *To Make a Nation: The Rediscovery of American Federalism* (Cambridge: Harvard University Press, 1992), and Rogan Kersh, *Dreams of a More Perfect Union* (Ithaca: Cornell University Press, 2001).

31. Madison, "Of Ancient & Modern Confederacies," in Myers, *The Mind of the Founder,* 69–81. See also Hamilton et al., *The Federalist Papers,* No. 9.

32. Richard Kay, "American Constitutionalism," in Larry Alexander, ed., *Constitutionalism: Philosophical Foundations* (New York: Cambridge University Press, 1998), 17.

33. For a broad-ranging discussion of the separation of powers, see M. J. C. Vile, *Constitutionalism and the Separation of Powers,* 2nd ed. (Indianapolis: Liberty Fund, 1998). On the centrality of constitutional frameworks, see Cindy Skach, *Borrowing Constitutional Designs: Constitutional Law in Weimar Germany and the French Fifth Republic* (Princeton: Princeton University Press, 2005), and "The Newest Separation of Powers," *I-Con,* 5, no. 1 (2007): 93–121.

34. Hamilton et al., *The Federalist Papers,* No. 47.

35. Ibid., No. 37.

36. Max Farrand, ed., *The Records of the Federal Convention of 1787,* vol. 2 (New Haven: Yale University Press, 1966), 34.

37. Aristotle, *The Politics* (New York: Cambridge University Press, 1988).

38. Paul O. Carrese, *The Cloaking of Power: Montesquieu, Blackstone, and the Rise of Judicial Activism* (Chicago: University of Chicago Press, 2003). See also Sheldon S. Wolin, *The Presence of the Past: Essays on the State and the Constitution* (Baltimore: Johns Hopkins University Press, 1989), and Anne Cohler, *Montesquieu's Comparative Politics and the Spirit of American Constitutionalism* (Lawrence: University Press of Kansas, 1988).

39. Hamilton et al., *The Federalist Papers,* Nos. 47 and 78.

40. Montesquieu, *The Spirit of the Laws* (New York: Cambridge University Press, 1989), book XI, ch. 6.

41. Ibid., ch. 4.

42. Montesquieu refers to republicanism, monarchy, and despotism, as well as following Locke in including the judicial power within the confines of executive power.

43. Walter Berns, "Judicial Review and the Rights and Laws of Nature," *The Supreme Court Review, 1979* (Chicago: University of Chicago Press, 1980), 77–79.

44. Alexis de Tocqueville, *Democracy in America,* trans. Harvey C. Mansfield and Delba Winthrop (Chicago: University of Chicago Press, 2000), 604.

45. Gary McDowell, "Private Conscience & Public Order: Hobbes & *The Federalist,*" *Polity* 25, no. 3 (Spring 1993): 435. See also Martin Diamond, "Democracy and The Federalist: A Reconsideration of the Framer's Intent," in Schambra, *As Far as Republican Principles Will Admit,* 17–36.

46. John Hart Ely, *Democracy and Distrust: A Theory of Judicial Review* (Cambridge: Harvard University Press, 1980), drawing out Harlan Fiske Stone's *Carolene Products Co. v. United States,* 304 U.S. 144 (1938), n. 4.

47. Gary J. Jacobsohn, *The Supreme Court and the Decline of Constitutional Aspiration* (Lanham, MD: Rowman and Littlefield, 1986), and *Apple of Gold: Constitutionalism in Israel and the United States* (Princeton: Princeton University Press, 1993). See also Sotirios A. Barber, *The Constitution of Judicial Power* (Baltimore: Johns Hopkins University Press, 1993), and *On What the Constitution Means,* for another, and potentially different, view of constitutional aspiration.

48. Hamilton et al., *The Federalist Papers,* No. 43, 276. As Charles R. Kesler's edited volume puts it in its apt title, the Constitution is aimed at *Saving the Revolution* instigated by the Declaration. See especially the essays be Kesler, "Federalist 10 and American Republicanism," and Thomas G. West, "The Rule of Law in *The Federalist."*

49. Abraham Lincoln, "The Perpetuation of Our Political Institutions," in Roy P. Basler, ed., *Abraham Lincoln: His Speeches and Writings* (New York: Da Capo Press, 2001), 81. Franklin Delano Roosevelt, "Fireside Chat on Reorganization of the Judiciary," March 9, 1937, www.fdrlibrary.marist.edu/030937.html (accessed June 13, 2007).

50. Sanford Levinson, *Constitutional Faith* (Princeton: Princeton University Press, 1989).

51. Hamilton et al., *The Federalist Papers,* No. 37, 225.

52. Lincoln, "The Perpetuation of Our Political Institutions," 81.

53. Roosevelt, "Fireside Chat on Reorganization of the Judiciary."

54. Lincoln, "The Perpetuation of Our Political Institutions," 81, 84.

55. Kesler, "Federalist 10 and American Republicanism," 29.

56. William Brennan, "The Constitution of the United States: Contemporary Ratification," lecture delivered at Georgetown University, October 12, 1985.

57. Bryan Garsten, *Saving Persuasion: A Defense of Rhetoric and Judgment* (Cambridge: Harvard University Press, 2006), 210.

58. Gary Jeffrey Jacobsohn, "The Permeability of Constitutional Borders," *Texas Law Review* 82 (June 2004): 1769–1818.

59. Keith E. Whittington, *Constitutional Interpretation: Textual Meaning, Original Intent, and Judicial Review* (Lawrence: University Press of Kansas, 1999), 172. See also Whittington, "The Road Not Taken: *Dred Scott,* Judicial Authority, and Political Questions," *Journal of Politics* 63, no. 2 (May 2001): 365–91.

60. *Marbury* at 174. Christopher Eisgruber, *Constitutional Self-Government* (Cambridge: Harvard University Press, 2001), for example, begins with the notion that our Constitution is a framework, but then very quickly argues that judges *should* interpret the Constitution based *on their notions of justice* (with very little concern about how this has worked out historically or the thought underlying the Constitution).

61. See Mark Tushnet, *Taking the Constitution Away from the Courts* (Princeton: Princeton University Press, 1998), 95–128 (preferring the thin Constitution of the preamble to the thick Constitution).

62. This has perhaps changed with the ratification of the Fourteenth Amendment, which arguably paved the way for the legalization of the Constitution, shifting our focus to rights (and courts) and away from constitutional structure. But such a reading relies on a legalist

view of the amendment, overlooking the fact that Congress was entrusted by way of section 5 with defending (and perhaps defining) constitutional rights. Furthermore, recent scholarship casts serious doubt on any special connection between rights—even in a bill of rights—and the judiciary, suggesting that the articulation of rights fits within a political view of the Constitution. See Akhil Reed Amar, *The Bill of Rights* (New Haven: Yale University Press, 1998), and John J. Dinan, *Keeping the People's Liberties: Legislators, Citizens, and Judges as Guardians of Rights* (Lawrence: University Press of Kansas, 1998).

63. Hamilton et al., *The Federalist Papers*, No. 51, 288. For a discussion of the solutions Madison rejected, see Burt, *The Constitution in Conflict*, 47.

64. Hamilton et al., *The Federalist Papers*, No. 51, 289, 290.

65. James Madison, June 17, 1789, in Charlene Bangs Bickford, Kenneth R. Bowling, and Helen E. Veit, eds., *Debates in the House of Representatives*, vol.11: *First Session: June–September 1789* (Baltimore: Johns Hopkins University Press, 1992), 899. See Jack Rakove, *Original Meanings: Politics and Ideas in the Making of the Constitution* (New York: Knopf, 1996), 345–48, and "Judicial Power in the Constitutional Theory of James Madison," *William and Mary Law Review* 43 (2002): 1513–47, discussing Madison and judicial review. See Charles A. Lofgren, "The Original Understanding of Original Intent?" and Jack Rakove, "Mr. Meese, Meet Mr. Madison," both in Rakove, ed., *Interpreting the Constitution: The Debate over Original Intent* (Boston: Northeastern University Press, 1990), 117–50, 179–94, discussing Madison and constitutional interpretation.

66. Stephen M. Griffin, *American Constitutionalism: From Theory to Politics* (Princeton: Princeton University Press, 1996), 41.

67. Rakove, *Original Meanings*, 348. Gary Jacobsohn notes that the consensus in Congress—unlike Madison's argument—did not question "the finality of the judicial determination of constitutionality," although that is not quite the same things as endorsing it. *The Supreme Court and the Decline of Constitutional Aspiration*, 123.

68. The repeal of the Judiciary Act of 1801 by the Judiciary Act of 1802 is also a prime example, but one I do not take up here.

69. Madison, June 17, 1789, in Bickford et al., *Debates in the House of Representatives*, 11:921.

70. Smith, June 16, 1789, in ibid., 876. See also the debates from May 19, 1789, Charlene Bangs Bickford, Kenneth R. Bowling, and Helen E. Veit, eds., *Debates in the House of Representatives*, vol. 10: *First Session: April–May 1789* (Baltimore: Johns Hopkins University Press, 1992), 726–27.

71. Madison, June 17, 1789, in Bickford et al., *Debates in the House of Representatives*, 11:926, 927.

72. Ibid., 11:927. See also Madison, "The Virginia Report," 303, 330, and Madison to Spencer Roane, September 2, 1819, both in Myers, *The Mind of the Founder*, 458.

73. Madison, June 17, 1789, in Bickford et al., *Debates in the House of Representatives*, 11:923, 900.

74. See Robert L. Clinton, Marbury v. Madison *and Judicial Review* (Lawrence: University Press of Kansas, 1989), 20–30 (for perhaps the most influential statement of this view), and Matthew Franck, *Against the Imperial Judiciary: The Supreme Court vs. the Sovereignty of the People* (Lawrence: University Press of Kansas, 1996), 65–91. See also Charles Hobson,

The Great Chief Justice: John Marshall and the Rule of Law (Lawrence: University Press of Kansas, 1996). Hobson suggests that Marshall's "defense of judicial review fully agreed with the 'departmental' theory of constitutional interpretation, according to which each of the three co-ordinate departments of government had final authority to interpret the Constitution when acting within its own sphere of duties and responsibilities" (67). Edward S. Corwin, *Court over Constitution: A Study of Judicial Review as an Instrument of Popular Government* (Princeton: Princeton University Press, 1938), 82, the scholar who coined the term departmentalism, surely meant "coordinate construction."

75. Jacobsohn suggests that Lincoln's views on judicial review, properly understood, also put it in this light. *The Supreme Court and the Decline of Constitutional Aspiration*, 95–112. John Agresto's departmentalism seems to be more along these lines as well, insofar as he puts emphasis on the dynamic of the checks and balances and interaction between the branches, *The Supreme Court and Constitutional Democracy*, 99–102. See also Louis Fisher, *Constitutional Dialogues: Interpretation as Political Process* (Princeton: Princeton University Press, 1988), 231–79, though Fisher seems to treat it all as mere politics, including judicial interpretation, thus neglecting central features of the separation of powers. This is also true of Corwin, *Court over Constitution*, 61, 69.

76. Roger Sherman had argued that Congress should allow for executive removal but not that it was constitutionally required. This sounds more like what Keith Whittington has dubbed "constitutional construction." Madison seemed to reject this argument insofar as it left it a question of legislative discretion rather than constitutional logic, June 17, 1789, Bickford et al., *Debates in the House of Representatives*, 11: 921, 926–27.

77. "But the proposed bank could not even be called necessary to the government; at most it could be but convenient." James Madison, "The Bank Bill, House of Representatives, 2 Feb. 1791" ("A bank there is not necessary, and consequently not authorized by this phrase"), and Thomas Jefferson, "Opinion on the Constitutionality of the Bill for Establishing a National Bank, 15 Feb. 1791," both in Philip Kurland and Ralph Lerner, eds., *The Founders' Constitution*, vol. 3 (Indianapolis: Liberty Fund, 1987), 245, 246. See also Alexander Hamilton, "Opinion on the Constitutionality of the Bank, 23 Feb. 1791," in ibid., 247–50.

78. This is true of the states as well, but my focus is on the national separation of powers.

79. Mark Graber, "The Jacksonian Origins of Chase Court Activism," *Journal of Supreme Court History* 25, no. 2 (2000): 18–19.

80. Madison, Helvidius, No. II, 68.

81. Gerard Magliocca, "Veto! The Jacksonian Revolution in Constitutional Law," *University of Nebraska Law Review* 78 (1999): 205–62. See also his *Andrew Jackson and the Constitution: The Rise and Fall of Generational Regimes* (Lawrence: University Press of Kansas, 2007).

82. Madison quoted in Rosen, *American Compact*, 172. See also Madison to Spencer Roane, September 2, 1819, and Madison to Reynolds Chapman, January 6, 1831, both in Kurland and Lerner, *The Founders' Constitution*, 3:259, 262.

83. In discussing *McCulloch*, perhaps the leading constitutional law casebook (Gerald Gunther and Kathleen Sullivan, *Constitutional Law*, 13th ed. [New York: Foundation Press, 1997]) gives a history of the debate prior to *McCulloch* and speaks of scholarly debate since

McCulloch but does not discuss Jackson's veto and the effective settlement of the issue for several decades seemingly against Marshall's opinion. Gunther and Sullivan acknowledge that "the McCulloch decision, important as it is, was no more the end than the beginning of the debate." Yet, they are speaking of the national legislature's ability to reach local affairs and not the power to establish a bank (99). Two leading books by political scientists fare no better. David O'Brien's *Constitutional Law and Politics,* 4th ed. (New York: W. W. Norton, 1998), gives a similar history and suggests that Marshall's interpretation seems correct and has been confirmed by subsequent Court opinions—namely, *The Legal Tender Cases* (1884) and *Katzenbach v. Morgan* (1966). But this comment eclipses a large portion of our constitutional history (1819–84) and focuses again on the Court, missing how the other branches seem to have settled a vital constitutional question without turning to the Court. Lee Epstein and Thomas Walker's *Constitutional Law* (Washington, DC: CQ Press, 1998), 4th ed., gives a history of the conflict prior to Marshall's opinion but says nothing of what came after 1819. This from two leading empirical political scientists! Walter Murphy, Sotirios Barber, James Fleming, and Stephen Macedo, eds., *American Constitutional Interpretation* (New York: Foundation Press, 2003), give a history of the conflict and Jackson's statement rejecting Marshall's opinion. But, then, this book specifically seeks to give an alternative view of the Constitution and questions of constitutional interpretation.

84. *McCulloch v. Maryland,* 4 Wheat. (17 U.S.) 316, 401 (1819).

85. *McCulloch* at 400–401.

86. Andrew Jackson, Veto Message, July 10, 1832, in Lerner and Kurland, *The Founders' Constitution,* 3:263–67.

87. Magliocca, "Veto!" 212.

88. Mark Graber, "Jacksonian Origins of Chase Court Activism," and "Naked Land Transfers and American Constitutional Development," *Vanderbilt Law Review* 53 (2000): 17–39, 71–122. See also Keith Whittington, *Political Foundations of Judicial Power: The Presidency, the Supreme Court, and Constitutional Leadership in U.S. History* (Princeton: Princeton University Press, 2007).

89. In his classic exegesis of checks and balances in *Federalist* 51, discussed previously, Madison never even mentions the judiciary. In fact, he rejects a check similar to judicial supremacy. One notable solution to keeping the majority in check, Madison says, is to create "a will in the community independent of the majority—that is, of the society itself." The Court, as an unelected and undemocratic branch of government seems suspiciously independent of society, a solution unacceptable to Madison. Hamilton et al., *The Federalist Papers,* No. 51, 321.

90. Madison to John Brown, October 12, 1788, "Remarks on Mr. Jefferson's 'Draught of a Constitution,'" in Myers, *The Mind of the Founder,* 65–66. Madison's argument must also be separated from arguments for legislative supremacy, the type that John Bannister Gibson made in *Eakin v. Raub,* 12 Sergeant & Rawle 330 (1825). Legislative supremacy, too, was unacceptable.

91. As Sylvia Snowiss has argued, this premise is based on a conceptual understanding of the Constitution as "supreme ordinary law," *Judicial Review and the Law of the Constitution,* 109–75. See also Snowiss, "The *Marbury* of 1803 and the Modern *Marbury,*" *Constitutional Commentary* 20, no. 2 (2003): 231–54.

92. *Marbury* at 176. For the political context of Marshall's decisions, see especially Mark Graber's articles on the Marshall Court: "The Passive Aggressive Virtues: *Cohens v. Virginia* and the Problematic Establishment of Judicial Power," *Constitutional Commentary* 12 (1995): 67–92; "Establishing Judicial Review: *Schooner Peggy* and the Early Marshall Court," *Political Research Quarterly* 51 (1998): 7–25; "Federalists or Friends of Adams: The Marshall Court and Party Politics," *Studies in American Political Development* 12 (1999): 229–66; "The Problematic Establishment of Judicial Review," in Howard Gillman and Cornell Clayton, eds., *The Supreme Court in American Politics: New Institutionalist Interpretations* (Lawrence: University Press of Kansas: 1999), 28–42.

93. Gibson does accept judicial review of state laws when they conflict with federal law, because the power is clearly derived from Article VI of the Constitution.

94. Larry Kramer has seized upon this notion to argue that the people themselves are the primary enforcers of our constitutionalism. As he argues, the fundamental misconception of those commentators who insist upon judicial supremacy "is the assumption not just that *someone* must have final authority to resolve routine constitutional conflicts, but that this someone must be a *governmental agency.*" Unlike Gibson, Kramer does accept that judicial review may operate within the contours of "popular constitutionalism." Larry Kramer, *The People Themselves: Popular Constitutionalism and Judicial Review* (New York: Oxford University Press, 2004), 107. See also Kramer, "*Marbury* and the Retreat from Judicial Supremacy," *Constitutional Commentary* 20, no. 2 (2003): 205–30.

95. *Eakin v. Raub* at 356.

96. See Snowiss, *Judicial Review and the Law of the Constitution,* 109–13; Clinton, *Marbury v. Madison and Judicial Review,* 97–101; Franck, *Against the Imperial Judiciary,* 66–75; Kramer, *The People Themselves,* 114–27; and Michael Stokes Paulsen, "Marbury in the Modern Era: The Irrepressible Myth of Marbury," *Michigan Law Review* 101 (2003): 2706–43, and "*Marbury's* Wrongness," *Constitutional Commentary* 20, no. 2 (2003): 358.

97. *Marbury* at 177–78.

98. See, for example, *City of Boerne v. Flores, Planned Parenthood v. Casey,* and *Cooper v. Aaron.*

99. Marbury at 179.

100. Clinton, Marbury v. Madison *and Judicial Review,* 99. Clinton suggests Marshall's logic applies only to cases of a *judicial* nature.

101. *Marbury* at 180.

102. *Marbury* at 179.

103. See J. Mitchell Pickerill, *Constitutional Deliberation in Congress: The Impact of Judicial Review in a Separated System* (Durham: Duke University Press, 2004), 30. See also Bruce Peabody, "Congressional Constitutional Interpretation and the Courts: A Preliminary Inquiry into Legislative Attitudes, 1959–2001," *Law & Social Inquiry* 29 (2004): 127–78.

104. *Casey* at 868. See Christopher Wolfe, ed., *That Eminent Tribunal: Judicial Supremacy and the Constitution* (Princeton: Princeton University Press, 2004), for a number of essays that take up *Casey.*

105. Christopher Wolfe, *The Rise of Modern Judicial Review: From Constitutional Interpretation to Judge-Made Law* (New York: Basic Books, 1986), 80–84; Clinton, Marbury v. Madison *and Judicial Review;* Franck, *Against the Imperial Judiciary;* and Hobson, *The Great*

Chief Justice, all insist that Marshall's opinion is much narrower than it has been made out to be by twentieth-century proponents of judicial activism. For Clinton, Franck, and Hobson, Marshall was simply claiming the right to interpret the judicial power and not to authoritatively settle the meaning of the Constitution for the other branches. For Wolfe, Marshall articulated "moderate" judicial review, which was grounded in norms of interpretation that narrowed the scope of judicial power.

106. *Marbury* at 177. Keith Whittington argues that judicial review, along these lines, can only be justified if the Court adheres to original intent, *Constitutional Interpretation,* 213–19.

107. See Madison's "The Virginia Report," in Myers, *The Mind of the Founder,* 307.

108. It was just this premise that Judge Gibson refused to grant Marshall in *Eakin v. Raub.* See Dean Alfange Jr., "*Marbury v. Madison:* In Defense of Traditional Wisdom," *The Supreme Court Review, 1993* (Chicago: University of Chicago Press, 1994), 413–44, and Robert Faulkner, *The Jurisprudence of John Marshall* (Princeton: Princeton University Press, 1968), 203–12.

109. Sylvia Snowiss, "From Fundamental Law to Supreme Law of the Land," *Studies in American Political Development* 2 (1989): 5. Although Snowiss argues that *Marbury* itself is far more limited. See also John E. Finn, "The Civic Constitution: Some Preliminaries," in Sotirios A. Barber and Robert P. George, eds., *Constitutional Politics: Essays on Constitution Making, Maintenance, and Change* (Princeton: Princeton University Press, 2001).

110. Faulkner, *The Jurisprudence of John Marshall,* 200.

111. *Boerne* at 516.

112. Kennedy continues, "When the political branches of the Government act against the background of a judicial interpretation of the Constitution already issued, it must be understood that in later cases and controversies the Court will treat its precedents with the respect due them under settled principles, including *stare decisis,* and contrary expectations must be disappointed." *Boerne* at 535. Kennedy's logic could plausibly be qualified if he is speaking only to "cases and controversies" before the Court, so the Congress cannot tell the Court how it should interpret the Constitution in a case before it. "RFRA [Religious Freedom Restoration Act] was designed to control cases and controversies, such as the one before us; but as the provisions of the federal statute here invoked are beyond congressional authority, it is this Court's precedent, not RFRA, which must control."

113. *Boerne* at 535.

114. *Powell v. McCormack,* 395 U.S. 486, 521 (1969).

115. Yet Marshall insists "the province of the court is, solely, to decide on the rights of individuals, not to inquire how the executive, or executive officers, perform duties in which they have discretion. Questions, in their nature political, or which are, by the constitution and laws, submitted to the executive, can never be made in this court" (*Marbury* at 170). This applies to the legislature as well: "Should Congress, in the execution of its powers, adopt measures which are prohibited by the Constitution . . . it would become the painful duty of this tribunal . . . to say that such an act was not the law of the land. But where the law is not prohibited, and is really calculated to effect any of the objects entrusted to the government, to undertake here to inquire into the degree of its necessity, would be to pass the line which

circumscribes the judicial department, and to tread on legislative grounds. This court disclaims all pretensions to such a power" (*McCulloch* at 423).

116. James R. Stoner Jr., *Common Law and Liberal Theory: Coke, Hobbes, and the Origins of American Constitutionalism* (Lawrence: University Press of Kansas, 1996), 197, the second passage quoting David Epstein. See also Stoner, "The Idiom of Common Law in the Formation of Judicial Power," in Bradford P. Wilson and Ken Masugi, eds., *The Supreme Court and American Constitutionalism* (Lanham, MD: Rowman and Littlefield, 1998), 47–68.

117. This is not meant to suggest these selections from *The Federalist* have less weight, just to highlight the tension between a legalistic understanding of the Constitution and a political understanding.

118. Hamilton et al., *The Federalist Papers*, No. 78, 435.

119. Ibid., 433, 438. See Carrese, *The Cloaking of Power*, 207–10, on Hamilton's judiciary and the "mixed regime."

120. Faulkner, *The Jurisprudence of John Marshall*, 201.

121. Hamilton et al., *The Federalist Papers*, No. 78, 392–93, and Wolfe, *The Rise of Modern Judicial Review*, 78–79.

122. Hamilton et al., *The Federalist Papers*, No. 70, 392. See also Nos. 57 and 71.

123. Martin Diamond, "The Separation of Powers and the Mixed Regime," in Schambra, *As Far as Republican Principles Will Admit*, 58–67. See also Joseph M. Bessette, *The Mild Voice of Reason: Deliberative Democracy and American National Government* (Chicago: University of Chicago Press); Jeffrey K. Tulis, *The Rhetorical Presidency* (Princeton: Princeton University Press, 1987); and Jessica Korn, *The Power of Separation: American Constitutionalism and the Myth of the Legislative Veto* (Princeton: Princeton University Press, 1996).

124. Hamilton et al., *The Federalist Papers*, No. 78, 439. See Jacobsohn, *The Supreme Court and the Decline of Constitutional Aspiration*, 57–73, discussing Hamilton's legal science. See also Barber, *The Constitution of Judicial Power*, 26–65, on *The Federalist* and judicial review.

125. Ralph Lerner, *The Thinking Revolutionary: Principle and Practice in the New Republic* (Ithaca: Cornell University Press, 1987), 124, 130.

126. *Marbury* at 167.

127. *Marbury* at 166.

128. *Marbury* at 178.

129. While the judiciary does use the language of law in speaking to the Constitution, this is based on the fact that the judiciary must approach the constitution through a legal lens, and not because it is given the power to reduce the constitution itself to legal rules. As Keith Whittington argues, given that the judiciary must always approach the constitution through the lens of legal interpretation, its role in the constitutional scheme should be limited by this fact, not expanded. *Constitutional Interpretation*. See also Stoner, *Common Law and Liberal Theory*, 197–211, and "The Idiom of Common Law in the Formation of Judicial Power," 56–61.

130. Madison to John Brown, October 12, 1788, "Remarks on Mr. Jefferson's 'Draught of a Constitution,'" in Myers, *The Mind of the Founder*, 65–66. See also Griffin, *American Constitutionalism*, 45.

131. Recall that Jefferson's greatest objection to Marshall's *Marbury* opinion was that the

Court had said that it could order the executive to deliver Marbury's appointment by way of a writ of mandamus. Jefferson's outrage stemmed from the fact that he thought this was a matter of executive discretion and, therefore, a *political* question. Marshall, of course, thought otherwise. Walter Murphy, *Congress and the Court: A Study in the American Political Process* (Chicago: University of Chicago Press, 1963), 7–19.

132. Laurence Tribe quoted in Sanford Levinson, *Constitutional Faith* (Princeton: Princeton University Press, 1989), 48. See also Tribe, *American Constitutional Law*, 3rd ed., vol. 1 (New York: Foundation Press, 2000), especially 118–206, on the separation of powers.

133. James W. Ceaser, *Presidential Selection: Theory and Development* (Princeton: Princeton University Press, 1979), and Tulis, *The Rhetorical Presidency.*

134. Alexander and Schauer, "On Extrajudicial Constitutional Interpretation," 1367.

135. *Boerne* at 529.

136. Corwin, *Court over Constitution,* 68. Perhaps this is why Thomas Reed Powell of the Harvard Law School used to tell his students not to read that Constitution because it would only confuse them.

137. Quoted in Jacobsohn, *The Supreme Court and the Decline of Constitutional Aspiration,* 133. In a similar vein, one of our most preeminent jurists, and one who frequently calls for rigorous empirical analysis, saw the mere possibility that Congress would have to take up a constitutional question in the wake of the 2000 presidential election as enough to cause a constitutional crisis: "We only know what *could* have ensued—and what could have ensued is fairly described as chaos." Yet Judge Posner bases his argument on speculation, not empirical evidence. Richard Posner, *Democracy's Deadlock: Breaking the 2000 Election* (Princeton: Princeton University Press, 2001).

138. Alexander and Schauer, "Defending Judicial Supremacy," 471.

139. Ronald Dworkin, *Law's Empire* (Cambridge: Harvard University Press, 1987).

140. Samuel Huntington, *American Politics: The Promise of Disharmony* (Cambridge: Harvard University Press, 1981).

Two • Congress, the Supreme Court, and the Meaning of the Civil War Amendments

1. Abraham Lincoln, "First Inaugural," in Roy B. Basler, ed., *Abraham Lincoln: His Speeches and Writings* (New York: Da Capo, 2001), 584. Lincoln's views here have more profoundly influenced our view of the American constitutional order than the Supreme Court's opinion in *Texas v. White,* 74 U.S. 700 (1868). In addition, John Calhoun's contrary constitutional vision, although perhaps viable in the antebellum era, is "out of bounds" after the Civil War. For a devastating critique of Calhoun and powerful explication of Lincoln's thought, see Harry V. Jaffa, *A New Birth of Freedom: Abraham Lincoln and the Coming of the Civil War* (Lanham, MD: Rowman and Littlefield, 2000).

2. Lincoln, "First Inaugural," 584.

3. See Mark Brandon, *Free in the World: American Slavery and Constitutional Failure* (Princeton: Princeton University Press, 1998), on the constitutional legitimacy of secession and various forms of constitutional failure. See also the discussion in David P. Currie, *The Constitution in Congress: Democrats and Whigs, 1829–1861* (Chicago: University of Chicago Press, 2005), 88–119.

4. Brandon, *Free in the World,* 167–99, goes so far as to suggest that Lincoln's argument against secession was anticonstitutionalist. See also Mark A. Graber, *Dred Scott and the Problem of Constitutional Evil* (New York: Cambridge University Press, 2006), for a critique of Lincoln as majoritarian democrat that goes a long way to blaming Lincoln for the Civil War. In powerful contrast, see Jaffa, *A New Birth of Freedom.*

5. Walter Murphy, "Who Shall Interpret?" *Review of Politics* 48, no. 3 (1986): 401–23. See also Harry V. Jaffa, *Crisis of the House Divided: An Interpretation of the Issues in the Lincoln-Douglas Debates* (Chicago: University of Chicago Press, 1959).

6. Rogan Kersh, *Dreams of a More Perfect Union* (Ithaca: Cornell University Press, 2001), 168–90, on Lincoln's more "moral Union."

7. Jaffa, *A New Birth of Freedom* and *Crisis of the House Divided.* See Wayne Moore, "The Fourteenth Amendment's Initial Authority: Problems of Constitutional Coherence," *Temple Political and Civil Rights Law Review* 13 (2004): 515–44, and "(Re)Construction of Constitutional Authority and Meaning: The Fourteenth Amendment and Slaughter-House Cases," in Ronald Kahn and Ken I. Kersch, eds., *The Supreme Court and American Political Development* (Lawrence: University Press of Kansas, 2006), 229–74, on reconstructing constitutional authority.

8. As Wayne Moore argues, the Democrats went from contesting the validity of the Fourteenth Amendment itself to contesting and narrowing its meaning; see "(Re)Construction of Constitutional Authority and Meaning: The Fourteenth Amendment and Slaughter-House Cases." And while neither *Court* nor *Congress* "speak" with a single voice, and there were profound disagreements in both, which I note throughout, I use the terms as a convenient shorthand reference.

9. Women in general were also abandoned, although the terms of original meaning were much less clear in regard to women. See *Bradwell v. Illinois,* 83 U.S. 130 (1873), but also note that Chief Justice Chase dissents.

10. Bruce Ackerman, *We the People: Transformations* (Cambridge: Harvard University Press, 1998). See also Stephen Skowronek, *The Politics Presidents Make: Leadership from John Adams to George Bush* (Cambridge: Harvard University Press, 1993), and Keith E. Whittington, *Political Foundations of Judicial Supremacy: The Presidency, the Supreme Court, and Constitutional Leadership in U.S. History* (Princeton: Princeton University Press, 2007).

11. See Jaffa, *A New Birth of Freedom,* 1–72, on equality as foundational to the American regime. In tracing out this constitutional development away from full equality, this chapter adds to other scholarship that challenges the conventional view of the Congress and the Court—that is, that the Court is a principled defender of constitutional rights (particularly of minorities), whereas the Congress is likely to dismiss such constitutional formalities. In this era, we see the almost complete reversal of this conventional wisdom.

12. Christopher Eisgruber, "Judicial Supremacy and Constitutional Distortion," in Sotirios A. Barber and Robert P. George, eds., *Constitutional Politics: Essays on Constitution Making, Maintenance, and Change* (Princeton: Princeton University Press, 2001), 72; John Finn, "The Civic Constitution: Some Preliminaries," in ibid., 54–60 (discussing the distinction between what he calls the "juridical" Constitution and the "civic" Constitution); William Harris, *The Interpretable Constitution* (Baltimore: Johns Hopkins University Press, 1993).

13. *City of Boerne v. Flores,* 521 U.S. 507 (1997).

14. Walter Murphy, "*Slaughter-House, Civil Rights,* and the Limits of Constitutional Change," *American Journal of Jurisprudence* 32 (1987): 1–17. See also Michael Zuckert, "Completing the Constitution: The Thirteenth Amendment," *Constitutional Commentary* 4 (1987): 259–83.

15. Lincoln, "The Dred Scott Decision," in Basler, *Abraham Lincoln: His Speeches and Writings,* 356.

16. *Dred Scott v. Sandford,* 60 U.S. 393 (1857). Compare with the Constitution of the United States, Article IV, Section 3, Clause 2.

17. Justice Benjamin Curtis, for example, a dissenter in *Dred Scott,* understood due process in manner that included "substance." See Stuart Streichler, *Justice Curtis in the Civil War Era: At the Crossroads of American Constitutionalism* (Charlottesville: University of Virginia Press, 2005), 109–15, also noting that Curtis's understanding would be drawn on by Justice John Marhsall Harlan. For a discussion of pre–Civil War due process, which would come to be dubbed "substantive" by its progressive critics, see James W. Ely Jr., "The Oxymoron Reconsidered: Myth and Reality in the Origins of Substantive Due Process," *Constitutional Commentary* 16 (1999): 315.

18. Lincoln, Fifth Debate, in Robert W. Johannsen, ed., *The Lincoln-Douglas Debates* (New York: Oxford University Press, 1965), 230. For a devastating critique of Taney, situating him within the contours of John Calhoun's rejection of the Declaration, see Jaffa, *A New Birth of Freedom,* 403–71. See also Lincoln, Fifth Debate, 219–20. In contrast, see Graber, *Dred Scott and the Problem of Constitutional Evil* (suggesting that Douglas is a "consensual democrat" and Lincoln is a "majoritarian democrat").

19. Lincoln, Fifth Debate, *Lincoln-Douglas,* 225. See Jaffa, *Crisis of the House Divided,* 302–7.

20. Lincoln, Speech at Peoria, Illinois, October 16, 1854, in Basler, *Abraham Lincoln: His Speeches and Writings,* 283–323.

21. Lincoln, First Debate, *Lincoln-Douglas,* 56.

22. James Madison in Ralph Ketcham, ed., *Selected Writing of James Madison* (Indianapolis: Hackett Publishing, 2006), 28.

23. Lincoln, First Debate, *Lincoln-Douglas,* 65, 55–57.

24. John C. Calhoun, *A Disquisition on Government,* in Ross M. Lence, ed., *Union and Liberty: The Political Philosophy of John C. Calhoun* (Indianapolis: Liberty Fund, 1992), 44.

25. Alexander Stephens, "Corner Stone Speech," in Henry Cleveland, ed., *Alexander H. Stephens, in Public and Private, with Letter and Speeches, Before, During, and Since the War* (Philadelphia: National Publishing Company, 1866), 721. Jaffa, *A New Birth of Freedom,* 219–20, also notes that Chief Justice Taney had, in 1818, put forward an understanding of the Declaration of Independence that is nearly indistinguishable from Lincoln's, lending powerful credence to Lincoln's own argument.

26. William Nelson, *The Fourteenth Amendment: From Political Principle to Judicial Doctrine* (Cambridge: Harvard University Press, 1988).

27. Michael Zuckert, "Congressional Power under the Fourteenth Amendment—the Original Understanding of Section Five," *Constitutional Commentary* 3 (1986): 136.

28. Ibid.

29. Rogan Kersh, *Dreams of a More Perfect Union*, 175, argues that Lincoln, in fact, sought to foster political conflict as part of a more perfect Union.

30. Rogers M. Smith, *Civic Ideals* (New Haven: Yale University Press, 1997), 308–17. See also Harold Hyman and William Wiecek, *Equal Protection under Law* (New York: Harper and Row, 1982).

31. Whether the Court got the meaning of the Fourteenth and Fifteenth amendments right, and how its interpretation of them has changed according to the times, is still heavily debated. Some scholars insist that the Supreme Court got the amendments wrong; while others insist that it trimmed the expansive powers of Congress in a correct interpretation of these amendments. Michael Kent Curtis, *No State Shall Abridge: The Fourteenth Amendment and the Bill of Rights* (Durham: Duke University Press, 1986); Akhil Reed Amar, *The Bill of Rights* (New Haven: Yale University Press, 1998); Smith, *Civic Ideals;* and William Nelson, *The Fourteenth Amendment* (Cambridge: Harvard University Press, 1988), are all skeptical of the Court's interpretation. Charles Fairman, *Reconstruction and Reunion, 1864–1888* (New York: Macmillan, 1987), argues that the Court got it right.

32. Skowronek, *The Politics Presidents Make*, and Ackerman, *We the People: Transformations*. See Pamela Brandwein, *Reconstructing Reconstruction: The Supreme Court and the Production of Historical Truth* (Durham: Duke University Press, 1999), on how arguments have changed over time.

33. *The Slaughter-House Cases*, 83 U.S. 36 (1873).

34. Ackerman, *We the People: Transformations*, 211.

35. For a critique of Ackerman's legalism, see Rogers Smith, "Legitimating Reconstruction: The Limits of Legalism," *Yale Law Journal* 108 (1999): 2039–75. See also Moore, *Constitutional Rights and Powers of the People*. On the Court's role in American politics during this period, see William Lasser, *The Limits of Judicial Power* (Chapel Hill: University of North Carolina Press, 1987), and Donald Grier Stephenson, *Campaigns and the Court* (New York: Columbia University Press, 1999), 81–106.

36. Bradley and Field, moreover, saw the Civil War amendments as reaffirming, rather than transforming, constitutional foundations.

37. Constitution of the United States, Amendment XIV, Section 1.

38. *Slaughterhouse* at 74.

39. *Barron v. Baltimore*, 32 U.S. 243 (1833).

40. *Corfield v. Coryell*, 6 F. Cas. 546, 551–52 (1823).

41. Ironically, Taney's *Dred Scott* opinion argues for the national vision against the state vision, but excludes blacks from the terms of national citizenship. So even if states may bestow some rights on free blacks, they cannot bestow citizenship.

42. Jacobus tenBroek, *The Antislavery Origins of the Fourteenth Amendment* (Berkeley: University of California Press, 1951).

43. Nelson, *The Fourteenth Amendment*, 154, 163.

44. *Slaughterhouse* at 81. For the "free labor" influence on Field, see Paul Kens, *Justice Stephen Field: Shaping American Liberty from the Gold Rush to the Gilded Age* (Lawrence: University Press of Kansas, 1997).

45. Robert J. Kaczorowski, "Revolutionary Constitutionalism in the Era of the Civil War

and Reconstruction," *New York University Law Review* 61 (1986): 863–940. See also tenBroek, *The Antislavery Origins of the Fourteenth Amendment.*

46. Zuckert, "Congressional Power under the Fourteenth Amendment," 135.

47. *Slaughterhouse* at 106. As Washington had put it in *Corfield* at 551, "The inquiry is, what are the privileges and immunities of citizens in the several states? We feel no hesitation in confining these expressions to those privileges and immunities which are, in their nature, fundamental; which belong, of right, to the citizens of all free governments; and which have, at all times, been enjoyed by the citizens of the several states which compose this Union, from the time of their becoming free, independent, and sovereign. What these fundamental principles are, it would perhaps be more tedious than difficult to enumerate."

48. *Slaughterhouse* at 106.

49. *Slaughterhouse* at 116.

50. Lincoln, Speech at Peoria, Illinois, October 16, 1854, in Basler, *Abraham Lincoln: His Speeches and Writings,* 291. This sentiment also found early expression in John Dickinson's "Letters from a Farmer in Pennsylvania," where he insists, given a lack of consent to the laws and taxes that govern us, "We are therefore—SLAVES." Letter VII, in Forrest McDonald, ed., *Empire and Nation* (Indianapolis: Liberty Fund), 44.

51. Lincoln, Seventh Debate, *Lincoln-Douglas,* 305.

52. tenBroek, *Antislavery Origins of the Fourteenth Amendment;* William Wiecek, *The Sources of Antislavery Constitutionalism in America, 1760–1848* (Ithaca: Cornell University Press, 1977); Eric Foner, *Reconstruction: America's Unfinished Revolution, 1863–1877* (New York: Perennial Classics, 2002).

53. *Slaughterhouse* at 106.

54. Lincoln, First Debate, *Lincoln-Douglas,* 53.

55. See Murphy, "*Slaughter-House, Civil Rights,* and the Limits of Constitutional Change," and Moore, "(Re)Construction of Constitutional Authority and Meaning."

56. *Slaughterhouse* at 119, 125, 129.

57. *Slaughterhouse* at 87–88 and at 119–20.

58. Lincoln, "Fragment on Free Labor, September 17, 1859," in Roy B. Basler, ed., *Collected Works of Abraham Lincoln,* vol. 3 (New Brunswick, NJ: Rutgers University Press, 1953), 463. See also Speech at Cincinnati, Ohio, September 17, 1859, and Address to the Wisconsin State Agricultural Society, Milwaukee, Wisconsin, September 30, 1859.

59. Ackerman, *We the People: Transformations,* 280.

60. Howard Gillman, *The Constitution Besieged: The Rise and Demise of Lochner Era Police Powers Jurisprudence* (Durham: Duke University Press, 1994), offers a far more persuasive telling of the constitutional vision of the Court during this era.

61. Hyman and Wiecek, *Equal Protection under Law;* Smith, *Civic Ideals,* 327; Alfred Kelly, Winfred Harbison, and Herman Belz, *The American Constitution: Its Origins and Development,* 7th ed., vol. 2 (New York: W. W. Norton, 1991), 346–50.

62. Nelson, *The Fourteenth Amendment,* 124.

63. Murphy, "*Slaughter-House, Civil Rights,* and the Limits of Constitutional Change." See also Walter F. Murphy, "Merlin's Memory: The Past and Future Imperfect of the Once and Future Polity," in Sanford Levinson, ed., *Responding to Imperfection: The Theory and Practice of Constitutional Amendment* (Princeton: Princeton University Press, 1995), 163–90,

and *Constitutional Democracy: Creating and Maintaining a Just Political Order* (Baltimore: Johns Hopkins University Press, 2007), 497–529.

64. *United States v. Reese,* 92 U.S. 214 (1876), and *United States v. Cruikshank,* 92 U.S. 542 (1876).

65. *Reese* at 217.

66. Robert Goldman, *Reconstruction and Black Suffrage: Losing the Vote in Reese and Cruikshank* (Lawrence: University Press of Kansas, 2001), 100.

67. *Reese* at 241–42 (Hunt dissenting).

68. David Currie, *The Constitution in the Supreme Court, 1789–1888* (Chicago: University of Chicago Press, 1985), 393–94; Smith, *Civic Ideals,* 336; Frank J. Scaturro, *The Supreme Court's Retreat from Reconstruction: A Distortion of Constitutional Jurisprudence* (Westport, CT: Greenwood Press, 2000), 41; Goldman, *Reconstruction and Black Suffrage,* 90–100.

69. Though Waite does invoke language that hints at the unconstitutionality of the whole statute. *Reese* at 217.

70. If we take the argument for judicial supremacy seriously, as a necessary first step for the Court to authoritatively settle questions of constitutional meaning, it must lay down fully theorized constitutional opinions that give the political branches clear guidance about constitutional meaning. As a corollary, the Court must follow its precedents to provide for stable constitutional meaning. The Court does not do this.

71. *Reese* at 216.

72. Charles Fairman, *Reconstruction and Reunion, 1864–1888,* vol. 2 (New York: Macmillan, 1987), 251.

73. Charles Fairman argues, "It is not to be doubted that if Congress had enacted the substance of Sections 3 and 4 in apt language, the validity of the legislation would have been affirmed." But it is to be doubted, because there is a powerful argument that Congress had already done just this and the Court had ignored it. *Reconstruction and Reunion, 1864–88,* 257. For a general critique of Fairman, see Curtis, *No State Shall Abridge,* 100–105.

74. "By the words 'as aforesaid,' the provisions respecting race and color of the first and second sections of the statute are incorporated into and made a part of the third and fourth sections." *Reese* at 242 (Hunt dissenting).

75. *Reese* at 246.

76. Thus Fairman's criticism of poor and sloppy prosecutions may well be true; yet that does not lead to the conclusion that Waite's opinion was correct. Indeed, Waite's opinion is just as sloppy. One could have upheld the Enforcements Acts, while rejecting specific prosecutions, which is what Clifford does.

77. Fairman, *Reconstruction and Reunion,* 244.

78. Kelly, Harbison, and Belz, *The American Constitution,* 346–50, suggest that the opinion was appropriate, as it clearly limited congressional action to the terms of the amendment. Yet Waite does not take up the fact that Congress, in sections 1 and 2 of the act, had already done this. *The American Constitution,* 358. As Currie argues, "the Court got around this difficulty by proclaiming . . . that it had not power to rewrite an overbroad statute." *The Constitution in the Supreme Court, 1789–1888,* 395.

79. *Cruikshank* at 549.

80. If the state first fails to protect these rights, as came out of later opinions, then Con-

gress could act. This is true, as well, for section 2 of the Fifteenth Amendment, which, as we saw in *Reese*, did not confer the right to vote, but the right not to be deprived of one's vote on the basis of race.

81. Both Field and Bradley, however, joined the Court's opinion, as they did in *Reese*.

82. *Cruikshank* at 552–53.

83. It "is nowhere alleged in these counts that the wrong contemplated against the rights of these citizens was on account of their race or color." *Cruikshank* at 555.

84. The Court's opinion is so sly on this fact that Lee Epstein, Jeffrey Segal, Harold Spaeth, and Thomas Walker, *The Supreme Court Compendium: Data, Decisions, and Developments* (Washington, DC: CQ Press, 1994), do not even list *United States v. Cruikshank* as a Court decision holding an act of Congress unconstitutional (because it does so by indirection rather than explicitly, which might suggest that *reading* Court opinions, rather than simply looking at the outcome, might be of some import), 96. Charles Warren, *The Supreme Court in United States History* (Boston: Little, Brown, and Company, 1922), 604; Kelly, Harbison, and Belz, *The American Constitution*, 357; Currie, *The Constitution in the Supreme Court*, 395–97; and Smith, *Civic Ideals*, 334–36, all treat the opinion as striking down an act of Congress. Indeed, all discuss it in explicit terms of the constitutional vision it offered up and not the narrow holding.

85. *Cruikshank* at 569.

86. Michael Les Benedict, "Preserving Federalism: Reconstruction and the Waite Court," *The Supreme Court Review, 1978* (Chicago: University of Chicago Press, 1979).

87. Warren, *The Supreme Court in United States History*, 608.

88. Herman Belz, *Emancipation and Equal Rights: Politics and Constitutionalism in the Civil War Era* (New York: W. W. Norton, 1978), 108–40, notes that the nationalization of rights did not necessarily entail national centralization. Yet, southern resistance invited an increasing national role if these rights were to be protected.

89. Smith, *Civic Ideals*, 335–36. In *Reese* and *Cruikshank*, important as they were, only two sections of the various enforcement acts were found unconstitutional and those sections were repassed (with little modification) shortly after the decisions were handed down. Goldman, *Reconstruction and Black Suffrage*, 109. See also Robert Goldman, *A Free Ballot and a Fair Count: The Department of Justice and the Enforcement of Voting Rights in the South, 1877–1893* (New York: Fordham University Press, 2001), 17.

90. Michael McConnell, "Originalism and the Desegregation Decisions," *University of Virginia Law Review* 81(1995): 1080.

91. Sections 3 and 4, which were struck down in *Reese*, were repassed, but never came before the Court.

92. Scaturro, *The Supreme Court's Retreat from Reconstruction*, 15.

93. See *Congressional Record*, 43rd Cong., 2nd sess., part III (1874), 1791. Mr. Boutwell, "I am not disposed to discuss the Slaughter-house decision, as it is called. It will stand legally and politically for what it is worth. It related to a particular case. In that case and in every other case like that, if there shall be another case like that, it is law; but it is not law beyond the case in which the opinion was rendered, and therefore for myself I dismiss that case as a legislator when I come to consider new propositions." Boutwell then insisted "it is not law beyond the case; it is not law with reference to the rights of the states generally, and certainly

is not law for the Senate when the Senate is engaged in considering a question which is a different question from that on which the court passed." Boutwell then offered a reading of the "privileges and immunities clause" akin to Field's and Bradley's dissents, although never mentioning them, the logic of which squarely rejected Miller's majority opinion, at 1793.

94. See ibid. at 1792.

95. Mr. Thurman: "I confess that I am amazed that in the face of the plain language of this section [privileges and immunities clause of the Fourteenth Amendment], in the face of the solemn decision of the Supreme Court of the United States adverse to this proposition [Civil Rights Act] it yet is pressed upon the Congress of the United States, and we are asked to do what the language of the Constitution does not authorize us to do, and what the solemn decision of our Supreme Court declares we have no power whatever to do." Ibid. at 1792.

96. Ibid. at 1796. Much of the debate expounded upon the Constitution itself, with no reference to the Supreme Court, with many congressmen making reference to the "plain meaning of the Constitution upon its face" and adding, "that every judicial exposition of that instrument sustains this reasonable view," when the Court supported their argument, but not relying on the Court's opinions alone (at 1797). Others expressed sympathy for the act but insisted it was unconstitutional given *their* reading of the Constitution: "I entertain, as strongly as any Senator, the sentiments which have inspired this bill; and in the present unhappy condition of the South, I would go to the extreme limit of our constitutional power to support any bill calculated to protect the colored people of the South or to restore order in that distracted section. But I cannot go beyond the limits of the Constitution" (at 1861). One senator (Carpenter) noted the vexing question of judicial supremacy against departmentalism, treating the question of "Who interprets?" as an open question, but noting that all agree that the Supreme Court settles legal questions when they are given jurisdiction in particular cases—that is, by the legislature, as a way to invoke its rights. He then noted that the *Slaughterhouse Cases* settled this issue for those bringing suit (if not for Congress as a general rule) (at 1862). He thus rejected the Civil Rights Act, given the Court's various opinions on the Enforcement Acts, as it would "involve the colored man in litigation in which he is certain to be defeated" (at 1863). In these same debates Senator Edmunds accuses the opponents of the Civil Rights Act (and the various previous acts) of willfully misreading the Civil War amendments—obstructing their meaning at every turn, and acting as if the Constitution had not been amended. He discoursed, at great length, on the nature of rights and equality under the Constitution without a single reference to a Court opinion (at 1869–70).

97. Scaturro, *The Supreme Court's Retreat from Reconstruction*, 114–28.

98. Fairman, *Reconstruction and Reunion*, 172.

99. *Slaughterhouse* at 71 (emphasis added), 81.

100. Assuming it was to follow Court opinions, Congress may need to interpret Court opinions in the very way that the Court interprets the Constitution in order to apply them to particular acts. Yet if we follow the logic of Alexander and Schauer, and other proponents of judicial supremacy, this, itself, is to enter forbidden terrain. The whole point of authoritative judicial settlement is that opinions "supplant the reasons upon which they are based." Those who wish to follow the terms of settlement are "no longer required to consult the reasons behind the settlement in determining how to act, they are also required not to heed

those reasons if, from their perspective, those reasons conflict with the terms of settlement." But as we have seen, Court opinions, especially on constitutional questions, do not necessarily operate in this way, telling the Congress "what ought to be done." Larry Alexander and Emily Sherwin, *The Rule of Rules: Morality, Rules, and the Dilemmas of Law* (Durham: Duke University Press, 2001), 12–13; Larry Alexander and Frederick Schauer, "On Extrajudicial Constitutional Interpretation," *Harvard Law Review* 110, no. 7 (1997): 1367, and "Defending Judicial Supremacy: A Reply," *Constitutional Commentary* 17 (2000): 455–82.

101. Warren, *The Supreme Court in United States History,* 2:600. Ackerman suggests that these issues were truly settled in the election returns of 1868: "With their hold on national power reconfirmed in the consolidating election, Republicans in the White House and Capitol Hill took aggressive steps to pack the Supreme Court with men who would vindicate their new vision of the Union." He misses that some of these putative transformative appointees led the charge in overturning the Republican Congress's constitutional vision when it came to bringing the promise of the Declaration to the newly freed slaves—namely, Waite and Bradley, both appointed by Grant and confirmed by a Republican Congress. *We the People: Transformations,* 211.

102. Michael W. McConnell, "The Forgotten Constitutional Moment," *Constitutional Commentary* 2, no. 1 (1994): 115–44, goes so far as the call the election of 1876 a "constitutional moment" in Ackerman's terms.

103. McConnell, "Originalism and the Desegregation Decisions," 1081.

104. Madison to Jefferson, October 17, 1788, in Marvin Myers, ed., *The Mind of the Founder: Sources of the Political Thought of James Madison* (Indianapolis: Bobbs-Merrill Company, 1973), 206.

105. Lincoln, First Debate, *Lincoln-Douglas,* 64–65.

106. Warren argues that confidence in the Waite Court was high: "When it is recalled that in every year from 1850 to 1873 (with the exception of the five years of the war) there had been Congressional legislation proposed in serious derogation of the Court's powers, the practical immunity from assault which occurred from 1873 to 1884 is a notable feature in its history." *The Supreme Court in United States History,* 2:563.

107. McConnell, "Originalism and the Desegregation Decisions," 1066.

108. See Jaffa, *A New Birth of Freedom,* 464, situating Stephens within the contours of John Calhoun's thought.

109. *Civil Rights Cases,* 109 U.S. 3 (1883).

110. *Civil Rights Cases* at 11. See Pamela Brandwein, "The Civil Rights Cases and the Lost Language of State Neglect," in Kahn and Kersch, *The Supreme Court and American Political Development,* 275–325.

111. *Civil Rights Cases* at 13.

112. *United States v. Harris,* 106 U.S. 629 (1882). In *Harris,* Justice Woods, who like Bradley had once embraced a far-reaching view of the Civil War amendments and Congress's ability to enforce them, found section 2 of the Ku Klux Act of 1871 unconstitutional. The act made conspiracies to deprive citizens of their rights a crime. Woods articulated the view that Bradley would more fully develop in the *Civil Rights Cases:* the Fourteenth Amendment only protected rights against state action or failure (the Fifteenth was rejected as a constitutional basis of the act as it did not, as Waite said in *Reese,* confer a right to vote). See also Woods in

United States v. Hall, 26 F. 79 (1871). Bradley's earlier opinions might be distinguished if they rely upon the Thirteenth and Fifteenth amendments, not the Fourteenth (*Harris* at 637, 643, 639, and 641–42).

113. Curtis, *No State Shall Abridge,* 170.

114. Frederick Douglass, *Life and Times of Frederick Douglass: His Early Life as a Slave, His Escape from Bondage, and His Complete History, Written by Himself* (New York: Collier Books, 1962), 551; on the drift of the Court generally, 539–53. See also Moore, *Constitutional Rights and Powers of the People,* 53–65.

115. Watching the retreat from Lincoln's constitutionalism in 1876, Frederick Douglass insisted that "measured by the sentiment of his country, a sentiment he [Lincoln] was bound as a statesman to consult, he was swift, zealous, radical, and determined: because of his fidelity to Union and liberty, he is doubly dear to us." Douglass, "Oration in Memory of Abraham Lincoln," in Herbert J. Storing, ed., *What Country Have I? Political Writings by Black Americans* (New York: St. Martin's Press, 1970), 46–56.

116. Quoted in Scaturro, *The Supreme Court's Retreat from Reconstruction,* 129 (emphasis added). Fairman catalogs similar newspaper reactions, attesting to the view that the cases were correctly decided, which is not precisely what they show; see *Reconstruction and Reunion,* 569–82.

117. *The Civil Rights Cases* at 26 (Harlan dissenting). See also Harold Hyman, *The Reconstruction Justice of Salmon P. Chase* (Lawrence: University Press of Kansas, 1997), 107–22, discussing Chase along these lines.

118. Frederick Douglass, "This Decision Has Humbled the Nation: An Address Delivered in Washington, D.C. on 22 October 1883," in John W. Blassingame and John R. McKivigan, eds., *The Frederick Douglass Papers, Series One: Speeches, Debates, and Interviews,* vol. 5: *1881–95* (New Haven: Yale University Press, 1992), 118.

119. Ibid., 119. Both Justice Bradley and Judge Woods (Bradley as a Supreme Court justice sitting in circuit and Woods as a circuit court judge) had given the Civil War amendments a broad-based reading in a controversy that would come before the Supreme Court as part of the *Slaughterhouse Cases.* There both justices embraced the logic that would later be articulated in Bradley's *Slaughterhouse* dissent, rejecting Miller's distinction between the "privileges and immunities" of state citizenship and the "privileges and immunities" of U.S. citizenship. Yet Bradley himself would implicitly reject this reading in his circuit court opinion in *Cruikshank,* which served as the doctrinal basis of Chief Justice Waite's opinion for the Supreme Court. Woods had further spelled out the "privileges and immunities" of U.S. citizenship in *United States v. Hall,* offering, after corresponding with Bradley, a broad reading of the "privileges and immunities" of U.S. citizenship, which included all rights expressly secured in the Constitution. He went further in saying that Congress, by way of section 5, could enforce these rights against "insufficient" state protection and not just overt discrimination.

120. Douglass also calls it "the RING-BOLT to the chain of your nation's destiny." "What to the Slave Is the Fourth of July?" in William L. Andrews and William S. McFeely, *Narrative of the Life of Fredrick Douglass, an American Slave, Written by Himself* (New York: W. W. Norton, 1997), 120.

121. Fairman, *Reconstruction and Reunion,* 565. While Bradley's opinion might plausibly

be read as asserting the "state failure" doctrine, rather than the narrower "state action" doctrine, Fairman notes that Bradley argued that Congress could not "deprive" white people of choosing their own company, which may well have limited Congress's ability to prohibit segregation in public spaces. Ibid., 564. Bradley had, in fact, cast the deciding vote on the special electoral commission that delivered the presidency to Rutherford Hayes as part of the Compromise of 1877. And that event intervenes between Bradley's *Slaughterhouse* dissent and his opinion in the *Civil Rights Cases*.

122. *Munn v. Illinois*, 94 U.S. 113 (1877).

123. *Allgeyer v. Louisiana*, 165 U.S. 578, 589–90 (1897).

124. See Charles A. Lofgren, *The Plessy Case: A Legal-Historical Interpretation* (New York: Oxford University Press, 1987).

125. *Civil Rights Cases* at 25.

126. *Plessy v. Ferguson*, 163 U.S. 537, 545 (1896). While the Court opinions in this time period seem to evolve with the nation's retreat from Reconstruction, the evolution of constitutional meaning is not always so clear. In *Ex Parte Yarbrough*, 110 U.S. 651 (1884), a year after *Harris* and a mere eight years after *Reese,* the Supreme Court came very close to saying that the Fifteenth Amendment conferred the right to vote, which was rejected in these earlier opinions. *Yarbrough* was based on the two sections of the Enforcement Act of 1870 that were found wanting (rather than explicitly declared unconstitutional) in *Reese*. This time the Court upheld the action. What is more, the Court took up the right to vote. Waite's opinion in *Reese* unequivocally stated that the Fifteenth Amendment confers no such right. This was reiterated in Justice Woods's opinion in *Harris* just the year before. But Miller's opinion stated that the Fifteenth Amendment "does, propio vigore, substantially confer the negro the right to vote, and Congress has the power to protect and enforce that right"; *Yarbrough* at 665. Miller does, just before, note that it is quite true that, as the Court said in Reese, the Fifteenth Amendment confers not the right to vote but only the right not to be discriminated against in the vote, that it may "operate as the immediate source of the right to vote." See also Goldman, *Reconstruction and Black Suffrage*, 115.

127. Justice Harlan: The Fourteenth Amendment does not "permit any public authority to know the race of those entitled to be protected in the enjoyment of rights"; *Plessy* at 554. See Frederick Douglass, "In Law Free; in Fact, a Slave: Address Delivered in Washington, D.C., on 16 April 1888," in Blassingame and McKivigan, *The Frederick Douglass Papers*, 372–73, arguing that Harlan "stood by the plain intention of the fourteenth amendment."

128. *Brown v. the Board of Education*, 347 U.S. 483, 493–95 (1954).

129. Even if the Court gets the Constitution wrong, proponents of judicial supremacy are fond of quoting Justice Brandeis: "in most matters it is more important that the applicable rule of law be settled than that it be settled right." Yet, they often fail to note Brandeis's subsequent sentence: "But in cases involving the Federal Constitution, where correction through legislative practice is practically impossible, this Court has often overruled its earlier decisions. The Court bows to the lessons of experience and the force of better reasoning[.]" *Burnet v. Coronado Oil & Gas Co.*, 285 U.S. 393, 406, 407–8 (1932) (Brandeis dissenting). On judicial supremacy and the settlement function, see Alexander and Schauer, "On Extrajudicial Constitutional Interpretation," 1371.

130. *Heart of Atlanta Motel, Inc. v. United States,* 379 U.S. 241 (1964), and *Katzenbach v. McClung,* 379 U.S. 294 (1964).

131. This reads Bradley's opinion as insisting upon "state failure," not "state action."

132. The state action limitation doctrine was itself altered by Supreme Court opinions, *Shelley v. Kraemer,* 334 U.S. 1 (1948). Moreover, in *Bell v. Maryland,* 378 U.S. 226 (1964), several members of the Court were prepared to reject the *Civil Rights Cases* outright. Constitutional doctrine was in the process of evolving on the Court—surely in relation to political changes—and was not simply held stable.

133. Congressional politics played a part as well, as the legislation was shifted to a more accommodating committee, away from southerners resistant to the legislation. Lucas A. Powe Jr., *The Warren Court and American Politics* (Cambridge: Harvard University Press, 2000), 234–38. See also Richard Valley, *The Two Reconstructions: The Struggle for Black Enfranchisement* (Chicago: University of Chicago Press, 2004), noting the successful entrenchment of civil rights the second time around.

134. *Civil Rights Cases* at 10. Fairman tries to insist that the commerce clause was not considered, but he ducks Bradley's logic. See *Reconstruction and Reunion,* 559.

135. Richard Cortner, *Civil Rights and Public Accommodations: The Heart of Atlanta and McClung Cases* (Lawrence: University Press of Kansas, 2001), 115.

136. Bradley's opinion in the *Civil Rights Cases* dealt with private discrimination in public accommodations: "Whether it might not be a denial of a right which, if sanctioned by the state law, would be obnoxious to the prohibitions of the Fourteenth Amendment, is another question" (at 21). He then went on to say, "The Fourteenth Amendment extends its protection to races and classes, and prohibits any State legislation which has the effect of denying to any race or class, or to any individual, the equal protection of the laws" (at 24). We might plausibly conclude from this that state-mandated segregation would be just such an unconstitutional distinction: "If the laws themselves make any unjust discrimination, amenable to the prohibitions of the Fourteenth Amendment, Congress has full power to afford a remedy under that amendment and in accordance with it" (at 25).

137. Brandwein, "The Civil Rights Cases and the Lost Language of State Neglect."

138. This, even after a series of Warren Court cases went some way to rejecting the logic of the *Civil Rights Cases.* Thus, while in *Boerne* and *United States v. Morrison,* 529 U.S. 598 (2000), the Rehnquist Court drew on elements of the *Civil Rights Cases,* the interpretation these opinions offered was rather different from the interpretation offered by the immediate Warren Court precedents, seemingly shifting "constitutional meaning" to the current of the Court.

139. See *United States v. Lopez,* 514 U.S. 549 (1995), and *United States v. Morrison.*

Three • *The Progressive Reconstruction of American Constitutionalism*

1. *Pollock v. Farmers' Loan and Trust Company,* 158 U.S. 601 (1895).

2. *United States v. E. C. Knight Co.,* 156 U.S. 1 (1895).

3. *In Re Debs,* 158 U.S. 564 (1895).

4. Charles A. Lofgren, *The Plessy Case: A Legal-Historical Interpretation* (New York: Oxford University Press, 1987).

5. Charles Warren, *The Supreme Court in United States History, 1836–1918* (Boston: Little Brown, 1922), 702.

6. Barry Friedman, "The History of the Countermajoritarian Difficulty, Part Three: The Lesson of Lochner," *New York University Law Review* 76 (2001): 1383–1455.

7. Sidney Milkis and Daniel Tichenor, "'Direct Democracy' and Social Justice: The Progressive Party Campaign of 1912," *Studies in American Political Development* 8 (Fall 1994): 329.

8. Herbert Croly, *Progressive Democracy* (New Brunswick, NJ: Transaction Publishers, 1914), 149–50.

9. Theodore Roosevelt, introduction to William L. Ransom, *Majority Rule and the Judiciary* (New York: Charles Scribner's Sons, 1912), 6.

10. Woodrow Wilson, *Constitutional Government in the United States* (New York: Columbia University Press, 1908), 172.

11. Alpheus Thomas Mason, *William Howard Taft: Chief Justice* (New York: Simon and Schuster: 1965), 75.

12. Sidney Milkis, *Political Parties and Constitutional Government* (Baltimore: Johns Hopkins University Press, 1998). William J. Novak, "The Legal Origins of the Modern American State," in Austin Sarat, Bryan Garth, and Robert Kagan, eds., *Looking Back at Law's Century* (Ithaca: Cornell University Press, 2002), notes that it has long been a progressive trope to see law as obstruction, even when utilizing the law in the "state-building" effort. See, for example, Woodrow Wilson, *The State* (Boston: D.C. Heath, 1889), and Stephen Skowronek, *Building a New American State: The Expansion of National Administrative Capacity* (Ithaca: Cornell University Press, 1981). As Skowronek argues, "Forged in the wake of a liberal revolt against the state, the American Constitution has always been awkward and incomplete as an organization of state power" (287). In contrast, see Novak, *The People's Welfare: Law and Regulation in Nineteenth-Century America* (Chapel Hill: University of North Carolina Press, 1996).

13. Herbert Croly, *The Promise of American Life* (Boston: Northeastern University Press, 1989 [1909]). About Lincoln's shrewd equivocations on full black equality, Croly said that "he had his sensible doubts about the equality between the negro and the white man" (94). TR invited Booker T. Washington to the White House, and Taft delivered speeches speaking to the necessity of living up the Fourteenth Amendment's promise—for example, "Southern Democracy and Republican Principles" in Lexington Kentucky, August 22, 1907, in Taft, *Collected Works,* vol. 1: *Four Aspects of Civic Duty and Present Day Problems* (Athens: Ohio University Press, 2001). Wilson, on the other hand, provided for the resegregation of the U.S. Civil Service.

14. In contrast, see William Howard Taft, *Our Chief Magistrate and His Powers* (Durham: Carolina Academic Press, 2002 [1916]).

15. Roosevelt, introduction to Ransom, *Majority Rule and the Judiciary,* 4.

16. Wilson, *Constitutional Government in the United States,* 54. See also Woodrow Wilson, *The New Freedom: A Call for the Emancipation of the Generous Energies of a People* (New York: Doubleday, Page, 1913), 46–47.

17. Wilson, *Constitutional Government in the United States,* 56. Woodrow Wilson, "Cabinet Government in the United States" and "Congressional Government," in Ronald J. Pes-

tritto, ed., *Woodrow Wilson: The Essential Political Writings* (Lanham, MD: Lexington Books, 2005), 134, 164, which both reject the separation of powers in favor of some version of the English system where the legislature and executive are combined. See, on Wilson's thought generally, Ronald J. Pestritto, *Woodrow Wilson and the Roots of Modern Liberalism* (Lanham, MD: Rowman and Littlefield, 2005).

18. Wilson, *Constitutional Government in the United States,* 56.

19. While the English Constitution had a single sovereign authority, in contrast, Wilson argued, the American Constitution rests on the principle of "having many sovereign authorities, and hoping that their multitude may atone for their inferiority." Situating this in terms of "development," Wilson argued that "so long as they [the people] adhere to the forms of such a constitution, so long as the machinery of government supplied by it is the only machinery which the legal and moral sense of such a people permits it to use, its political development must be in many directions narrowly restricted because of an insuperable lack of open and adequate channels." Wilson, "Congressional Government," in Pestritto, *Woodrow Wilson,* 164, 165.

20. At least the Roosevelt of the 1912 election. His earlier views, as elaborated by Jeffrey K. Tulis, *The Rhetorical Presidency* (Princeton: Princeton University Press, 1987), are more clearly aimed at upholding the Constitution.

21. James W. Ceaser, *Nature and History in American Political Development* (Cambridge: Harvard University Press, 2006).

22. Croly, *The Promise of American Life,* 27–52.

23. Wilson, *Constitutional Government in the United States,* 199, and "Congressional Government," 163. See Tulis, *The Rhetorical Presidency,* and James W. Ceaser, *Presidential Selection: Theory and Development* (Princeton: Princeton University Press, 1978), on the intellectual foundations of the "modern" presidency.

24. See Ken I. Kersch, *Constructing Civil Liberties: Discontinuities in the Development of American Constitutional Law* (New York: Cambridge University Press, 2004), on the deconstructive aspects of progressive thought, which involved "erasing" the constitutional past. For traditional scholarly accounts of the period, see, for example, Alpheus Thomas Mason, *The Supreme Court from Taft to Burger* (Baton Rouge: Louisiana State University Press, 1979), *Harlan Fiske Stone: Pillar of the Law* (New York: Viking, 1956), and "The Core of Free Government, 1938–40: Mr. Justice Stone and 'Preferred Freedoms,'" *Yale Law Journal* 65 (1956): 597–628; Robert McCloskey, *The American Supreme Court,* 2nd ed. (Chicago: University of Chicago Press, 1994); and William Leuchtenburg, *The Supreme Court Reborn* (New York: Oxford University Press, 1994). For leading revisionist accounts, see Howard Gillman, "The Collapse of Constitutional Originalism and the Rise of the Notion of the 'Living Constitution' in the Course of American State-Building," *Studies in American Political Development* 11 (Fall 1997): 191–247, "Preferred Freedoms: The Progressive Expansion of State Power and the Rise of Modern Civil Liberties Jurisprudence," *Political Research Quarterly* 47, no. 3 (September 1994): 623–53, and *The Constitution Besieged: The Rise and Demise of Lochner Era Police Power's Jurisprudence* (Durham: Duke University Press, 1993); Bruce Ackerman, *We the People: Transformations* and *We the People: Foundations* (Cambridge: Harvard University Press, 1991 and 1998); and Stephen Griffin, *American Constitutionalism: From Theory to Politics* (Princeton: Princeton University Press, 1998).

25. Tulis, *The Rhetorical Presidency.* See also Daniel Stid, *The President as Statesman: Woodrow Wilson and the Constitution* (Lawrence: University Press of Kansas, 1998).

26. While the plebiscitary nature of the modern presidency is rooted in the progressive vision of democracy, with the executive acting on behalf of the popular will, this progressive shift in our view did not wholly displace the constitutional foundations of the presidency. Rather, the plebiscitary presidency overlays the constitutional presidency, and these conflicting visions and institutional features remain in tension with one another, occasionally coming into open conflict—in the 2000 election, for example. Stephen Skowronek and Karen Orren have dubbed these conflicting visions "intercurrence" in *The Search for American Political Development* (New York: Cambridge University Press, 2004). Bruce Ackerman attempts to locate this change in Thomas Jefferson, but conflates popular sovereignty with a plebiscitary presidency. *The Failure of the Founding Fathers: Jefferson, Marshall and the Rise of Presidential Democracy* (Cambridge: Harvard University Press, 2005).

27. Keith E. Whittington, "The Political Foundations of Judicial Supremacy," in Sotirios A. Barber and Robert P. George, eds., *Constitutional Politics: Essays on Constitution Making, Maintenance, and Change* (Princeton: Princeton University Press, 2001), 270. See also Whittington, *Political Foundations of Judicial Supremacy: The Presidency, the Supreme Court, and Constitutional Leadership in U.S. History* (Princeton: Princeton University Press, 2007).

28. Donald Morgan, *Congress and the Constitution* (Cambridge: Harvard University Press, 1966), 142; Melvin Urofsky and Paul Finkelman, *A March of Liberty: A Constitutional History of the United States*, vol. 2: *From 1877 to the Present* (New York: Oxford University Press, 2002), 535. Scott James argues that the act merely federalized the common law, which only limited "unreasonable" restraints upon trade, but was reinterpreted by the executive branch for largely political reasons. Scott James, "Prelude to Progressivism: Party Decay, Populism, and the Doctrine of 'Free and Unrestricted Competition' in American Antitrust Policy, 1890–1897," *Studies in American Political Development* 13 (Fall 1999): 288–336. See also William Letwin, *Law and Economic Policy in America: The Evolution of the Sherman Antitrust Act* (New York: Random House 1965); Martin J. Sklar, *The Corporate Reconstruction of American Capitalism, 1890–1916: The Market, the Law, and Politics* (New York: Cambridge University Press, 1988); and James W. Ely Jr., *The Chief Justiceship of Melville Fuller, 1888–1910* (Columbia: University of South Carolina Press, 1995).

29. Mark A. Graber, "The Nonmajoritarian Difficulty: Legislative Deference to the Judiciary," *Studies in American Political Development* 7 (1993): 52. James notes that the act was misnamed, as Sherman's original intent was altered by the final bill; see "Prelude to Progressivism," 294.

30. Morgan, *Congress and the Constitution*, 154.

31. Edward Corwin, "The Anti-Trust Act and the Constitution," *Virginia Law Review* 18, no. 4 (1932): 369.

32. Taft in David Potash and Donald F. Anderson, eds., *The Collected Works of William Howard Taft*, vol. 5: *Popular Government & The Anti-Trust Act and the Supreme Court* (Athens: Ohio University Press, 2003), 174–75.

33. Morgan, *Congress and the Constitution*, 144.

34. James, "Prelude to Progressivism," 313.

35. Taft, *The Anti-Trust Act and the Supreme Court*, 202.

204 Notes to Pages 71–72

36. Although that is not to say that Fuller was a simpleminded "formalist" and Harlan was a sophisticated "realist." See Barry Cushman, "Formalism and Realism in Commerce Clause Jurisprudence," *University of Chicago Law Review* 67 (2000): 1089–1150.

37. Owen Fiss, *The Troubled Beginnings of the Modern State* (New York: Macmillan, 1994), 114. See also Alan Furman Westin, "The Supreme Court, the Populist Movement and the Campaign of 1896," *Journal of Politics* 15, no. 1 (1953): 3–41. This is true, too, of Donald Grier Stephanson Jr., *Campaigns and the Court: The U.S. Supreme Court in Presidential Elections* (New York: Columbia University Press, 1999), 117.

38. *United States v. Trans-Missouri Freight Association*, 166 U.S. 290 (1896); *United States v. Joint Traffic Association*, 171 U.S. 505 (1898); and *Addyston Pipe and Steel Co. v. United States*, 175 U.S. 211 (1899).

39. Letwin, *Law and Economic Policy in America*, 136. Some members of the Congress, who were dependent on executive prosecutions to enforce the act, insisted that the executive was not enforcing the law vigorously enough, or that the Court was deliberately distorting it. On the other hand, Cleveland's subsequent attorney general, even while bringing prosecutions, called for Congress to amend and clarify the act. And Cleveland himself insisted that antitrust laws had proved ineffective, "not because of any lack of disposition or attempt to enforce them, but simply because the laws themselves as interpreted by the courts do not reach the difficulty."

40. Stephenson, *Campaigns and the Court*, 126. In *Pollock,* the Court held that a national tax on incomes more than $4,000 (less than 1 percent of the population at the time) was an unconstitutional "direct" tax. The *Pollock* opinion caused far more of a public opinion storm than *Knight,* as it was seen to run counter to Supreme Court precedents—one dating back to the Founding generation—that suggested such a moderate tax was constitutional. In *Pollock* I the Court struck down a section of the income tax provision of the Wilson-Gorman Tariff Act of 1894, distinguishing between a tax on income and a tax on real estate, which was equated with a direct tax and, therefore, read as unconstitutional. Attorney General Olney petitioned for a direct rehearing, suggesting the executive branch did not buy the Court's opinion and sought to change it immediately (Fiss, "Troubled Beginnings," 97). In *Pollock* II (1895) the Court struck down all provisions of the income tax, but in doing so, seemingly rejected early Supreme Court opinions—*Hylton v. United States* (1796) and *Springer v. United States* (1881). Moreover, the Court, under pressure from Congress, public opinion, and the president upheld a similar tax on corporations in *Flint v. Stone Tracy Company* (1909) prior to the enactment and ratification of the 16th Amendment (which, of course, made the income tax constitutional).

41. Westin, "The Supreme Court, the Populist Movement and the Campaign of 1896," 27.

42. *In Re Debs* at 599.

43. John Semonche, *Charting the Future: The Supreme Court Responds to a Changing Society, 1890–1920* (Westport, CT: Greenwood Press, 1978), 218.

44. Taft, *The Anti-Trust Act and the Supreme Court,* 202.

45. *E. C. Knight* at 210 quoting *Gibbons v. Ogden,* 9 Wheat. 1, 189. The power is "plenary," Harlan insisted, as "it may be exercised whenever the subject exists" (*Knight* at 196 quoting *Gibbons* at 195). In *Addyston,* Peckham similarly insisted that Congress's commerce power

was plenary: "The reasons which may have caused the framers of the Constitution to repose the power to regulate interstate commerce in Congress do not, however, affect or limit the extent of the power itself" (*Addyston* at 228).

46. *E. C. Knight* at 34. See also *Kidd v. Pearson*, 128 U.S. 1 (1888). In fact, neither Harlan nor Fuller cite the Tenth Amendment, but rest their arguments wholly on the reach of the commerce power. On the *Knight* decision and its relation to *Gibbons v. Ogden*, see the exchange between Robert Lowry Clinton, "Judicial Review, Nationalism, and the Commerce Clause: Contrasting Antebellum and Postbellum Supreme Court Decision Making," and Howard Gillman, "The Struggle over Marshall and the Politics of Constitutional History," and Clinton's "John Marshall's Federalism: A Reply to Professor Gillman," *Political Research Quarterly* 47, no. 4 (1994): 857–90. See also a second exchange: Howard Gillman, "More on the Origins of the Fuller Court's Jurisprudence: Reexamining the Scope of Federal Power over Commerce and Manufacturing in Nineteenth-Century Constitutional Law," and Wallace Mendelson, "John Marshall and the Sugar Trust: A Reply to Professor Gillman," and "Nullification via Dual Federalism A Second Response to Professor Gillman," *Political Research Quarterly* 49, no. 2 (1996): 405–44. Richard Epstein, *How Progressives Rewrote the Constitution* (Washington, DC: Cato, 2006), argues that *E. C. Knight* and its line of decisions may have exceeded Marshall's view of the commerce power in *Gibbons*, 35.

47. *McCulloch v. the State of Maryland*, 17 U.S. 316, 423 (1819).

48. Theodore Roosevelt, "From the President's Message at the Opening of the Second Session of the Fifty-Seventh Congress," December 2, 1902, in *The Roosevelt Policy*, vol. 1 (New York: Current Literature Publishing Company, 1919), 182, 183.

49. Croly, *Promise of American Life*, 169, 34.

50. Croly, *Progressive Democracy*, 274.

51. Tulis, *The Rhetorical Presidency*, 110.

52. Ceaser, *Nature and History in American Political Development*, 62–63.

53. Roosevelt, *The Roosevelt Policy*, 1:248–49.

54. Ibid., 1:266. The Interstate Commerce Commission (ICC) had been established in 1887 as the nation's first administrative commission. Thomas Cooley, whose famous treatise on constitutional limitations had a profound influence on the thought of the period, was the ICC's first chair, suggesting that national regulation was indeed consistent with the constitutional thought of the era. In fact, prior to the Hepburn Act, when the ICC attempted to exercise rate-making power, the Court rejected that as inconsistent with the original act establishing the commission: given the separation of powers, one could not assume that Congress had confirmed an agency with legislative power (rate fixing) if such a power was not clearly bestowed. But Congress seemed to confirm this view when it amended the act in 1903 with the Elkins Act, but even against the backdrop of the Court's opinion it did not confer the ICC with the power to set rates.

55. Semonche, *Charting the Future*, 209.

56. Skowronek, *Building the New American State*, 261: The Court's "actions suggested that it would now use judicial discretion more cautiously so as to move with, rather than against, the mounting political pressures for change, and that in doing so, it would readjust its position in the new state on its own terms."

57. Roosevelt, *The Roosevelt Policy*, 1:83.

58. *Northern Securities Co. v. United States*, 193 U.S. 197 (1904).

59. Croly, *The Promise of American Life*, 356–37.

60. Croly, *Progressive Democracy*, 220.

61. Croly, *The Promise of American Life*, 358–59.

62. Taft, "The Present Issues of the Two Great Parties," in *The Collected Works of William Howard Taft*, vol. 2: *Political Issues and Outlooks* (Athens: Ohio State University Press, 2003), 21. Taft's conclusion is not so clear, as the logic of both the Court and the Roosevelt and Taft administrations underwent a number of important changes, yet these cases reached a stable understanding of antitrust.

63. Taft, *The Anti-Trust Act and the Supreme Court*, 195–96.

64. *Northern Securities* at 305. The government's brief referred to *E. C. Knight* once, but only to note that the action here had a direct effect on interstate commerce (at 315). *Champion v. Ames*, 188 U.S. 321 (1903).

65. *Champion* at 355. For Harlan, this regulation was itself a regulation of interstate commerce. Fuller, in dissent, disagreed.

66. *Northern Securities* at 334. In dissent, Justice White: "The plenary authority of Congress over interstate commerce . . . is thus conceded." The question at issue in *Northern Securities*, however, "is not commerce at all" (at 368). In contrast, Harlan argued, "there was no actual investment, in any substantial sense, by the Northern Securities Company in the stock of the two constituent companies. It was, in form, such a transaction, it was not, in fact, one of that kind" (at 353–54).

67. Tinsley E. Yarbrough, *Judicial Enigma: The First Justice Harlan* (New York: Oxford University Press, 1995), viii.

68. *Northern Securities* at 402–3. This case does not conform to progressive lore in another matter was well. Justice Brewer, often vilified as a reactionary, upheld the government's action in a concurring opinion.

69. *Lochner v. New York*, 198 U.S. 45, 76 (1905).

70. See especially George Lovell, *Legislative Deferrals: Statutory Ambiguity, Judicial Power, and American Democracy* (New York: Cambridge University Press, 2003).

71. *Lochner* at 75.

72. *Swift & Co. v. United States*, 196 U.S. 375 (1905), itself seemed at odds with *Hopkins v. United States*, 171 U.S. 578 (1898), which limited Congress's power to regulate interstate commerce on stockyard sales of out-of-state cattle, not seeing this movement as part of the flow of interstate commerce.

73. As Holmes argued, "Therefore the case is not like United States v. E. C. Knight Co., 156 U.S. 1, where the subject matter of the combination was manufacture and the direct object monopoly of manufacture within a State. However likely monopoly of commerce among the States in the article manufactured was to follow from the agreement it was not a necessary consequence nor a primary end. Here the subject matter is sales and the very point of the combination is to restrain and monopolize commerce among the States in respect of such sales. The two cases are near to each other, as sooner or later always must happen where lines are to be drawn, but the line between them is distinct." *Swift & Co.* at 297.

74. Cushman, "Formalism and Realism in Commerce Clause Jurisprudence," 1129.

75. G. Edward White, *The Constitution and the New Deal* (Cambridge: Harvard University Press, 2000).

76. Loren Beth, *The Development of the American Constitution* (New York: Harper and Row, 1971), 141. There is a question of whether TR's reading was consistent with the original terms of the Sherman Act, but it certainly shows that the act itself left this discretion to the executive branch by relying on it, through the courts, to enforce the act's terms. See Richard Wagner, "A Falling Out: The Relationship between Oliver Wendell Holmes and Theodore Roosevelt," *Journal of Supreme Court History* 27, no. 2 (2002): 114–37.

77. Theodore Roosevelt, *The New Nationalism* (New York: Outlook Co., 1911).

78. Milkis, *Political Parties and Constitutional Government*, 59–61. Tulis, *The Rhetorical Presidency*. See also Stid, *The President as Statesman*. See also Friedman, "The Lesson of Lochner," 1443, on the 1912 election and the Court, and "The Birth of an Academic Obsession: The History of the Countermajoritarian Difficulty, Part Five," *Yale Law Journal* 112 (2002): 152–259.

79. Steven G. Calabresi, "The Libertarian-Lite Constitutional Order and the Rehnquist Court," *Georgetown Law Journal* 93 (2005): 1023–60, argues that the Sixteenth and Seventeenth amendments were central to preserving the progressive vision. See also Ralph A. Rossum, *Federalism, the Supreme Court, and the Seventeenth Amendment: The Irony of Constitutional Democracy* (Lanham, MD: Lexington Books, 2001).

80. Taft, *Our Chief Magistrate*, 138. Referring to Jefferson's, Jackson's, and Lincoln's stance against judicial supremacy, Taft said it was not necessary to dispute "these distinguished men." He went on, "it is sufficient to say that the Court is a permanent body, respecting precedent and seeking consistency in its decision, and that therefore its view of the Constitution, whether binding on the Executive and the legislature or not, is likely ultimately to prevail as accepted law."

81. Croly, *Progressive Democracy*, 253, 126. See also Novak, "The Legal Origins of the Modern American State," 258, arguing that scholars of American political development continue to embrace "the classic Progressive trope: law as obstruction."

82. Croly, *Progressive Democracy*, 220.

83. Milkis, *Political Parties and Constitutional Government*, 61.

84. Roosevelt, *The Roosevelt Policy*, 605, 600.

85. Roosevelt, *The New Nationalism*, 257.

86. Ibid., 39–40. As Roosevelt would argue, "the people could not decide in a more conflicting fashion, could not possibly make their decision conflict with one another to a greater degree, than has actually been the case with the courts." Roosevelt, introduction to Ransom, *Majority Rule*, 14–15. See also Croly, *Progressive Democracy*, 233.

87. Henry Cabot Lodge, *Alexander Hamilton* (Boston: Houghton Mifflin, 1898), 182. Wilson even praised Lodge's biography in "Congressional Government"; Pestritto, *Woodrow Wilson*, 163.

88. Henry Cabot Lodge, "The Democracy of Abraham Lincoln," in his *The Democracy of the Constitution; and Other Addresses and Essays* (New York: Charles Scribner, 1915), 138. Others, like Nicholas Murray Butler, president of Columbia, also engaged in this effort, writing *True and False Democracy* (New York: Scribner's Sons, 1915), as well as later defenses of the Constitution, such as *Building the American Nation: An Essay of Interpretation* (New

York: Scribner's Sons, 1939). Butler would be attacked by Roosevelt for his adherence to the judiciary against the people. See also Herman Belz, *A Living Constitution or Fundamental Law? American Constitutionalism in Historical Perspective* (Lanham, MD: Rowman and Littlefield, 1998), 57–75.

89. Lodge, "The Democracy of Abraham Lincoln," 139.

90. Stid, *The President as Statesman*, 156–59.

91. Wilson, *The New Freedom*, 48.

92. Ibid., 49. See also Wilson, "The Authors and Signers of the Declaration of Independence," in Pestritto, *Woodrow Wilson*, 97–106, and "Address at Independence Hall: The Meaning of Liberty," July 4, 1914, www.presidency.ucsb.edu/ws/print.php?pid=65381 (accessed June 15, 2007). As Wilson put it in the latter, "Have you ever read the Declaration of Independence or attended with close comprehension to the real character of it when you have heard it read? If you have, you will know that it is not a Fourth of July oration. The Declaration of Independence was a document preliminary to war. It was a vital piece of practical business, not a piece of rhetoric; and if you will pass beyond those preliminary passages which we are accustomed to quote about the rights of men and read into the heart of the document you will see that it is very express and detailed, that it consists of a series of definite specifications concerning actual public business of the day." Wilson even insisted that to understand the Declaration, we should omit the first two paragraphs, rejecting it is a philosophical foundation for government. See Pestritto, *Woodrow Wilson*, 56.

93. Wilson, *The New Freedom*, 50.

94. Ibid., 25.

95. Milkis and Tichenor, "'Direct Democracy' and Social Justice," 327.

96. Morton Keller, "Social and Economic Regulation in the Progressive Era," in Jerome Mileur and Sidney Milkis, eds., *Progressivism and the New Democracy* (Amherst: University of Massachusetts Press, 1999), 122. Progressives like Croly and Walter Lippmann were often harsh critics of Wilson's inability—or unwillingness—to act against Congress, to remain in "drift." See Walter Lippmann, *Drift and Mastery* (Madison: University of Wisconsin Press, 1985), 101–12.

97. *Loewe v. Lawlor*, 208 U.S. 274 (1908).

98. William Wiecek, *The Lost World of Classical Legal Thought: Law and Ideology in America, 1886–1937* (New York: Oxford University Press, 1998); Corwin, "Anti-Trust," 286; Lovell, *Legislative Deferrals*, 112.

99. *Duplex Printing v. Deering*, 254 U.S. 443 (1921). See also Lovell, *Legislative Deferrals*, 99–160.

100. Kersch, *Constructing Civil Liberties*, 168–69. Taft also rejected the application of the act to unions in several instances.

101. Wilson, *Constitutional Government in the United States*, 170, 171.

102. Quoted in Mason, *William Howard Taft*, 75.

103. *Hammer v. Dagenhart*, 247 U.S. 251 (1919). Day tried to distinguish this case from the likes of the oleomargarine case, by saying that Congress could prevent harmful goods from moving in interstate commerce, but not goods that were, in themselves, unharmful—and nothing about the products produced with child labor was harmful per se. See Walter Murphy, *Congress and the Court: A Study in the American Political Process* (Chicago: University

of Chicago Press, 1963). See also Stephen B. Wood, *Constitutional Politics in the Progressive Era: Child Labor and the Law* (Chicago: University of Chicago Press, 1968).

104. *Bailey v. Drexel Furniture Company*, 259 U.S. 20 (1922). Alpheus Thomas Mason in his biography of Taft suggests that Taft was being wildly inconsistent. But Mason himself was engaged in a reconstructive effort to place the progressive and New Deal justices in line with John Marshall's nationalism, *Williams Howard Taft*, 260–61.

105. *Bailey* at 40–41. See *McCray v. United States*, 195 U.S. 27 (1904), as well as opinions upholding the Pure Food and Drugs Act of 1906 (*Hipolite Egg Co. v. United States*, 220 U.S. 45 [1911]) and the Mann Act (*Hoke v. United States*, 227 U.S. 308 [1913]). *McCray*, the oleomargarine case, is especially troublesome, as it upheld an extensive congressional tax on yellow-colored margarine (a tax that was hard to read as a revenue measure, as uncolored margarine was barely taxed), which entered the forbidden territory of manufacture, was not in the "current of commerce," and did not have a significant impact on commerce. Nor was it "unhealthy."

106. *Stafford v. Wallace*, 258 U.S. 495, 518–19 (1922). The current of commerce theory adopted by a unanimous Court in *Swift*, even if relying on the "public interest" of the business, sat uneasily alongside *E. C. Knight's* formal distinction between manufacturing and commerce. Moreover, Fuller's insistence that Congress may reach only those things that have a "direct" rather than "indirect" affect upon commerce in *Knight* had itself been qualified—if not overturned—by the Court's various opinions in antitrust.

107. *Adair v. United States*, 208 U.S. 161 (1908).

108. *Loewe v. Lawlor*.

109. *Employers Liability Cases*, 207 U.S. 463 (1908). Also, in *Ex parte Young*, 209 U.S. 123 (1908), the Court enjoined a state officer from proceeding against a corporation on the grounds that the law was unconstitutional. In the wake of *Young*, the states appealed to Congress and President Roosevelt, who took up the issue, and Congress, in 1910, passed a statute forbidding such injunctions, unless it was heard in a court with three federal judges (one of whom must be at least a circuit court judge). The Elkins-Mann Act, see Warren, *The Supreme Court in United States History*, 717.

110. Fiss, *Troubled Beginnings of the Modern State*, 166.

111. Abraham Lincoln, "Annual Message to Congress, December 3, 1861," in Gore Vidal, ed., *Lincoln: Selected Speeches and Writings* (New York: Library of America 1992), 325.

112. Roosevelt, *The New Nationalism*, 128. As I noted in the previous chapter, Lincoln's criticism of property in slaves was not a criticism of property as a liberty or the rights of property. It was, rather, a rejection of property in human beings and the moral equivalence between property in human beings and other types of property.

113. Ibid., 136.

114. Ibid., 245.

115. The government's defense of section 10 illustrates the unsettled state of interstate commerce, as it drew upon the Court's recent commerce clause opinions: "The right of individuals or corporations to make contracts and do business is at all times subservient to the power of Congress to regulate interstate commerce, and common carriers are subject to greater control than private individuals by the State or Congress . . . on account of the public nature of such business" (*Adair* at 64).

116. See Lofgren, *The Plessy Case*, 156–64, discussing such classifications and the regulation of public health, welfare, and morals.

117. *Lochner* at 66–67.

118. *Adair* at 175.

119. *Adair* at 175. The Court was responsive to Congress's broader reading of commerce on occasion. After it struck down an act regulating both interstate and intrastate employment relations as part of interstate commerce, in a second Employer's Liability decision the Court upheld a congressional reenactment that made the law applicable to employees in interstate commerce only, falling into line with Roosevelt's insistence, in a private letter to Justice Day, that if the reasoning of the first Employer's Liability case persisted, "we should not only have a revolution, but it would be absolutely necessary to have a revolution, because the condition of the worker would become inoperable." Urofsky and Finkleman, *A March of Liberty*, 579.

120. *Adair* at 179. For a discussion of the common-law link between liberty of contract and the commerce clause, see James R. Stoner Jr., *Common-Law Liberty: Rethinking American Constitutionalism* (Lawrence: University Press of Kansas, 2003), 125–47.

121. Roscoe Pound, "Liberty of Contract," *Yale Law Journal* 18, no. 7 (1908): 454. See also Pound, "Mechanical Jurisprudence," *Columbia Law Review* 8, no. 8 (1908): 605–23.

122. *Adair* at 191.

123. *Lochner* at 75. See also Albert W. Alschuler, *Law without Values: The Life Work, and Legacy of Justice Holmes* (Chicago: University of Chicago Press, 2000).

124. Gillman, *Constitution Besieged*, 131; Barry Cushman, *Rethinking the New Deal Court: The Structure of a Constitutional Revolution* (New York: Oxford University Press, 1998), 109–38; and Friedman, "The Lesson of Lochner," see Holmes as breaking with the jurisprudence of the day; whereas White, *The Constitution and the New Deal*, 246–47, sees Holmes as working within the framework of guardian review. For a general discussion of revisionism, see Gary D. Rowe, "Lochner Revisionism Revisited," *Law & Social Inquiry* 24 (1999): 221–52; David Bernstein, "*Lochner* Era Revisionism, Revised: *Lochner* and the Origins of Fundamental Rights Constitutionalism," *Georgetown Law Journal* 82 (2003): 1–60, and "*Lochner's* Legacy's Legacy," *Texas Law Review* 92 (2003): 1–64.

125. Lovell, "'As Harmless as an Infant': Deference, Denial, and *Adair v. United States*," *Studies in American Political Development* 14 (Fall 2000): 223.

126. Ibid., 223.

127. Warren, *The Supreme Court in United States History*, 715.

128. Taft, *The Anti-Trust Act and the Supreme Court*, 195.

129. Croly, *The Promise of American Life*, 387.

130. Ibid., 278–79.

131. Croly, *Progressive Democracy*, 55.

132. Learned Hand, *The Bill of Rights* (New York: Antheum, 1963).

133. Learned Hand, "Due Process of Law and the Eight-Hour Day," *Harvard Law Review* 21, no. 7 (1908): 495–509.

134. Wilson, *The New Freedom*, 8–10, 13.

135. Croly, *Progressive Democracy*, 385.

136. Hadley Arkes, "*Lochner v. New York* and the Cast of Our Laws," in Robert P. George,

ed., *Great Cases in Constitutional Law* (Princeton: Princeton University Press, 2000), 104. See also David Bernstein, "The Story of Lochner v. New York: Impediment to the Growth of the Regulatory State," in Michael C. Dorf, *Constitutional Law Stories* (New York: Foundation Press, 2004), 325–75; Bernard Seigan, *Economic Liberties and the Constitution* (Chicago: University of Chicago Press, 1980); and Paul Kens, *Lochner v. New York: Economic Regulation on Trail* (Lawrence: University Press of Kansas, 1998).

137. Wilson, "The Study of Administration," *Political Science Quarterly* 2, no. 2 (1887): 214.

138. Wilson, *Constitutional Government,* 16.

139. Ibid., 14. Situating America against England in constitutional development, in "Congressional Government," Wilson wrote, "The English Constitution was at that time in reality much worse than our own; and, if it is now superior, it is so perhaps because its growth has not been hindered or destroyed by the too tight ligaments of a written fundamental law"; in Pestritto, *Woodrow Wilson,* 164.

140. Wilson, *Constitutional Government,* 5. Indeed, Wilson speaks of four stages of constitutional development where in the last stage we get a near merger of the people and the government as one, "in which the leaders of the people themselves became the government, and the development was complete" (28).

141. Kersch, *Constructing Civil Liberties,* 152.

142. See, for example, *Yick Wo v. Hopkins,* 118 U.S. 356 (1886).

143. Charles Warren, "The Progressiveness of the United States Supreme Court," *Columbia Law Review* 13, no. 4 (April 1913): 294–313, and "A Bulwark to the State Police Power—The United States Supreme Court," *Columbia Law Review* 13, no. 8 (December 1913): 667–95.

144. Warren, "The Progressiveness of the United States Supreme Court," 294.

145. Warren, "A Bulwark to the State Police Power," 668.

146. Croly, *Progressive Democracy,* 368.

147. Epstein, *How Progressives Rewrote the Constitution*, 106–7. See Kersch, *Constructing Civil Liberties,* 147–54.

148. *Meyer v. Nebraska,* 262 U.S. 390 (1923), and *Pierce v. Society of Sisters,* 268 U.S. 510 (1925). Modern defenders of "privacy" would try to rescue these cases, without considering their constitutional foundations. See especially *Griswold v. Connecticut,* 381 U.S. 479 (1925).

149. See *Muller v. Oregon,* 208 U.S. 412 (1908), upholding a maximum-hour law for women. The Court's opinion was unanimous and written by Justice Brewer, a leading proponent of liberty of contract and, though often forgotten in our age, a leading proponent of women's equality (along with Justice George Sutherland, another Court "reactionary"). See also *Bunting v. Oregon,* 243 U.S. 426 (1917), where it upheld a general ten-hour workday.

150. *Adkins v. Children's Hospital,* 261 U.S. 525 (1923). See also Stoner, *Common-Law Liberty,* arguing that there was a more doctrinaire movement from the earlier common-law understandings during this period, 140–45.

151. Wiecek, *The Lost World of Classical Legal Thought,* 157.

152. Elihu Root, *Experiments in Government and the Essentials of the Constitution* (Princeton: Princeton University Press, 1913), 78.

153. Wilson, *Constitutional Government in the United States,* 158, 68.

154. Stid, *The President as Statesman,* 151–67.

Four • Discontinuities in the "Constitutional Revolution of 1937"

1. Franklin D. Roosevelt, Two Hundred and Eighth Press Conference, May 29, 1935, in *The Public Papers and Addresses of Franklin D. Roosevelt,* vol. 4: *The Court Disapproves,* comp. Samuel I. Rosenman (New York: Random House, 1938), 205. See also Bruce Ackerman, *We the People: Transformations* (Cambridge: Harvard University Press, 1998), 327.

2. Franklin Delano Roosevelt, "Fireside Chat on Reorganization of the Judiciary," March 9, 1937, www.fdrlibrary.marist.edu/030937.html (accessed June 13, 2007).

3. Robert Jackson, *The Struggle for Judicial Supremacy: A Study of a Crisis in American Power Politics* (New York: Knopf, 1941), xv.

4. Quoted in Howard Gillman, "The Collapse of Constitutional Originalism and the Rise of the Notion of the 'Living Constitution' in the Course of American State-Building," *Studies in American Political Development* 11 (Fall 1997): 231.

5. Jackson, *The Struggle for Judicial Supremacy,* xv.

6. Cass R. Sunstein, *The Second Bill of Rights: FDR's Unfinished Revolution and Why We Need It More Than Ever* (New York: Basic Books, 2004), 75.

7. Franklin Delano Roosevelt, "Commonwealth Club Address," in *The Public Papers and Addresses of Franklin D. Roosevelt,* vol. 1: *The Genesis of the New Deal,* comp. Samuel I. Rosenman (New York: Random House, 1938), 752, 754, 756.

8. Kevin McMahon, *Reconsidering Roosevelt on Race: How the Presidency Paved the Road to Brown* (Chicago: University of Chicago Press, 2004); Sidney Milkis, *The President and the Parties: The Transformation of the American Party System since the New Deal* (New York: Oxford University Press, 1993); and Sunstein, *The Second Bill of Rights.*

9. Robert Bork, *The Tempting of America: The Political Seduction of the Law* (New York: Free Press, 1990); Raoul Berger, *Government by Judiciary: The Transformation of the Fourteenth Amendment,* 2nd ed. (Indianapolis: Liberty Fund, 1998); and Antonin Scalia, "Originalism: The Lesser Evil," *University of Cincinnati Law Review* 57 (1989): 849–54. Keith E. Whittington, *Constitutional Interpretation: Textual Meaning, Original Intent, and Judicial Review* (Lawrence: University Press of Kansas, 1999), offers a more principled argument for original intent, grounding it in the principles of popular sovereignty and the nature of a written constitution, rather than as a way to limit judicial will. This also suggests that revisionist scholars of American constitutional development like Howard Gillman cannot so easily cast the Court's protection of "unenumerated" privacy rights as part of the New Deal Constitution, rejecting the putative "double standard"—if *Roe,* then *Lochner*—as inapposite under the (New Deal) Constitution. See Howard Gillman, "Preferred Freedoms: The Progressive Expansion of State Power and the Rise of Modern Civil Liberties Jurisprudence," *Political Research Quarterly* 47, no. 3 (1994): 649–50. See also Ackerman, *We the People: Transformations,* 390, and Stephen M. Griffin, *American Constitutionalism: From Theory to Politics* (Princeton: Princeton University Press 1996), 162.

10. Barry Friedman, "The Birth of an Academic Obsession: The History of the Countermajoritarian Difficulty, Part Five," *Yale Law Journal* 112 (2002): 153–259, tries a different angle. Friedman gives a persuasive history of this academic obsession, which, he argues, is rooted in the progressive critique of the Lochner Court. Friedman argues, though, that this

obsession is inapplicable to the constitutional debates, including the public reaction to judicial decisions, which follows the New Deal era. It may well be that we should get over this
dilemma, as Friedman argues, but his advice to "liberals" at times seems to suggest that they
should stop worrying about justifying judicial review in such terms and focus on the
results—do you like the outcome? Elsewhere, "The History of the Countermajoritarian
Difficulty, Part Three: The Lesson of Lochner," *New York University Law Review* 76 (2001),
1390, Friedman argues that judicial review should be justified more in terms of public acceptance of judicial outcomes than the "legal" reasoning such decisions are based upon. But
even this move, troublesome as it is, would seem to take us back to debates about *Roe* and
Lochner: isn't *Roe,* perhaps, just as illegitimate under these terms as *Lochner* was? So if this is
the true "lesson of Lochner," then this old debate remains just as potent (at least in this
area).

11. Ken I. Kersch, "The New Deal Triumph as the End of History? The Judicial Negotiation of Labor Rights and Civil Rights," in Ronald Kahn and Ken I. Kersch, eds., *The Supreme
Court and American Political Development* (Lawrence: University Press of Kansas, 2006),
169–226.

12. The era may be more unique for the constitutional thought that it fostered, rather
than its constitutional politics. While scholars tend to focus on the "Constitutional Revolution of 1937," in many ways the most important development was the change in constitutional thought during the Progressive Era, which not only shaped the New Deal breakthrough, but it continues to structure and shape our jurisprudential debates.

13. *Louisville Joint Stock Bank v. Radford,* 295 U.S. 555 (1935), written by Justice Brandeis.

14. The "hot oil" cases struck down sections of the National Industrial Recovery Act,
Panama Refining Company v. Ryan (1935).

15. *Schechter Poultry Corp. v. United States,* 295 U.S. 495, 553 (1935).

16. In fact, many in the administration—Homer Cummings, for example—were quietly
happy to see it go.

17. *Schechter* at 543.

18. *United States v. E. C. Knight,* 156 U.S. 1 (1895).

19. *Schechter* at 546. Hughes did cite his opinion in the *Minnesota Rate Cases,* 230 U.S.
352 (1913), noting that local matters could be regulated if they had an impact on interstate
commerce and were affected with a "public interest," which was true of railroads. Cushman,
in fact, points out that all of these cases dealt with railroads. See Barry Cushman, "Formalism and Realism in Commerce Clause Jurisprudence," *University of Chicago Law Review* 67
(2000): 1133.

20. Jackson, *The Struggle for Judicial Supremacy,* 78. See also Keith E. Whittington, *Political Foundations of Judicial Supremacy: The Presidency, the Supreme Court, and Constitutional
Leadership in U.S. History* (Princeton: Princeton University Press, 2007).

21. See Alpheus Thomas Mason, *The Supreme Court from Taft to Burger* (Baton Rouge:
Louisiana State University Press, 1979), and Edward Corwin, "The Anti-Trust Act and the
Constitution," *Virginia Law Review* 18, no. 4 (1932): 355–78. In the *Shreveport Rate Case,* 234
U.S. 342 (1914), for example, Hughes's opinion argued that Congress's "paramount authority
always enables it to intervene at its discretion for the complete and effective government of

that which has been committed to its care, and, for this purpose and to this extent, in response to a conviction of national need, to displace local laws by substituting laws of its own. The successful working of our constitutional system has thus been made possible." But Mason and Corwin ignore Hughes's insistence on "that which has been committed to" Congress's care. And while Hughes would argue, "In such cases, Congress must be judge of the necessity of federal action" (*Shreveport* at 351), this did not reject the Court's looking at a law's constitutionality, which was distinct from its necessity.

22. *Stafford v. Wallace*, 258 U.S. 495, 521 (1922) (which Justice Sutherland joined).

23. *Schechter* at 549. This lead Corwin to insist that "the Court's application here [in *Schechter*] of the distinction between 'direct' and 'indirect' effects upon interstate commerce represents an attempt to revive a precedent forty years old, and one which subsequent adjudication had almost completely discredited." Corwin dramatically overstates his case. Corwin, "The Schechter Case—Landmark, or What?" in Richard Loss, ed., *Corwin on the Constitution*, vol. 2 (Ithaca: Cornell University Press, 1987), 351.

24. *Schechter* at 554.

25. Roosevelt, Two Hundred and Eighth Press Conference, May 29, 1935, 209.

26. Roosevelt, Campaign Address, Detroit, Michigan, October 2, 1932, 774.

27. James W. Ceaser, *Nature and History in American Political Development* (Cambridge: Harvard University Press, 2006), 66.

28. Felix Frankfurter, *The Commerce Clause under Marshall, Taney, and Waite* (Chapel Hill: University of North Carolina Press, 1937), 2. See also Howard Lee McBain, *The Living Constitution: A Reconsideration of the Realities and Legends of Our Fundamental Law* (New York: Workers Bookshelf, 1927).

29. There is, still, a debt to Woodrow Wilson's understanding of constitutional government and the meaning of constitutional "development"; see *Constitutional Government in the United States* (New York: Columbia University Press, 1908), 1–24, 28. See also Charles R. Kesler, "The Public Philosophy of the New Freedom and the New Deal," in Robert Eden, ed., *The New Deal and Its Legacy: Critique and Reappraisal* (New York: Greenwood Press, 1989), 155–66.

30. Jackson, *The Struggle for Judicial Supremacy*, 78.

31. Ibid., 79.

32. Frankfurter, *The Commerce Clause under Marshall, Taney, and Waite*, 42.

33. This is Gary J. Jacobsohn's contention in *Pragmatism, Statesmanship, and the Supreme Court* (Ithaca: Cornell University Press, 1977), 190–91. As Jacobsohn notes, in a series of lectures on the Supreme Court prior to his being appointed Chief Justice, Hughes approvingly quoted Justice Sutherland's language from *Euclid v. Ambler County*, 272 U.S. 365 (1926), that the "application of constitutional principles" is given a degree of elasticity while the meaning of those principles remains the same (182). Sutherland, of course, drew on this very language to criticize Hughes's opinion in *Home Building and Loan Association v. Blaisdell*, 290 U.S. 398 (1934). In contrast to Jacobsohn, see Hadley Arkes, *The Return of George Sutherland: Restoring a Jurisprudence of Natural Rights* (Princeton: Princeton University Press, 1994), 243–50. If Jacobsohn is right, the most profound difference might be between Hughes and Sutherland on the one hand, and Justice Cardozo on the other. This is perhaps made more plausible by the fact that Hughes incorporated language into his *Blaisdell* opinion

from Cardozo's concurring opinion, which was never issued, that spoke more clearly of evolving meaning. For Cardozo's concurrence, see Walter F. Murphy, James E. Fleming, Sotirios A. Barber, and Stephen Macedo, *American Constitutional Interpretation*, 3rd ed. (New York: Foundation Press, 2003), 223–26.

34. *Schechter* at 529.

35. Charles A. Lofgren, "The Origins of the Tenth Amendment: History, Sovereignty, and the Problem of Constitutional Intention," in his *Government from Reflection and Choice: Constitutional Essays on War, Foreign Relations, and Federalism* (New York: Oxford University Press, 1986), 70–115.

36. For a powerful argument that the fundamentals of the New Deal, particularly "big government," nationalism, and a powerful presidency, flow from the fundamentals of the original Constitution, see Jeffrey K. Tulis, "The Constitutional Presidency in American Political Development.," in Martin L. Fausold and Alan Shank, eds., *The Constitution and the American Presidency* (Albany: SUNY Press, 1991), 133–47. Tulis's argument is all the more interesting as he rejects the notion of an evolutionary constitution where constitutional ends are wholly open. See also Herbert J. Storing, "The Problem of Big Government," in Joseph Bessette, ed., *Toward a More Perfect Union* (Washington, DC: AEI Press, 1995), 287–306.

37. All quotations are from Roosevelt, "Commonwealth Club Address," 752. In his May 29, 1935, press conference, FDR did seem to insist that the Constitution would have to change with "emergency." As FDR said in shocked reaction to the Court's *Schechter* decision, "But the Supreme Court has finally ruled that extraordinary conditions do not create or enlarge constitutional power" (206–7).

38. For such a view, see Sotirios Barber, *Welfare and the Constitution* (Princeton: Princeton University Press, 2003), 92–93.

39. Ackerman, *We the People: Transformations*, 306. It is also far from clear that the public supported a "constitutional transformation," as Ackerman suggests. See Barry Cushman, "Mr. Dooley and Mr. Gallup: Public Opinion and Constitutional Change in the 1930s," *Buffalo Law Review* 50 (2002), 73–74.

40. As Ken Kersch notes, the Wagner Act was in fact drafted largely behind closed doors by lawyers, and thus he finds it difficult to believe that the act provided a democratic ratification of the New Constitutional Revolution, as Bruce Ackerman makes out; see *Constructing Civil Liberties: Discontinuities in the Development of American Constitutional Law* (New York: Cambridge University Press, 2004), 179.

41. Sidney Milkis, *Political Parties and Constitutional Government* (Baltimore: Johns Hopkins University Press, 1998), 84.

42. Ibid., 81.

43. Sunstein, *The Second Bill of Rights*, 26.

44. Wilson, *Constitutional Government*, 4, 5.

45. Roosevelt, "The Commonwealth Club Address," 753.

46. Sunstein, *The Second Bill of Rights*, 26–27.

47. Cass R. Sunstein, in *The Partial Constitution* (Cambridge: Harvard University Press, 1993), and "Lochner's Legacy," *Columbia Law Review* 87 (1987): 873, treats all "baselines" as

equal, because they all require some form of regulation. In contrast, see Hadley Arkes, *Beyond the Constitution* (Princeton: Princeton University Press, 1990).

48. Sunstein, *The Second Bill of Rights,* 160. When Roosevelt's attorney general, Homer Cummings, was called before Congress to testify on the act, he also demurred as to its constitutionality: "advising the subcommittee 'to push it through and leave the question to the courts.'"

49. Franklin Delano Roosevelt, Address at the Democratic Victory Dinner, Washington, DC, March 4, 1937, in *The Public Papers and Addresses of Franklin D. Roosevelt: 1937,* vol. 6: *The Constitution Prevails,* comp. Samuel I. Rosenman (New York: Macmillan, 1941), 116.

50. Ibid.,118.

51. *United States v. Butler,* 297 U.S. 1 (1936).

52. *United States v. Butler* at 78, 79.

53. *United States v. Butler* at 85. "It is a contradiction in terms to say that there is a power to spend for the national welfare, while rejecting any power to impose conditions reasonably adapted to the attainment of the end which alone would justify the expenditure." As the court had said, "But the adoption of the broader construction [Hamiltonian] leaves the power to spend subject to limitations" (at 66). Roberts continued, "We are not now required to ascertain the scope of the phrase 'general welfare of the United States' or to determine whether an appropriation in aid of agriculture falls within it" (at 68).

54. Stone reiterated this in dissent in *Morehead v. Tipaldo,* 298 U.S. 587, 636 (1936), where the Court struck down a New York state minimum-wage law. Stone insisted that *Nebbia v. New York,* 291 U.S. 502 (1934), which upheld a state regulation of the price of milk, redefined the public-private distinction in such a way that made it inconsistent with the Court's earlier minimum-wage opinions. These earlier opinions—most notably *Adkins*—adhered to a distinction between public and private that the Court had rejected in *Nebbia.* Thus, following *Nebbia,* the Court should uphold the current minimum-wage case and, thereby, explicitly reject its precedents. Barry Cushman persuasively suggests that *Nebbia,* authored by Justice Roberts, was inconsistent with *Tipaldo,* but that the Court was not considering the broad constitutional question—as Stone called for—but only the narrow question of whether the New York law could be distinguished from the Court's earlier precedent in *Adkins.* Roberts, thinking it could not, voted with the majority on this narrow question, even if it pulled against the thrust of his reasoning in *Nebbia.* See Cushman, *Rethinking the New Deal Court: The Structure of a Constitutional Revolution* (New York: Oxford University Press, 1998), 84–105.

55. *Carter v. Carter Coal Co.,* 298 U.S. 238, 292 (1936).

56. In fact, Sutherland offered a long exposition on the very nature of the Union and the Constitution to situate his reading of the commerce power. "The effect of the labor provisions of the [act] primarily falls upon production and not upon commerce. [P]roduction is a purely local activity. It follows that none of these essential antecedents of production constitutes a transaction in or forms any part of interstate commerce" (*Carter v. Carter Coal* at 298). Sutherland then spun out direct and indirect effects: "The word 'direct,'" Sutherland reasoned, "implies that the activity or condition invoked or blamed shall operate proximately—not mediately, remotely, or collaterally—to produce the effect" (at 307–8). He continued: "The distinction between a direct and an indirect effect turns, not upon the magni-

tude of either the cause or the effect, but entirely upon the manner in which the effect has been brought about."

57. *Home Building and Loan Association v. Blaisdell* at 448–49. See also Arkes, *The Return of George Sutherland*, 243–50.

58. *Carter v. Carter Coal* at 309. "[T]he conclusive answer is that the evils are all local evils over which the federal government has no legislative control. . . . Such effect as they may have upon commerce, however extensive it may be, is secondary and indirect. An increase in the greatness of the effect adds to its importance. It does not alter its character."

59. *Carter v. Carter Coal* at 318. Even so, Hughes departed from the Court on the price-fixing provisions, insisting it was separable and, while not then properly before the Court, may be constitutional.

60. *Carter v. Carter Coal* at 306.

61. *Carter v. Carter Coal* at 327. "Mining and agriculture and manufacture are not inter-state commerce considered by themselves, yet their relation to that commerce may be such that for the protection of the one there is need to regulate the other. Sometimes it is said that the relation must be 'direct' to bring that power into play. In many circumstances such a description will be sufficiently precise to meet the needs of the occasion. But a great prin-ciple of constitutional law is not susceptible of comprehensive statement in an adjective." He argued that the Court should not reach the question of hours and wages.

62. "Within rulings the most orthodox, the prices for intrastate sales of coal have so inescapable a relation to those for interstate sales that a system of regulation of the one class is necessary to give adequate protection to the system of regulation adopted for the other" (*Carter v. Carter Coal* at 328).

63. Barry Cushman, "Lost Fidelities," *William and Mary Law Review* 41 (1999): 95–145, and Richard Friedman, "Switching Time and Other Thought Experiments: The Hughes Court and Constitutional Transformation," *University of Pennsylvania Law Review* 42, no. 6 (1994): 1892–1984.

64. While the Court was not an explicit issue in the 1936 election, this sentiment was central to FDR's constitutional reconstruction in the election's aftermath. See William Leuch-tenburg, "When the People Spoke, What Did They Say? The Election of 1936 and the Acker-man Thesis," and Laura Kalman, "Law, Politics, and the New Deal(s)," *Yale Law Journal* 108, no. 8 (1999): 2077–2114, 2105–2214.

65. Franklin Delano Roosevelt, Second Inaugural, in *The Public Papers and Addresses of Franklin D. Roosevelt: 1937*, vol. 6: *The Constitution Prevails*, 2.

66. Roosevelt, Address at the Democratic Victory Dinner, Washington, DC, March 4, 1937, 117.

67. Ibid., 120.

68. All quotations are from Roosevelt, "Fireside Chat on Reorganization of the Judi-ciary."

69. Ibid. See also McMahon, *Reconsidering Roosevelt on Race*, 71.

70. Compare this to Alexander Hamilton's insistence in *Federalist* 84 that "the Constitu-tion is itself, in every rational sense, and to every useful purpose, A BILL OF RIGHTS." Ham-ilton, James Madison, and John Jay, *The Federalist Papers*, introduction and notes by

Charles R. Kesler, ed. Clinton Rossiter (New York: Signet Classics, 1999), 514. See also Arkes, *Beyond the Constitution*, 58–80.

71. Roosevelt, Message to Congress on the State of the Union, January 11, 1944, in *The Public Papers and Addresses of Franklin D. Roosevelt*, vol. 9: *War and Aid to Democracies*, comp. Samuel I. Rosenman (New York: Macmillan, 1945), 40.

72. McMahon, *Reconsidering Roosevelt on Race*, 78.

73. As Cushman argues, based upon polls of the era, "In none of these polls did Roosevelt's proposal ever command the support of a majority. In fact, the Court packing episode seemed only to harden the views of the Court expressed in the April 1936 Fortune survey. In this issue published in July of 1937, 23.1% of those questioned agreed that the Court had 'recently stood in the way of the people's will,' while 43.1% contended that the Court had 'protected the people against rash legislation.'" Cushman, "Mr. Dooley and Mr. Gallup," 69.

74. FDR even titled his 1938 volume of papers and addresses, *The Continuing Struggle for Liberalism. The Public Papers and Addresses of Franklin D. Roosevelt: 1938*, vol. 7, comp. Samuel I. Rosenman (New York: Macmillan, 1941).

75. Kersch, *Constructing Civil Liberties*, 179.

76. In drafting the National Labor Relations Act—known as the Wagner Act for its sponsor—Leon Keyserling, a young Harvard Law graduate working on Senator Wagner's staff, carefully laid out a "Findings and Policy" explaining the purpose of the legislation and squarely rooting it in the "current of commerce" theory. In defending the legislation, Senator Wagner himself drew on Hughes's earlier opinions permitting the regulation of unfair labor practices that created a burden on interstate commerce and even quoted Taft. See Peter Irons, *The New Deal Lawyers* (Princeton: Princeton University Press, 1982), 227, 232–33. Thus in attempting to distinguish this second round of New Deal legislation from the first round, the lawyers drafting and then arguing the National Labor Relations Act constitutionality before the courts were more careful than the National Recovery Act lawyers arguing the first round of legislation. See also Cushman, *Rethinking the New Deal Court*, and Richard Cortner, *The Jones and Laughlin Case* (New York: Knopf, 1970).

77. Roosevelt, Address at the Democratic Victory Dinner, Washington, DC, March 4, 1937, 120.

78. As Justice McReynolds noted in dissent, however, it is difficult to imagine these cases being upheld, no matter how carefully the law was crafted, given the Court's earlier reasoning: "A more remote and indirect interference with interstate commerce or a more definite invasion of the powers reserved to the states is difficult, if not impossible, to imagine."

79. *West Coast Hotel Co. v. Parrish*, 300 U.S. 379, 391 (1937).

80. *West Coast Hotel* at 391. See also James R. Stoner Jr., *Common-Law Liberty: Rethinking American Constitutionalism* (Lawrence: University Press of Kansas, 2003), 140–45.

81. *National Labor Relations Board v. Jones and Laughlin Steel Corp.*, 301 U.S. 1, 31 (1937). In its brief, the government drew heavily on *Stafford v. Wallace* and argued that *Schechter* and *Carter* were not applicable.

82. *Jones & Laughlin* at 36. Yet Hughes did not bind congressional regulation to the "current of commerce theory" alone: "We do not find it necessary to determine whether these features of defendant's business dispose of the asserted analogy to the 'stream of commerce' cases. The instances in which that metaphor has been used are but particular, and not exclu-

sive, illustrations of the protective power which the Government invokes in support of the present Act. The congressional authority to protect interstate commerce from burdens and obstructions is not limited to transactions which can be deemed to be an essential part of the flow of interstate or foreign commerce."

83. *Jones & Laughlin* at 36–37.

84. As Cushman suggests, even in the wake of Hughes's opinion many thought both *Schechter* and *Carter Coal* were still good law. *Rethinking the New Deal Court*, 169.

85. *Jones & Laughlin* at 37.

86. It was also consistent with the logic of Cardozo's dissent in *Carter v. Carter Coal*. "We are asked to shut our eyes to the plainest facts of our national life and deal with the question of direct and indirect effects in an intellectual vacuum." *Jones & Laughlin* at 41.

87. The 1938 act was based on Congress's commerce power, not its power to tax and spend, but it was not clear at the time how far-reaching the commerce power was. The new Agricultural Adjustment Act was upheld in *Mulford v. Smith* (1939).

88. The act was upheld in *Sunshine Anthracite Coal Company v. Adkins* (1940).

89. *United States v. Darby*, 312 U.S. 100, 115 (1941). "Whatever their motive and purpose, regulations of commerce which do not infringe some constitutional prohibition are within the plenary power conferred on Congress by the Commerce Clause."

90. *United States v. Darby* at 115–16.

91. Stone then insisted that, "the motive and purpose of a regulation of interstate commerce are matters for the legislative judgment upon the exercise of which the Constitution places no restriction and over which the courts are given no control" (*United States v. Darby* at 115).

92. *Wickard v. Filburn*, 317 U.S. 111 (1942). This was very clearly a "durable shift in governing authority," which was far removed from even Cardozo's insistence in *Schechter* that "to find proximity here is to find it everywhere." G. Edward White, "Constitutional Change and the New Deal: The Internalist/Externalist Debate," *American Historical Review* 10, no. 4 (2006): 40. In the same issue, see Laura Kalman, "The Constitution, the Supreme Court, and the New Deal," 1052–80, and William E. Leuchtenburg, "Comment on Laura Kalman's Article," 1052–93.

93. Franklin Delano Roosevelt, Message to Congress, January 6, 1941, in *The Public Papers and Addresses of Franklin D. Roosevelt*, vol. 9, comp. Samuel I. Rosenman (New York: Macmillan, 1942), 663, 672.

94. Roosevelt, State of the Union, January 11, 1944, 41.

95. Barber, *Welfare and the Constitution*, and Sunstein, *The Second Bill of Rights*.

96. McMahon, *Reconsidering Roosevelt on Race*, 33.

97. McMahon, *Reconsidering Roosevelt on Race*, illustrates how "civil rights" for African Americans were advanced by the executive branch, through the courts, in just this manner.

98. For this view, see Barber, *Welfare and the Constitution*.

99. This is Sunstein's view in *The Second Bill of Rights*.

100. Gary J. Jacobsohn, *The Supreme Court and the Decline of Constitutional Aspiration* (Lanham, MD: Rowman and Littlefield, 1986), 29. Others, of course, continue to see this as a grand opportunity to create the "modern" Constitution. See William Wiecek, *The Birth of*

the Modern Constitution: The United States Supreme Court, 1941–1953 (New York: Cambridge University Press, 2006).

101. Barber, *Welfare and the Constitution*, 3.

102. Jacobsohn, *Pragmatism, Statesmanship, and the Supreme Court*, 171–72. "With this understanding, the mental gymnastics, for example, of those who were advocates of judicial self-restraint prior to 1937 and then suddenly found themselves defending judicial activism (while concurrently groping for a principled way in which to explain the abrupt reversal of their judicial philosophy), might have been avoided." In a similar fashion, Whittington's argument for originalism begins from constitutional principles and is thus quite different from conservative arguments for originalism like Bork's and Scalia's. See Whittington, *Constitutional Interpretation*, 17–46.

103. *Butler* at 79.

104. Max Lerner, "Constitution and Court as Symbols," *Yale Law Journal* 46, no. 8 (1937): 1290–1319. "If these groups succeed in their efforts to make out of the Constitution once more . . . an 'instrument' for the common interest, the Constitutional symbol will get renewed strength; but the path toward such a reshaping of the Constitutional symbol lies necessarily through the decline and fall of the symbol of the divine right of judges."

105. Barry Friedman, "The History of the Countermajoritarian Difficulty, Part Four: Law's Politics," *University of Pennsylvania Law Review* 148, no. 4 (2000): 1046. Friedman might properly be labeled "post-revisionist" in that he takes revisionist scholarship seriously and yet is not a "traditionalist," but has begun to merge the insights of both. Revisionists, however, easily go along with this "post-1937" view. As Howard Gillman puts it, "The eventual collapse of this constitutional tradition signaled the rise of a new American Republic organized around a different understanding of the proper use of legislative power." Gillman, *The Constitution Besieged: The Rise and Demise of Lochner Era Police Powers Jurisprudence* (Durham: Duke University Press, 1993), 15.

106. Laura Kalman, *The Strange Career of Legal Liberalism* (New Haven: Yale University Press, 1996), 5; C. Herman Pritchett, *The Roosevelt Court: A Study in Judicial Politics and Values* (New York: Macmillan, 1948).

107. Pritchett, *The Roosevelt Court*, 46.

108. Frankfurter's jurisprudence as often been identified as "ordered liberty." While I accept this characterization, I suggest that ordered liberty is something to be identified by a discreet judicial mind—so it is the proper state of mind that is central to limiting judicial discretion.

109. See Geoffrey P. Miller, "The True Story of Carolene Products," *The Supreme Court Review, 1987* (Chicago: University of Chicago Press, 1988), 397–428.

110. *United States v. Carolene Products*, 304 U.S. 144, 152 (1938). Stone referred to these as "regulatory legislation affecting ordinary commercial transactions," which no longer posed constitutional issues. Stone offered three essential qualifications where there would be a "narrower scope for the operation of the presumption of constitutionality": (1) when legislation appears to violate a specific prohibition of the Constitution, especially the Bill of Rights; (2) when legislation "restricts those political processes which can ordinarily be expected to bring about repeal of undesirable legislation"; and (3) when legislation impinges upon "discrete and insular minorities" that cannot be expected to appeal effectively to the

democratic process. Stone added the section on the Bill of Rights at the request of Chief Justice Hughes. Murphy, et al., *American Constitutional Interpretation*, 683–87.

111. John Hart Ely, *Democracy and Distrust: A Theory of Judicial Review* (Cambridge: Harvard University Press, 1980). See Michael Sandel, *Democracy's Discontent: America in Search of a Public Philosophy* (Cambridge: Harvard University Press, 1996), on the rise of the procedural republic and value neutrality in modern liberalism.

112. Jackson, *The Struggle for Judicial Supremacy*, 285.

113. See especially H. N. Hirsch, *The Enigma of Felix Frankfurter* (New York: Basic Books, 1981).

114. Hand's one exception is freedom of speech, *The Bill of Rights* (New York: Atheneum 1968), 69.

115. See Jacobsohn, *Pragmatism, Statesmanship and the Supreme Court*, 114–60.

116. Mark Silverstein, *Constitutional Faiths: Felix Frankfurter, Hugo Black, and the Process of Judicial Decision Making* (Ithaca: Cornell University Press, 1984), 128.

117. "But to the legislature no less than to courts is committed the guardianship of deeply-cherished liberties. Where all the effective means of inducing political changes are left free from interference, education in the abandonment of foolish legislation is itself a training in liberty. To fight out the wise use of legislative authority in the forum of public opinion and before legislative assemblies rather than to transfer such a contest to the judicial arena, serves to vindicate the self-confidence of a free people." *Minnersville School District v. Gobitis*, 310 U.S. 586, 600 (1940).

118. *West Virginia State Board of Education v. Barnette*, 319 U.S. 624, 648 (1942).

119. *Dennis v. United States*, 341 U.S. 494, 526–27 (1951). Frankfurter pushed this line of thinking in two free-speech cases, taking further aim at footnote 4: "It has been suggested, with the casualness of a footnote, that such legislation is not presumptively valid and it has been weightily reiterated that freedom of speech has a 'preferred position' among constitutional safeguards." See also *Kovacs v. Cooper*, 336 U.S. 77, 95 (1949). "Those liberties of the individual which history has attested as the indispensable conditions of an open as against a closed society come to this Court with a momentum and respect lacking when appeal is made to liberties which derive from shifting economic arrangements." But Frankfurter went on to say, even so, "these are matters for the legislative judgment controlled by public opinion" (*Kovacs* at 97).

120. Silverstein, *Constitutional Faiths*, 143.

121. Jacobsohn, *Pragmatism, Statesmanship, and the Supreme Court*, 140.

122. *Rochin v. California*, at 342 U.S. 165, 170–71(1952). "To practice the requisite detachment and to achieve sufficient objectivity no doubt demands of judges the habit of self-discipline and self-criticism, incertitude that one's own views are incontestable and alert to tolerance toward views not shared. But these are precisely . . . the qualities society has a right to expect from those entrusted with ultimate judicial power."

123. Jacobsohn, *Pragmatism, Statesmanship, and the Supreme Court*, 141. See also Silverstein, *Constitutional Faiths*, 142–55.

124. *Rochin* at 172.

125. *Baker v. Carr*, 369 U.S. 186, 270 (1962).

126. Silverstein, *Constitutional Faiths*, 134.

127. Silverstein notes that Black did join Justice Cardozo's famous opinion in *Palko v. Connecticut*, 302 U.S. 319 (1937), which exemplified Frankfurter's notion of "ordered liberty" that so horrified Black. Yet, as Silverstein argues, Black joined the opinion his first year on the Court largely out of respect for Cardozo and prior to working out his textualist jurisprudence that rejected such subjective notions in its quest to ground judicial will. *Constitutional Faiths*, 141.

128. *Rochin* at 75.

129. Silverstein, *Constitutional Faiths*, 136.

130. Leslie Friedman Goldstein, *In Defense of the Text: Democracy and Constitutional Theory* (Lanham, MD: Rowman and Littlefield, 1990), 41–66.

131. *Adamson v. California*, 332 U.S. 46 (1947).

132. *Griswold v. Connecticut*, 381 U.S. 479, 511 (1965). "The due process argument . . . here is based on the premise that this Court is vested with the power to invalidate all state laws that it considers to be arbitrary, capricious, unreasonable, or oppressive, or this Court's belief that a particular state law under scrutiny has no 'rational or justifying' purpose, or is offensive to 'a sense of fairness and justice.' If these formulas based on 'natural justice,' or others which mean the same thing are to prevail, they require judges to determine what is or is not constitutional on the basis of their own appraisal of what laws are unwise of unnecessary."

133. *Dennis* at 580. "So long as this Court exercises the power of judicial review . . . I cannot agree that the First Amendment permits us to sustain laws suppressing freedom of speech and press on the basis of Congress' or our own notions of mere 'reasonableness.' Such a doctrine waters down the First Amendment so that it amounts to little more than an admonition to Congress."

134. Brutus, XI, in Herbert J. Storing, *The Anti-Federalist*, selected by Murray Dry (Chicago: University of Chicago Press, 1985), 165.

135. A point Black noted in a footnote in *Adamson* at 78, n. 6.

136. *Adamson* at 62.

137. *Twining v. New Jersey* 211 U.S. 78, 121 (1908). This position was also held, arguably, by Justices Field and Bradley in their *Slaughterhouse* dissents, *Slaughter-House Cases*, 83 U.S. 36 (1873).

138. *Adamson* at 67.

139. Sunstein, *The Second Bill of Rights*, 179.

140. To return to an old argument that has been neglected, we should recall that Justice Brandeis's most famous opinion in defense of freedom of speech is premised on the Court's protecting rights like liberty of contract. In *Whitney* Brandeis suggests that, "Despite arguments to the contrary which had seemed to me persuasive, it is settled that the due process clause of the Fourteenth Amendment applies to matters of substantive law as well as to matters of procedure. Thus all fundamental rights comprised within the term liberty are protected by the Federal Constitution from invasion by the States." Brandies then insisted, "The power of the courts to strike down an offending law is no less when the interests involved are not property rights, but the fundamental personal rights of free speech and assembly" (*Whitney v. California*, 274 U.S. 347, 373–74 (1927). But the Court, for Brandeis, should really be protecting neither under due process. Justice Sutherland, on the other hand, accepted

both of these as part of liberty under due process: "the states are precluded from abridging the freedom of speech or of the press by force of the due process clause of the Fourteenth Amendment." In insisting upon this point, Sutherland argued that the Court had "concluded that certain fundamental rights, safeguarded by the first eight amendments against federal action, were also safeguarded against state action by the due process of law clause of the Fourteenth Amendment[.]" Turning to the very substantive due process cases that Brandeis thought had been wrongly decided, Sutherland insisted, "The word 'liberty' contained in that amendment embraces not only the right of a person to be free from physical restraint, but the right to be free in the enjoyment of all his faculties as well" (*Grosjean v. American Press Co.*, 297 U.S. 233, 233–34 [1936]). What happens, though, when we reject Sutherland's logic? Can we then protect some rights under liberty, but not others? If we reject *Lochner*, must we then reject Brandeis's opinion in *Whitney?* This was the dilemma that confronted the New Deal justices, which required a reconstruction of the very meaning of liberty and a rewriting of these earlier cases. See, generally, Mark A. Graber, *Transforming Free Speech: The Ambiguous Legacy of Civil Libertarianism* (Berkeley: University of California Press, 1991).

141. I focus on *Griswold* because it is a high-profile case that cannot be connected to the New Deal. Cases under the first amendment also illustrate the conflict we saw previously with Stone, Frankfurter, and Black, but, arguably, they can be situated within one or another strand of New Deal thinking. The due process line of cases vividly shows this conflict, but until *Griswold,* the Court attempts to negotiate around due process in cases such as *Edwards v. California,* 314 U.S. 160, and *Skinner v. Oklahoma,* 316 U.S. 535 (1942). This is most evident in *Bolling v. Sharpe,* 347 U.S. 497 (1954), the D.C. companion case to *Brown v. the Board of Education,* where the Court engages in substantive due process but calls it equal protection, even though the Fifth Amendment does not have an equal protection clause. Along with *Brown,* this case would be sharply criticized for its sloppy logic but could plausibly be situated within New Deal understandings (though I raise serious questions about his in the next chapter). This is simply not true of *Griswold.*

142. *Nomination of Robert H. Bork to Be Associate Justice of the Supreme Court of the United States: Hearings before the Senate Committee on the Judiciary,* 100th Cong., 1st sess. (1987), 249. Bork, *The Tempting of America,* 184–85, would later qualify this position, attempting to construct the amendment in accord with original intent.

143. *Griswold* at 484, 481–82.

144. *Griswold* at 511–12.

145. *Griswold* at 522.

146. *Griswold* at 500–501.

147. *Griswold* at 501. "Judicial self-restraint will not, I suggest, be brought about in the 'due process' area by the historically unfounded incorporation formula. It will be achieved in this area, as in other constitutional areas, only by continual insistence upon respect for the teachings of history, solid recognition of the basic values that underlie society, and wise appreciation of the great role that the doctrines of federalism and separation of powers have played in establishing and preserving American freedoms."

148. "In determining which rights are fundamental, judges are not left at large to decide cases in light of their personal and private notions. Rather, they must look to the 'traditions

and conscience of our people' to determine whether a principle is 'so rooted . . . as to be ranked fundamental'" (*Griswold* at 496).

149. *Griswold* at 496.

150. Randy Barnett, *Restoring the Lost Constitution* (Princeton: Princeton University Press, 2004). See also Gillman, "Preferred Freedoms."

151. Wayne Moore, *The Constitutional Rights and Powers of the People* (Princeton: Princeton University Press, 1996), 105–51, and Hadley Arkes, *Natural Rights and the Right to Choose* (New York: Cambridge University Press, 2002), 11–33.

152. Hamilton et al., *The Federalist Papers*, No. 84, 513.

153. As Gillman argues, "The same skepticism that called into question the ability of judges to discern true public purposes has been deployed against judges who struggle to identify fundamental rights." Gillman chastises critics of the Court, especially conservative critics, who "use the lore of *Lochner* as a weapon in their struggle against the modern Court's use of fundamental rights as a trump on government power." This conservative critique, however, is rooted in the Constitutional Revolution of 1937. Gillman, *The Constitution Besieged*, 204.

154. This seems to be precisely what Goldberg is doing. Douglas's nod at the close of his opinion to the right of marriage "older than the Bill of Rights" might be on firmer ground, but he does not rest his opinion on this logic, *Griswold* at 486–87.

155. Perhaps these two can be reconciled in a Burkean fashion where our constitutional identity emerges out of this historical process.

156. *Lawrence v. Texas*, 539 U.S. 558 (2003).

Five • Unsettling the New Deal and the Return of Originalism

1. Quoted in Sidney Milkis, *The President and the Parties: The Transformation of the American Party System since the New Deal* (New York: Oxford University Press, 1993), 263.

2. William Leuchtenburg, *In the Shadow of FDR: From Harry Truman to Bill Clinton* (Ithaca: Cornell University Press, 1993), 225.

3. William Leuchtenburg, *The Supreme Court Reborn: The Constitutional Revolution in the Age of Roosevelt* (New York: Oxford University Press, 1995), 213.

4. Ronald Reagan, First Inaugural, www.reaganfoundation.org/reagan/speeches/speech.asp?spid=6 (accessed June 22, 2007).

5. See, for example, Sotirios A. Barber, *Welfare and the Constitution* (Princeton: Princeton University Press, 2003), and Stephen Holmes and Cass R. Sunstein, *The Cost of Rights: Why Liberty Depends on Taxes* (New York: W. W. Norton, 1999).

6. Johnathan O'Neill, *Originalism in American Law and Politics: A Constitutional History* (Baltimore: Johns Hopkins University Press, 2005).

7. Edwin Meese III, "Interpreting the Constitution," in Jack Rakove, ed., *Interpreting the Constitution: The Debate over Original Intent* (Boston: Northeastern University Press, 1990).

8. Ken I. Kersch, "The New Deal Triumph as the End of History? The Judicial Negotiation of Labor Rights and Civil Rights," in Ronald Kahn and Ken I. Kersch, eds., *The Supreme Court and American Political Development* (Lawrence: University Press of Kansas, 2006).

9. Keith E. Whittington, *Political Foundations of Judicial Supremacy: The Presidency, the*

Supreme Court, and Constitutional Leadership in U.S. History (Princeton: Princeton University Press, 2007). See also Sheldon Goldman, *Picking Federal Judges: Lower Court Selection from Roosevelt to Reagan* (New Haven: Yale University Press, 1997), 3, and Kevin McMahon, *Reconsidering Roosevelt on Race: How the Presidency Paved the Road to Brown* (Chicago: University of Chicago Press, 2004).

10. On the political foundations of judicial supremacy and efforts by presidents to work through the court, see Whittington, *Political Foundations of Judicial Supremacy.*

11. *Planned Parenthood v. Casey,* 505 U.S. 833, 868 (1992), and *City of Boerne v. Flores* 521 U.S. 507, 529 (1997).

12. This was also true of progressives and New Dealers, though they also had a specific legislative agenda that the Court often resisted.

13. Jean-Jacques Rousseau, *The Social Contract and the First and Second Discourses* (New Haven: Yale University Press, 2002), 16.

14. Andrew E. Busch, *Reagan's Victory: The Election of 1980* (Lawrence: University Press of Kansas, 2006), 174.

15. John O. McGinnis, "Reviving Tocqueville's America: The Rehnquist Court's Jurisprudence of Social Discovery," *California Law Review* 90, no. 401 (2002): 485–571.

16. *Nomination of Robert H. Bork to Be Associate Justice of the Supreme Court of the United States: Hearings before the Senate Committee on the Judiciary,* 100th Cong., 1st sess. (1987), 249. See also Randy Barnett, *Restoring the Lost Constitution: The Presumption of Liberty* (Princeton: Princeton University Press, 2004).

17. This line of argument insists upon *enumerated powers* and *enumerated rights* without thinking how these two elements fit into the whole of the Constitution.

18. Busch, *Reagan's Victory.* See also Harvey C. Mansfield Jr., *America's Constitutional Soul* (Baltimore: Johns Hopkins University Press, 1991), 25–27.

19. Bruce Ackerman, *We the People: Transformations* (Cambridge: Harvard University Press, 1998), 389–92.

20. Stephen Skowronek, *The Politics Presidents Make: Leadership from John Adams to George Bush* (Cambridge: Harvard University Press, 1993), 428, 416.

21. Marc Landy and Sidney Milkis, *Presidential Greatness* (Lawrence: University Press of Kansas, 2000), 225, 198.

22. Ackerman, *We the People: Transformations,* 391.

23. Skowronek, *The Politics Presidents Make,* 39. Donald Grier Stephenson, *Campaigns and the Court* (New York: Columbia University Press, 1999), focuses almost exclusively on the Court and abortion. James Simon's *The Center Holds* (New York: Simon and Schuster, 1996) speaks about the failure of the conservative revolution, but does not even have a chapter on federalism!

24. Landy and Milkis, *Presidential Greatness,* 4.

25. Whittington, *Political Foundations of Judicial Supremacy,* 22–25.

26. Stephen Gottlieb, *Morality Imposed* (New York: New York University Press 2000). Arguably, this is the message of Ackerman's "multiple origins originalist" *We the People* as well, insofar as Reagan failed to create a "new" origin and thus was bound by the New Deal origin.

27. Milkis, *The President and the Parties,* 228. Even Nixon, who insisted upon a "strict

construction" of the Constitution and spoke more actively of federalism than any president until Reagan, never questioned the fundamentals of the New Deal constitutional order in terms of governmental power.

28. Mark Tushnet, *The New Constitutional Order* (Princeton: Princeton University Press, 2003), and Thomas M. Keck, *The Most Activist Court in History:* (Chicago: University of Chicago Press, 2004). On judicial appointments and the Great Society, see Goldman, *Picking Federal Judges,* 154–97.

29. Alexis de Tocqueville, *Democracy in America,* trans. Harvey C. Mansfield and Delba Winthrop (Chicago: University of Chicago Press, 2000), vol. 2, iv, ch. 6, 662.

30. *Congressional Quarterly,* October 3, 1981, 1922.

31. Franklin D. Roosevelt, Message to Congress on the State of the Union, January 11, 1944, in *The Public Papers and Addresses of Franklin D. Roosevelt,* vol. 9, comp. Samuel I. Rosenman (New York: Macmillan, 1945), 40. Reagan said that he left the Democratic Party when it left Jefferson's principles of limited government. In some sense, this cast the argument as how these things should be best provided for. See Andrew E. Busch, *Ronald Reagan and the Politics of Freedom* (Lanham, MD: Rowman and Littlefield, 2001), 6.

32. Reagan, Second Inaugural, www.reaganfoundation.org/reagan/speeches/speech.asp ?spid=22 (accessed June 22, 2007).

33. Jeffrey K. Tulis, *The Rhetorical Presidency* (Princeton: Princeton University Press, 1987), 181, goes so far as to say that "Democrats now talk like Republicans." While this was certainly true of New Democrat presidential contenders, it is arguably less so of congressional Democrats, or those who ran for president after Bill Clinton.

34. Skowronek, *The Politics Presidents Make,* 416–29, and Landy and Milkis, *Presidential Greatness,* 219–26. See also Stephen Skowronek, *Building a New American State: The Expansion of National Administrative Capacities* (New York: Cambridge University Press, 1982), 34–35.

35. Mansfield, *America's Constitutional Soul,* 52.

36. Cass Sunstein has, in a much overwrought manner, taken up arms against a return of the "constitution-in-exile." *Radicals in Robes: Why Extreme Right-Wing Courts Are Wrong for America* (New York: Basic Books, 2005).

37. Martin Diamond, "The Forgotten Doctrine of Enumerated Powers," *Publius* 6, no. 4 (1976): 187–93.

38. See especially Akhil Reed Amar, *The Bill of Rights: Creation and Reconstruction* (New Haven: Yale University Press, 1998) and *America's Constitution: A Biography* (New York: Random House, 2005). See also Jack Balkin, "Abortion and Original Meaning," Yale Law School Public Law Working Paper No. 119. Available at SSRN: http://ssrn.com/abstract=925558.

39. William J. Brennan Jr., "The Constitution of the United States: Contemporary Ratification," in Jack N. Rakove, ed., *Interpreting the Constitution: The Debate over Original Intent* (Boston: Northeastern University Press, 1990), 25.

40. John Hart Ely, *Democracy and Distrust: A Theory of Judicial Review* (Cambridge: Harvard University Press, 1980). Even Ronald Dworkin, once emblematic of "noninterpretivism," now uses the language of interpretivism and original meaning and intent, while declining to be called on "originalist." See Dworkin, *Justice in Robes* (Cambridge: Harvard

University Press, 2006). See also Sotirios A. Barber and James Fleming, *Constitutional Interpretation* (New York: Oxford University Press, 2007).

41. Edwin Meese III, "Perspective on the Authoritativeness of Supreme Court Decision: The Law of the Constitution," *Tulane Law Review* 61 (1987): 979–90.

42. Michael Kinsley called it "Meese's Stink bomb," *Washington Post,* October 29, 1986, A19; Ronald Dworkin, *Freedom's Law: The Moral Reading of the American Constitution* (Cambridge: Harvard University Press, 1996) (essays that originally appeared in the *New York Review of Books*); Laurence Tribe, *Constitutional Choices* (Cambridge: Harvard University Press, 1985). Sanford Levinson and Sotirios Barber (among others) rejected Reagan's constitutional reconstruction but agreed with departmentalism. See Levinson, *Constitutional Faith* (Princeton: Princeton University Press, 1989), and Barber, *On What the Constitution Means* (Baltimore: Johns Hopkins University Press, 1984) and *The Constitution of Judicial Power* (Baltimore: Johns Hopkins University Press, 1993).

43. O'Neill, *Originalism in American Law and Politics,* 43–66. See also Laura Kalman, *The Strange Career of Legal Liberalism* (New Haven: Yale University Press, 1996), 13–59.

44. Lucas A. Powe Jr., *The Warren Court and American Politics* (Cambridge: Harvard University Press, 2000).

45. Ken I. Kersch, *Constructing Civil Liberties: Discontinuities in the Development of American Constitutional Law* (New York: Cambridge University Press, 2004), 16.

46. See especially Benjamin Cardozo, *The Nature of the Judicial Process* (New Haven: Yale University Press, 1921), and his withheld concurring opinion in *Home Building & Loan Association v. Blaisdell,* in Walter Murphy et al., *American Constitutional Interpretation* (New York: Foundation Press, 2003), 224–26.

47. Brennan, "The Constitution of the United States."

48. Ibid., 33. In contrast, see Howard Gillman, "Party Politics and Constitutional Change: The Political Origins of Liberal Judicial Activism," in Kahn and Kersch, *The Supreme Court and American Political Development*, 138–68.

49. Brennan's own logic might push in this direction, but, like many proponents of a living constitution, he seems to think it must move in a "progressive" direction and, therefore, with History.

50. George Thomas, "New Deal 'Originalism,'" *Polity* 33, no. 1 (2000): 151–61. See also G. Edward White, *The Constitution and the New Deal* (Cambridge: Harvard University Press, 2000), 27.

51. Kersch, "The New Deal Triumph as the End of History?"

52. In doing so, I do not mean to suggest that these scholars are being disingenuous about the arguments they put forward. The project of creating and maintaining constitutional authority is necessarily a political one. See George Thomas, "Popular Constitutionalism: The New Living Constitutionalism," *Studies in Law, Politics, and Society* 44 (2008): 75–107.

53. As an isolated case, Rehnquist's opinion for the Court in *National League of Cities v. Usery* (1976) held out limitations on Congress's power under the commerce clause, but did so indirectly by way of state sovereignty. See Charles A. Lofgren, "The Origins of the Tenth Amendment: History, Sovereignty, and the Problem of Constitutional Intention," in his *Government from Reflection and Choice: Constitutional Essays on War, Foreign Relations, and Federalism* (New York: Oxford University Press, 1986).

54. Mark Tushnet, "Living in a Constitutional Moment? *Lopez* and Constitutional Theory," *Case Western Reserve Law Review* 46 (1996): 845–75, and *The New Constitutional Order.*

55. Mark Tushnet, *Taking the Constitution Away from the Courts* (Princeton: Princeton University Press, 1998), 19, 154, 11.

56. *Casey* is also very difficult to situate within the contours of popular constitutionalism insofar as it insists on the preeminent role of the Court. See Thomas, "Popular Constitutionalism."

57. Cass R. Sunstein, *One Case at a Time: Judicial Minimalism on the Supreme Court* (Cambridge: Harvard University Press, 1998).

58. Cass R. Sunstein, *The Second Bill of Rights: FDR's Unfinished Revolution and Why We Need It More Than Ever* (New York: Basic Books, 2004).

59. Sunstein, *Radicals in Robes,* 49, 53–78.

60. Ibid., 237.

61. As Keith Whittington argues, this inverts the political consequences of these cases: "in brief, *Casey* is about stopping political debate and legislative action. *Lopez* and its brethren are about redirecting political activism into different channels. Ultimately, *Casey* is intended to have substantial political and policy consequences. By contrast, *Lopez* has only modest policy consequences." Whittington, "The Casey Five versus the Federalism Five: Supreme Legislator or Prudent Umpire," in Christopher Wolfe, ed., *That Eminent Tribunal: Judicial Supremacy and the Constitution* (Princeton: Princeton University Press, 2004), 184. Yet under the guise of minimalism, Justice O'Connor could play an extraordinarily powerful role as the interpreter of the Constitution insofar as her opinions were often so "fact specific" that only she could understand them. This is difficult to reconcile with minimalism in any meaningful sense.

62. Larry Kramer, *The People Themselves: Popular Constitutionalism and Judicial Review* (New York: Oxford University Press, 2004), 220. Like the scholarly works of Tushnet and Ackerman, this is an extraordinarily illuminating piece of scholarship that develops powerful arguments for the people's role in constitutional interpretation and persuasively rejects judicial supremacy.

63. Ibid., 229. At times, popular constitutionalists seem to be more enamored of Rousseau's "General Will" than the constitution—a constitution that was, after all, also binding on the people, even if they might, at times, be its defenders.

64. Reagan, "Farewell Address," www.reaganlibrary.com/reagan/speeches/farewell.asp (accessed December 1, 2007).

65. Busch, *Ronald Reagan and the Politics of Freedom*, 21. See also on Madison, Charles A. Lofgren, "The Original Understanding of Original Intent?" and Jack Rakove, "Mr. Meese, Meet Mr. Madison," both in Rakove, ed., *Interpreting the Constitution,* 117–50, 179–94.

66. See, for example, Jeffrey K. Tulis, "The Constitutional Presidency in American Political Development," in Martin L. Fausold and Alan Shank, eds., *The Constitution and the American Presidency* (Albany: SUNY Press, 1991), 133–47, and Herbert J. Storing, "The Problem of Big Government," in *Toward a More Perfect Union* (Washington, DC: AEI Press, 1995), 287–306. Both of these pieces recapture arguments made for "big government," which are rooted in the original constitution and not by way of "constitutional transformation" or an evolving constitution.

67. Ackerman, *We the People: Transformations,* 26 (emphasis in original).

68. *Roe v. Wade,* 410 U.S. 113 (1973).

69. *Planned Parenthood v. Casey,* 505 U.S. 833 (1992).

70. For similar arguments that focus on the "governing coalition" or political regimes, but that offer far more subtle and nuanced accounts, see J. Mitchell Pickerill and Cornell Clayton, "The Rehnquist Court and the Political Dynamics of Federalism," *Perspectives on Politics* 2, no. 2 (2004): 233–48, and "Guess What Happened on the Way to Revolution? Precursors to the Supreme Court's Federalism Revolution," *Publius* 34, no. 3 (2004): 85–114; Mark Tushnet, *A Court Divided: The Rehnquist Court and the Future of Constitutional Law* (New York: W. W. Norton, 2005); and Jack M. Balkin and Sanford Levinson, "Understanding the Constitutional Revolution," *Virginia Law Review* 87, no. 6 (2001): 1045–1109. For an excellent critique of this emerging literature, see Thomas Keck, "Party Politics or Judicial Independence? The Regime Politics Literature Hits the Law Schools," *Law & Social Inquiry* 32, no. 2 (2007): 511–44.

71. Though see Landy and Milkis, *Presidential Greatness,* 224.

72. For a much more sober take on Reagan's ambitions, see Whittington, *Political Foundations of Judicial Supremacy,* 274–83.

73. This argument repeatedly flared up between Felix Frankfurter and Hugo Black. See Mark Silverstein, *Constitutional Faiths: Felix Frankfurter, Hugo Black, and the Process of Judicial Decision-Making* (Ithaca: Cornell University Press, 1984), and C. Herman Pritchett, *The Roosevelt Court: A Study in Judicial Politics and Values, 1937–1947* (Chicago: University of Chicago Press, 1948).

74. O'Neill, *Originalism in American Law and Politics,* 28–36.

75. *Roe* at 174.

76. *Griswold v. Connecticut,* 381 U.S. 479, 522 (1965) (J. Black dissenting).

77. John Hart Ely, *Democracy and Distrust* and "The Wages of Crying Wolf: A Comment on *Roe v. Wade,*" *Yale Law Journal* 82 (1973): 920–49. See also Kalman, *The Strange Career of Legal Liberalism,* 1–10.

78. James W. Ely Jr., "The Oxymoron Reconsidered: Myth and Reality in the Origins of Substantive Due Process," *Constitutional Commentary* 16 (1999): 315–47, illuminating how critics dubbed this long-held understanding of due process "substantive" to discredit it.

79. O'Neill, *Originalism in American Law and Politics,* 112, 168. See also Gary J. Jacobsohn, *The Supreme Court and the Decline of Constitutional Aspiration* (Lanham, MD: Rowman and Littlefield, 1986), 57–58, and Sotirios A. Barber, *The Constitution of Judicial Power* (Baltimore: Johns Hopkins University Press, 1993), 121–29.

80. Hadley Arkes, *Beyond the Constitution* (Princeton: Princeton University Press, 1990), 14.

81. See Edward Corwin, *The Higher Law Background of American Constitutional Law* (Ithaca: Cornell University Press, 1955).

82. James Wilson, Pennsylvania Ratifying Convention, November 28, December 4, 1787, in Philip B. Kurland and Ralph Lerner, *The Founders' Constitution* (Indianapolis: Liberty Fund, 1987), 1:454.

83. Raoul Berger, *Government by Judiciary: The Transformation of the Fourteenth Amend-*

ment, 2nd ed. (Indianapolis: Liberty Fund, 1998), 273–301, and Robert Bork, *The Tempting of America: The Political Seduction of the Law* (New York: Free Press, 1990), 51–67.

84. Barry Friedman, "The Birth of an Academic Obsession: The History of the Countermajoritarian Difficulty, Part Five," *Yale Law Journal* 112 (2002): 253–54.

85. See Justice Holmes's dissenting opinion in *Adkins v. Children's Hospital,* 261 U.S. 525 (1923).

86. Quoted in Leuchtenburg, *The Supreme Court Reborn,* 234. See also Friedman, "The Birth of an Academic Obsession." Again, Friedman points to the historical contingency of this dilemma, but that itself hardly makes it less powerful if it was the preoccupation at the heart of New Deal constitutionalism, other than to suggest that we should forge a new understanding of judicial review, leaving the preoccupations of the New Dealer's behind us. But this opens the possibility, surely, for a return to older understandings of the Constitution as well.

87. Herbert Wechsler, "Toward Neutral Principles of Constitutional Law," *Harvard Law Review* 73 (1959): 1–35.

88. Bork, *The Tempting of America,* 139–41.

89. Alexander M. Bickel, *The Least Dangerous Branch: The Supreme Court at the Bar of Politics* (New Haven: Yale University Press, 1962). See also O'Neill, *Originalism in American Law and Politics,* 164.

90. Bork, *The Tempting of America,* 140. To some degree, by focusing on historical original intent, this wave of originalism shares the historicism of the progressives. For subsequent waves of originalism, which depart significantly from Bork and Berger, see Keith E. Whittington, *Constitutional Interpretation: Textual Meaning, Original Intent, and Judicial Review* (Lawrence: University Press of Kansas, 1999); Barnett, *Restoring the Lost Constitution* and "An Originalism for Nonoriginalists," *Loyola Law Review* 45 (1999): 611–54; and Vasan Kesavan and Michael Stokes Paulsen, "The Interpretive Force of the Constitution's Secret Drafting History," *Georgetown Law Journal* 91 (2003): 1114–1214.

91. Quoted in Ralph A. Rossum, *Antonin Scalia's Jurisprudence: Text and Tradition* (Lawrence: University Press of Kansas, 2006), 36. See also James R. Stoner Jr., *Common-Law Liberty: Rethinking American Constitutionalism* (Lawrence: University Press of Kansas, 2003), 2–3.

92. Bork, *The Tempting of America,* 57. "Yet legal reasoning must begin with a body of rules or principles or major premises that are independent of the judge's preferences. That, as we have seen, is impossible under any philosophy of judging other than the view that the original understanding of the Constitution is the exclusive source for those exterior principles" (265). See also Raoul Berger, *Government by Judiciary: The Transformation of the Fourteenth Amendment* (Indianapolis: Liberty Fund, 1998).

93. But what if it doesn't? This raises a profound question that subsequent originalists have taken up. See Stanley C. Brubaker, "The Countermajoritarian Difficulty: Tradition versus Original Meaning," in Kenneth D. Ward and Cecilia R. Castillo, eds., *The Judiciary and American Democracy: Alexander Bickel, the Countermajoritarian Difficult, and Contemporary Constitutional Theory* (Albany: SUNY Press, 2005), 110.

94. See William Harris II, "Bonding Word and Polity: The Logic of American Constitu-

tionalism," *American Political Science Review* 76, no. 1 (1982): 34–45, which attempts to situate different views of interpretation within the constitutional enterprise.

95. Antonin Scalia, "Originalism: The Lesser Evil," *University of Cincinnati Law Review* 57 (1989), 863. See Rossum, *Antonin Scalia's Jurisprudence*, 44–48.

96. Scalia, "Originalism," 863–64.

97. Scalia's originalism is a bit different than Bork's insofar as he has shown a willingness to draw on unenumerated rights that are clearly part of our history and tradition. See, for example, Scalia's opinion in *Michael H. v. Gerald D.*, 491 U.S. 110 (1989). See Rossum, *Antonin Scalia's Jurisprudence*, 27–51, 127–65.

98. See Arkes, *Beyond the Constitution*, 21–39. See also Barber, *The Constitution of Judicial Power*, 73–78.

99. Bork, *The Tempting of America*, 20–26.

100. *Adamson v. California*, 332 U.S. 46, 75 (1947). As Black says about the Court's abandoning this "natural law formula," "I believe that formula to be itself a violation of our Constitution, in that it subtly conveys to courts, at the expense of legislatures, ultimate power over public policies in fields where no specific provision of the Constitution limits legislative power." Like Scalia and Berger, Bork essentially accepts the post New Deal jurisprudential development of "strict scrutiny" as put forward in *Carolene Products*, accepting the presumption of constitutionality and two-tier review, moving in stride with justices Frankfurter, Stone, and Black. While there are disagreements here, they are essentially on what liberties strict scrutiny should be applied to, as we saw in Scalia's *Lawrence* dissent.

101. Bork, *The Tempting of America*, 81.

102. O'Neill, *Originalism in American Law and Politics*, 40. This was profoundly different than the post–New Deal balancing of "fundamental rights."

103. In this, interestingly, they also reject the notion, put forward at times by FDR, that the New Deal was consistent with original constitutional ends. As Herbert Storing put it, modern big government is "today's manifestation of the original decision for big government" that is part of the enduring character of our government based on the founders' principles. Storing, "The Problem of Big Government," 304, 288.

104. Justice Cardozo's notion of "ordered liberty," embraced by Frankfurter and the second Harlan, is the one strand of jurisprudence from the New Deal breakthrough that could accommodate such rights and often bears a resemblance to the Court's pre–New Deal substantive due process thinking; see *Palko v. Connecticut*, 302 U.S. 319 (1937). Stone's understanding, as developed by *Carolene Products*, n. 4, could accommodate unenumerated rights that were linked to democracy itself, but that is clearly not true in these cases.

105. Stephen M. Griffin, *American Constitutionalism: From Theory to Politics* (Princeton: Princeton University Press, 1996), 168. It is possible to argue that in the realm of liberty of contract the circumstances had changed so much, that to be true to the principle, we could no longer defend it on its old terms. This might, then, preserve the logic of due process in others areas (which would preserve Court opinions such as *Meyer v. Nebraska*). But this is not the argument progressives or New Dealers put forward in the midst of such change. (See Howard Gillman, *The Constitution Besieged: The Rise and Demise of Lochner Era Police Powers Jurisprudence* [Durham: Duke University Press, 1993], for the possible first line of argument.) Moreover, if we recognize historical change as legitimately altering constitutional

interpretation, there is no reason to preclude the return of "liberty of contract." Indeed, the changes wrought in the last years of the twentieth century may make the return of "dual federalism" viable. See, for example, Keith Whittington, "Dismantling the Modern State? The Changing Structural Foundations of Federalism," *Hastings Constitutional Law Quarterly* 25 (1998): 483.

106. See Jeffrey K. Tulis, "On the State of Constitutional Theory," *Law & Social Inquiry* 16, no. 4 (1991): 711–16.

107. Which could be plausible, but one could easily accept *Griswold* and reject *Roe*. See, for example, Charles Fried, *Order and Law: Arguing the Reagan Revolution* (New York: Touchstone, 1991), 71–88, who, for Reagan and Bush, argued that the Court could preserve *Griswold* while rejecting *Roe*. Fried argues that Justice Harlan's argument in *Griswold* finds support in Frankfurter's and Cardozo's notion of "ordered liberty." As I argued in the preceding chapter, if any strand of New Deal jurisprudence would have led to *Griswold*, it would have to be Frankfurter's. Yet, as one scholar of American constitutional development has argued, Frankfurter's jurisprudence was the one strand that was clearly rejected over time. See Keck, *The Most Activist Supreme Court in History,* 37–66. This would seem to make *Griswold* even more difficult to situate within the New Deal breakthrough if, that is, it has any coherence other than as an always evolving constitution.

108. Bruce Ackerman, *We the People: Foundations* (Cambridge: Harvard University Press, 1991), 131–62, and *We the People: Transformations,* 390–403. For a far more persuasive account of privacy rights amid the project of state building, see Ken I. Kersch, "The Reconstruction of Constitutional Privacy Rights and the New American State," *Studies in American Political Development* 16 (September 2002): 61–87.

109. Bruce Ackerman discusses *Brown* as an interpretive synthesis of our multiple-origins Constitution based on the Founding, Reconstruction, and New Deal in both volumes of *We the People.* Yet he does not say a word about *Bolling* in either. In *Reconsidering Roosevelt on Race,* Kevin McMahon persuasively argues that the Court took up a new institutional role in the wake of the New Deal that helped pave the road to *Brown.* Yet this role, as McMahon describes it, was largely deference to the executive. McMahon does not discuss *Bolling* or attempt to situate its logic in a broader constitutional setting. This is also true of Michael J. Klarman, *From Jim Crow to Civil Rights: The Supreme Court and the Struggle for Racial Equality* (New York: Oxford University Press, 2004). Klarman's only mention of *Bolling* is to note that "Because a practice that the Court had just invalidated in the states could not possibly be permitted in the capital of the free world, the justices ruled in the companion case of *Bolling v. Sharpe* that the Due Process Clause of the Fifth Amendment imposed identical restrictions on the District of Columbia" (292). McMahon and Klarman offer subtle and detailed accounts of how the Court was following the political branches. These accounts suggest that we could expect the same possible behavior from the Court in the wake of Reagan's victories. But this is precisely what Ackerman tries to deny. For the uneasy state of civil rights and labor rights in the New Deal, which challenges their easy merger, see Kersch, "The New Deal as the End of History?"

110. *Bolling v. Sharpe,* 347 U.S. 497, 500 (1954).

111. Bork, *The Tempting of America,* 83. Conservatives have also wrestled with this di-

lemma, often ducking how *Bolling* fits with *Brown*. Some have rejected *Brown* as unjustified by original intent (as much as they like the moral result). See Earl Maltz, "*Brown v. the Board of Education* and Originalism," in Robert P. George, ed., *Great Cases in Constitutional Law* (Princeton: Princeton University Press, 2000), 136–53, and Christopher Wolfe, *The Rise of Modern Judicial Review: From Constitutional Interpretation to Judge-Made Law* (New York: Basic Books, 1986), 259–62.

112. Ackerman, *We the People: Foundations,* 142.

113. Kersch, "The Reconstruction of Constitutional Privacy Rights and the New American State," 86.

114. Whittington, *Political Foundations of Judicial Supremacy,* 266. In some sense, this captures much of the literature on "political regimes."

115. See especially *United States v. Darby,* 312 U.S. 100 (1941).

116. Bork, *The Tempting of America,* 57. See also Raoul Berger, *Federalism: The Founder's Design* (Norman: University of Oklahoma Press, 1987).

117. Ronald Reagan, Executive Order 12612-Federalism, October 26, 1987, www.reagan. utexas.edu/search/speeches/speech_srch.html (accessed June 20, 2007). See also Martin Diamond, "The Ends of Federalism," *Publius* 3, no. 2 (1973): 190.

118. Reagan, Executive Order 12612-Federalism, October 26, 1987. See also Busch, *Ronald Reagan and the Politics of Freedom,* 6.

119. See Executive Order 12612-Federalism, October 26, 1987.

120. See also Meese, "Interpreting the Constitution," 17.

121. Busch, *Ronald Reagan and the Politics of Freedom,* 15. See also Fried, *Order and Law,* 148–60.

122. Ronald Reagan, Statement on Signing the Federal Debt Limit and Deficit Reduction Bill, September 29, 1987, www.reagan.utexas.edu/search/speeches/speech_srch.html (accessed June 20, 2007). See also Alexander Hamilton, James Madison, and John Jay, *The Federalist Papers,* introduction and notes by Charles R. Kesler, ed. Clinton Rossiter (New York: Signet Classics, 1999), No. 70, 421.

123. Thomas Jefferson, "Opinion on the Constitutionality of the Bill for Establishing a National Bank," in Philip Kurland and Ralph Lerner, eds., *The Founders' Constitution,* vol. 3 (Indianapolis: Liberty Fund, 1987), 246.

124. Meese, "Interpreting the Constitution," 16.

125. David E. Kyvig, *Explicit and Authentic Acts: Amending the U.S. Constitution, 1776–1995* (Lawrence: University Press of Kansas, 1996), 447–55, argues that Reagan supported many conservative amendments for the same kind of rhetorical purposes.

126. *New York v. United States,* 505 U.S. 144 (1992).

127. *Lopez* and *United States v. Morrison,* 529 U.S. 598 (2000).

128. *New York v. United States* and *Printz v. United States,* 521 U.S. 898 (1997).

129. *Seminole Tribe of Florida v. Florida,* 517 U.S. 44 (1996); *Florida Prepaid Postsecondary Education Expense Board v. College Savings Bank,* 527 U.S. 627 (1999); *College Savings Bank v. Florida Prepaid Postsecondary Education Expense Board,* 527 U.S. 666 (1999); *Alden v. Maine,* 527 U.S. 706 (1999); *Kimel v. Florida Board of Regents,* 528 U.S. 62 (2000); *Trustees of the University of Alabama v. Garrett,* 531 U.S. 356 (2001). This line of decisions is, perhaps, the most

radical aspect of the Rehnquist Court's jurisprudence with questionable constitutional foundations.

130. See McGinnis, "Reviving Tocqueville's America."

131. Alexis de Tocqueville, *The Old Regime and the Revolution* (Chicago: University of Chicago Press, 1998), 10.

132. Goldman, *Picking Federal Judges*, 285.

133. Busch, *Ronald Reagan and the Politics of Freedom*, 43.

134. David Yalof, *Pursuit of Justices: Presidential Politics and the Selection of Supreme Court Nominees* (Chicago: University of Chicago Press, 1999), 143. David O'Brien suggest that the Reagan judges may well be his most enduring legacy, "The Reagan Judges: His Most Enduring Legacy?" in Charles O. Jones, ed., *The Reagan Legacy: Promise and Performance* (Chatham: Chatham House Publishers, 1988), 60–100. See also Goldman, *Picking Federal Judges*, 285–345.

135. Reagan attempted to entrench his constitutional reconstruction by way of judicial appointments, the Department of Justice, and the Office of Legal Policy and by way of executive orders and presidential signing statements, in what Cornell Clayton calls the "judicialization of politics." *The Politics of Justice: The Attorney General and the Making of Legal Policy* (New York: M. E. Sharpe, 1992), 146–55. At the same time, see Fried, *Order and Law*, 132–71, on attempts to limit and confine the administrative state within the separation of powers.

136. Busch, *Ronald Reagan and the Politics of Freedom*, 41.

137. Whittington, *Political Foundations of Judicial Supremacy*, 276–77.

138. Keck, *The Most Activist Court in History*, on the tension between conservatives' insistence on limited government and judicial restraint.

139. Mansfield, *America's Constitutional Soul*, 31.

140. Ralph A. Rossum, *Federalism, the Supreme Court, and the Seventeenth Amendment: The Irony of Constitutional Democracy* (Lanham, MD: Lexington Books, 2001), argues that the Seventeenth Amendment removed the Court from this role altogether.

141. Keck, *The Most Activist Court in History*, 7–8.

142. See Ken Kersch, "Justice Breyer's Mandarin Liberty," *University of Chicago Law Review* 73 (2005): 759–822, for a critique of such views.

143. Ronald Reagan, Remarks on the Supreme Court Nomination of Robert H. Bork to Law Enforcement Officials in Los Angeles, California, August 28, 1987, www.reagan.utexas .edu/search/speeches/speech_srch.html (accessed on June 21, 2007). See also Reagan, Remarks during a White House Briefing for United States Attorneys, October 21, 1985, "I want judges of the highest intellectual standing who harbor the deepest regard for the Constitution and its traditions, one of which is judicial restraint," and Reagan, Letter Accepting the Resignation of Robert H. Bork as United States Circuit Judge, January 14, 1988, where he praised Bork's "unswerving commitment to the doctrine of judicial restraint," www.reagan .utexas.edu/archives/speeches/1985/102185a.htm (accessed June 21, 2007).

144. Meese, "Interpreting the Constitution," does say that where constitutional principle is clear, "it should be followed," which would seem to invite strong judicial review.

145. Tulis, *The Rhetorical President*, 189–202. Tulis even calls Reagan *the* rhetorical president, 192. At the same time, Tulis notes that his speeches were carefully and logically crafted

unlike the many laundry list speeches that have become the norm in the rhetorical presidency (191).

146. *Cooper v. Aaron,* 358 U.S. 1, 18 (1958).

147. Meese, "The Law of the Constitution," 987.

148. Reagan's description of "the Reagan Revolution," in his "Farwell Address."

149. Busch, *Ronald Reagan and the Politics of Freedom,* 36.

150. On the "political safeguards" of federalism, see Herbert Wechsler, "The Political Safeguards of Federalism: The Role of the States in the Composition and Selection of the National Government," *Columbia Law Review* 54 (1954): 543–60; Jesse H. Choper, *Judicial Review and the National Political Process* (Chicago: University of Chicago Press, 1980); and Larry Kramer, "Putting Politics Back into the Political Safeguards of Federalism," *Columbia Law Review* 100 (2000): 215–93. The insistence that the Court cannot enforce federalism because it has "political safeguards" in the national political process is at odds with a Madisonian understanding insofar as Madison persistently insisted on multiple and overlapping methods for maintaining the Constitution. So we could have both "political safeguards" and judicial review.

151. Edwin Meese III, "The Attorney General's View of the Supreme Court: Toward a Jurisprudence of Original Intention," *Public Administration Review* 45 (1985): 701–4, 702.

152. *Garcia v. San Antonio Metropolitan Transit Authority,* 469 U.S. 528, 580 (1986) (J. Rehnquist dissenting). See also Lofgren, "The Origins of the Tenth Amendment: History, Sovereignty, and the Problem of Constitutional Intention."

153. *Lopez* at 609 (J. Souter dissenting).

154. Given, the Court said, "cumulative effects."

155. Quoted in Barry Cushman, *Rethinking the New Deal Court: The Structure of a Constitutional Revolution* (New York: Oxford University Press, 1998), 221.

156. *Lopez* at 628 (J. Breyer dissenting, emphasis in original).

157. *Jones & Laughlin* at 37.

158. Justice Thomas's concurring opinion helps draw this out, as he urges a complete repudiation of the New Deal cases as constitutionally unfounded (*Lopez* at 585, J. Thomas concurring).

159. *New York v. United States,* at 156–57.

160. *Darby* at 124.

161. *Morrison* at 614. See also Ronald Rotunda, "The Commerce Clause, the Political Questions Doctrine, and Morrison," *Constitutional Commentary* 18 (2001): 319–34.

162. *Lopez* at 564–65.

163. *City of Boerne v. Flores,* 521 U.S. 507, 535–36 (1997).

164. Meese, "Perspective on the Authoritativeness of Supreme Court Decision," 979.

165. Pickerill and Clayton, "The Rehnquist Court and the Political Dynamics of Federalism" and "Guess What Happened on the Way to Revolution?" This is especially true of the Republican Party platforms, which speak of "a decentralization of the federal government and efforts to return decision making power to state and local elected officials."

166. Keith Whittington, "James Madison Has Left the Building," *University of Chicago Law Review* 72 (2005): 1137–58, reviewing J. Mitchell Pickerill, *Constitutional Deliberation in*

Congress: The Impact of Judicial Review in a Separated System (Durham: Duke University Press, 2004).

167. For a full discussion of the importance of the Court's cases, particularly in historical perspective, see Steven G. Calabresi, "The Libertarian-Lite Constitutional Order and the Rehnquist Court," *Georgetown Law Journal* 93 (2005): 1023–60.

168. *Federal Maritime Commission v. South Carolina State Ports Authority,* 535 U.S. 743, 787 (2002). See also *Morrison* at 654–55 (J. Souter dissenting). Writing in the *New Republic* ("Our Discriminating Court: Federal Offensive," April 9, 2001), Jeffrey Rosen insisted that the Court's federalism opinions put the "New Deal legacy of a powerful federal government" at stake. Rosen has gone on to suggest that "the resurrection of a tradition of liberal restraint . . . seems more relevant today than at any time since the New Deal" ("Breyer Restraint: A Modest Proposal," *New Republic,* January 14, 2002). See also Linda Greenhouse, "The High Court's Target: Congress," *New York Times,* February 25, 2001.

169. Leuchtenburg, *The Supreme Court Reborn,* 236.

170. Even when there has been a divide among "Reagan's justices" on the reach of national power, there has been a foundational agreement that there are limits to national power and that the Court has a role in maintaining those limits within the separation of powers.

In *Gonzales v. Raich,* 545 U.S. 1 (2005), for example, Justice Scalia concurred in the Court's opinion holding that the Controlled Substances Act might be applied even to marijuana grown for medical purposes and personal use. But he rested his opinion on the necessary and proper clause in conjunction with the commerce clause. And when he turned to the commerce clause, he cited *NRLB v. Jones & Laughlin Steel,* 301 U.S. 1 (1937). In this, Scalia seemed to reject the full reach of *Wickard,* 317 U.S. 111 (1942).

171. Karen Orren and Stephen Skowronek, "Beyond the Iconography of Order: Notes for a 'New Institutionalism,'" in Lawrence C. Dodd and Calvin Jillson, eds., *The Dynamics of American Politics: Approaches and Interpretations* (Boulder, CO: Westview Press, 1994), 311–30.

Conclusion

1. Alexis de Tocqueville, *Democracy in America,* trans. Harvey C. Mansfield and Delba Winthrop (Chicago: University of Chicago Press, 2000), 232.

2. Walter F. Murphy, *Constitutional Democracy: Creating and Maintaining a Just Political Order* (Baltimore: Johns Hopkins University Press, 2007), 10.

3. Alexander Hamilton, James Madison, and John Jay, *The Federalist Papers,* introduction and notes by Charles R. Kesler, ed. Clinton Rossiter (New York: Signet Classics, 1999), No. 85. Even Brutus, arguing against the Constitution, said we cannot strive for perfection, as even those urging ratification of this Constitution admit it is imperfect. Brutus I in Herbert J. Storing, ed., *The Anti-Federalist* (Chicago: University of Chicago Press, 1985).

4. Woodrow Wilson, *Constitutional Government in the United States* (New York: Columbia University Press, 1908), 56. See Robert A. Goldwin, "Of Men and Angels: A Search for Morality in the Constitution," in Robert H. Horwitz, ed., *The Moral Foundations of the American Republic* (Charlottesville: University of Virginia Press, 1986), 24–41.

5. Wilson, *Constitutional Government in the United States,* 49–51. In contrast, see Martin Diamond, "Democracy and The Federalist: A Reconsideration of the Framers' Intent," in William A. Schambra, ed., *As Far as Republican Principles Will Admit: Essays by Martin Diamond* (Washington, DC: AEI Press, 1992), 17–36, pointing out that *The Federalist* did not presuppose a harmony of interests or that democracy would necessarily lead to unity.

6. Herbert Croly, *Progressive Democracy* (New Brunswick, NJ: Transaction Publisher, 1998).

7. Jean-Jacques Rousseau, *The Social Contract and the First and Second Discourses* (New Haven: Yale University Press, 2002), 171. See Wilson, *Constitutional Government in the United States,* 56–57.

8. Rousseau, *The Social Contract and the First and Second Discourses,* 170.

9. Ibid., 172.

10. Wilson, *Constitutional Government in the United States,* 49–50. See also Croly, *Progressive Democracy,* 211, "The socially righteous expression of the popular will is to be brought about by frank and complete confidence in its own necessary and ultimate custodian." Croly went on to reject the traditional notion of a constitution as binding the polity: "Any particular method of securing order, such as that prescribed by the Constitution, must not be exalted from a method or an instrument into a Higher Law" (227).

11. This is especially true of Bruce Ackerman, who explicitly suggests that his "dualist democracy" is rooted in an unbound popular sovereignty. *We the People: Foundations* (Cambridge: Harvard University Press, 1991), 3–33. In *We the People: Transformations* (Cambridge: Cambridge University Press, 1998), Ackerman even calls the people's voice "the prophetic voice" (3). See also Mark Tushnet, *Taking the Constitution Away from the Courts* (Princeton: Princeton University Press, 1998), and Larry Kramer, *The People Themselves: Popular Constitutionalism and Judicial Review* (New York: Oxford University Press, 2004). For a critique, see George Thomas, "Popular Constitutionalism: The New Living Constitutionalism," *Studies in Law, Politics, and Society* 44 (2008): 75–107.

12. Kramer, *The People Themselves,* 248–49.

13. Ibid., 8.

14. This tends to place more constitutional weight on elections than they can bear. It also points to the difference between constitutional democracy and popular constitutionalism. In the former, constitutional authority depends on winning elections under formal rules, not on reading the popular meaning of an election in a manner that can then alter the constitution.

15. See Patrick J. Deneen, *Democratic Faith* (Princeton: Princeton University Press, 2005).

16. As Madison put it, while insisting that the people themselves were the best guardians of their rights, "after establishing a government they should watch over it, as well as obey it." Note that he says, "obey it." James Madison, "Who Are the Best Keepers of the People's Liberties," in Ralph Ketcham, ed., *Selected Writings of James Madison* (Indianapolis: Hackett Publishing, 2006), 228.

17. William Harris II, *The Interpretable Constitution* (Baltimore: Johns Hopkins University Press, 1993), 201–2.

18. Jeffrey K. Tulis, "Constitution and Revolution," in Sotirios A. Barber and Robert P. George, eds., *Constitutional Politics: Essays on Constitutional Making, Maintenance, and Change* (Princeton: Princeton University Press, 2001), 116–27, and Martin Diamond, "The Separation of Powers and the Mixed Regime," in Schambra, *As Far as Republican Principles Will Admit*, 58–67. Jed Rubenfeld, *Revolution by Judiciary: The Structure of American Constitutional Law* (Cambridge: Harvard University Press, 2005), argues that constitutional law features such radical reinterpretations.

19. Harris, *The Interpretable Constitution,* 165. For an excellent discussion of the logic of amendment, see Sanford Levinson, "How Many Times Has the United States Constitution Been Amended?" in Sanford Levinson, ed., *Responding to Imperfection: The Theory and Practice of Constitutional Amendment* (Princeton: Princeton University Press, 1995), 13–36.

20. Popular constitutionalists do not argue for the alteration of what Sanford Levinson has called the "hard wired" features of the Constitution. *Our Undemocratic Constitution* (New York: Oxford University Press, 2006). By "hard wired," though, Levinson simply has in mind language that is so clear it could not be subject to radical transformation.

21. Gary Jeffrey Jacobsohn, "An Unconstitutional Constitution? A Comparative Perspective," *I-CON* 4, no. 3 (2006): 464.

22. Murphy, *Constitutional Democracy,* 508. See also Carl Schmitt, *Legality and Legitimacy* (Durham: Duke University Press, 2004), 58: "When a constitution envisions the possibility of constitutional revisions, the constitution does not intend to provide, for example, a legal method for the elimination of its own legality, still less the legitimate means to the destruction of its legitimacy." Hadley Arkes, *Beyond the Constitution* (Princeton: Princeton University Press, 1990), might be seen as making a similar argument about constitutional substance limiting constitutional text specifically within the idiom of American constitutionalism.

23. The Declaration of Independence, "He has combined with others to subject us to a Jurisdiction foreign to our Constitution, and unacknowledged by our Laws; giving his assent to their Acts of pretended Legislation[.]"

24. Murphy, *Constitutional Democracy,* 516. See also Tulis, "Constitution and Revolution," where he notes that it is difficult to imagine a "Lockean people" becoming Rousseauian, though one could imagine the reverse.

25. Akhil Reed Amar, "Popular Sovereignty and Constitutional Amendment," in Levinson, *Responding to Imperfection,* 89–115.

26. James Wilson, Pennsylvania Ratifying Convention, December 4, 1787, in Philip Kurland and Ralph Lerner, eds., *The Founders' Constitution,* vol. 1 (Indianapolis: Liberty Fund, 1987), 62. For a discussion of Wilson suggesting his endorsement of unqualified popular sovereignty, see Akhil Reed Amar, *America's Constitution: A Biography* (New York: Random House, 2005), 297.

27. Thomas Jefferson to James Madison, September 6, 1789, in Kurland and Lerner, *The Founders' Constitution,* 1:68.

28. Abraham Lincoln, First Debate, in Robert W. Johannsen, ed., *The Lincoln-Douglas Debates* (New York: Oxford University Press, 1965), 55–56.

29. James Madison, "The Law of Nature and Majority Rule" and "A Memorial and

Remonstrance against Religious Assessments," in Ralph Ketcham, ed., *Selected Writings of James Madison* (Indianapolis: Hackett Publishing, 2006), 28, 21.

30. Much of modern political science tends to collapse this distinction insofar as it is concerned with empirical analysis removed from normative concerns.

31. Sotirios A. Barber, *On What the Constitution Means* (Baltimore: Johns Hopkins University Press), 18.

32. This distinction can also be a very easy process.

33. Gary Jeffrey Jacbosohn, "Constitutional Identity," *Review of Politics* 68, no. 3 (2006): 394.

34. This tendency is evident in the political regimes literature, which treats constitutional change as what comes out of the electoral process.

35. James W. Ceaser, *Nature and History in American Constitutional Development* (Cambridge: Harvard University Press, 2006).

36. Edmund Burke, *Reflections on the Revolution in France* (New Haven: Yale University Press, 2003), 210.

37. George Washington, Farewell Address, September 19, 1796, in Kurland and Lerner, *The Founders' Constitution*, 1:681.

38. Washington, Farewell Address, 681, where he insisted that adhering to "powers properly distributed and adjusted" was the Constitution's surest guardian.

39. See Mark E. Brandon, *Free in the World: American Slavery and Constitutional Failure* (Princeton: Princeton University Press, 1998), 19–20, on various forms of constitutional failure (different from those I suggest later).

40. Murphy, *Constitutional Democracy*. See also Arkes, *Beyond the Constitution*, 40–57.

41. Whittington speaks of this in terms of the presidency and constitutional leadership. *The Political Foundations of Judicial Supremacy: The Presidency, the Supreme Court, and Constitutional Leadership in U.S. History* (Princeton: Princeton University Press, 2007). On how the separation of powers fosters responsibility, see Mark Blitz, *Duty Bound: Responsibility and American Public Life* (Lanham, MD: Rowman and Littlefield, 2005).

42. James Madison, The Virginia Report, in Marvin Meyers, *The Mind of the Founder* (New York: Bobs Merrill, 1973), 303. See also Hamilton et al., *The Federalist Papers*, No. 10, 74.

43. Ken Kersch captures the variation of the Court even on the vaunted issue of rights, "The Court, it turns out, is doctrinal and political, an obstacle and a hope, active and restrained, and formalistic and pragmatic. Its jurisprudence is in some areas transformed by critical elections, and in others left relatively unchanged. It embraces new ideological visions, at times as wholes, but at others only in part. It resists change, negotiates change, and initiates change." *Constructing Civil Liberties: Discontinuities in the Development of American Constitutional Law* (New York: Cambridge University Press, 2004), 37.

44. Jack Balkin, ed., *What Brown v. the Board of Education Should Have Said* (New York: New York University Press, 2002).

45. *Brown v. the Board of Education*, 347 U.S. 483, 494–95 (1954).

46. *Brown* at 495.

47. *Congressional Record*, 84th Cong., 2nd sess., vol. 102, part 4 (March 12, 1956), 4459–60.

48. Robert Burt, *The Constitution in Conflict* (Cambridge: Harvard University Press, 1992), 353–56.

49. Lucas A. Powe Jr., *The Warren Court and American Politics* (Cambridge: Harvard University Press, 2000), 217–27. See also Gerald N. Rosenberg, *The Hollow Hope: Can Courts Bring about Social Change* (Chicago: University of Chicago Press, 1991), 42–71.

50. See, for example, *Parents Involved in Community Schools v. Seattle School District*, 551 U.S. (2007).

51. *Cooper v. Aaron*, 358 U.S. 1, 18 (1958).

52. The Hearing of the Senate Judiciary Committee, Confirmation Hearing for Judge John G. Roberts to Be Chief Justice of the United States. Federal News Service, September 15, 2005. The Supreme Court also partly avoided this issue; see *Hamdan v. Rumsfeld*, 126 S. Ct. 2749 (2006).

53. See, for example, the exchange between Senator Charles Schumer of New York and John Roberts in Roberts's Senate Confirmation Hearings, September 14, 2005.

54. Edward S. Corwin, *The President: Office and Powers, 1787–1984* (New York: New York University 1984).

55. For recent cases, see *Dellmus v. Bush*, 752 F. Supp 1141 (D.D.C. 1990), and *Doe v. Bush*, 323 F. 3d 133 (1st Cir. 2003).

56. Alexander Hamilton, Pacificus, No. I, in Morton J. Frisch, ed., *The Pacificus-Helvidius Debates of 1793–1794* (Indianapolis: Liberty Fund 2007).

57. James Madison, Helvidius, No. I, 56, in ibid.

58. Helvidius, No. II, 68–69, in ibid.

59. Helvidius, No. IV, in ibid.

60. Harvey C. Mansfield Jr., *Taming the Prince: The Ambivalence of Modern Executive Power* (Baltimore: Johns Hopkins University Press, 1993), 255. See also George Thomas, "As Far as Republican Principles Will Admit: Presidential Prerogative and Constitutional Government," *Presidential Studies Quarterly* 30, no. 3 (2000): 534–52.

61. See, for example, Joint Resolution to Authorize the Use of United States Armed Forces against Iraq (2002), Public Law 107–243, October 16, 2002.

62. *INS v. Chadha*, 462 U.S. 919 (1983).

63. Individual rights claims are different from claims about the separation of powers generally and need not turn on judicial supremacy. See, for example, *Hamdi v. Rumsfeld*, 542 U.S. 507 (2004). President George W. Bush's claims to extraordinary executive power also have roots in earlier executive claims, particularly those of FDR. For a discussion of FDR's claims, see Clinton Rossiter, *Constitutional Dictatorship: Crisis Government in the Modern Democracies* (Princeton: Princeton University Press, 1948).

64. Hamilton insisted that his Pacificus essays be included in the 1802 edition of *The Federalist*. Frisch, *The Pacificus-Helvidius Debates*, xv. On such a civic mind-set, see John E. Finn, "The Civic Constitution: Some Preliminaries," in Barber and George, *Constitutional Politics*.

65. Save by way of illustration of the separation of power generally. Again, questions of individual rights may be different.

66. Whittington, *The Political Foundations of Judicial Supremacy*, 293.

67. Ibid., 295.

68. John Maynard Keynes, *The General Theory of Employment, Interest, and Money* (New York: Harcourt Brace, 1935).

69. Edmund Burke, Address to the British Colonists of North America in Isaac Kramnick, ed., *The Portable Edmund Burke* (New York: Penguin Books, 1999), 280.

70. Tocqueville, *Democracy in America*, 662.